PELICAN BOOKS

A320

CICERO AND THE ROMAN REPUBLIC

Frank Richard Cowell was educated at the Roan School, Greenwich, and, after war service, at King's College London and at the London School of Economics. From 1929 to 1931 he held a Rockefeller Research Fellowship in the Social Sciences in the United States of America and in Europe. He began his civil service career on publicity work for H.M. Stationery Office. From July 1939 to November 1946 he was in the Foreign Office, serving for three years with the British Mission to General de Gaulle's French National Committee. He was Secretary of the United Kingdom National Commission for Unesco from 1946 until 1958. In 1952 he was awarded the C.M.G.

Frank Cowell is also the author of *History, Civilization and Culture* (1952), *Culture in Private and Public Life* (1959), *Everyday Life in Ancient Rome* (1962), *Leibniz* (1968), and *Values in Human Society* (1968).

CICERO
AND THE ROMAN REPUBLIC

F. R. COWELL

PENGUIN BOOKS
BALTIMORE · MARYLAND

Penguin Books Ltd, Harmondsworth, Middlesex, England
Penguin Books Inc., 7110 Ambassador Road, Baltimore, Maryland 21207, U.S.A.
Penguin Books Australia Ltd, Ringwood, Victoria, Australia

—

First published 1948
Published in Pelican Books 1956
Second edition 1962
Third edition 1964
Fourth edition 1967
Reprinted 1968

—

Copyright © F. R. Cowell, 1948, 1962, 1964, 1967

—

Made and printed in Great Britain
by C. Nicholls & Company Ltd
Collogravure Plates printed by Harrison & Sons Ltd
Set in Monotype Times

10408

CONTENTS

LIST OF PLATES

Acknowledgement is made to the following for permission to reproduce photographs: Messrs Alinari, Florence, for Plates 6a and b, 7b, 8, 9b, 11a and b, 13b, 15a and b, 17b, 23, 24b, 30; Messrs Anderson, Rome, for Plates 5a, 18b, 31; Messrs Mansell for Plates 16b and 26a; Les Archives Photographiques, Paris, for Plates 14a to c; The Trustees of the British Museum for Plates 9a, 19, 20, 24a, 25a, 32a; Messrs Brogi, Florence, for Plates 16a, 26b; The Clarendon Press, Oxford, and Dr I. A. Richmond for Plate 18a; Istituto Geografico de Agostini, Rome, for Plates 13a, 17a; The Metropolitan Museum, New York, for Plates 2a, 7a, 10a and b, 29; Mr Ernest Nash, New York, for Plates 4, 5b, 32b; Ny Carlsberg Glyptotek, Copenhagen, for Plates 21a and b, 22a and b, 27; The Director of the Victoria and Albert Museum and the Keeper of the Wellington Museum for Plate 1.

LIST OF MAPS AND DIAGRAMS

Specially drawn for this edition by Donald Bell-Scott

TO THE MEMORY OF
MY MOTHER AND
FATHER

FOREWORD

WITH the beginning of the year 1959 Cicero's fame entered its twenty-first century. It is given to few human beings to remain a figure of interest, still remembered and still admired, two thousand years after their death, but such is the singular quality of Cicero that he with Julius Caesar alone among the Romans of the Republic have so far evoked such commemoration.

By this tribute of remembrance to two outstanding personalities of the ancient world, the twentieth century testifies also to a sustained interest in the tremendous drama of the crash of the Roman Republic in which they both lost their lives.

The bimillenaries of Julius Caesar and of Cicero serve to draw attention once more to the early Roman way of life and to the great story of the rise, decline, and fall of that Republican form of government under which the Romans conquered the world. What Polybius said about it two thousand one hundred years ago, and a century at least before it had worked out to its tragic climax, may still explain something of the magic that has enabled it to engross the attention of mankind ever since he confessed to its enthralling interest. 'Can anyone be so indifferent or idle', he asked, 'as not to care to know by what means and under what kind of polity, almost the whole inhabited world was conquered and brought under the dominion of the single city of Rome, and that too within a period of not quite fifty-three years?'

To that great theme this small work is devoted. It has now been revised for the third time and I hope improved in one or two details so that it may continue to serve as an introduction to the story of the rise and fall of the Roman Republic as it is seen from the perspectives of our own day and from those offered by the life, times, and opinions of Marcus Tullius Cicero.

RICHARD COWELL

March 1964

FROM THE PREFACE TO THE
FIRST EDITION

To tell once more the story of an earlier period of the history of mankind so that it may come alive in the minds of those who read it has been the motive inspiring so much good work in the past that any new attempt necessarily seems to require a considerable defence and apology.

The best justification would no doubt be the discovery of important new facts throwing fresh light upon the events of bygone days. Unfortunately the history of the Roman Republic has not yet benefited by epoch-making novelties that still remain among a scholar's dreams. The lost books of Livy have not yet been found. Unless the sands of Egypt or the dust of Herculaneum still conceal valuable papyri, parchments or inscriptions on stone or bronze from that vast amount of Latin writing that seems to have disappeared for ever, or unless modern marvels of infra-red photography reveal more of the text of classical authors obliterated from vellum or parchment to make a clean page for monkish scribes in the Middle Ages, the probability of modifying in any substantial manner what we believe to be the story of the rise, the development and the collapse of the Roman Republic now seems faint indeed.

Nevertheless many writers in the last hundred years have shown that the old record can be seen in a new light when re-interpreted from a fresh point of view. Several pages would be required to pay homage to the distinguished scholars, from Niebuhr and Mommsen in the nineteenth century to Professors Tenney Frank and Hugh Last in our own day, upon whom all others who write on the subject must necessarily and heavily depend.

They have shown that the history of the Roman Republic cannot be regarded as a dead and static story to be repeated without change from one generation to another. Unlike mere compilers of manuals, they have proved that it can be made a living story able to illuminate the workings of the human spirit and the behaviour of men in society.

Inspired by their example I have sought to interpret the fascinating story of the Roman Republic in the light of a special interest in the operation of economic, political and social forces – but not,

I trust, to the neglect or undue subordination of all that which, in the art of war, in literature, art, general science, building and civil engineering, has so long and so justly been regarded as among the achievements upon which the fame of Rome securely rests.

For the text I alone of course am answerable, but the burden of so formidable a responsibility has been notably lessened by Harold Mattingly and Ronald Syme, each of whom has read the proofs and saved me from many blunders. Such, however, is the authority they both command in Roman Studies, and so far do I fall short of their high standards of scholarship, that I should ill repay their generosity and kindness by trying to get credit for my own wares through the authority and trust their names inspire.

In the United States the book appears with an introduction by Professor Allan Nevins, who thereby increases my debt to him for many kindnesses begun during the war years when he shared in the dangers and inconveniences of war-time London – when, I may perhaps add, this book was begun as an occupation in the black-out and during frequent air-raids.

RICHARD COWELL

February 1948

In reprinting the above preface I have omitted a reference to my indebtedness to the late Dr. Otto Neurath, and to the Isotype Institute which he founded, because the present Penguin edition does not contain the coloured Isotype charts which were included in the 1948 edition in the hope that they would give greater clarity and precision to the account of the following topics:

The Geology of Central Italy
The Growth of Roman Territory
The Expansion of Roman Power in Italy
The Growth of Plebeian Power in Rome
The Roman World in the Age of Cicero
The Political Organization of Italy
Rome's Near Neighbours and Allies, 298 B.C.
The Lost Literature of Rome
The Expansion of Roman Power in the Mediterranean

Readers interested in what is believed to be the first attempt to
apply a novel form of visual aid to the study of the history of
Rome are accordingly referred to the earlier edition of this book
published in the United Kingdom by Sir Isaac Pitman and Sons
Ltd and in the United States of America by Chanticleer Press
Inc., New York.

Line drawings in black and white are however provided in this
edition as well as the full series of 32 pages of photogravure plates
originally reproduced. The technical planning and production of
the first edition was undertaken by Messrs Adprint Ltd.

FOREWORD TO THE FOURTH EDITION

Gratification at the continuing demand for this book deepens
my indebtedness to all those who continue to push forward the
frontiers of knowledge about the Ancient Romans and from
whose labours I endeavour to profit. Among those whose work is
done, I continue to venerate the memory of Harold Mattingly
and Dr Hugh Last, both of whom helped me by their generous
encouragement and advice. To them and to others whose aid has
been acknowledged in previous editions, I am now gratefully able
to add the name of another very active historian of Roman times,
Mr P. A. Brunt, Fellow of Oriel College Oxford and formerly a
colleague during the Second World War. In the light of his
comments on several specific points I have been able to make
improvements which I am happy to acknowledge, without of
course implying that he necessarily agrees with all the rest of the
book. I have again made other minor corrections and revised the
Bibliography.

1966   F.R.C.

INTRODUCTION

WHEN the affairs of a country are in a bad way it is useful to remember Oliver Cromwell's advice to look back to the time when things went well and to try to see what subsequently went wrong. Complete success in such a task is rarely possible, but partial success would clearly repay the effort involved if it helped to unravel something of the tangled story of the rise and decline of great nations. The manhood of Cicero as that of his more famous contemporary Julius Caesar was spent in the momentous years from about 90 B.C. to 43 B.C., a period that saw the decline and ruin of that old Republican form of government through which, within the previous 200 years, the Roman State had risen to unparalleled heights of power, wealth and glory.

By what steps the Romans arrived at this commanding position, what wars they fought and what victories they won, is told in every history of the Republic. Over 2,000 years now separate us from the struggles in which that one small and obscure tribe, settled on the banks of the River Tiber in the middle of Italy, slowly emerged victorious after constant warfare against other neighbouring tribes. The wavering fortunes of war, the bloodshed, the heroism, the exaltation of the victors, the dumb misery of the defeated were vivid urgent realities then; but for us today they can exist only in imagination and they cannot therefore seem of much account in comparison with the horrors endured by all those who have survived the tremendous crisis of 1914–18 and the still more deadly crisis of 1939–45.

Romans, Etruscans, Samnites, Sabines, Volscians, their enemies and allies have long since mouldered away. The sands of Africa have obliterated what remained of the Carthaginian Empire. Debris and dust have mounted slowly year by year throughout fifteen centuries to cover the ruins of the Roman Forum where excited crowds used to gather to hear the eloquence of Cicero and the commanding oratory of Caesar. But those questions of human rights and wrongs, of the best way to use political power and of the correct management of economic affairs, to which they and many other Romans endeavoured to find the right answers, still continue to vex mankind and to puzzle and perplex their leaders.

The martyrdom that was Cicero's reward for his vain opposition to dictatorship has in our own time ennobled the lives of millions of liberty-loving people who have been struck down at the behest of modern dictators and tyrants. This dreadful ordeal compels the survivors to return with passionate interest to those grand questions of human destiny that have always been forced upon the leaders of mankind. For we have now been made to see that these historic problems are indeed personal problems for everyone and that they cannot be indifferently left to political leaders alone.

Faced as we are with such a task, it is natural to look back to other periods in which men were also confronted with the same problems. That is why every new generation must look at history afresh. We do so not merely out of a rather childish curiosity to find parallels and precedents, still less with the sinister and dangerous intention of rewriting history as our own praise or apology. A compelling motive to historical study must surely always be to profit by that deepening awareness of the true nature of our own problems and possibilities which comes from a real understanding of the past. History is then a double-edged tool. By getting to grips with our own problems through its aid we are able to see more clearly into the working of the social forces of our own time. Armed with this greater insight we are in turn so much the better equipped in our effort to understand the operation of the social forces at work in past ages.

Despite the fact, therefore, that the events in the history of Rome have been narrated afresh in almost every generation, and in every land, and although the lives and characters of the chief personalities in that great drama have been described again and again, the work of reinterpretation cannot cease. As we learn more about the arts of government and administration, as we develop our knowledge of economics, agriculture and trade, and above all as we seek to penetrate deeper into the mind of man and into social psychology, we naturally hope to look to the past with more understanding eyes. The fact that so great a task can hardly ever be brought to an end must be a sufficient excuse for any attempt, however partial and imperfect, to deal with it at all.

It is in this spirit that an effort has been made in the pages that follow to understand the Age of Cicero, to see how he and his countrymen were formed by a style and way of life not of their own devising, how they tried to reshape their inheritance, what strains and stresses they endured and how far by their own efforts they were able to modify the destiny of mankind.

'Rome was not built in a day' is the enduring, proverbial testimony to the complicated story that this book seeks to tell. For the origins of many truly Roman aspects of the period around Cicero reach back through the mists of time. The activities of Caesar, Pompey, Brutus, Cato, Antony and the other celebrated figures of Cicero's age do not make sense unless they are seen in the light of this long evolution. It is a story in which the promise of great achievement is indeed realized but, despite great success, the end is ultimately a chaos that seems to have been unavoidable. The Roman Republic did not fall before external foes. It had not been permanently crippled or weakened by long wars against powerful neighbours.

What, then, were the faults and weaknesses that brought it to disaster? Were they due to defects in Roman political life or to a faulty machinery of government? Were they the result of an unsound economic system which discouraged the production and upset the distribution among all the people of the good things of this world? Was Roman law unjust, producing social discontent and resentment? Or did the trouble spring from some deeper cause, traceable perhaps to some fundamental change in men's attitude towards life? If so, was it a matter of altered social relationships between one class and another, between rich and poor, between the old families and fashionable society on the one hand and the unknown 'common man' on the other, between the free and the slaves or between the Romans and the Italians or the Romans and foreigners? Beyond all these possible sources of weakness was there a failure of old religious and moral beliefs and a decay of old habits that had in the last resort been the true source of the vitality of the State?

Such seem to be the main questions that arise as we read about Cicero and endeavour to understand the circumstances in which he was placed, the troubles and anxieties with which he had to contend and the extraordinary difficulties facing the men of his time who tried to put the Roman world to rights.

CICERO AND THE ROMAN REPUBLIC

*

Chapter One

ROME TAKES THE LEAD IN ITALY

753–265 B.C.

'THE City, the City, my dear Rufus – stick to that and live in its full light! Residence elsewhere – as I made up my mind in early life – is mere eclipse and obscurity to those whose energy is capable of shining in Rome.' The gusto and unmistakable note of enthusiasm in these words ring down the ages through the 2,000 years that divide the man who wrote them from our own time. They excite curiosity. What manner of man was he and what were the deep satisfactions which life in that city afforded? The City was, of course, Rome and the writer was Marcus Tullius Cicero, at that time fifty-six years of age and proconsul or governor, for the year 50 B.C., of Rome's distant province of Cilicia in Asia Minor.

Had there been a Roman Dictionary of National Biography, it might have summarized the story of Cicero's career briefly as follows:

MARCUS TULLIUS CICERO, of the tribe Cornelia. Son of Marcus Tullius Cicero, *eques*. Born at Arpinum a.d. III Non. Ian. A.U.C. 648 [3 January 106 B.C.]. Served in the army in the Social War, A.U.C. 665 [89 B.C.]. Student of philosophy and rhetoric in Rome, Athens and Rhodes. Pleader in the Roman Courts, A.U.C. 666–676 [88–78 B.C.] Elected Quaestor, served at Lilybaeum in Sicily, A.U.C. 679 [75 B.C.]. Senator, A.U.C. 680 [74 B.C.]. Curule Aedile, A.U.C. 685 [69 B.C.]. Praetor Urbanus, A.U.C. 688 [66 B.C.]. Consul, A.U.C. 691 [63 B.C.], when he suppressed the conspiracy of Catiline and was acclaimed Father of his country. He opposed Julius Caesar who indirectly procured his exile in A.U.C. 696 [58 B.C.]. Recalled, A.U.C. 697 [57 B.C.]. Augur, A.U.C. 701 [53 B.C.]. Proconsul of Cilicia for the year A.U.C. 703–704 [51–50 B.C.]. In the defence of the Republican constitution he joined

Gnaeus Pompeius Magnus in the Civil War against Julius Caesar, A.U.C. 705 [49 B.C.]. Pardoned by Julius Caesar on the defeat of Pompeius, he returned to Italy, A.U.C. 706 [48 B.C.], but retired from political life on the overthrow of the Republican constitution. He wrote philosophical and literary works until the assassination of Julius Caesar on Id. Mar. A.U.C. 710 [15 March 44 B.C.], when he sought to arouse and direct the opposition to M. Antonius. The alliance between Antonius and Octavianus made the task of restoring the Republican constitution hopeless and doomed its chief supporters. Cicero did not live to see the reconstruction of the Roman State under Octavianus but was proscribed and beheaded attempting to leave Italy, a.d. VII Id. Dec. A.U.C. 711 [7 December 43 B.C.]. Married Terentia, A.U.C. 677 [77 B.C.]: one son, M. Tullius Cicero, born A.U.C. 689 [65 B.C.], daughter Tullia, born A.U.C. 678 [76 B.C.]. Divorced, A.U.C. 708 [46 B.C.]. Married Pubililia, A.U.C. 708 [46 B.C.]. Again divorced, A.U.C. 708 [46 B.C.].

Almost all trace of Cicero's eager enthusiasm, his zest for life and action, his intensity of feeling and warm human sympathies have evaporated from so dry and condensed a summary. Some of the words it contains, like Tribe, Quaestor, Aedile, Praetor for example, sound strangely to twentieth-century ears. The dating 'A.U.C.' above is the Roman year measured ('*ab urbe condita*') from the year of the supposed foundation of Rome by Romulus, in the year 753 B.C. according to our reckoning. The equivalent dates B.C. in our chronology are given in brackets.

If Cicero the man is to come alive in our imagination we want to see, beyond his life-story, his dignity and his offices, something of his country and his people. We want a vision, however imperfect and fleeting, of the crowded scenes at Rome, the swirl of white togas among the gilded statues in the sunlit Forum, the hum of humanity at the chariot races in the great Circus suddenly swelling in volume to thunder as the speed-crazed drivers whip their horses to fury on the last lap of a race.

Who were these men and women by the hundred thousand among whom Cicero walked 2,000 years ago? What were their worries and their difficulties? How did they try to escape from them or solve them? How did they live and work and what were their opinions about the nature, the duties and the destiny of mankind? How was it that Cicero was murdered and what provoked the intense political upheavals and civil war in which he perished? Through history alone it may be possible to find clues to the answers to some of these questions. There is much we shall never know. We have to pick our way with what care and luck

we may among the scattered relics which have survived the wreck
of Rome. By piecing together such remnants of the record a
tolerably clear picture of the main outlines of the grand story of
the Roman Republic should emerge. It is an amazing story.
Cicero and his contemporaries might well have glowed with pride
and an intense national self-satisfaction when they looked back
upon the dogged determination, the endurance and bravery of
their forefathers who in the short space of three or four generations had conquered the known world. Cicero himself makes it
abundantly clear in his own writings that the history of the
Republic was a subject that absorbed and fascinated him. It is
true that his interest in it did not arise from that detached intellectual curiosity towards the past that characterizes modern
scholarship. Cicero, like the rest of his countrymen, was a busy
man. History for him was useful if it pointed a moral and adorned
some tale he wanted to tell, the better to sway the opinions of his
hearers.

Few Englishmen attain manhood today without learning something about the critical events in their nation's history. King
Alfred's victory over the Danes, the defeat of King Harold by the
Normans, the grant of the great Charter by King John, the overthrow of the Spanish Armada by the Elizabethans, the work of
Oliver Cromwell, the Revolution of 1688, the battles of Trafalgar
in 1805 and of Waterloo in 1815, the Reform of Parliament and of
administration in the nineteenth century and the development of
the public social services in the twentieth century are so many
milestones in the long march of the English people through
history, now followed in imagination, often haltingly and often
without real understanding, by the schoolboys and schoolgirls
who study the English tradition. The achievements of Christopher
Columbus, of the 'Mayflower' pioneers, the battle of Bunker
Hill, the ride of Paul Revere, the life-work of George Washington
and of Abraham Lincoln are similarly part of the grand story of
the growth of the United States with which all its young citizens
become familiar. In the same way in Cicero's day the Romans
heard from their cradles the epic story of the rise of Rome, and of
the mighty deeds of their forebears. At an early age they learned
to hate the name of King, to fear the tribes of Gaul, to thrill at the
story of Roman triumphs over the Etruscans, Greeks, Carthaginians and the rest of their Mediterranean neighbours. Indelibly

associated with many such stirring events were the names of
national heroes – Lucius Brutus who led the revolt that drove the
last Etruscan King from Rome; Cincinnatus who left his plough
to lead the Romans against the Aequi in 458 B.C.; Camillus who
saved the city from the Gauls seventy years later; Appius
Claudius, the blind Censor of 312–308 B.C. who devoted his life
to the Republic and inspired its struggle against the Greek King
Pyrrhus. The great renown of these and other historical figures
was kept alive in Roman minds by the loyalty of the Romans to
their ancestors and by the devotion of Roman fathers who trained
their sons to reverence the memory of the mighty deeds of the
men whose achievements made up the heroic story of the rise and
grandeur of Rome. A rapid glance at some of the main lines of
this oft-told story may help to fix Cicero's age in better perspective in the long vista of the ever-changing and developing history
of Rome. Without such an historical introduction more than half
the story of Cicero himself and the men of his age would remain
untold, because their activities can only be understood as a part
of the slow development of Roman social life and politics.

Traditions of Early Rome

Although when Cicero was a boy it was little more than 400
years since Rome had been ruled by kings, memory of them
had become hazy and their history was uncertain. Some records
used to be made in those early years, but they were probably
few and meagre chronicles of the high priest, consisting of bare
notes of wars, famines, eclipses, weather conditions, prodigies
and pestilence. Until the evidence of recent archaeological
investigations threw doubt on the story, it was confidently
believed, on the authority of Livy, whose history of Rome was
written a few years after Cicero's death, that all these early
archives had been lost when Rome was burned by the Gauls, the
barbarian invaders from the North, at the beginning of the fourth
century B.C. (around 390 B.C.). The archives, however, were
stored in various temples and these, it is now thought, survived
the invasion. Later Roman historians got what they could from
these early records, but modern notions of patient research
through masses of documents had not yet been born and some
later scholars have been bitter at what they consider the laziness

of the Roman writers. The records were, in any case, probably inadequate for anything like a full account of early Rome.

Legends supplied what history lacked. Stimulated, it seems, by a remark of Cicero's, Macaulay among others believed that the stories of the early days of Rome, beginning with its supposed foundation by Romulus in 753 B.C., had for many generations been preserved as ballads. If so, they had already been forgotten by Cicero's day, although the stories they enshrined were still part of the heritage of every Roman. 'The loves of the Vestal and the God of War ... the she-wolf, the shepherd's cabin, the recognition, the fratricide, the rape of the Sabines, the death of Tarpeia, the fall of Hostus Hostilius, the struggle of Mettus Curtius through the marsh, the women rushing with torn raiment and dishevelled hair between their fathers and their husbands, the nightly meetings of Numa and the Nymph by the well in the sacred grove, the fight of the three Romans and the three Albans, the purchase of the Sibylline Books, the crime of Tullia, the simulated madness of Brutus, the ambiguous reply of the Delphian oracle to the Tarquins, the wrongs of Lucretia, the heroic actions of Horatius Cocles, of Scaevola and of Cloelia, the battle of Regillus won by the aid of Castor and Pollux, the defence of the Cremera, the touching story of Coriolanus, the still more touching story of Virginia, the wild legend about the draining of the Alban Lake, the combat between Valerius Corvus and the gigantic Gaul' are, as Macaulay said, some among the many poetic legends about the early Roman State. They no longer, as he supposed, 'at once suggest themselves to every reader', but they may still be read in the pages of Livy, in the many histories of later writers and in the stirring, energetic verse of Macaulay himself. Although, for the last hundred years at least, they have generally been regarded as fictions, they have the merit of showing what actions and ideals the Romans thought worthy of admiration. To strike out these early legends entirely would be to lose this valuable insight into the greatness of the Roman spirit. Fearful no doubt of such a result, many people have agreed with Goethe, who used to say that if the Romans were great enough to invent such stories we should at least be great enough to believe them. Belief is perhaps rather a strong word in this connexion but, true or false, there can be no doubt about their powerful influence in shaping the thoughts and actions of mankind, not only in ancient Rome but in modern Europe, where for centuries they have figured prominently in the lessons of schoolboys and in the study and recreation of maturer minds.

Cicero was under no illusions about the historical value of much of what, in his day, passed for the story of early Rome and particularly the story of the achievements of early Romans whose later descendants relied heavily upon the assumed glory of their ancestors to redeem their own very real shortcomings. They had, he said, referring particularly to the written traditions repeated on all ceremonial occasions, particularly as funeral orations, 'filled our history with lies. They tell of events which never took place, imaginary triumphs, an excess of consular ancestors ... collected by including men from obscure families who happened to bear the same name'. It was foolish, he thought, to demand in a matter such as the early traditions of Rome 'the kind of truthfulness expected of a witness in court rather than of a poet'. In history on the other hand 'the standard by which everything is judged', he said, 'is the truth'.

The truth was sufficiently impressive, and Cicero, like all cultivated Romans, as well they might, took a great interest in the history and traditions of his country, for, from the most inauspicious beginnings, Rome had achieved in a mere three or four hundred years a position of predominance in the known world. Constant and often bitter warfare had been the price of supremacy. Surrounded on all sides by more numerous, richer, and apparently more powerful peoples, the men of Rome in the seventh and sixth centuries B.C. possessed no obvious advantages that would enable them to survive in a struggle with their neighbours. A small, inconspicuous tribe, they occupied no strong natural fortress, but were settled on seven small hills overlooking the largest river of Central Italy as it swept down, yellow with sand and silt, to traverse the narrow coastal plain to the sea. From this centre they would emerge every day to work on their small plots each of probably about five to ten acres in the flat and fertile country around, retiring again behind the city's protective defences or walls every night. Theirs must have been a hard life in which hand labour with the hoe predominated. Carried on for centuries with relatively little change and with very slow progress, it was hardly the kind of life to encourage great ambitions. Merely to succeed in holding such a site was an undoubted achievement, but not by itself a guarantee of future greatness.

The Romans always believed in later years that their early ancestors had been gifted with extraordinary qualities of tenacity, patience, frugality, capacity for hard work, and a constitutional inability ever to admit defeat. The life they led was certainly the sort to breed such qualities. They were specially manifest in the army and in the organization of the government.

The first political task of the Roman people had been to secure independence from the Etruscans, their powerful neighbours who occupied the north-western shores of Italy. These strange people remain one of the mysteries of history. Their origin is obscure, their manner of life and their civilization can be imagined only by putting together the scanty facts that archaeologists discover with the spade. For although many of their inscriptions on tombstones survive, almost nothing else remains to give a clue to their language. At an early period the Etruscan realm in Italy included Rome, and the Latin and Campanian plains. It seems clear that the Etruscans developed a relatively highly cultivated civilization. Under Etruscan domination Rome seems to have flourished and grown considerably. It was helped by its one natural strategic asset. Its hills, although not very high, served as a stronghold commanding the crossing of the Tiber in the middle of the coastal plain. A bridge at this site could be protected as it could nowhere else from the Central Apennines to the sea. Hence an important trade route from north to south lay through Rome, a circumstance from which the Romans were able to profit, as people in similar circumstances usually have profited, by levying tolls. Helped by their fertile soil to increase their numbers, and by their control of a salt-yielding area on the coast and of an important trade route to increase their wealth, the Romans had already made their home, in this early period, one of the strongest and most important cities in the whole of Italy. No other city in the peninsula had a larger temple than that at Rome. There were other impressive buildings all enclosed within walled fortifications of greater extent than those of any other settlement except those of Tarentum, one of the Greek cities in the south of Italy. At length the Romans thought themselves strong enough to seek independence from their overlords. Etruscan political and military ascendancy consequently came

to an end when the leading men of Rome succeeded in expelling
the last of the proud Tarquin Kings traditionally in 510 B.C.

Freedom was thereby won, but at considerable cost. Etruscan
enmity became a lasting and serious hazard. The closing of the
north–south trade route through Rome was an immediate consequence of independence. The Romans were forced back upon
their own resources, which meant concentration upon agriculture
as a means of livelihood. For a century at least the going was
hard and Rome declined rather than progressed. The Etruscans
by-passed them by putting their north–south commerce on the
sea-route well out of the reach of Rome. A lengthy period of
defence and consolidation was therefore necessary before Rome
could expand and provide the food required by her growing
numbers. Under a Republican form of government the Romans
gradually built up their strength.

The strategic picture was essentially simple. The Romans were
one among several peoples cultivating the small but fertile coastal
plain of Latium. They were separated from another and a yet
more fertile plain of about the same size (Campania) by a mountainous mass. The hinterland was also all mountainous and its
glens and passes were controlled by hardy mountain races.
There were Umbrians and Sabines flanking the Etruscans in the
north. More formidable than either were the Samnites occupying
the whole of the central range. Their dominion extended behind
and beyond Latium and Campania down to the Adriatic coast.
The men on the plains had what the hill-men often lacked, ample
crops of grain, vegetables and fruits. The hill-men had what the
men on the plains often wanted, well-watered grazing for animals.
Clashes between the two were naturally to be expected, particularly as the growth of population pressed everywhere upon the
means of subsistence. The first essential in such conditions was
union between the men on the plains and foothills – Romans,
Latins, and Campanians. The near neighbours of Rome, the
Latins to the south, came to terms only after the fierce battle of
Lake Regillus (497 B.C.), in which defeat was narrowly averted,
the legends assert, by the intervention of the twin gods Castor and
Pollux. The Romans secured independence, equality and the
promise of perpetual peace by guaranteeing the same advantages
to the Latins. Both promised mutual aid against common enemies.
Such was the *foedus Cassianum*, one of the oldest public documents

in the history of Rome, which Cicero remembered seeing copied on bronze tablets before the rostra in the Forum at Rome.

Roman policy, rough and brutal as it so often was, knew how to use some at least of its victories with a moderation and restraint rare if not unknown in a barbaric age. The Romans improved upon the usual practice of always stealing land, of enslaving whole populations or of taxing the survivors. Instead Rome sought to secure and maintain alliances with the other peoples of the plains. To this quality as much as anything else must the rise and greatness of Rome be attributed. Statesmanlike distinctions were made in dealing with the vanquished. Some were granted Roman citizenship, others were admitted to half the privileges of citizens, the more recalcitrant were given no citizen rights until, under Roman government, they had earned the privilege by good behaviour. The fighting over, the Romans and the Latins became at first allies, later fellow-citizens and ultimately one people. In this way other neighbouring tribes, such as the Hernici, either by choice or by necessity joined the complicated Roman-Latin coalition. The struggles with the hill-men, the Volscians, the Umbrians, Sabines and Samnites, then began in earnest and they led to more difficult and more persistent warfare. At first the Romans were hard pressed in defensive struggles against the Latins until their victory at Lake Regillus (the date of which is traditionally given as 497 B.C.). Intermittent wars with the Sabines lasted from about 505 B.C. to 449 B.C. The Aequi and Volsci were more formidable opponents who were not overcome until the Battle of Algidus, 431 B.C., after strife lasting something more than fifty years. The great power at this time was still Rome's old masters, the Etruscans, and with them a forty years' peace treaty was made after ten or eleven years' fighting, in 474 B.C.

The Romans turned to the offensive during the last quarter of the fifth century B.C. On the east they overcame the Aequi (423 B.C. to 393 B.C.) and the Volsci (about 431 B.C. to 393 B.C.). A great step forward was made when the formidable Etruscan city of Veii, north of the Tiber, was finally overthrown after a ten years' struggle in 396 B.C. Two other Etruscan towns involved in this struggle were also overcome, Capena in 395 B.C. and Falerii in 394 B.C. While these neighbours fought and snarled at each other, a truly formidable danger to them all lurked beyond the River Po and the mountains of the north.

From far and legendary lands of forest and winter snow, swarms of wild nomadic Gaulish tribes crossed the mountain ranges and passes of the Alps to loot, burn and destroy in the sunny land of Italy. Streams of stricken refugees and the glow of burning villages on the horizon would be the only warning that the devouring hordes were at hand. In the year 390 or 387 B.C., the horror reached Rome. The city fell, except for the Capitol, the citadel perched on its small rocky eminence. For six months the fate of this sole small stronghold was perilous. The final disaster was narrowly averted, legend says, by the sacred geese giving the alarm as a scaling party of Gauls had all but gained a foothold on the Capitol. The Gauls were bought off by a large ransom and they withdrew again to the north. It was an experience Rome never forgot. The work of their forefathers for over a hundred years seemed entirely undone. In international affairs as in politics, prestige is a product of expectations about future conduct based upon present performance. The past, however solid or brilliant, counts for little. Disasters to proud and powerful nations therefore rarely come singly. So Rome found. Crushed by defeat, the Romans soon saw that their hard-won good name in Italy was also forfeit so that, as Livy recorded in a later age, 'it was clear to all that the Roman name was menaced not only with the hate of her enemies, but also with the scorn of her allies'. The Romans had to buckle to and vindicate afresh their pre-eminence in Central Italy. The Etruscans, despite their own heavy losses at the hands of the Gauls, took the offensive against Rome from the north between 388 B.C. and 386 B.C. Rome was unable to retaliate until 359 B.C. when after eight years' fighting another forty years' truce was concluded with the Etruscans (351 B.C.) who thereafter gave little trouble. (See the map pp. 22–3.)

Meanwhile to the east, Rome attacked the Aequi in 389 B.C., next the Hernici, Rome's old allies, in 386/385 B.C. Not until 358 B.C. was Rome able to settle accounts with the Hernici, after having declared war on them again in 362 B.C.

The Volsci on the south-east were tougher foes. They also had struck when Rome's fortunes seemed low in 389 B.C. After a bitter struggle they were beaten off in 386–385 B.C. but they renewed their onslaughts in attacks lasting until 377 B.C. until they were finally crushed in a war lasting from 348 to 338 B.C.

Even the Latins had no scruples in breaking away from their

old ally, and Rome was hard put to it between 389 B.C. and 354 B.C. to restore her paramount position to the south in Latium. The task was not finally completed until, with the aid of the Samnites between 340 B.C. and 338 B.C., Rome finally broke up the Latin League and dictated her own terms of peace to its members in the decisive treaty of 338 B.C., a statesmanlike settlement which bound the Latins and Romans in a new confederacy.

Aided by a succession of able men, the might of Rome was painstakingly restored. Of them all the name of Camillus is outstanding. For a quarter of a century he was the man to whom Romans looked in times of trouble, and he did not fail them. He and the men around him were succeeded by others famous in the traditions of Rome, T. Manlius Torquatus, thrice Consul (347 B.C., 344 B.C. and 340 B.C.), and M. Valerius Corvus, Consul in 348 B.C., 346 B.C., 343 B.C. and 335 B.C. Rome again became a strongly fortified town, military colonies were planted at strategic points, and the army was reformed by abandoning the phalanx or serried, horde formation and introducing open order fighting by spear throwers. After 381 B.C., when Tusculum was the first to be so privileged, former enemies were bound to Rome by being given rights as Roman citizens. In the last half of the fourth century B.C. this method of augmenting the size of the citizen body, and consequently of the army, was increasingly used.

About thirty years after the sack of Rome, the Gauls returned on their plundering raids. The details of their various incursions are confused. There is no doubt, however, that the Romans were thickly beset by troubles from both the Gauls and their nearer neighbours. Northwards against the Etruscans, eastwards against the Aequi and Hernici and southwards against the Volsci and Latins, the Romans had to fight doggedly for fifty years before securing themselves in Central Italy. Had the Gauls given up their nomadic way of life and achieved a well-laid plan of conquest and settlement, the story might have been very different. For Rome would have been hopelessly outnumbered by the Gauls. Nothing but their superior intelligence and will to conquer enabled the Romans to survive the Gaulish menace. Then the Romans had to reckon with the Samnites to the South and they also called forth all the military power the Romans could muster. Their task of imposing their leadership upon their neighbours became very much more difficult when some of these tough highlanders took the mad risk of inviting the Gauls to help them against Rome.

The wars with the Samnites began badly for Rome with defeat and humiliation at the Caudine Forks, where disarmed Roman survivors of the battle were marched under a yoke of spears (321 B.C.). War was renewed five or six years later. Thereafter the Gauls reappeared in force to join the Samnites. They were routed after one of the decisive battles in Roman history, at Sentinum (295 B.C.), in which the Consul P. Decius Mus met a hero's death to turn the day for Rome. The Etruscans, Umbrians and Samnites, who had joined the Gauls against Rome, did not sustain the fight for much longer, and successively made their peace, until, with the unconditional surrender of the Samnites in 290 B.C., the might of Rome was once again supreme in Central Italy. The power of the Etruscans seems finally to have collapsed at this time, as a result of their own inability to organize themselves and to withstand the destructive attacks of the Gauls. Rome profited not merely by the elimination of a once powerful and dangerous enemy but also by being able eventually to succeed to the Etruscan heritage. That unity which Italy failed to oppose to the barbarian, Rome, by instinct or design, sought to achieve by her own strength aided by wise diplomacy. The Gauls with ever-renewed force returned in 285 B.C., still formidable, but they were again defeated and this time they were driven north of the Rubicon. Land was taken from them, and added to the Roman public domain. Again in the following year yet another tribe of Gauls got to within fifty miles of Rome before they were hurled back. The northern frontier was thereafter fairly secure for nearly 200 years. Three generations of Rome's manhood between 400 and 280 B.C. had, in constant and often desperate warfare, brought their country from insignificance to a position of enviable distinction in the Italian peninsula. Their strength had been forged amid fiery trials. Thus prepared, Rome was able to face the yet graver perils which the future was to bring.

The expansion of Greece into Italy seemed likely at one time to include the territory of Rome itself, but the Etruscans had proved too strong for the Greek invaders in the northern half of the peninsula. The whole of the south of Italy including the rich island of Sicily fell, however, under Greek sway. The civilization of Greece was thereby brought very near to the Romans but a century at least was to elapse before the Romans began to take any interest in it. Then they got involved in Greek affairs by coming to the rescue of the Greek city of Thurii, whose leaders appealed to Rome for help against their enemies the Lucanians instead of to the Greeks of Tarentum, whose 'protection' was becoming too expensive. This annoyed the Tarentines, who sank some Roman ships. Rome declared war (281 B.C.). The Tarentines found a brilliant leader in Pyrrhus, one of the younger successors of Alexander the Great, whose own meteoric career had recently come to an end after he had carried the arms of Greece to the confines of the known world and had returned laden with immense treasures from the East (323 B.C.). The Romans then faced a formidable foe and narrowly escaped disaster at Heraclea in the south of Italy, on the bay of Tarentum (280 B.C.). Eventually they gained the mastery. Pyrrhus was called back by troubles at home and Rome secured an undisputed leadership of the whole of South Italy, after reducing the many Greek settlements along the southern coast.

In the ten years between 281 B.C. and 272 B.C. Rome was within sight of securing the ascendancy which she finally won by 265 B.C., when she became supreme in Italy south of the territory of the Gauls beyond the River Po. Sicily, however, still remained outside the Roman orbit. So did the other Mediterranean islands, Corsica and Sardinia.

The full story of these struggles of Rome with her neighbours is blurred and many details have been lost. Until comparatively recently, when economic causes have been suggested as a simple explanation of these early wars, their sole interest lay in their political results and in the light they threw upon the character and the methods of the Romans. Many of the actual wars were probably similar in nature to and on much the same scale as the clashes in the Middle Ages between the Saxon kingdoms of the Heptarchy or the tribal feuds dividing the semi-barbaric clans of Scotland or tribes of Ireland. The amount of authentic history concerning Rome's often desperate and perilous struggles was of less account, even in Rome itself, than the rich crop of heroic tales mixed with legends, some of which have been referred to briefly above. They survived to stimulate Roman patriotic sentiment and family pride and to increase the respect and deference shown in later ages to the noble or patrician families

bearing the same names as the renowned heroes in many stirring
and dramatic scenes in battles long ago.

Economic motives alone do not fully account for these
struggles although Rome certainly profited as a result of them.
The Romans needed more food and they got it by winning better
agricultural land, not by migrating overseas as the Greeks had
done or by taking to trade and commerce as the Phoenicians were
doing. Success in warfare brought very real advantages in this
early age, when wealth was more obviously bound to the soil
than it is in modern times. There was no richer booty for a
growing community than fertile land and slave labour with which
to work it. For this reason the rank and file of the Roman people
were often quite as ready to vote for war as were their leaders.
It says much for Roman restraint that her wars had other
objects and that by no means all of the vanquished automatically
forfeited to the Romans their land and liberty. Rome's territory
increased from about 600 square miles at the time of the capture
of Rome by the Gauls, to about 9,600 square miles after winning
supremacy in Italy. The new resources enabled the Romans to
plant out their younger sons and landless citizens to become
colonial dependants of the mother city. They naturally were a
privileged class among the conquered. As long as Rome was liable
to attack by its neighbours, the motive force in founding such
colonies would be strategical rather than merely economic and
the colonists would be armed outposts of Rome. They marched
to their new homes in military formation as though embarking
upon a new campaign. Some of the newly won territory was given
in small lots to the rank and file. Some was taken for the public
domain and then leased to swell the fortunes of the wealthier
classes, who obviously were best able to pay the rental and the
cost of the labour required to work the land.

Slavery was already a feature of life in Rome, as indeed it was
fairly generally at this time in most Mediterranean countries. The
fact that Rome's first slaves were people of Italy, and near
neighbours at that, meant that they could be absorbed into the
social life of Rome with little difficulty. Moreover slaves did not
at first form the bulk of the labour force, because the men of Rome
were mostly independent farmers in a small way who worked
hard themselves. Those who did not possess farms of their own
worked as hired labourers for the landowners. Many forces

conspired to lighten the lot of the Italian slaves. The defeated tribes and peoples from whom they came were brought under Roman rule and given some, but not all, of the privileges of Roman citizenship. Trade and business relationships and later intermarriage with the Romans followed. By degrees a greater community of interest was established. That some generations passed before this policy took effect says nothing against the soundness of instinct that seems to have led the Romans to adopt it. If slavery had stopped at that, the entire history of Rome might have been very different. For slavery under such conditions was a much milder fate than it became later when vast hordes of men and women were imported wholesale from their homes in the Eastern and Western Mediterranean. It was one thing to be a slave from the neighbouring hills of Rome amongst a people not very dissimilar in manners, customs, and language, and in much the same land as the slaves' own territory, but it was a very different thing to be a slave torn from hearth and home and transported hundreds of miles across the sea like cattle to an alien land where the language and the habits were entirely new. Yet the Romans do not seem to have treated the foreign slaves less favourably than the local slaves, particularly in the all-important matter of granting them freedom. Huge numbers of alien people were imported into Rome as slaves and later set free. They and their descendants so greatly diluted the old Roman stock that by Cicero's time the inhabitants of Rome were fast becoming a different breed from the heroes of the fourth century B.C. and from the men with whom his grandfather rubbed shoulders along the Sacred Way and in the crowded Forum.

The Golden Age of the Roman Republic

Romans of later days not surprisingly looked back upon the early period of the rise of their Republic from the fifth to the third century B.C. as the days in which the finest qualities of their race found fullest expression. No doubt the Roman habit of venerating their ancestors explains something of this attitude. In Rome, moreover, as in most ancient lands, nobody believed that, as a matter of course, the future would be better than the past. On the contrary, the Golden Age of the Greeks and Romans, like the Garden of Eden of the Hebrews, was a state from which imperfect men had steadily fallen. Inevitably also reformers in later Rome gave point to criticisms of their contemporaries and justified their own discontents by depicting a time when, so they said, selfishness was swamped by public spirit, when contentment with a few modest necessities of life left no place for envy or avarice, and when men were brave because they were strong, with a simple faith in their country and their gods.

> Then none was for a party;
> Then all were for the State;
> Then the great man helped the poor,
> And the poor man loved the great:
> Then lands were fairly portioned;
> Then spoils were fairly sold:
> The Romans were like brothers,
> In the brave days of old.

Nevertheless, when all allowance is made for the influence of such habits of mind, it seems that Romans had some solid reasons for believing that their forerunners were men of no common stamp. It was a fact which other non-Roman peoples in Italy could hardly deny, especially at a time when Rome controlled the whole world and they were themselves anxious to be counted as Romans and admitted to the privileges of Roman citizenship.

What were the special qualities that won supremacy for Rome? Certainly not mere numbers; their Latin neighbours were as numerous. Certainly not mere wealth; the Etruscans and Greeks were richer. How else could Roman success be explained save by the force of human personality? Nowhere, thought Cicero, was it possible to find a people possessed of so many excellent qualities as the old Romans. They had, he said, true greatness of soul, a nature at once deeply serious, calm, steadfast, loyal and trustworthy. We have learned in our own day that there are few more misleading imaginative exercises than that of generalizing about the supposed character of so large and complex an organism as a nation. Nevertheless we have succeeded in finding one or two clues promising a greater insight into national characteristics. Of them language is assuredly one. The form and character of the Latin language offers one means of testing the truth of what might be dismissed as merely a product of Cicero's patriotic imagination. For the style and manner of speech are an index of the man and

Latin has characteristics of a special kind. Latin sentences are direct and to the point, virile, energetic, austere and dignified. Because they were an essentially practical people, the Romans chose concrete words in preference to abstractions. Simplicity and a terse vigour of speech are the foundation of their language. The few remains of early Roman writing we possess show little other quality. When a more sophisticated and involved style was developed a century or two later, particularly after Cicero had left the marks of his imperishable genius upon the language of his forefathers, a rigid discipline of thought and expression is still observable in Roman writings, especially in the careful marshalling of subordinate sentences and clauses around the main theme.

During the two and a half long centuries of struggle and triumph of the early Republic of Rome in Italy there was no native literature of any consequence. Not until Rome had begun to find itself in wars of expansion abroad did there seem to develop a consciousness of individual character and history sufficiently strong to stimulate self-expression. Then, when Romans began to interest themselves in the history of their city, they wrote in Greek, just as in the Middle Ages men of learning wrote in Latin because the vernacular European languages were little understood outside their borders and they also lacked words and phrases in which they could express themselves to an educated audience. Not for the Romans of the heroic age were the graces and the elegance of the highly cultivated Greeks, whom, in fact, most of them despised. Blunt, direct, practical and determined, the creators of the Republic showed well enough in their speech what manner of men they were. The indications that language affords need confirmation from other quarters. It is forthcoming in many anecdotes and in the more substantial evidence provided by the known achievements of the early Romans. A general picture emerges of a stolid matter-of-fact and puritanical people, intensely loyal to their family, their State and their gods, willingly accepting such authority with perfect discipline; a quality described by the Latin word *pietas*. Every true Roman valued this quality and sought it for himself, so that he could be described as *pius*. The words meant more than our modern words 'piety' and 'pious' which are now used in a religious sense alone. The satisfaction of being one of a social group, sharing in common loyalties, common tasks and common triumphs, answers one of the most deep-seated cravings of human beings. In primitive communities life seems to have no meaning or value to the individual unless it affords this satisfaction. It is a satisfaction all the deeper because it provides a natural outlet for human affections and it helps to develop them. There was plenty of love and affection in the apparently stern Roman household. In modern societies, despite the extent to which individuals have freed themselves to live according to their own ideas, the need for contact and community within the family or with some group or society is still very evident. Otherwise human energies and affections are blunted and, lacking a worthwhile purpose, develop frustration, disillusionment and boredom with their usual accompaniment of bad temper, aggressiveness and mental illness. Most people seem unable to achieve peace of mind and sometimes cannot sustain themselves without the assurance of support from the system of common beliefs, sentiments and values that society or community alone can afford. Often men demand no more from life than such assurance. A remark by one of the early visitors to Japan in the nineteenth century illustrates the overwhelming importance of the social framework for the individual: 'It is a singular fact that in Japan, where the individual is sacrificed to the community, he should seem perfectly happy and contented; while in America, where exactly the opposite takes place and the community is sacrificed to the individual, the latter is in a perpetual state of uproarious clamour for his rights.' This was written in 1859 but the principle applies very widely in all ages.

With the Romans of the early Republic, the community spirit and a readiness of the individual to sacrifice himself to it was a natural and spontaneous thing. Since life had no meaning apart from the survival of the State, the individual was reckless in its defence. No Roman in any circumstances could regard himself as vanquished – 'a peculiarity', said the observant Greek, Polybius, in the days of Cicero's grandfather, 'which they have inherited from their ancestors'. This was the key to the real strength of the Republic. The other well-known virtues of the Romans followed from it; their manliness and courage in battle (*virtus*), their sobriety, their consciousness of their responsibilities, their disciplining of the emotions (*gravitas*) and their readiness to give single-minded attention to the practical needs of the hour (*simplicitas*). With it all went a precise formality by which almost all their actions were measured and undertaken, and a high sense of honesty. Theirs was a community spirit fostered first in the home which the Romans venerated and cherished with a passion and tenacity that seem to have been new in the development of civilization. The head of the home, the father of the family, was the first source of authority and discipline, qualities which, in the early centuries of Rome, he seems to have exercised in full measure. This marked supremacy of the Roman male points to a patriarchal form of society. Inevitably therefore it suggests the view held today by some students of social organization that it would probably have been predominantly a rather hard, militarist and even cruel society, as the patriarchal society of Prussia has been in modern history. It is not difficult to discern such tendencies in Roman society, but the respect which the Roman father enjoyed extended also to his wife. The Roman matron held a high position in the family second only to that of her husband. These robust family and household units in turn owed all their loyalty to the Republic. They were the Republic. To pay such tributes to the Roman character is to echo the highly idealized picture that men of the age of Cicero and ever since have always held up for the admiration of the world.

Such a glorification of the early Romans has no doubt served various purposes of which the chief seems to have been the moral aim of stirring up others to imitate them. And it has served this purpose with some success not only in the Republic and later Empire of Rome, but in more modern times as well. Shakespeare confessed to a vivid awareness of the heroic Roman pattern of life when he made the noble Horatio declare at the culminating point of Hamlet's tragedy, 'I am more an antique Roman than a Dane'.

As long as history is regarded as 'philosophy teaching by examples' drawn from real life, this tendency to write up the virtues of past ages will persist. So long also will classical scholars be tempted to seek to enhance the value of their subject by dwelling with enthusiasm upon the moral worth of the Romans. So long also will it be a thankless task to propose any less generous revaluation of what has so generally been accepted as the grandeur that was Rome. It would be nearer the truth to take the view that the best Roman characters of the early Republic, over-idealized as they have been, were the fine product of a simple and primitive state of society that could not by any conceivable means have been restored once it had faded away. Cicero and very many who have followed him did not seem to realize that it was not by harking back to models in the past, but by resolutely facing the problems of their own time, that they could hope to create conditions in which the human personality could grow and expand to the extent of embracing qualities and achievements of which the Romans of the early Republic, despite their many admirable characteristics, would not have been capable.

Roman Citizenship and the Beginnings of International Relations

In the ancient world a beaten enemy ran a serious risk of being killed, enslaved or forced to find a ruinous ransom as the price of his life. To Rome belongs the credit of much reducing these evil practices, not indeed of abolishing any of them, for her record is darkened by crimes and atrocities as black as any to be found on the pages of history.

Rome often went beyond extermination, cruelty and repression, to arrive at an understanding with her former enemies. Characteristically, among the oldest of her religious officials were the *Fetiales*. They were priestly ambassadors employed to advise upon war and peace, to act as spokesmen to the enemy, to endeavour to lead him to acknowledge the justice of the Roman cause and, if persuasion failed, to perform the religious ceremonies attendant upon the declaration of war without which the Roman conscience was not completely clear. To the *Fetiales* also was committed the duty of attending the declaration of peace with proper ceremony. The religious scruples to which the 'college' of *Fetiales* bears witness may often have seemed to Rome's victims to be mere humbug. But methods of declaring war which we have experienced in our supposedly more advanced civilization do not entitle the twentieth century to be over-scornful of the techniques of a barbarous age.

The Romans, like the dwellers on the plains in all ages, had more often been the victims of mountain-dwelling raiders than in the habit themselves of raiding the mountaineers. The plainsman is consequently the first to develop a healthy respect for law and order. In an age when life was cheaply held, and before the notion of justice between nations had begun to develop, it was no mean achievement of victorious Romans to turn their former enemies into allies, whose descendants ultimately fought to become, and were later proud to be, citizens of Rome. From Ariminum in the north to Brundisium in the south, a complicated system of treaty states, independent towns, citizen colonies and Latin cities and colonies were connected with Rome, not as the head of a federal union, but as leader of Italy. It is said that the idea of a federal union had early been proposed to Rome by her Latin neighbours on the basis that half the Roman Senate and one Consul should be chosen by the Latins (about 340 B.C.). Determined to retain independence of action as a conquering power, the Romans rejected a policy that would have left Rome a federal Capital. They backed their refusal by fighting and defeating the Latins (341 – 338 B.C.). This 'No' to the Latins has been said to mark a turning point in the history of Italy and of the world. From this time the political organization of Italy under Roman domination began to take shape.

The bonds between Rome and the other inhabitants of Italy were of various sorts. (See diagram, pp. 22–3.)

Citizen Colonies. Those who had gone from Rome with full citizenship to settle on newly won Roman domains or in newly formed and strategically situated Roman colonies, remained citizens of Rome. Because of their distance from Rome, their rights were nominal rather than real as far as taking part in public assemblies and elections at Rome was concerned. Nevertheless they remained for legal purposes Romans, on the Roman soil – the *Ager Romanus*. A man who was not already a Roman citizen, by joining such new communities, became *civis Romanus* himself. The citizen colonies thus opened a way whereby Roman franchise might be acquired.

Municipalities. Some old Latin towns, such as Lanuvium and Nomentum, were included in the Roman State as *municipia*, their inhabitants becoming full Roman citizens but being allowed to retain their own system of local government. The inhabitants of other Italian towns at a greater distance from Rome, such as Fundi and Formiae, were not at first given full

ROME · ALLIES, ENEMIES

ETRUSCI

AEQUICULI

VE

Sutrium

Nepete

SABINI

Capena

Carseoli

Alba Fucens

5   6

Nomentum

9

7

8

Tibur

ROMA   Gabii

MAR

1   2

AEQUI   Aletrium

3   4

10

Praeneste   Anagnia

Tusculum

HERNICI   Verulae

Velitrae   Cora

Ferentinum

II

Signia

Arpinum

Lavinium

12   Norba   13   Frusino

Ardea

14   Fregellae

Setia

Antium   Satricum

Privernum   Fabrateria

15   VOLSCI

16 Fundi

Circei   Formiae

Tarracina

D.B.S

& NEIGHBOURS · 298 B.C.

STINI

● ROMAN CITIZENS WITH VOTES · *Cives Romani.*

○ ROMAN CITIZENS WITH-OUT VOTES · *Cives sine suffragio.*

▣ 'LATIN' ALLIES · *Socii Latini nominis*

PELIGNI

□ OTHER ALLIES · *Socii*

S I

◎ COLONY OR CITY OF ROMAN FOUNDATION

○ CITY OF NON-ROMAN FOUNDATION

Sora

Allies   Enemy Tribes

SAMNITES

ROMAN TRIBES *of Cives Romani*

Aquinum

Inter-amna

Suessa

Minturnae

1	*Succusana*	9	*Aniensis*
2	*Esquilina*	10	*Arnensis*
3	*Palatina*	11	*Scaptia*
4	*Collina*	12	*Maecia*
5	*Sabatina*	13	*Teretina*
6	*Stellatina*	14	*Pomptina*
7	*Clustumina*	15	*Poplilia*
8	*Tromentina*	16	*Oufentina*

citizenship. They had all the rights of citizenship except the right to vote in Rome's public assemblies or to hold a political office. They became *cives sine suffragio*, a kind of half-citizen. Until the political organization of Roman lands was completed in 241 B.C., the territories of these half-citizens were about five times as large as those of Rome.

Latin Colonies and Cities. Roman citizen colonies were supplemented by colonies formed jointly with the neighbouring Latins. The Latin colonists could not complain that Rome was careless of their rights and privileges. The municipal authorities of which they formed part had their own constitution, which was not a lifeless copy of that of Rome. They elected their own magistrates and sometimes struck their own coinage. Rome left them to conduct their own census and to mobilize their own troops for the Roman Army, in which they served as distinct units under their own officers. They shared with Rome in the booty won in war. Most of the old Latin cities had the same advantages. They were specially favoured allies as '*socii Latini nominis*' for they possessed the right of owning Roman land, of inheriting property from a Roman and of trading by Roman methods and under the protection of Roman courts. Theirs was, in fact, the whole collection of privileges admitting equality with Romans as far as the laws of property and trade were concerned (the *ius commercii*). It is important to note that the Latin peoples did not possess these links with each other – at least such links would not be recognized by Roman law.

They did not, however, have full rights as Roman citizens and the privileges they once possessed of acquiring such rights simply by migrating to Rome were progressively limited to those who left a son in the colony (177 B.C.) and later to those who had held office or risen to special eminence in their own community. In imposing these restrictions, the Romans were not without support from the colonies who were alarmed by the fear of depopulation, particularly after 265 B.C., when the attractions of Rome as the metropolis of the Italian world had become much more powerful.

Men from the Latin colonies who chanced to be in Rome when public assemblies were being held had the right of voting, a privilege they may have been given in compensation for the refusal to allow them to leave their colony to take up residence in Rome.

Italian Allies. More numerous than the citizen colonies and the Latin allies and colonies were the lands of the other allied Italian peoples. The details of the carefully devised treaties and agreements binding them to Rome, where they are still known, are less important than the general fact that each depended individually upon Rome. All were bound to supply troops for Rome's wars and not to conduct a foreign policy of their own. In return they were allowed full freedom in running their own internal affairs and were guaranteed military protection.

It was a guarantee that the Romans were proud to keep, but their ability to sustain their pride and to maintain the honour of the Roman State was put to the most gruelling test very shortly after the foundation of Rome's policy for Italy had been laid. Less favoured than the Latins, these Italian allies were excluded from the political life of Rome until Cicero's day, when the Samnites, Marsians, Umbrians and others turned upon Rome and fought a bitter civil war (90–89 B.C.) before they were able to win any promise of better treatment. Long before Cicero's day Rome had to struggle with the Italians for mere survival.

The Romans Consolidate Their Position in Italy

When it is said that Rome gained 'supremacy in Italy' by the middle of the third century B.C., it does not mean that a harsh Roman central government was forcibly imposed, stamping out local Italian customs, languages, institutions and political life. The Romans did not behave as the Nazis did during their brief, although far too long, supremacy in Europe. There were no Roman equivalents of Gauleiters, storm-troopers; no Russian tanks ready to stifle everything through which distinctive national characteristics become manifest. On the contrary, the Romans left the Latins, Volscians and Sabines very much to their own devices as far as their internal affairs were concerned. They paid Rome no taxes.

Maybe Rome found it difficult to provide an adequate administration for those territories. Perhaps the idea of doing so never occurred in those early days, when government was far from being the well-organized, efficient machine that it became with the invention of the professional civil service in the nineteenth century. Perhaps it was unnecessary for Rome forcibly to try to romanize her neighbours, for in the end the various Italian peoples no doubt went some of the way towards meeting the Romans by showing themselves willing to link their fortunes with those of the stronger, richer and more progressive Roman community. In politics, as in other spheres of life, nothing succeeds like success, and the ample evidence of Roman prowess showed the Italian world that the Romans were allies worth having. The device of creating 'half-citizens' proved very valuable because for the first time it showed the Romans that political loyalty could be given both to a local community and to the larger State of which the community was a subordinate part.

Whatever the reason, the result amply justified Roman policy. Whether by mere instinct, plain good sense, or by intelligent foresight, Roman statesmanship triumphed through the implicit recognition it gave to the fundamentally important psychological fact that men get along well together only as long as they are allowed to keep their self-respect and are satisfied in working together. What is a nation, if it is not, as Renan has said, the memory of a common achievement and 'the desire to work together for common aims? Rome, like all other political combinations, had in the long run no other cement to hold it together than this free energy of co-operation springing from the wills of the men of the many tribes, races and nations drawn, attracted, or temporarily compelled into association with it. 'Rome was an amalgamation.' Such was the verdict of the great German historian of Rome, Theodor Mommsen. The Romans themselves were aware of the fact, indeed Cicero's brother himself described Rome as 'a city made up of the meeting of many peoples'. As it began in Italy, so it was to go on in the Mediterranean and in Europe, adding and attracting new territories to adhere to its political system. Peoples such as the Germans, whose ways of life were so fundamentally different from those of Rome would see nothing to attract them in the complex city life of the Mediterranean and hence would naturally never wish to join it. The Etruscans, Rome's next-door neighbours, had an alien, un-Italian way of life and were never able to assimilate easily the Roman way.

Plenty of support can be found in Roman history for the notion that men are naturally aggressive and like fighting. But deeper than ingrained bellicosity lie differences that are more profound than the racial antagonism that is often regarded as a sufficient explanation of conflict. Mere physical peculiarities such as colour of skin, shape of nose, type of hair, and so forth are superficial. It is incompatibilities in manners, traditions, beliefs, and practices that are really serious because they may easily be so pronounced that they are irreconcilable. Then conflict or separation is inevitable. Primitive peoples may kill missionaries bringing another culture. Cultivated people not fired with missionary zeal may find it too repulsive to live among the uneducated and uncouth of their own or any other race, whatever the colour of their skin. For them there is a clash of values in which everything that gives meaning and value to life is felt to be at stake. Men will make desperate efforts to defend their traditions, practices, beliefs, standards and way of life even at the cost of war or exile. The early Romans, Etruscans and Gauls could not accept each others' way of life. Later, when the Romans had become much more sophisticated, the Etruscans no longer seemed so strange. When the Gauls later still assimilated Roman ways, the two races could live in peace. The Greek, Italian and Roman ways of life, although dissimilar, were not fundamentally so. Completely irreconcilable hatreds did not arise, although jealousies and unequal civic privileges long rankled, ultimately to burst out in fierce rebellion.

Unless this loosely knit character of the Roman State is remembered, it will seem a paradox, if not an actual contradiction of the historical achievement of the early Republic, to learn that 200 years later, in Cicero's time, Rome again became involved in bitter warfare with those same Italian neighbours over whom it had ostensibly 'triumphed' in the third century B.C. The truth is, however, that a composite political unit such as the Roman Republic can endure as long as it has sufficient attractions to keep its various component parts content and satisfied with the programme of joint activity devised by the leading partner. Should that force no longer live up to its promise of leadership, the parts will fall away, as they were later to fall away from the Roman Empire in its decadence and as they have in more recent times fallen away from once great Empires such as those of Spain and of Austria.

Chapter Two

ROME TAKES THE LEAD IN THE
MEDITERRANEAN
264–201 B.C.

OF all the peoples with whom the Romans had dealings, none was better organized than the Carthaginians. Theirs was the strength of a trading people who had long since found foreign trade so profitable that they had developed it to such an extent that they knew that they must trade in order to live. Based upon the city of Carthage on what is now the Gulf of Tunis, they controlled the two islands of Sardinia and Corsica, to their immediate north, as well as Sicily to the east. The sea was their element and over the Western Mediterranean their power was unchallenged. The wealth of their traders found attractive investment in the fertile soil of North Africa where a landowning aristocracy grew and gained influence in the State. The division of the interests of its governing classes between trade and agriculture was, however, to become a source of political weakness rather than of strength. The power of the Carthaginians was moreover insecurely based. Their agriculture depended upon gangs of slaves. Their armies and fleets were largely manned by mercenaries. Carthage was supposed to have been the first foreign power with which the young Republic of Rome had concluded an alliance, for an old tradition asserts that there had been a treaty in the first year of the Republic, 509 B.C. During the struggle with the Greeks, Rome had concluded another alliance with the Carthaginians. Peace between Rome and Carthage became more precarious after Rome's victory over Pyrrhus and the Greeks of Southern Italy, when jealousy and suspicion began to grow on both sides. The Carthaginians had narrow ideas on the subject of sea-borne commerce. They were in the habit of sinking at sight any foreign vessel they encountered in the Western Mediterranean. The Romans, not then being in any way dependent upon sea trade, did not particularly resent such action. The most obvious bone of contention between Rome and Carthage was the island of Sicily lying at the toe of Italy. Along its ample coastline, many gangs of pirate-brigands had hiding-places from which they would emerge to plunder the Italian mainland. In accepting an alliance with some of them, the Romans trespassed upon Carthaginian preserves. War, likely enough on more general grounds, there-upon resulted (264 B.C.).

The First Punic War, 264–241 B.C.

The momentous wars with Carthage, which thus began, were undoubtedly the supreme testing time for Rome. There were several periods in the second half of the third century B.C. when timid souls must have thought it an open question whether Aryan Romans and Italians or Semites from North Africa would secure control of the entire Mediterranean and so dominate the whole of the known world. But the Romans were not timid and theirs was the greater strength, founded four-square upon the sturdy men who farmed the soil of Central Italy.

The First Carthaginian, Phoenician or 'Punic' War lasted for twenty-three years (264–241 B.C.). In it Romans were forced into new forms of warfare, above all at sea, an element shunned and feared and upon which they never ventured with any pleasure. Aided by their allies, notably by seafaring western Greeks, who also had many old scores to settle with the Phoenicians, the Romans improvised successfully.

A fleet was created. Rowers were trained – at first on dry land, so it is said. The new fleet would not have availed the Romans against the better equipped and more experienced Carthaginians, unless they had succeeded in developing new tactics. The ortho-dox form of naval warfare as practised by the Carthaginians was to manoeuvre their vessels so that their heavily strengthened prow drove into the enemies' ships. The tactics were either ramming by a direct blow or striking a glancing blow so as to slice off the enemy's oars and thereby render him helpless against later ramming.

What the Romans did was to make floating forts out of their ships, manning them with Roman infantry, in addition to the rowers. The great physical strain on the rowers made it impossible for them to row and fight as well. As the Carthaginians came up alongside, trusting to their superior speed and momentum to cripple the rowing-power of the Romans, they were made fast by grappling-irons. Roman soldiers poured on board and slaughtered the unarmed and half-exhausted crew. The Carthaginian navy went down to defeat in the face of this startling new manoeuvre. But a naval victory or two could not alone win the war. The Romans did not have it all their own way at sea. Their losses were indeed, for that age, of staggering dimensions. They suffered more from shipwreck and storms than from the Carthaginian navy. Altogether they are said to have lost more than 500 ships, each with a crew of about 300 and 120 fighting men. Apart from some initial successes they owed their final victory to the fact that while both sides made many blunders, the Carthaginians made most. With dogged determination the Romans kept up the struggle. They invaded North Africa, but were unable to make good their easy victories there.

In the end Carthage sued for peace (242 B.C.). The result of twenty-three years' war was Roman control over all Sicily, except the small independent kingdom centred around the ancient Greek city of Syracuse. These long Sicilian campaigns had some unexpected results. Young, uncultivated Roman soldiers found themselves among a far more cultivated and civilized people. The master hand of Greek creative genius was evident all around them in the architecture of homes and temples, in the elegance of their fine furnishings and household equipment, in the consummate skill of Greek sculptors and potters and, above all, in the quick intelligence of the people. Something of the supremacy of the spirit of Greece in literature must also have become apparent to Romans who, in the sunny amphitheatres of many a Greek city, listened for the first time to the tragedies of Euripides and to the comedies of Menander. There were other products of the conquest of a more material kind, destined to exercise a sinister influence upon Roman policy and on the Roman character in the years to come. Money was forthcoming in the shape of a large indemnity from Carthage payable over ten years. It was badly needed in Rome to pay for the vast expense of the long war (241 B.C.). A new and more lasting source of wealth was gained, for Rome inherited from the former rulers of Sicily a tithe payable in grain. Nearly half a million bushels of wheat, sufficient at first to last the city for half a year, were annually supplied free of charge by the Sicilians. It was imported and sold in Rome, the proceeds going to the Treasury. It might be thought that the Roman farmers would object to this competition, but there are no records of any complaints on this score in the public assemblies of the citizen farmers. The truth must be that the wheat was needed. Before long, as much again as the free tithe of nearly half a million bushels was bought for the Roman market. In adopting the methods of Oriental despotism by acquiring a dependency yielding tribute, the Romans took a different line from that which they had hitherto followed with their Latin neighbours. Sicily received a Roman ruler who combined the duties of military commander, judge, and administrator. The Sicilians were in his power, and henceforward they remained part of the Roman dominion, well-protected, apart from a disastrous slave rebellion (p. 43) and Verres (p. 225).

The Second Punic War, 218–201 B.C.

The difficulties and dangers of the First Punic War, great as they were, paled to insignificance in comparison with the perils of the Second Punic War. After their initial victory in the first war the Romans seemed in little danger. Their power in Italy had steadily increased, aided by the prestige and the more substantial prizes of victory. They had spanned the Adriatic to gain a foothold in Illyria; ties with Greece were strengthened by alliances. Determined action was taken against the Gauls who again flooded south through Etruria. They were defeated at Telamon (225 B.C.); and Rome, strong with the legionary might of an army of 150,000 men, drove them northwards beyond the River Po. A Roman census at this time revealed a potential force of 700,000 infantry and 70,000 cavalry. About a third of these forces were Roman citizens who were therefore out-numbered two to one by their Latin, Samnite, Sabellian, Etruscan and other allies.

The Carthaginians, after being crippled at home by a fierce struggle with the mercenary army, whom they tried to cheat out of their pay, and weakened by their government of timid wealthy merchant princes, before long found a leader of genius in a young soldier, Hannibal, of the distinguished Barca family. It would be nearer the truth to say that he imposed himself upon them rather than was chosen by them. He seized his opportunity when the Carthaginians sought in Spain a compensation for the power they had lost and were continuing to lose further east. For after their first war with Rome, Sardinia and Corsica had been taken from them by the Romans, over and above the agreed terms of the treaty of peace. Later Roman historians themselves condemned this high-handed theft, but the senators who decided upon it had obvious motives for their action.

When the trade of Spain began to go southwards direct to Carthage instead of eastwards through Marseilles, the people of Marseilles lost a great part of their livelihood. They had therefore a strong motive to stir up the Romans against Carthage. There was also a war party in Carthage and there is a dramatic story of the way in which young Hannibal and his brother had been trained to seek vengeance on Rome. He had no other policy towards Rome than war, but it was a war for prestige and revenge rather than for more substantial prizes. After building up and training an army in Spain, Hannibal attacked and captured the city of a Roman ally, Saguntum, and carried the war, which he thereby precipitated, into the heart of Italy by his famous march, with his elephants, over the Alps. The breath-taking surprise caused by this exploit, later matched by the crushing defeats he inflicted upon the might of Rome, has obscured the fact that it was in itself a confession of weakness. If Hannibal and the Carthaginians had been able to retain command of the sea, this long and costly land journey, in which almost half his seasoned troops perished, would never have been undertaken. Nevertheless, once he was in Italy no Roman army, no Roman general, was a match for Hannibal. Until the last battle in 202 B.C. he suffered no major defeats, but dealt Rome one mighty blow after another, beginning in the north, followed up in the centre, in the misty ambush near Lake Trasimene, and reaching a devastating climax in the south on the fatal field of Cannae (216 B.C.).

Not until the final collapse of her Empire did the Roman arms again suffer such disasters from a foreign foe as Hannibal inflicted upon them. Two Roman armies had been exterminated with their commanding Consuls, leaving the invader free to roam and wreck Italy at his will. Hannibal's one mistake was not to capture Rome. Probably his lack of siege equipment made the task impossible; but why he did not try, and what would have been the consequence had he succeeded, have been the subject for perennial debate ever since.

Despite his military genius, he was unable to recruit the allies he had hoped to find among the enemies of Rome. He did not find it difficult to win over the Gauls in the north. His great surprise was the attitude of Rome's Italian allies, who seem to have regarded his promises of liberation from the hated yoke of Rome with no more enthusiasm than Irish, Egyptians, Africans and Indians displayed in our own time towards the pledges of freedom from British thraldom so persuasively proffered by Germans and Japanese. Some Italians in the south might conceivably have succumbed to very skilful diplomacy backed with overwhelming military success if Hannibal's conquest had been rapid. Instead it was long-drawn-out and all the while his army was living on Italian lands and taking their produce. The Italians also greatly feared the Gauls and the Gauls had no reason to love them. Hannibal apparently counted upon harnessing these fundamentally incompatible forces to serve his war machine, but was unable to rouse all the Italian peoples to his side. The few who fell into his clutches later incurred the stern vengeance of Rome.

Active support within Italy might have been unnecessary had Hannibal not suffered from the weakness and inefficiency of the rulers of Carthage at home. In his isolated, exposed situation he was bound to fail unless he was fed by constant streams of supplies and reinforcements. The Carthaginians no longer had command of the sea and they could not, even had they so wished, which is not very evident, have supported him with men and resources on the scale he needed. Moreover Hannibal himself did not succeed in capturing a good seaport at which he could receive supplies. Had he been adequately reinforced and equipped with heavy siege material, he might have reduced the many fortress towns of Italy and taken Rome. For there is no doubt that Hannibal had indeed brought the fortunes of the Republic to a low ebb.

The slaughter had been appalling: 15,000 citizen farmers and the best of their officers at Trasimene; at least 50,000 more at Cannae, involving the loss of the legions, cavalry, arms, standards, men and horses of two armies; another army of 25,000 and a Consul-elect lost in Gaul. These heavy blows were accompanied by a succession of other disasters and cruel disappointments: revolts in Sicily, defeats in Spain. The Treasury was empty and the State bankrupt. A general scarcity of supplies, of money and of food prevailed, and it could not be made good as long as farms in the most fertile parts of Italy were going up in smoke and while oxen broken to the plough were driven off by thousands to the slaughter to feed the hordes of foreign soldiers living on the country. A full picture of the nameless horrors endured by the wretched inhabitants of Italy can only be imagined.

Sometimes panic swept the country, and Rome itself did not escape some ugly scenes in one of which two Gauls and two Greeks were buried alive as a human sacrifice to propitiate the gods. Yet the one word which was not heard from Roman lips was 'Peace'. The Senate was magnificent in its refusal to despair of the Republic. When, in 211 B.C., Hannibal marched up to the walls of Rome, the site of his camp was calmly put up to auction in the city and it realized its full normal price. At the same time reinforcements were sent by sea from the city to the Roman troops engaging the Carthaginians under Hannibal's brother, Hasdrubal, in Spain.

The Romans no longer feared the Carthaginian navy or the ally from the East, Philip of Macedon, whom the Carthaginians brought into the war against them. The Romans were sufficiently strong at sea to be able to prevent an invasion of Italy from the Balkans.

The desperate struggle in Spain had been going badly for Rome. In 210 B.C., however, a young soldier, Publius Cornelius Scipio, was sent in command of all Roman forces there at the unprecedentedly early age of twenty-four. It was a command previously held by his father and his uncle, both members of the proud Cornelian family. They had been defeated and killed by the Carthaginians two years before. He revenged his family and succeeded in turning the tide of war in Rome's favour, but was not able to prevent Hasdrubal leaving Spain with an army of over 50,000 men to join his brother Hannibal in Italy. A new crisis occurred when this formidable new army entered Italy and faced a Roman army in the north in 207 B.C. The best troops of the army watching Hannibal in the south were suddenly marched north to unite against the new invader. The alarm and excitement in Rome was intense. There were now two Hannibals in Italy where the name of one alone was able to inspire chill and terror in the stoutest heart. While the citizens of Rome spent restless days and nights in an agony of apprehension and sickening fear, battle was joined

on the Metaurus river where a great Roman triumph avenged
the defeat of Cannae. Hannibal was said to have realized that his
brother's defeat and death spelt ruin for him also, but he remained in South Italy for another four years. Nevertheless, life in
Rome was beginning to take a more normal course. Before long,
in 204 B.C., a Roman army, again under Scipio, sailed to Africa.
The best indication that the tide of war had truly turned was
then evident. The Carthaginians recalled Hannibal, Scipio had
justified the extraordinary trust the people had shown in appointing him to the command in Spain, and his was the undying glory
of defeating Hannibal at Zama in central Tunisia (202 B.C.).
Hannibal escaped but the Carthaginian defeat was final. One of
the decisive battles of the world, Zama marked the final eclipse
of the Phoenicians as a first-class power in the Mediterranean
world. The relief and joy which this victory must have brought
to the Romans and indeed to the whole of Italy can best be
imagined by recalling the magnitude of the disasters they had
endured through long years of defeat.

Whether the Romans knew it or not their victory had done
more than eliminate a dangerous enemy; it had put world
domination within their grasp. A small City State which, less than
a hundred years previously, was still fighting hard to survive
among its own neighbours in Italy, suddenly emerged as a
potential ruler of the world. It was the turning-point in the history
of the Republic. In so far as it is ever possible to win security
against external enemies, the Romans had achieved it. Delivered
from their enemies, they were free to serve new causes without
fear.

They had to prove themselves equal, not only to the opportunity of seizing world power, but to the much more difficult task
of using that power wisely, now it was theirs. For use it they must.
There could be no going back to live in peace with reduced
commitments and no ambitions. Power inescapably involves
responsibility also. The opportunity was plainly theirs. They were
the strongest power in the Mediterranean. They had most men
and the best-disciplined army of citizen soldiers. None but the very
reckless would now challenge Rome, but some were found to do
so among minor eastern potentates and the successors of
Alexander the Great.

Wars in the East and the Beginnings of Rome's
Provincial Empire after 200 B.C.

The chief power to the east at the beginning of the second century B.C. was the Kingdom of Macedonia, then including parts of the present-day Bulgaria, Albania and Yugoslavia. An uneasy struggle with the federated Greek cities (in the Achaean League) and cantons (in the Aetolian League) had left King Philip of Macedonia paramount power in the Balkans. Resenting the presence of the Romans in Illyria he had made a treaty with Hannibal three years after Hannibal's march into Italy. With Antiochus, King of Syria, Philip planned (203 B.C.) to divide the outlying possessions of Egypt. Success in such an enterprise would have created two powers in the East which might have succeeded in making difficulties for Rome. He began by attacking Greek cities and islands, selling their inhabitants as slaves. Several Eastern States, including Rhodes and Egypt, appealed to Rome for help. Loth as the soldier farmers were to embark on fresh wars after the ruinous fight with Carthage, their leaders in the Senate of Rome nevertheless determined to take up the challenge. The anti-war party were able to appeal not merely to the war-weariness of the Romans but they argued that to declare war on Philip would transgress their ancestral rules, and the law of the *Fetiales* which forbade all except defensive wars on behalf of Rome and her allies. The lands appealing for help were not allies. It was therefore with some difficulty that the Senate got the necessary vote for war from the assembly of the people.

The Romans, commanded by Titus Quinctius Flamininus, speedily defeated King Philip of Macedon at the battle of Cynoscephalae (197 B.C.). In the following year, at the renowned Isthmian Games, thronged by visitors from all parts of Greece, Flamininus announced through a herald, amid scenes of hysterical enthusiasm, not merely salvation from the Macedonian oppressor but the restoration of full freedom to Greece. 'The Roman Senate and the Consul Titus Quinctius, having overcome King Philip and the Macedonians, leave free, without garrisons or tribute, and governed by their ancestral laws, the Corinthians, Phocians, Locrians, Euboeans, Achaeans of Phthiotis, Magnesians, Thessalians and Perrhaebians.'

The combination between Philip of Macedonia and Antiochus

of Syria had been broken. Roman commissioners warned Antiochus to be careful: 'No Greek was henceforth to be attacked or subjugated by anyone.' This was not the language of economic or any other kind of imperialism but of disinterested, almost sentimental politics contrasting in a striking manner with the normal relationships between the strong and the weak. It was not an attitude in which the Romans persisted for very long.

To vindicate such high-sounding declarations was another matter. By intervening so thoroughly in the confused and troubled politics of Greece and the Near East, the Romans had put their heads into a very active beehive. They were inevitably involved in thorny diplomatic problems arising from the jealousies, the boundary disputes, and the bitter rivalries of the Greek peoples. By supporting constituted authority, they embittered and made desperate the multitudes of poor struggling Greeks who sought some relief in their desperate economic plight. They speedily discovered that generosity and altruism on their part created as many problems as it appeared to solve. Flamininus did his best and in 194 B.C., after four winters in Greece, withdrew all his troops and sailed home. Rome was not to get out of foreign entanglements so easily. In such troubled waters her enemies had great temptations to fish. Antiochus sought in Egypt the support he had lost when Rome eliminated his ally, Philip of Macedon. By marrying his daughter to Ptolemy V he gave to Egypt the first Queen Cleopatra whose descendant, the seventh of that name, was to exercise, 150 years later, so sinister an influence upon the politics of the Roman Republic.

His careful diplomacy, clever intrigues and cunning schemes against his neighbours and against Rome were powerfully stimulated by the great Hannibal, now a refugee from Carthage at the Syrian Court. In 192 B.C. Rome was provoked sufficiently to declare war. The campaign was entrusted to Lucius Scipio, who took his brother, the victor at Zama, the great Scipio Africanus, as his deputy or Chief of Staff. Antiochus, who had invaded Greece, met his first reverse in the famous pass of Thermopylae (191 B.C.) and his final overthrow at the decisive battle of Magnesia (January 189 B.C.). The Roman armies returned weighed down with plunder (188 B.C.), but that was an incident of war, not the beginning of economic imperialism.

The Romans quitted Asia Minor, as they had left Greece, without exacting the payment of tribute and without intending to return.

The supremacy of Rome by land and sea, already in sight after the overthrow of Carthage, now became a plain and evident fact. The policy of the Senate had been crowned with a success probably far more complete than the most sanguine Senators had expected. Their urge to action had been no imperialistic determination to conquer and subdue. Fear of foreign aggression might well have been a sufficient motive. They had lived through the miseries of Hannibal's invasion of Italy and they had every reason to resolve that never again should a foreign power or combination of foreign powers repeat that shattering experience.

Roman diplomacy had never been busier than it must have been during the whole of the second century B.C. From this great distance in time it is impossible to follow it in all its intricate detail. It is also unnecessary to do so provided that it is never forgotten that any broad general picture of the developing situation is apt to lead to over-hasty generalizations and to alleged explanations which may be nothing more than the events themselves artificially foreshortened, seen in a false perspective and linked together in a pattern that would probably have seemed strangely unreal to the Romans of the time.

It is true that one by one Spain, Macedonia, Greece, North Africa, Syria, Gaul fell under Roman domination. But these conquests, which gave Rome world power, were not carefully elaborated, stage by stage, by Roman Senators and magistrates as part of vast plans for world supremacy akin to those in the modern world avowed by forces such as the Nazi or the Communist Party.

What actually happened from year to year was the arrival in Rome of envoys from foreign kings, States and cities asking for treaties of friendship, telling tales about the misbehaviour of their neighbours and appealing for help, whether in the form of a Roman arbitrator, or Roman threats against their enemies or by armed intervention of the Roman legions.

The Romans had to ask themselves what lay behind all these confused claims and counterclaims. It was not always easy to discover the answer. There were no resident Roman ambassadors or diplomatic representatives and no newspaper correspondents. No streams of trustworthy reports were flashed to Rome from small far-away, unknown countries as they now are to modern capital cities, to be read by people familiar with the history and background of world affairs.

Gradually the Senators learned the facts. They were undoubtedly complicated. A sample of some of the many questions with which the Senate had to grapple in the first two or three decades of the second century B.C. would include such problems as the following: What was the relationship of King Attalus of Pergamum to the Celts of Galatia? What were the rights and the treaty obligations of each of the many rich and important free Greek cities of Asia Minor? Who had the rightful claim to the territories of Phrygia, Pisidia, Lycaonia? Was Antiochus of Syria entitled to lord it over Cilicia? Should the Ptolemies of Egypt possess South Syria? How could the Aetolian League be prevented from stirring up trouble for Rome in the Balkan peninsula and in the Near East? What lay behind the diplomatic manoeuvres of Philip of Macedon, how strong was he, was he ill-intentioned towards Rome and, if so, should he be checkmated and, if so, how? Was it true that Philopoemen, General of the Achaean League, had annexed the city of Sparta, destroyed its walls and sold thousands of its inhabitants into slavery and, if so, what was Rome's position under the Roman-Spartan treaty of 191 B.C.?

These and scores of other tricky problems were forced upon the attention of Rome's ruling classes. The prestige of the Senate naturally grew by dealing with them, for they were all questions far above the heads of the ignorant toiling masses of Rome.

Greece and the Mediterranean world therefore came to incite Rome to action long before Romans had developed any ambitions to become the supreme rulers of the known world. The truth is surely that the Romans were inevitably drawn into new activities from which they incurred new responsibilities so that in the end, as it has been said with equal plausibility of England, the Republic 'acquired an Empire in a fit of absent-mindedness'. To believe otherwise would be to indulge in the childish fantasy that requires every story to have either a hero or a villain before it becomes interesting or plausible.

These campaigns had, however, been highly remunerative in booty, captives, treasure and indemnities. War indemnities from Carthage, booty from the East and from Spain probably provided nearly a quarter of the public expenses of the Republic in the period 200–160 B.C. These sums were over and above the works of art and other movable property of inestimable worth brought back in the baggage trains of the Roman conquerors. Troubles in the East continued to flicker and to flare up from time to time. Hannibal, who must have worn out his valiant spirit in the endeavour to galvanize the Eastern peoples against Rome, tried to rally one after another for the fight until at last he too was forced to take his own life to avoid being surrendered to Rome by the King of Bithynia, the last potentate whom he advised in war against Rome (about 183 B.C.). The Macedonians were slow to learn their lesson. Perseus, the son of Philip of Macedon, rashly provoked a further clash with Rome (171 B.C.) which led to the final extinction of Macedonia as an independent power at the battle of Pydna (168 B.C.). His overthrow and capture revealed, when his archives fell into Roman hands, that prominent Greeks had secretly helped him against Rome. Rome did not overlook such double-dealing. Macedonia was divided into four independent states and an effort was made to isolate each from the other, commercially and socially (167 B.C.). In that year Macedonia began to pay an annual tribute to Rome, equal to half only of the amount levied by its former king, and from that year also Romans in Italy were relieved of the necessity of paying taxes themselves to the Roman Treasury. Savage reprisals were taken against the Greek allies of Perseus, particularly in Epirus, where 150,000 Greeks were herded into the slave market. The Roman Senate was responsible for this cruelty, not the commander of the victorious Roman army, the veteran Consul L. Aemilius Paulus, nicknamed 'Macedonicus' in honour of his victory.

Self-government under the impossible conditions imposed by Rome proved no solution to the Macedonian problem and in 146 B.C. Rome took the country over as a Roman province, under the rule of a Roman governor. Greece continued to be a troublesome land. In 146 B.C. its Roman protectors, stung by unruly behaviour, sacked and burnt Corinth as though it also had earned the fate of Carthage which was obliterated in the same year and for no better reason. Greece, nominally free, remained in uneasy partnership with Rome for more than another century. The authority of the Roman governor in Macedonia gradually extended into Greece which was not, however, organized as a

province (Achaea) until after the collapse of the Roman Republic
(27 B.C.).

In the West, Rome, like a dog worrying a hedgehog, was trying
to reduce Spain. Before the end of the Second Punic War, Spain
had been organized into two Roman provinces (205 B.C.),
Nearer and Further Spain. Rome wanted three things from Spain
above all else: metals, recruits and corn. They were not to be had
without a determined effort, but Rome did not leave such tasks
half completed. The pressure of Roman greed provoked formidable revolts by 197 B.C., which were not finally stamped out until,
in 133 B.C., after incredible suffering, Numantia, defended by
4,000 men, was overcome by a force of 20,000 Romans aided by
40,000 Iberian auxiliaries commanded by Scipio Aemilianus. He
was the famous son of the victor at Pydna, L. Aemilius Paulus,
and he had been adopted by the son of Scipio Africanus into the
proud family of the Cornelii. Thereafter until the overthrow of the
Roman Republic, Spain seems to have been treated with harsh
brutality, valued for what could be got out of it at no matter
what expense in suffering and degradation to its native races and
to the slaves toiling in the mines. The slaughter of Roman citizen
farmers in the Spanish wars seriously weakened the Republic.

More important than winning a fortune is the use made of it
and the lasting consequence of its possession. The troubles as well
as the grandeur of Rome date from this time. What they were
and how they worked out will be more fully seen in the sequel.
Here it is necessary to note that Rome's conquests throughout
the Mediterranean world, and especially those made in the more
highly civilized lands of Greece, Syria and Asia Minor, greatly
stimulated the natural inclination of the Romans to go after easy
loot. (See diagram, p. 42.)

Realizing the predatory nature of the Roman power it is tempting to conclude that the Romans were nothing better than a well-
organized gang of robbers and murderers whose chief title to
fame is that they succeeded. Nothing succeeds like complete
success especially when it means that the victors and not the
vanquished write the history of the event.

The Roman conscience was not entirely clear. Reviewing the
rise of Rome a hundred years and more later, Cicero tried to
pretend that the Roman practice of declaring wars by heralds (the
Fetiales) made aggression lawful but he was honest enough to

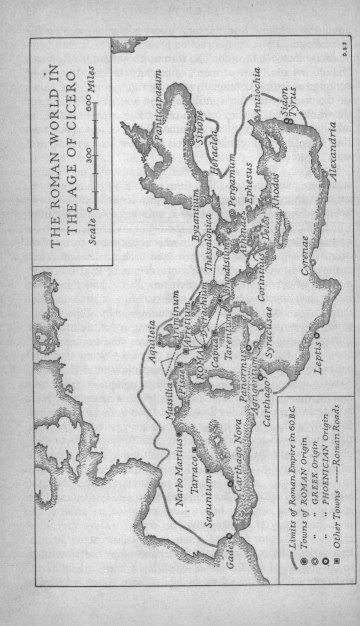

THE ROMAN WORLD IN
THE AGE OF CICERO

Scale 0   300   600 Miles

Limits of Roman Empire in 60 B.C.
Towns of ROMAN Origin
  "   " GREEK Origin
  "   " PHOENICIAN Origin
Other Towns ----Roman Roads

Panticapaeum
Sinope
Heraclea
Byzantium
Pergamum
Athenae
Ephesus
Corinthus
Delos
Rhodos
Antiochia
Sidon
Tyrus
Cyrenae
Alexandria
Thessalonica
Dyrrachium
Brundisium
Tarentum
Syracusae
Agrigentum
Panormus
Capua
ROMA
Arretium
Ariminum
Aquileia
Pisae
Massilia
Narbo Martius
Tarraco
Saguntum
Carthago Nova
Gades
Carthago
Leptis

D.&.S

admit that many of Rome's wars 'were made very much for the sake of captives and the destruction of rival cities . . . a matter not without offence to the gods'. So it came about that the Romans, 'indeed the most just of men', once embarked on a career of conquest ended by 'continually coveting and laying violent hands on the property of others until they have acquired possession of the whole world'. If they were to obey the dictates of justice, he added, 'that is to say if they restored all that belonged to others they would have to return to hovels and lie down in misery and want'.

In ignoring the extent to which the Roman Republic grew strong by successful brutality at the expense of weaker nations, we should therefore not merely be false to history, as even a few intelligent Romans themselves saw it, but we should lose sight of a valuable help to understanding their character and perhaps a source of their weakness. A nation which behaved as the Romans ultimately did towards the Greeks and other civilized peoples, enslaving the weaker but much more intelligent race, exhibited a strain of callous brutality which was likely to be stimulated rather than appeased by its easy victory. Just as one of the most damning revelations of the fundamental brutality of the prison-states of our own time has been their enslavement of the nations they conquered and occupied, so the Romans would equally stand condemned for their behaviour were it not for the fact that the age in which they lived accepted it as part of the nature of things. Yet Romans who gave free run to their impulse to dominate and enslave outsiders were not likely to be able to restrain such impulses when the evil day dawned for them to be turned against fellow-Romans. Then their very virtues became a curse because their inability to acknowledge defeat dreadfully embittered their civil dissensions. Such a view of the matter may help to explain why the internal troubles of the Republic became so acute in the first century B.C., a time in which no foreign power offered a serious threat to Rome. Cicero himself remarked that this age was stained by cruelties worse than those known at any time in the previous history of the Republic, no doubt because they were cruelties by Romans against Romans in Rome, and not by Roman legionaries fighting in foreign lands. His words would also apply to the horrors of the Slave War which had twice wrought havoc and destruction in the island of Sicily: once between 135 and

132 B.C., and a second time from 104 to 99 B.C., twenty-five years before he was a Quaestor there. A hundred thousand revolted slaves were said to have perished on that last occasion, most of whom were lucky if they were spared the torture of crucifixion by being slain on the battlefield.

In addition to their brutalizing and debasing effects, Roman foreign conquests had another tremendous consequence. The armies of slaves imported from the Eastern Mediterranean who remained to increase and multiply on Italian soil were people of a very different stamp from the Romans of the ancient Republic. Excitable, often nervous and timid, they had little of the stolid, stalwart, robust self-reliance of the true Roman. Small wonder, for they had been torn out of their own customary ways of living and replanted in alien soil. The political and social background of very many of them had been one of age-long subjection to autocrats and tyrants. They and their ancestors knew nothing of the Roman custom of law-making by assemblies of the people. Some Roman masters and some households may have done much to train their slaves to understand and adopt Roman ways, but otherwise no special steps were taken by the Romans to assimilate them to Roman ways of life and thought. They therefore had little or no compensation for the tragedy of losing almost everything that had given meaning and value to their lives. They were, it is true, allowed their Oriental emotional religions, for the Romans, except in times of great alarm and danger, do not seem to have indulged in religious persecution. By this means they opened the way for a steadily growing influence from the Near East and thereby entirely changed the character of the Roman people. The true nature of this change is not to be explained by invoking racial characteristics. The far more significant matter of loyalty to differing cultural values is what is really in question. With more truth than it was once mischievously said about the 'melting-pot' in which immigrants to the U.S.A. are supposed to be turned into fully fledged American citizens, it seems that, when Italy was flooded with slave immigrants, the only thing that melted was the pot.

Such in a brief, bare and far from adequate summary were some of the outstanding events in the early development of the Roman Republic. The results of the steady expansion of territory and influence are best seen on a map (see p. 42).

Although in Cicero's day not very much seems to have been known about the detailed history of these early times, nobody could be ignorant of the fact that it was then that the foundations of the might and majesty of the Roman State were laid. Whatever may have been the unrecorded defeats, the brutalities, the meanness, the bad faith and the hidden evil of those distant times, the positive achievements they bequeathed could not be questioned or scorned. Rome was the most important city in the world. On what was its power based? How had it been affected by its fierce struggle for survival?

The Roman Army

As it is evident that Rome attained predominant power first in Italy and then in the Mediterranean by fighting for it, the obvious place to look for the secret of Roman success is in the Roman Army. By what magic were the hardy little farmers of the Tiber plain able to assert themselves? The answer is not to be found in any secret of unusual physical strength or merely in a superiority of numbers. The Romans were of course good soldiers. The army was, with farming, their largest single industry, and concentration and specialization upon soldiering brought its own rewards in increased skill and above all in improved organization.

It must never be forgotten that in those early days there were no secret armaments to give one tribe or nation a long start over its competitors. Swords, daggers, spears, bows and arrows and stones were the only implements, and everybody had them. Helmets, shields, body armour of leather or of metal were also nobody's monopoly. The Roman foot-soldier, who made up the army in the legion, or legions, commanded by a Consul, went campaigning with as much of it as he could get – and carry. The distinction is important, for in addition to armour and arms (usually a dagger and a short thrusting sword and one or more short heavy spears to hurl at the enemy), the legionary carried a 'pack' of auxiliary equipment – spade, hatchet, saw, basket, cooking-pot, several stakes, and rations for half a month (largely of wheaten meal). These alone weighed 43 lb or 60 Roman pounds (*librae*). His arms and armour weighed as much again. All this gear had to be carried, for baggage trains of mules were often something of a luxury and reserved for tents and such siege equipment in the way of mechanical slings, scaling ladders or battering rams as might be needed and available.

Roman victories were won by Roman infantry living, it seems, largely upon a diet of wheaten porridge and vegetables. Cavalry troops were not unknown but they were rarely important. The Romans never learned to use them effectively in war, partly perhaps because the stirrup had not yet been invented.

The troops were indeed the prime agents of Rome's victories but the consistent success of Roman arms was not won by a ferocious horde of well-armed warriors however numerous. The secret of their success was their willingness to submit to organization and discipline. The credit for discovering how to turn an armed horde into a victorious army is, it seems, due to the Greeks. They were the first to invent an order of battle in which drilled men acting together as a unit in formation (a *phalanx*) were able to overcome unorganized enemies many times more numerous who sought to engage their opponents in battles which were nothing more or less than a vast number of single hand-to-hand encounters. It was, in fact, this striking achievement of the Greek intellect in the service of the Greek will-to-victory that saved Mediterranean civilization from an Oriental domination by the Persian hordes.

The Romans copied the Greek phalanx, probably after seeing it used against them by their Etruscan neighbours, adapted it at first to their own feudal organization and improved it after their overwhelming defeat by the Gauls in 390 B.C. In this way the Roman Legion was created. Every schoolboy and schoolgirl making a first acquaintance with Latin prose by way of Caesar's *Commentaries* is familiar with the organization of the legion. In its early form it reflected the social structure of the Roman State. Every soldier provided his own arms and equipment, which meant that every soldier had a farm or other property enabling him to acquire his outfit. The landless poor did not fight. The well-to-do, able to bring a horse, constituted the cavalry. The legionary organization provided the framework of the political organization of the Republic. The legion itself, divided into thirty maniples of two companies ('centuries') each, consisted usually of 4,000 to 5,000 men. Its theoretical strength was 6,000 men. Three or four 'armies' of this small size made up the effective striking force of the early Roman State. The troops were ranged in three separate lines corresponding roughly to three age groups – the younger men (*hastati*) in front, the middle age group (*principes*) in the second line. Both these classes were armed with a short sword and one or two heavy spears which they were able to hurl up to a range of about thirty yards. The third line, bringing up the rear of each maniple, were seasoned veterans called *triarii*. They had a sword and a long spear, not for throwing, but for thrusting at the enemy. The veterans were a form of reserve, and if the day went so badly that the decision had to be left to them, the situation was regarded as highly critical.

Every maniple or regimental unit of 100 to 120 men was made up of two 'centuries' or companies (of fifty to sixty men) each commanded by a centurion. There were several degrees of rank and importance in the centurion class. The leading centurion (*primipilus*) was an officer of sufficient standing to attend a council of war. No common soldier could rise higher in the ranks than the position of leading centurion; that is to say he could never command a legion. The higher command was reserved for men of senatorial rank. Below the centurions there were a dozen lesser officers (*principales*) who may perhaps be regarded as the non-commissioned officers. Each legionary commander also had his personal staff of adjutants and clerks.

Accompanying every solid legionary corps was a force of lightly armed skirmishing troops (*velites*) numbering about 1,200 men. The order of battle of a legion no doubt varied according to the commander's judgement of every new situation but in theory it was a chequer-board formation, every maniple being separated from the next by a space equivalent to its own length.

The imposing strength of this formation is at once evident. The solid maniples were a powerful striking force. When within twenty or thirty yards of the enemy they were able, by a sudden barrage of hundreds of heavy spears, to throw him into momentary confusion before charging him with their swords which they used like bayonets. A thrust two inches deep in a vulnerable spot was, they found, much more deadly than a slashing cut. Primitive surgery was unable to cope with internal wounds, although quite deep cuts to the bone would heal while the bone would protect a vital organ. A thrust, moreover, exposed very little of the legionary's arm, whereas a slashing motion involved raising the arm high above the head.

A sudden attack delivered in this style by the front line of maniples could be repeated as the second line came into action, and there yet remained the third line to dismay the enemy ranks.

The strength of the legionary formation lay not merely in the solidity of the maniples nor yet in their high and valuable mobility and flexibility as fighting units. The legion, unlike the phalanx, was strong on the flank as well as in the centre; it was also able to deal with a surprise attack in the rear; all most important tactical advantages. But above all the legion, like the phalanx by which it had been inspired, had the supreme merit of harnessing the consciousness of strength which men derive from action in union with their fellows. The old adage that strength lies in union is abundantly illustrated in the military achievements of the phalanx and legion in antiquity. Not merely did the legionary organization go far towards eliminating the tendency of the faint-hearted to flee, so providing a guarantee against that sudden panic flight to which a mere horde is always prone, but it multiplied and amplified the confidence and will-to-victory of the stout-hearted by assuring him that his fellow soldiers all around him would not fail. The organized phalanx and particularly the better-organized legion was the supreme embodiment of deliberate, collective human purpose which antiquity has to offer. The military interpretation of the history of Greece and still more of Rome provides a more valuable insight into their development than does the economic interpretation of history which has proved so fruitful in the great age of commerce and industry in which we now live. Such a military interpretation must include much more than a mere dull record of the successive campaigns and battles in which military power became manifest. It involves insight into the nature of that power, the conditions of its development and the consequences of its employment. From such a deeper and more general point of view alone is it possible to understand how the phalanx and the legion were as decisive for the protection of a dawning European civilization against the threat of sudden obliteration by Oriental, Semitic, or Germanic barbarians as it is thought the atomic marvels of our own age might be against new races of barbarians. Designed to meet different conditions, the phalanx and legion cannot very well be compared. When Greek and Roman met in war in Southern Italy the day was hotly contested and the legion was not uniformly victorious. At Heraclea in 280 B.C. the Roman defeat was partly due to the surprise sprung by the Greeks who charged the Romans with elephants, an ancient equivalent of the 'tank' of modern warfare. The might of Greece had, however, far decayed by the time the Roman legions had reached their first full development.

Successful warfare is not usually enumerated among the causes of the wealth of nations, but it would be unrealistic and unhistorical to overlook the fact that war, as much as agriculture, industry, or commerce, was at the basis of such civilization as the Romans achieved. Organized in their legions, the Roman people fought their way to victory. In the same organization they gave their votes upon political questions involving the destiny of their country. For he who fought could hardly be denied a vote, so close is the link between military autocracy and democratic politics.

The political aspect of military organization is reflected in the later development of the Roman army. In the year after Cicero's birth, Roman arms sustained a terrible defeat at the hands of the Germans at Arausio (105 B.C.). The result, as it had been after the more disastrous defeat of Rome by the Gauls early in the fourth century, was to force through a thorough reorganization of the Roman army, which was at once undertaken by a bluff country-bred soldier, Gaius Marius, who hailed from Cicero's own district of Arpinum. He supplemented and largely replaced the old conscript citizen army of poorly paid short-service landowning citizen soldiers by a professional paid body of long-service volunteers recruited from the citizen body as a whole, whether they owned land or property or not. He swept away the old division of juniors, seniors and veterans (*hastati, principes* and *triarii*), armed all the legionaries alike, replaced the old regimental standards by the uniform silver eagle and regrouped the thirty maniples of the legion into ten cohorts of three maniples each. The cohort had been used by P. Scipio in Spain. In so reshaping or 'streamlining' the Roman army, Marius did far more than revitalize it as a fighting unit. What he changed was not merely the organization of an army but the very fabric of the social body of Rome. It was not part of his plan; but the economic condition of Rome, particularly the widespread distress among small-scale farmers, conspired with his plans to produce new political strains, tensions and forces in the politics of the great city. The Roman legionaries, now all on an equality under their centurions, were all dependent upon their pay and such largesse as their commander could win for them from the enemy as booty or extort from the Roman Senate as a gratuity in the shape of money or land or both. The early legionaries had been drawn from all classes of citizens except the poorest, and they provided their own equipment. In the age of Cicero none but the poorer classes enlisted. The State then found their equipment.

Whereas the soldiers of the citizen army of the Republic had their own means of livelihood and were most anxious to return to it as soon as possible, the men of the new model army had every reason to stay in the ranks, where alone they had an assured living and from which alone they could expect some provision for their old age. The Romans left the recruitment as well as the command of their armies to the general appointed to lead them. When that commander was one of the two elected chief magistrates of the State (Consuls) for the year, such procedure was quite normal. But during Cicero's lifetime extraordinary commands for more than one year's campaign, conferred by vote of the people, began to replace the consular commands. When that happened a new executive power of tremendous weight was created in the State, rivalling and easily able to supplant the power of the Consuls, the titular heads of the Republic. It was a power all the greater because, in accordance with old custom, the Roman soldier was required to take a solemn oath of loyalty, not to the Roman State but to his commander. The commander of an army was thus elevated into a position of importance such as he had never had before. Service under a successful general was naturally looked upon as a promising gamble and recruits willingly gave him all their loyalty. The consequences of this break with the past cut deeply, as will be seen in the sequel, into the whole social and political framework of the Roman Republic. Romans were soon to suffer terribly from their inability or dangerous disinclination to develop their State administrative service and to see to it that the Romans who volunteered in the new army put loyalty to the Republic before devotion to their general and to their own self-interest.

It is time to turn from wars and conquests which are a part of the story of the military survival and expansion of Rome, to look into the state of affairs within the city and to discover if possible

something about the farmers, workmen, middle classes, busin___
men and politicians whose activities give meaning and reality to
the words 'The Roman Republic'. It is on the whole a grim and
ominous record.

A Turning Point in the History of the Republic

The years after the victories over Carthage, Macedonia and Syria
bequeathed the troubles and difficulties with which Cicero and his
generation struggled and fought and by which they were finally
overpowered. Questions of military organization and the strategy
of war became of less account than the urgent economic and
political problems at home.

Every kind of public question was involved. First and foremost
were the difficulties of the sturdy Roman farmers, the backbone
of the State. The triumph of the Roman Republic was above all
their triumph. Common sense would seem to have demanded that
they should not merely be saved from ruin, but be actively protected and encouraged. Remarkable as Roman common sense
was, it did not succeed in this task. Many evils flowed from its
failure. The political system gradually got out of gear. It was not
reshaped to deal with the entirely new situation resulting from
the victories of the Roman legions in Italy and in the Mediterranean lands. Roman society remained divided. Greed for large
possessions in land and above all the fearful consequences of
allowing slavery to become the prime motive power of the
economic life of the country further and dangerously undermined
the stability of the Republic. Greatly as Rome had expanded and
prospered, the Old Roman traditions and beliefs no longer held
all the people together. They were therefore in no condition to
govern their own country, still less to administer their Empire

Chapter Three

THE ROMAN FARMER

Antiquity and Social Prestige of Agriculture

'OF all gainful occupations,' Cicero once said, 'nothing is better, nothing more pleasing, nothing more delightful, nothing better becomes a well-bred man than agriculture.'

Cicero, therefore, like other political leaders, senators, and respected members of the best Roman society, was one of the landed gentry. They were landowners because landowning gave social distinction which other ways of earning an income did not confer. In the absence of any permanent national debt there were no gilt-edged securities into which money could be invested. Landownership was one of the very few profitable investments open to the wealthy. As long before Cicero's day as 218 B.C. the Roman people had agreed by a plebiscite to prohibit Senators and their sons from owning cargo ships of a size allowing them to engage in overseas trade. They were also forbidden to take government contracts. In one of the earliest Latin works that have survived, the old Roman tradition a hundred years before Cicero's time had been described as follows: 'To obtain money by trade is sometimes more profitable, were it not so hazardous, and likewise money-lending, if it were as honourable.' In Cicero's day many Romans had become rich by engaging in trade, by lending money and by undertaking public contracts. They thereby renounced any political ambitions and could not aspire to a higher status than that of the social class below the politicians, that of the *equites* (see p. 114). Many had estates also as the Senators had because agriculture was always the main source of wealth in the Ancient World.

Cicero succeeded in adding to his inherited estates, thanks to his professional earnings. These he gained through his great skill as a public speaker in the defence of men accused before the Roman people. He did not, to be sure, accept fees. That was 'not done'. His clients however found ways and means of repaying him in more substantial coin than gratitude. He was able to receive indirect presents and especially legacies from people he had helped. In this way he was able to buy his expensive town house and his ornamental country estates. He was also driven by his irregular but usually substantial income to borrow money, which he seems to have done cheerfully and heavily. We do not know accurately what his income was, which is less surprising because he often seems to have been just as ignorant himself. It was not a subject upon which he worried over-much. The sort of thing he said to his banker and friend Atticus was, 'Do not consider what my purse demands, about which I care nothing, but what I want.'

As eldest son he inherited his ancestral home and substantial farm at Arpinum on the death of his father about 64 B.C. He had already acquired two country properties on his own account; one was at Formiae, the other, which he loved best all his life, was at Tusculum, only fifteen miles from Rome, where the town of Frascati stands today. It was probably modest in size because land so near the city was very expensive. Other villas acquired later as his fame and fortune grew were at Pompeii, where a villa reputed to have been his has been unearthed, Antium, Cumae, Astura and Puteoli. Exactly how many such country properties he owned is not known for certain. They have been variously estimated as eight, twelve, or nineteen.

Apart from the estates, he seems to have owned one or two small houses which served as country cottages where he could spend a night or two when travelling. Inns were plentiful in Italy but were evidently not frequented by the best society, who when travelling always preferred a roof of their own or the hospitality of friends.

Cicero's larger country properties included several farms managed by bailiffs, and worked by slaves. They probably paid their way and yielded a modest contribution to his annual income. All except Tusculum and the family estates in the Volscian hills were situated on or near the sea in the plains of Latium and Campania. Here were the lands which had nourished the Roman people and their Latin allies from the earliest times.

None of the well-to-do Romans of Cicero's time depended upon this territory for a livelihood as their predecessors and ancestors had done. The stately villas and country residences to be found there had become pleasant retreats from the heat, dust and noise of Rome. Some of them also supplied their owners with fresh fruit, vegetables, salads and flowers, but nearer Rome they often depended upon the city markets even for supplies of this sort. Latium and Campania were no longer the sole granary of Rome, whence came the raw material of that coarse wheaten porridge on which Roman legions had conquered the world.

Changing Nature of Roman Agriculture

In the story of this change lies the explanation of many of the troubles and difficulties by which the Roman Republic was beset and from which it never recovered. For although Rome was a warrior state and an imperial power, its roots were in the land. The country was not exuberantly rich like the valley of the Nile, but then, as now, Italy had many fertile tracts within the area where the olive and the vine flourish and where men do not perish from cold in the short winter. With proper management, it was capable of supporting a larger population than that of other Mediterranean lands.

The key to Roman agriculture is the geological formation of Central Italy. (See the outline map on page 124.) Less than 3,000 years before the birth of Cicero active volcanoes were deluging the Latin plain with ash and lava; periodically forests sprang up only to be buried again under new storms of volcanic ash. Fifty or more craters of extinct volcanoes can still be seen in little more than twenty miles around Rome. As they gradually became extinct the volcanic soil was fertilized by the annual growth and decay of thick crops of grasses, leaves and vegetation. Forests of beech, oaks, laurels and myrtle succeeded. The prehistoric tribes lived in a very different Italy from that of Cicero's day. Their landscape was one of forests, woods and groves. It gradually changed as the wood was cut down for fuel, for building materials and to enlarge the cultivable land needed by the growth of the early inhabitants, whose ancestors had begun to come into Italy from the Danube and the central Alps some 2,000 years before Cicero's day.

Those who were first to exploit the soil of the Latin plain reaped a rich reward. There was, however, a limit to the productivity of the soil, which at length was unable to keep pace with the increase in population. Difficulties arose as the trees disappeared and as the surface soil, no longer retained by natural forests and grasses and kept moist by forest conditions, began to be washed down to the sea by the torrential rains falling on the hills and mountains which form the backbone of Italy.

Desperate efforts were made to retain the soil. By what must have required a great and well-organized communal effort, an elaborate system of drains, gulleys, tunnels and dams was constructed to channel the rain streams to the sea without taking the precious soil as well. Remains of these long-forgotten tunnels still abound. Such doubtless was the origin of the trenches and underground passages rediscovered to the cost of the Allied armies by the German defenders of Cassino in 1944.

As the land became less fertile the difficulty of finding food for the growing population of Rome became more and more burdensome. The bare annals of the early Republic record frequent famines as well as frequent wars. There may indeed have been a close connexion between them, for it seems reasonable to suppose both that the Romans, the Latins and the hill tribes needed more land and that they found they could get it only by fighting for it. Lack of food caused trouble within the Roman community as much as it did for Rome's neighbours. It set the landless men and the farmers with small plots, the poor men, against those endowed with more acres. Their antagonism very largely explains the political and social cleavage of the early Republic, for the two warring parties, the plebeians and the patricians, were roughly the party of the poor and landless against the freeholders and the men of wealth. In 393 B.C., after a victory over the citizens of Veii, a town a few miles north of Rome, sufficient land was confiscated to give every citizen an allotment of 7 *iugera* equalling 4⅜ English acres. It was not by any means a fortune, but it stands comparison with the three acres and a cow, once proclaimed in nineteenth-century England as a respectable ambition for a working man. Gains of this sort transformed Romans into an independent citizen body with its roots in the soil and so endowed with a vital stake in the Republic.

The soil of the plains immediately around and south of Rome was a relatively thin volcanic deposit over rocks. Artificial fertilizers were almost unknown. Farmers relied upon animal manure and wood-ash to replenish the soil and they never had enough. The Roman countryside could not therefore have supported an intensive cultivation indefinitely even if the eroding action of rains from the mountains had not washed much of it away. As it was, the plains of Latium were already becoming unable to support arable farming and the food crops had gradually to give way to grass. But the summer heat burned off the grass by July and for three months at least green fodder had to be sought elsewhere. In the light of such facts, the wars with the hill tribes, the Volscians, Sabines, and Samnites, in the fourth and third centuries B.C. assume a new significance. Whether fought for that purpose or not they had the useful result of giving Roman farmers access to badly-needed summer pasture for the flocks and herds of the Latin plain.

The conquest of a rich wheat- and grain-producing area in the island of Sicily after the First Punic War must have been a useful addition to the food supply of Rome. In Cicero's day three-quarters of a million bushels (3 million *modii*) were taken every year as a tax or tithe from Sicily, sufficient then to meet the needs of the army and to feed the entire city population for about two months in the year. As much again as this free tithe of grain was bought on the Sicilian market. The rest of Italy had to provide for itself from its own resources, for which probably about 60 million bushels a year would have been necessary for a population of about 5 million.

By the middle of the third century B.C., there was no longer an excess of population. The man-power of Rome was indeed insufficient to found and sustain all the military colonies which the rulers of the Republic insisted upon maintaining in strategic areas of Italy. Plainly Romans had no compelling reasons to turn their energies into industry, commerce, and emigration as, for instance, the Greeks had been forced to do when their growing numbers had outstripped their slender agricultural resources.

The orderly development of Roman agriculture and of Roman political life had, however, received a rude shock in the Second Punic War which created difficulties that gave a permanent twist to the Republic from which it never recovered. We need no reminder of the great and grievous cost of war to the victors as well as to the vanquished. The high cost of Hannibal to the Romans as of Hitler to Europe cannot be measured by any scale of quantities in which mankind habitually reckons, least of all in terms of money. War's hideous tale of loss and destruction is first and foremost a story of human suffering and misery, of the slaughter of the bravest and best of a nation's manhood, of degradation and a general lowering of standards, and finally of mere material deprivation and loss. The last-mentioned is the least of war's evils and the only one it is possible to repair fairly quickly if sufficient men survive.

The Second Punic War and its Aftermath: 200 B.C.

In so far as history is a search for the underlying explanation of the changes in the fortunes of mankind, it must account, if it can, for the altered nature of Rome and the Romans after they had achieved mastery in the Mediterranean.

The very nature and duration of the supreme struggle with Carthage left deep scars, giving a sinister twist to the destiny of Rome. Colossal losses in men and in property all but shattered the stability of the old Republic. Rome, maimed and broken, now had a vast and immediate task of reconstruction which could not wait. Inevitably the plans hurriedly adopted would form the foundation for the future development of the State. One thing at least was clear: Rome was the leader of Italy. The responsibility of her statesmen was therefore heavy.

Throughout fourteen hard years Romans had been forced to expend every ounce of energy they possessed in resisting, on their own territory, enemies who seemed invincible. Where these enemies could not take the produce of the land for themselves – and they brought thousands of hungry mouths – they destroyed it. Those of the free farmers of Italy who had not become corpses on the blood-stained fields of the Trebia, Trasimene, Cannae, the Metaurus, in Spain and in facing the Gauls, were either still under arms or refugees within the walled cities. Most of those who had possessed slaves lost them. Farm villas, barns, sheds and all their contents had gone up in smoke. The livestock had been taken. Of these animals the ox held the place of honour. It was, as Aristotle had said, 'the poor man's slave'. It drove the plough, pulled the heavy carts, supplied meat, milk and hides. In Cicero's day it was widely believed that the very name Italy had been derived from the word for bullocks (*vituli*). The oxen of Italy represented much of its capital wealth and they had disappeared. It takes three years to produce a cow capable of bearing calves, and Romans did not believe that a young ox should be broken to the plough before it was three years old. Horses also, which were used for human transport rather than in agriculture, were not broken in before they were two or three years old. Farms would also need to be restocked with mules, pigs, goats, sheep, dogs and poultry. Every kind of implement from the heavy ploughs and waggons to the harrows, rakes, threshing flails, baskets, winnowing fans, forks and shovels had somewhere to be found. All these things represented what economists understand by fixed and circulating capital or material equipment. Not until it disappears in some catastrophe such as war, do men begin to realize to what extent the comfort and convenience of their own lives have been sustained by their anonymous and unknown predecessors. So it must have been in Italy. Land had lain idle and become infested with weeds and undergrowth which multiply and spread in the climate of Italy with dismaying rapidity. The best agricultural practice in Cicero's day considered that cultivated land required at least two ploughings before seeding. When at last the implements had been remade, seeds had to be provided and a whole season elapse before any crops could be harvested. These are the realities behind the glib phrases in history books which tell how Hannibal 'devastated and ravaged the land of Italy'. This is why warfare in a self-sufficient agricultural country in ancient times meant the threat of death by starvation to thousands who did not fall before the swords, spears and arrows of the enemy. No wonder that recovery from the aftermath of war could be a slow and painful process. Little wonder also, that the small men who were faced with so overwhelming a task of reconstruction were sunk in indebtedness.

Those of the citizen farmers who survived the blood-stained fields of battle returned with glory, but they came back with little else. They certainly had not been able to amass much money from their meagre pay or from their share of the booty. Neither would coins have helped very much in the universal dearth and scarcity of farm stock and equipment. There was only one way for a poor farmer to re-establish himself and his family on a farm and make it a going concern. He was forced to borrow stock, seed and equipment from a wealthier man. Indeed the constant dependence of the poor small cultivator upon the rich, universally found among the agricultural countries of the world, is still characteristic wherever economic institutions such as co-operative buying and marketing organizations, agricultural credit banks or State aid in other forms have not been developed. Once in debt the small man was in the power of his creditor. Laws about property and debt were made, as all Roman laws were made, by the property-owners, hard-fisted successful farmers, who went to great lengths to force their debtors to repay.

In the struggle to re-establish agriculture the advantage went to the wealthier in more ways than one. During the war, when the Treasury was empty and the State bankrupt, it was their money that bought food and arms and paid the soldiers in the field. Peace brought more tempting outlets for investment. There was much more land than the small man could cultivate. Derelict farms were to be had very cheaply. About a million acres of arable land and another million suitable for cattle-ranching lacked occupiers. Unable to meet the clamour for repayment of the war loans, the State made over, at a low valuation and on a nominal annual lease, the lands falling into the public domain. They were transferred in large lots of 500 or 1,000 *iugera* (312½ and 625 English acres). (A Roman *iugerum* was equal to 100 English square poles or 3,025 square yards, that is ⅝ acre. Two *iugera* were therefore equal to 1¼ acres.) There had been a law passed in 367 B.C. (the Licinian Rogation) limiting the amount of public land any one man could occupy. Its details are by no means clear but it was traditionally believed to fix the maximum holding at 500 *iugera* and the number of cattle to 100 head with 500 sheep. It was a law which the wealth-seeking Romans found it convenient to ignore as time went on.

The new leases of public land after the Second Punic War were meant to serve as a reminder that the freehold was the property of the Roman people. It was a little-heeded reminder. Prompt advantage was taken of the bargain and Romans who had done well in spite of or because of the wars became proud owners of broad acres. They belonged to the well-to-do from whose ranks came most of the officials responsible for collecting the rents. They were unlikely to be very exacting landlords. Soon there was much more liquid capital looking for investment. Not very long after the victory over Carthage and Macedon, the Republic began to pay dividends from the booty of its successful wars. The equivalent of twenty-five years' revenue from one of the main taxes (*tributum*) was refunded by the State in 187 B.C., out of booty brought back by Cn. Manlius from his campaign in Asia Minor. Many of the great estates which, in Cicero's day, three or four generations later, were denounced as the ruin of Italy had their origin in this period.

It is sometimes said that Romans copied the huge slave ranches they found in conquered Carthage, but slavery was already an ancient institution in Rome. The simultaneous availability of large tracts of uncultivated farm land and of a glut of slaves as the prize of successful war must have been an opportunity too obvious to escape the attention of the victorious but impoverished Senators and leading men of Rome.

Everything pushed them to exploit the situation. Their notion of a dignified way of living was a life devoted to public affairs supported by a prosperous farm. With this ideal in view the Senators had accepted in 218 B.C. a law forbidding them and their sons to engage in overseas commerce. In practice they were not above turning their hands to other sources of gain and many of them found ways of evading the law. But the fact remained that agriculture was supposed to be and usually was their main interest. Politics and landowning were very closely linked. Disraeli's disparaging reference to 'the territorial constitution' of the England of his time is an apt label for the Roman constitution also.

In defence of the decisions of the political leaders of Rome after the war with Hannibal it can at least be said that at the time there was no other obvious way to deal with the problem of reconstruction. Thousands of citizen farmers had gone. The survivors could not farm the whole area intensively. It was inevitable that more arable land should become pasture on which a few slaves tended flocks and herds. Many of the able-bodied poor who were not content to work as hired labourers, shepherds and cowherds turned northwards and sought among the Celtic settlements of the Po valley the livelihood their fatherland no longer provided.

Not until the natural growth of population in two or three generations had repaired the ravages of war and again created a land-hungry peasantry did all the disadvantages of the large ranch estates become apparent. By that time the large estates had become vested interests to their occupiers by whom they had been improved and handed down as a family inheritance.

An Agricultural 'New Deal' Required

It had never been an accepted principle in Roman society, as it has quite recently become among us, that the State owed all its citizens the means of a livelihood. One bold spirit seems indeed to have tried to win his countrymen over to this view. After the First Punic War, in 232 B.C., C. Flaminius, then a Tribune of the people (not to be confused with the later Flamininus, the liberator of Greece), succeeded against strong opposition in having some public land, recently taken from a raiding tribe from the north in the *Ager Gallicus*, divided up into small freehold lots instead of being leased in larger lots for the benefit of the State Treasury. Flaminius, who gave his name to the great highway leading from Rome to the land of the Gauls (the *via Flaminia*) and to the *Circus Flaminius* in the city of Rome, clearly had much sound sense on his side, but his precedent was not popular with the rulers of Rome, who wanted large estates for themselves and were against giving up the annual lease payments to the Treasury. It was an innovation in the custom-bound, legalistic Roman manner of regarding property which was not forgotten. In after years, when new generations had replaced those slain in the struggle against Hannibal, many men again began with insistence to demand the renewal of the policy of Flaminius.

By the middle of the second century B.C. there were over 300,000 Roman citizens and fathers of families where there had been around 200,000 when Hannibal was defeated in 202 B.C. This fact appears from occasional census figures of men citizens and freedmen which are the only population figures we have. They allow an approximate estimate of the numbers in ancient Rome.

CENSUS FIGURES

NUMBER OF ROMAN CITIZENS (MEN OVER 17 YEARS OF AGE)

264 B.C.	292,234	194 B.C.	143,704	147 B.C.	322,000
251 B.C.	297,797	189 B.C.	258,318	142 B.C.	328,442
246 B.C.	241,212	179 B.C.	258,294	136 B.C.	317,933
240 B.C.	260,000	174 B.C.	269,015	130 B.C.	318,823
234 B.C.	270,713	169 B.C.	312,805	125 B.C.	394,736
225 B.C.	291,200	164 B.C.	337,452	115 B.C.	394,336
209 B.C.	137,108	159 B.C.	328,316	85 B.C.	463,000
204 B.C.	214,000	154 B.C.	324,000	69 B.C.	900,000

The number of mouths to feed was at the very least probably three or four times as great as the number of adult male citizens. The foreign wars had provided new armies of slaves from whom new generations of slaves were born in the slave marriage unions which the Romans permitted and encouraged. Many of them won their freedom and so became Roman citizens. From about 230 B.C. they were all enrolled in four urban tribes but after 189 B.C. this restriction no longer applied to their sons who henceforth might be enrolled in any tribe in which they had property (see p. 152). The blunt fact seems to have been that their former masters wanted them there so as to be able to control their votes.

Hands were therefore available to resume the intensive cultivation demanded by the soil of Latium (south of Rome) and of Campania (south of Latium). The toil was exacting but, even had our modern machinery been invented, it would have found little employment on so difficult a soil. Over wide stretches of the Latin plain where there was now but a thin top-soil, deep ploughing was impossible and the relatively light wooden ploughs did not turn the sod. Consequently every arable patch had to be cross-ploughed, the clods then broken by gangs of labourers each armed with a mattock, and the whole re-harrowed. The same gangs served to cut and harvest the crop by hand. So hard and costly a method of production made corn-growing an unattractive investment in such areas and the large labour force employed could probably earn little more than the bare necessities of life. That was all the labourers could expect because they were mostly slaves.

By this time what had once been a thickly populated arable area had long since given way to large tracts of grass supporting sheep, goats and oxen tended by a few slaves, wild men living a lonely life on standards little better than those of the animals they watched. Where cultivation was still possible, in fertile pockets among the Alban hills south of Rome for example, the more remunerative olive tree and the vine took the place of the cereal crops. Already marshy wastes were spreading on the plains where soil washed down from the mountains formed stagnant pools. The plains near the coast became the breeding-ground of mosquitoes and the source of malarial diseases which enfeebled the population. This plague had not got very far in

Cicero's time. Campania remained more fertile; 'the most beautiful estate belonging to the Roman people' was Cicero's proud description of it. He told his Roman countrymen that it was 'the main source of your riches, your chief supply in time of war, the foundation of your revenues, the granary from which your legions are fed'. It was cultivated, he said, 'by a most virtuous and moderate common people . . . excellent farmers and excellent soldiers'. This connexion in Cicero's thought between farmers and soldiers was in the best Roman tradition, although around Rome smallholders faced mounting difficulties.

But livestock, olives and vines were not within the range of the smallholder. All require considerable capital. The vine does not yield a vintage for five years. An olive grove requires fifteen years before it begins to pay. Cicero's century saw the vine and olive spread steadily. They were both crops giving their owners a vested interest in peace and security, for the loss of vines and olive trees represented a crippling loss of wealth.

A free citizen could not hope to sustain a spacious mode of life by harvesting grain near Rome and he probably did not try to do so. Already a hundred years earlier, in his farming manual written after the Second Punic War, old Cato the Censor had advised his fellow citizens to concentrate their energies according to the following list of priorities:

> Vines – if good-quality grapes could be grown.
> Garden crops – if there was a local water supply to irrigate the soil.
> Willows – to provide the many baskets and panniers needed in a fruit-growing country.
> Olives – for oil used as food and as a fuel to feed a burning wick in lamps.
> Pasture
> Grain
> Timber
> Orchard
> Oak – mainly as a source of acorns for pigs.

Cicero told another story according to which Cato recommended successful cattle-raising as the best policy in managing an estate. When asked 'What next?' he replied 'Raising cattle with tolerable success.' 'What third?' 'Raising cattle with slight success.' 'What fourth?' 'Raising crops.' Cato may have been thinking of the Latin plains when he said this. Generations of men accustomed to hard work in wresting a livelihood from the soil developed a very sound knowledge of the best combination and rotation of crops. Nowhere does the sound, practical common sense of the Romans show to better advantage than in the use made of their land. Greatly as it had declined in value owing to over-cultivation (in the absence of sufficient natural and artificial fertilizers) and owing to erosion, there were favoured spots still where deep alluvial deposits and the possibility of irrigation yielded a steady succession of good crops of cereals, vegetables, peas and beans.

Much of this farm land was managed by a trusted slave as a bailiff with his slave wife. Under their command would be a gang of anything up to about fifty slaves housed in barracks or pens frequently under miserable conditions, fed like cattle as cheaply as was consistent with their continuance in productive labour. Cato, who had the most cheese-paring notions of profit and loss, recommended readers of his manual to be always on the watch to make sure that their bailiffs did not swindle them. He thought they would always take advantage of a careless master. So he carefully advised the would-be farmer to cross-examine the bailiffs. If their excuse for slack work was that the weather was too bad for work on the land, then he should ask why was not a lot of indoor work done such as mending harness or repairing wine vats? If he was told that the slaves had been ill, he should ask why they had been given full rations. His advice to sell all cattle and slaves when they were no longer fit to work is in character. The fate of such discarded slaves in days when Roman citizens themselves, for all their privileges, had no guarantee of a livelihood if their own failed them, is not pleasant to contemplate. However, Cato was regarded as somewhat eccentric in his own day and a hundred years after Cato's death there was a new race of slaves, and, if Cicero is an example, a more considerate class of employer.

We do not know how many slaves the Romans owned in Cicero's day, but they must have covered Italy in hundreds of thousands. In the second century and afterwards they began to be of very different types and were no longer Italians like the slaves of the earlier Republic. Instead of the natives of Italy a motley crew of foreigners, Syrians, Greeks, Numidians, Gauls, Sardinians, were now planted on Italian soil and they began to increase and mutliply. However useful and pleasant it may have seemed for the Romans to have all their hard work and all their dirty work done for them for next to nothing, the results in practice were bad. Slavery, a great evil from the standpoint of the slaves, proved to be a great evil to the free Romans also. Rich Romans in the last decades of the Republic, owning perhaps hundreds of slaves, employed them for every conceivable household task and for most manufacturing and industrial jobs: spinning, weaving, baking, brewing, shoe-making, book-copying and so on. Obviously they profited to the extent that they did not have to do such jobs themselves. But neither were they able to employ free labourers for such work. Consequently a race of independent craftsmen and manufacturers was deprived of work. Slaves, mostly lacking the incentive which stimulates free workers, could not be expected to work so well. Indeed they were not all required to work hard. Many of them in Rome and in large towns were maintained as evidence of the wealth of their owners and thus as a sheer drag on the productive energies of the Republic. In more ways than one therefore Roman society and Roman life were weakened and impoverished by the huge slave colony in their midst.

The Roman landowners who employed armies of slaves on their olive groves and vineyards, on their cattle ranches and on their harvest fields, also deprived their poorer fellow citizens of the opportunity to live that sturdy life of the independent peasant smallholder whose exertions had created the Republic. Cato may again speak for the traditions of old Rome: 'Our ancestors when they would praise a worthy man would call him a husbandman, a good farmer. ... It is from the farming class that the bravest men and sturdiest soldiers come, their calling is most highly respected, their livelihood is most assured and is looked on with the least hostility and those who are engaged in that pursuit are least inclined to be disaffected.' Cicero's words, echoing those of old Cato, have already been quoted to illustrate this old Roman tradition of thinking of farmers as soldiers. From their ranks had come the conscript legions to fight Rome's wars while the slaves and the freedmen stayed behind. All male citizens and their sons were liable to serve in the army until they were forty-six years old. It was this farming class by whose energy, bravery and successes the Republic had been preserved and enlarged. The problem of Roman agriculture was so serious precisely because it was also a military and political problem. The men who farmed the land fought to maintain and extend the State. It was by their votes that the leaders of the State were chosen. Reformers who sought to maintain a healthy, prosperous body of agricultural smallholders were not conscious partisans in a class war. They wished to conserve the force which had created the Republic and to avoid the necessity of recruiting a professional paid army. Despite the plain good sense of their policy, they were doomed to fail to maintain the citizen levies. The social class of Rome midway between the relatively few rich men and the many paupers and slaves was diminishing. The evil did not stop there. The hordes of foreign slaves rendered desperate by loss of liberty and ill-treatment turned on their owners whenever a good opportunity arose. Fierce reprisals were taken against them. Evidence from a slave was not accepted in a Roman law court unless it had been extracted under torture. The death of a Roman at the hands of one of his slaves might result in the whole slave household being slaughtered in revenge. Riots and open revolt became more frequent and from 139 to 71 B.C. a series of armed risings by rebellious slaves were put down with great difficulty and at the cost of much loss of life and still more loss of property.

The danger was becoming obvious to reflective men in the days of Cicero's father and grandfather. Two such were the brothers Tiberius and Gaius Gracchus whose mother, the famous Cornelia of the proud race of the Scipios, was a daughter of Scipio Africanus who defeated Hannibal. As a child she had been used to seeing her mother take a prominent part in public life. When in turn she became one of the leaders of Roman society, it was perfectly natural for her to gather together in a kind of *salon* her wide circle of friends. Her dignified position in social life, her generous hospitality, her fondness for literary men and cultivated Greeks, contributed to allow her to radiate an influence which, until perhaps the invention of television, none but aristocratic societies have known how to elicit from unusually gifted and intelligent women. Her fame extended beyond the city of Rome and beyond Italy. Ptolemy VIII in vain besought her to marry him and to become Queen of Egypt. Her sons were among the first children of the Roman aristocracy to get their education under pronounced Greek influence. For the first time, therefore, the clear cold rationalism of the inquiring Greek mind was grafted upon the conservative, literal-minded, tradition-bound Roman stock from which Rome's leaders were drawn. The result was of tremendous consequence, not merely to the unfortunate Gracchi brothers, but to the Republic of Rome as well.

The elder brother, Tiberius, elected as representative or 'Tribune' of the people (see p. 176) for 133 B.C., thought he saw a solution for some at least of the troubles of his countrymen if the leases on public lands which had been let in large holdings after the Second Punic War could be cancelled, and the land so made available be let out again, but subdivided into small holdings. Many free peasant farmers would then replace the slave labour employed by the large landowners.

Tiberius Gracchus, thanks to the prominent position of his family in Roman society, was no doubt able to discuss the matter with some of the most experienced and wisest of the statesmen of his time. He is said to have laid his plans with great care. Anticipating trouble from the wealthy occupiers of Rome's public lands, he no doubt did his best to disarm their hostility. He proposed to leave them with 500 *iugera*, and, if the holder had two sons, he might retain an additional 250 *iugera* for each of them, or a maximum holding of 1,000 *iugera* which is equivalent to 625 English acres. Now the maximum amount of public land any man was able to lease had already been fixed according to an old law of the Republic, the Licinian-Sextian Law of 368–367 B.C., at 500 *iugera*. So Tiberius proposed to make over to the existing occupants, or 'possessors', not less than the maximum which they were in any case supposed to observe, but possibly twice as much. This not inconsiderable estate, legally the property of the Roman people, Tiberius offered free of all dues. At first he also promised to compensate possessors forced to surrender land in excess of this maximum for the improvements they had made during their tenure.

Tiberius Gracchus, unlike C. Flaminius, did not propose to give the land to the needy Romans, Latins and Italians, but to let them have it at a small annual rent. He soon got a favourable vote for his programme in the public assembly in which the citizen farmers still had a majority whenever they were willing to come to Rome to give their vote. The landowners were normally able to control the assembly because these farmers rarely would turn out in force to make what for many of them was a long and expensive journey to the city. When the country farmers were thus absent from Rome the wealthy landowners were able to rely upon their bands of retainers, or clients, and freedmen to carry the day, with perhaps a judicious amount of bribery both indirect and direct. The presence of the country farmers in Rome, attracted as they would have been by a scheme as promising as that presented to them by Tiberius Gracchus, forced the landowning and governing class to other tactics. It was easy to oppose political action in Rome. All that the landowners or Senators had to do was to put up another Tribune to tell Tiberius to stop. Such a command, or 'veto', of a Tribune was enough to hold up any new measure. There were ten Tribunes and the Senators found one of them willing to oppose Tiberius.

Exasperated by this political manoeuvre, so clearly contrary to his notion of the public interest and to the wishes of the citizen assembly, Tiberius took the daring and unprecedented step of getting his colleague and opponent removed from the office of Tribune by asking the public assembly to pass a special vote deposing him. Never before, so far as it is known, had the Roman people voted a man out of the office to which they had elected him. To dismiss a Tribune was not merely to break with tradition, but also to strike at the Tribune's authority. For a Tribune, able as he was by law to oppose any new measure, should also be able to oppose the bill removing him.

By means of this unconstitutional procedure, Tiberius succeeded in having his land law passed. A Commission of three men was set up to supervise the details and a very thorny and thankless task they found it. But Tiberius did not survive to help them. It was dangerous to upset settled political traditions and to disturb so conservative and hide-bound a people as the Romans. Tiberius Gracchus was killed in a riot provoked by his opponents when he came forward for re-election (133 B.C.).

As a result of his activity it has been estimated that perhaps some 70,000 citizens became landowners. The more enduring result of his work was its political lesson. He had served notice upon Rome that the age-old political supremacy of the Roman

Senate and the almost immemorial constitutional practice of the Republic were henceforward liable to be challenged by any ambitious man who was able to speak in the name of the Roman people.

Ten years later, Gaius Gracchus, his younger brother, made the lesson abundantly clear. He had been one of the Commissioners supervising the execution of his brother's land settlement scheme until its opponents succeeded in bringing its work to an end, as they fairly soon did. Despite the opposition, Gaius succeeded in getting himself elected as Tribune with nine colleagues, none of whom was opposed to his programme (124 B.C.).

From the none too trustworthy accounts which remain of his activities in the brief two years 123 B.C. and 122 B.C., it is at least clear that he succeeded in reviving, re-stating, amplifying and enforcing once more his brother's law dividing up the leaseholds on some large estates on the public lands into many smaller ones. His fierce energy and reforming zeal were everywhere apparent. He grappled manfully with the problem of unemployment which was then at the root of so much of the discontent at Rome, just as it has proved to be a curse of the more highly developed, complicated economic societies of our own day. He tried all the obvious remedies: land settlement on his brother's lines; colonization overseas, including the site of ruined Carthage; public works, especially roads to cheapen the movement of agricultural produce in Italy and so to make farming pay (the road-making because it was casual labour, was probably done by free men); and finally the reduction and stabilization of the market price of the staple food of the Roman and Italian people – wheat. He had large granaries built and he sold corn at a standard low price.

Of all his schemes the wheat subsidy has usually been singled out ever since for special attack. Possibly he regarded it as no more than a temporary expedient to deal with the very real and acute distress he saw around him and for which his other policies were devised as their long-term cure. When very large numbers of men are in danger of starvation, statesmen with no administrative machinery able to give immediate relief are forced to improvise first aid. So the British Government found in the severe economic crisis which was the aftermath of the war of 1914–18, and so the United States Government found in the yet more severe crisis following the economic depression beginning in September 1929. Gaius Gracchus did not give wheat away to the poor and needy. That much more serious step was reserved for a more famous Roman to provoke. But because Julius Caesar allowed one of his agents to bribe the dregs of Rome at State expense, it does not follow that Gracchus had the same policy. It cannot be denied, however, that the cheap grain in Rome had important political consequences from which Gracchus could hardly fail to benefit. For one thing it helped to ensure his popularity with the masses and for another it struck at the political strength of those of his opponents, and they were many, who used their wealth to buy the support of a band of clients to whom they doled out gifts of corn, especially at election time.

Gaius Gracchus, like all practical men of affairs in a democracy, could not afford to neglect the stricly 'political' aspect of his various plans. That is to say, he had to win support for them from as many voters as possible and he also had to be vigilant in detecting and providing against the counter-measures planned by his enemies to bring him down as they had brought down his brother ten years earlier. How he attracted the small farmer to support him is sufficiently obvious from his land settlement and road-making schemes. His need for political support went much beyond the easily-won applause of the hungry city crowds. Nothing, clearly, could mollify his enemies in the Senate. With a brother's death to avenge in a cause which he had made his own, it was not likely that he would seek to buy favours in the head-quarters of the landowning classes.

About fifty years earlier a new force, the men of the business, trading and moneyed interest, the *equites* (p. 114), were making themselves felt in Roman politics. They had risen to influence and power in the State since the end of the Second Punic War and had become a party to be reckoned with in the political balance of forces in Rome where they occupied a key position. Aided by the *equites* and by the small farmers and city mob, Gaius Gracchus was able to get sufficient support to outvote the great landowning class from whom the Senators were mainly chosen. The help of the business men was only to be had at a price. As we know little of the private lives of any of them, it would be rash to generalize about their character merely on the strength of what we can put together as a fair description of their aims and

motives. To say that they cared for one thing alone with passionate interest and determination, and to say that that one thing
was money, may seem rather a crude manner of dismissing a set
of hardworking, intelligent human beings. However, the record of
their acts and the remarks of men such as Cicero, devoted to their
interest and springing from their ranks, makes it very difficult to
give any other verdict. Gaius Gracchus gained their temporary
support at the price of the helpless subject races of the Romans in
the overseas provinces. He put the *equites* in the way of getting
lucrative business in the Eastern dependencies by handing over to
them the work of collecting the taxes. Joined with their other
business interests, it undoubtedly added substantially to their
income. 'Farming the taxes', as this system of tax-collecting is
called, is the only method open to States which do not possess
and will not create proper administrative services to undertake
essential State business. It appears to be a way of getting public
administration done on the cheap, because no salaried tax-
collectors then have to be carried on government pay-rolls. The
economy is however apparent and never real because there can
never be any check upon the amounts collected from the tax-
payers. The State, of course, fixed the amount to be collected and
knew how much the public treasury received, but not the total
amount actually collected from the victims of the tax-farmers.
Although the law laid down rules which were theoretically fair
and uniform for all tax-payers, all too often the tax-farmers
were able to flout these rules; they went out for what they could
get.

To introduce such a system was bad enough for the wretched
provincials, but the second privilege with which Gaius Gracchus
rewarded his supporters among the business men was yet more
disastrous. The one hope of provincials groaning under the
injustice of a Roman governor or other official was an appeal to
Rome and perhaps a prosecution of the offender in a Roman
court. The case would then be tried before Roman judges who
by long tradition were a jury of Senators: in other words of
Roman landowners legally excluded from overseas trade and
commerce. No doubt these men were under the strongest
pressure from the business men with whom they naturally had
the closest ties. They intermarried, met each other socially, and
the Senators, like Cicero, no doubt often borrowed money from

wealthy business men such as Cicero's banker friend, Atticus. Yet they were men of honour for the most part whose sense of justice and dignity kept them from acting as though everything which increased their profits must necessarily be the right action. When Gaius Gracchus took this 'jury' service away from the Senators and gave it to the *equites* or business men, he annoyed the Senators but at the same time he removed the one hope that the provincials had of demanding justice. In other words he went far towards making the business men judges in their own cause. An upright Roman provincial governor who would not run his province as far as possible for the greater ease and enrichment of the Roman business men was liable on some trumped-up charge to face a jury consisting of the very men he had refused to help. It was no light matter. One such governor, P. Rutilius Rufus, falsely accused in 92 B.C. on his return to Rome by vindictive business men, was driven into exile by their spiteful attacks. He went back to live as an honoured figure among the very people he was falsely convicted of oppressing.

Thus it came about that attempts made in the last quarter of the second century B.C. to deal intelligently with the problem of agricultural distress and unemployment led to a general upheaval over the whole field of administration and government. C. Gracchus was an early example of a man who thought it essential to plan and not to drift. He was ahead of his time in that his contemporaries had not been shaken out of their routine way of living and were very annoyed with any busybody who tried to rouse them to face their problems with resolution and determination. He was not up to the requirements of the situation, which not merely included a thorough understanding of the nature and causes of the evils and difficulties facing his countrymen, but demanded also a plan to take care of them and at the same time ability to win general assent to the plan itself. It has been given to few men in any age to fulfil three so exacting requirements but it is difficult to see how the respected name of statesmen can be awarded to men who fall short of them all.

The Gracchan 'New Deal', with its redistribution of public lands and its attempt to reduce the cost of living, aroused intense opposition but the enemies of Gaius were unable to strike at him openly on account of either of these two main foundations of his policy. Both were naturally assured of strong backing from the rural proletariat of agricultural labourers and ruined farmers and from the urban proletariat of unemployed city dwellers. It was not until Gaius proposed a measure to which these two proletarian groups were antagonistic that his enemies saw their chance. This opportunity was given them when he talked of admitting the Italian peoples to share the advantages of Roman citizenship. The rank and file then showed themselves every bit as jealous and selfish as the ruling classes they were so ready to attack. Themselves on the verge of destitution, they were not prepared to see Italians qualify for cheap corn or for admission to their games and gladiator shows. The Roman agricultural masses were equally opposed to allowing Italians a share in any distribution of public land on an equal footing with themselves. By playing upon these fears, the aristocracy and governing classes were able to deprive Gaius of the support he needed when he stood for election for a third term of office. Then they passed to the attack on his plans for founding a colony on the site of Carthage. The record of these critical years is very defective but it seems that his enemies put up a man from their own ranks, M. Livius Drusus, as a Tribune to overbid Gracchus with lavish promises to the mob which they did not mean to honour, and which they knew would not be accepted by the people as a whole. In the excitement resulting from such provocation the two parties came to blows. The Senators and *equites* brought up their armed slaves with the result that Gaius and 3,000 of his supporters lost their lives.

The death of Gaius Gracchus in 121 B.C. halted the gallant but premature effort he and his brother had made to think of some way for their countrymen to get out of the many difficulties by which they were beset. In these days of national planning and large-scale public enterprises it is not easy to give the Gracchi all the credit due to them for their pioneer work in trying to lead men to see that if their customary, habitual and unreflective way of life had landed them in a bad mess, then they ought to take warning that a change had become necessary and realize that it was up to them to organize themselves and to create new conditions for human co-operation to replace the traditional pattern of life that had failed. This is a hard lesson that has by no means been generally accepted and acted upon today. In the days of the Gracchi not merely was the idea of State-planned economic reforms very new but the means and machinery for carrying out the plans did not exist. The Roman Republic had no national civil service. As soon, therefore, as Gaius Gracchus had been disposed of it was not difficult to put a stop to his land settlement schemes also. No attempt seems to have been made, however, to undo the work of the land resettlement commission. To that extent the Gracchi had made a small but positive contribution to practical agricultural policy. It was accepted, and by a law in 111 B.C. the leaseholds were turned into freeholds so that thereafter all those still on their plots of public land lived rent-free. So of course did the leaseholders on the larger plots up to 1,000 *iugera* or the few of still greater acreage that had not been subdivided by the Gracchan land commission.

More significant by far than any transfers of plots of land by the Gracchi was the new spirit of conflict that their activities had brought into Roman public life. For the first time Romans had slain Romans in political strife. Whatever else they had done, the Gracchi had lined up the poor against the rich and proclaimed the stakes for which both should fight. Men had murdered each other who should have settled their differences in true Roman fashion by peaceful discussion and by planned re-adjustment in their way of life. Henceforth some uneasy ghosts were to haunt the Forum and the Senate House.

The Failure of the Agricultural Reformers and its Political Consequences

The economic forces moulding Roman agriculture were too strong to be diverted from their course by the well-meaning efforts of the Gracchi. The two ill-fated brothers were not able to deal with more than a part of the agricultural problem of the Roman Republic, and it was not the most important part. It would no doubt have been a substantial gain if they had succeeded in establishing a race of prosperous Roman middle-class farmers on the two million acres of public lands of Latium and Campania. But this was only one-seventh of the Roman lands. The forces of nature were taking their revenge and the thin top-soil on the treeless, sunbaked Latin coastal plain was becoming fit for little but grazing. The movement towards cattle-raising on large ranches was being forced upon those who sought a livelihood from the land around Rome. The rest of Italy, being less affected by such developments, remained predominantly a country of small farms. The difficulties and the crisis here to be described, therefore, related solely to the Roman lands.

The example set by the Gracchi may have delayed the process for a while on some tracts of public land, but not on land in private ownership. When therefore after 111 B.C. the former public lands became private property they were again at the mercy of 'natural economic forces'. Wealthy Romans whose respectability made it necessary for them to figure as landowners and whose greed or lavish tastes drove them to make every penny out of their property, bought up the farms of the small men. Large estates run by slave labour continued therefore to be the order of the day. Very soon the efforts spent by the Gracchi were proved to have been in vain. Cicero tells us very little of any sturdy country farmer neighbours of his on his various estates. He speaks of the bailiffs who managed his properties and of his gardeners who were not as active as they ought to have been. Less of a snob than most of his well-to-do friends, he yet makes a slighting reference to the mean social position occupied by those who worked on the land with their own hands. He makes a still more slighting reference to the land-proud aristocracy clinging stupidly to lands no longer yielding them an income sufficient to pay the interest on the mortgages for which they had pledged their land. The fate of the small Roman farmer was a problem to which Cicero must have given thought, but it does not seem to have spurred him to urgent action, neither does he seem to have realized that it was one of the danger spots of the Roman Republic.

In his early career he seems to have been more willing to help the poor than he became later on in his public life. One test of his attitude is the references he made to the Gracchi. At the height of his career in 63 B.C. when he was one of the two Consuls or co-presidents of the Roman Republic, it fell to his lot to oppose an ultra-radical land settlement programme more drastic than anything devised by the Gracchi. He then told the electors of Rome that the Gracchi were 'two most illustrious men, two most able men, two men most thoroughly attached to the Roman people. . . . Nor am I a Consul of such opinions as to think it wrong, as most men do, to praise the Gracchi, by whose counsels and wisdom and laws I see that many parts of the Republic have been greatly strengthened.'

Three years later a new agrarian law was being vehemently pushed. Cicero's attitude was simple: 'I, with the full assent of a public meeting, proposed to omit all clauses which adversely affected private rights . . . for the landed gentry form the bulk of our party's forces. . . . If it was put on a sound footing, I thought that two advantages would accrue – the dregs might be drawn from the city and the deserted portions of Italy be repeopled.'

As he grew older he became more frightened of drastic reform and he ended by saying of the Gracchi that they were not approved of by the good in their lifetime and were deservedly put to death. Property to the matter-of-fact Romans was something very real and tangible and it was well defended and protected by custom and by law. Agriculture was the supremely important activity by which property was to be acquired. To deprive one man of his property, unless he was an enemy of the State, and to give it to another, could not, in their eyes, seem a plausible method of solving anybody's problems.

Where Cicero detected no major evil and demanded no immediate remedy, the unreflective rank and file would not be likely to do better. Many independent farmers were consequently driven off the land to make way for large-scale cattle ranches. There was a drift to the city where what had been the life-blood of the Republic soon lingered in poverty, squalor and neglect. Slaves took the jobs of free labourers who, tenacious of their privileges as citizens and possessing votes in the public assemblies, were an ever-present source of trouble in Rome. Frustrated by their lack of employment, by their inability to support themselves or their families, by their degradation to a level often no better than that of freedmen, perhaps of slaves, they were all the more likely to become embittered by the pomp and parade of the well-to-do members of the governing and trading families. They ended by not wanting to work upon the land or anywhere else. Their smouldering resentment could easily be fanned to a flame powerful to destroy but impotent to create. They were therefore a constant source of anxiety to the majority of wealthy Romans, who only wanted one thing from the politicians, and that was to be left alone in the enjoyment of their possessions. Such was one result of free competition in economic relations. Extended as it soon was in political relations it produced the same fierce 'every man for himself' attitude. It led, in fact, to economic and political anarchy. Before long, ambitious and unscrupulous men soon discovered the power latent in the distress of the plebeian masses who had votes in the public assembly of Roman citizens.

Chapter Four

ROMAN INDUSTRY: TRADE, MONEY
AND COMMUNICATIONS

Some Industries

CICERO, together with a small favoured band of men and women around him in Rome and Italy, enjoyed a highly developed civilization with many amenities in the shape of good housing, rich food, large staffs of servants and slaves, luxurious furnishings, and opportunities to travel. Resources on such a scale clearly could not have been at his disposal had the Romans remained nothing more than a nation of farmers and smallholders.

Despite the great preponderance of the farming community it is clear from the indirect evidence which has survived that there was, in addition, a very considerable industry and trade. Yet little or nothing is known about it in any precise detail. The workshops, factories, manufacturing, trading and distributive industries which loom so large as the foundations of the complex civilization of the twentieth century are misty, uncertain activities in the first century B.C. What is certain is that many such activities were in full swing in Cicero's Rome; that they employed thousands of busy workers, slave and free; and that their products were of a respectably high quality considering that they depended almost, if not entirely, upon the labour of human muscular strength unaided by anything except animal power and a limited range of crude tools. Machinery and mechanical power as we know them today were unknown in the age of Cicero.

Two of the best-known agricultural handbooks of the Republican period have survived, but there are no similar sources of first-hand information about other activities whereby Romans could earn a living. Consequently what little we know about the industrial life of Rome at the close of the Republic, and earlier, depends upon chance remarks scattered here and there in the books of Roman writers, often combined with the more certain evidence from actual examples of Roman crafts and a few Roman inscriptions dug up by the spade.

Many objects have been discovered by chance, but planned excavations have yielded much also, especially on the sites of the two towns Herculaneum and Pompeii, which were buried under huge deposits of dust and ashes during an eruption of Vesuvius in A.D. 79, just over 120 years after the death of Cicero. When this calamity occurred Italy had probably progressed considerably in wealth and luxury, but many articles then in use would still have had a very familiar look to Cicero.

Industrial crafts over wide stretches of Italy were slow to change because their development was limited by the relatively modest, unprogressive and traditional needs of home and farm and of the army. Slave labour consequently supplied a very great deal of the everyday needs of country households for such things as rough pottery, basketware, clothes and shoes. But in Cicero's time an entirely self-sufficient household, even in country districts, was the exception rather than the rule.

A hundred years before the time of Cicero, Cato the Censor, in his manual for Roman farmers, itself the oldest surviving prose work in the Latin language, showed that a considerable division of labour already existed between various districts in Italy, but he tells us little more.

'Tunics, togas, blankets, smocks and shoes', he said, 'should be bought at Rome; caps, iron tools, scythes, spades, mattocks, axes, harness, ornaments and small chains at Cales and Minturnae; spades at Venafrum, carts and sledges at Suessa and in Lucania, jars and pots at Alba and at Rome; tiles at Venafrum, oil mills at Pompeii and at Rufrius's yard at Nola; nails and bars at Rome; pails, oil urns, water pitchers, wine urns, other copper vessels at Capua and at Nola; Campanian baskets, pulley-ropes and all sorts of cordage at Capua, Roman baskets at Suessa and Casinum.'

From the early adaptation of Greek comedies made for the Roman stage by Plautus and Terence it is also clear that other specialized trades already existed in the first half of the second century B.C. Clothing workers, for example, had already separate crafts, as fullers, dyers, wool-workers, veil-makers, girdle-makers, muff-makers and linen-workers.

There is nothing surprising about such specialization. From an early age, crafts requiring a relatively large amount of equipment or unusual skill as well as those depending upon the transport of heavy raw materials naturally tended to become localized and concentrated.

Metal Industries. The copper and bronze industry at Capua was of great antiquity. Its products, some striking examples of which may be seen in plates 2, 6 and 7, were still in great demand in Cicero's day. Over those centuries there was growing concentration of workers in this one place. It would be misleading to speak of it as factory production, which might conjure up a picture of smoking chimney stacks, huge furnaces, whirring wheels, transmission belts and armies of workers pouring through the factory gates. Nothing on this modern scale was known anywhere in antiquity. A workshop employing fifty or more men would have seemed a very large establishment indeed in those days. Machinery was unknown, for the few primitive mechanical aids used by the Romans, such as grinding-mills, cannot be likened to modern engineering products. It was nearly 2,000 years after Cicero's day before a way was found to harness the expansive energy of steam to work a pump and to drive a wheel. This great invention marks off our industrial age from the handwork era of earlier times, as another world. A simple estimate made before the discovery of atomic power of the units of power at the disposal of people such as the Romans using solely their own muscles aided by a domestic animal or two, compared with Englishmen and Americans able to call upon the mechanical contrivances of steam power and electricity, showed a comparison of the order of 80 units of the average Roman against over 2,000 units of the average Englishman and over 2,800 of the average American. In this mechanical sense every Englishman had the aid of at least twenty-five times the power at the disposal of each Roman of the Republic, and the difference becomes more striking every year.

Just as the nearby copper ores accounted for the early concentration of industry at Capua, so also iron ore imported from Elba explains the iron and steel industry of Puteoli, situated at the north of the bay of Naples (now called Pozzuoli, the only good port within hundreds of miles of Rome). Without iron, steel and copper the Roman army could not have become the force it proved to be. Before joining the ranks, every citizen in the armies of the early Republic had to bring with him his own sword, steel-pointed spear, metal helmet and breastplate. Every community

therefore needed its own blacksmith. A multitude of small
smithies rather than anything in the nature of large-scale production was the rule. It was not till the later Republic that such
equipment was provided by the State. Manufacturing methods
were and remained primitive. The iron and steel industry in
particular was held back because the Romans did not know how
to develop sufficient heat to melt the metal. Coal was unknown
and the Romans had to rely upon small wood-burning furnaces.
They could not therefore produce cast iron because without a
more intense heat in the furnaces the metal could not be run in a
molten state into moulds. The good-quality steel of the Roman
broadsword and other weapons and tools was achieved at the cost
of persistent forging and reforging.

With bronze and copper the situation was different. Copper and
silver both melt at a lower temperature than iron, and both
copper and bronze are therefore much easier and consequently
cheaper to manufacture. Bronze, an alloy of copper and tin, melts
at a lower temperature than pure copper. The Egyptians discovered
this fact and it was also known to the Greeks. Bronze pots, pans,
jugs, plates, vases, vats, buckets, large butts or containers for wine,
olive oil, or water, were made in Capua in vast numbers. In-
numerable specimens of them have been found scattered all over
Mediterranean lands and Western Europe. The makers' names
which many of them bear are also found on the tombs of wealthy
families in Capua, so it is highly probable that the flourishing
industry of the town supported an active overseas trade besides
supplying the home market. As the earlier quotation from Cato
shows, Capua was already the recognized centre for all manner of
copper household and farm utensils. A hundred years after Cato,
the workmen of Capua, mostly slaves but some of them perhaps
free labourers for whom local agriculture no longer offered employment, were turning their hands to articles demanding greater
skill and taste in their production than did the plain and domestic
utility goods that he commended. The simple life no longer held
much attraction for Romans who had grown wealthy or who had
seen their neighbours grow wealthy on the spoils of war. One of
the fruits of conquest was a taste for finer things. 'It was through
the Army serving in Asia' in the first half of the second century
B.C., said Livy, 'that the beginnings of foreign luxury were
introduced into the city.'

The loot paraded through the streets of Rome after a successful campaign in the East was stacked with such things as bronze-framed couches, pedestal tables and other rare furniture, as well as luxurious bedspreads, tapestries and other fabrics wrought with an exquisite skill far beyond that of the native Romans. Among the troops of captives who became slaves were some craftsmen who may have helped to create such marvels. One way of making money was to employ slaves to turn out articles which could be sold in the markets of Rome and other Italian cities. So the workmen of Capua began to make in more sophisticated styles bronze lamps, lamp-stands, braziers for charcoal fires, tables, tripods, and all manner of decorative luxury articles.

Cicero speaks with affection of a decorative lamp-stand which his brother had ordered for him in the Greek island of Samos and which he often used when hard at work before sunrise or late at night. Such a lamp would burn olive oil. Petroleum products were of course unknown. The custom of adorning one's house with statues and portrait-busts, which the Romans copied from the Greeks, also gave the bronze-workers of Capua a steady trade. Greek slaves or ex-slaves were no doubt numerous among the ranks of the artists and designers who made models from which moulds to cast the copies were taken. Cicero took a great delight in statuary, but he and the few Romans of cultivated taste sought the genuine products of the famous sculptors of Greece just as many people today prefer the furniture of Chippendale and Sheraton to modern factory products, however soundly constructed. There were not enough originals to go round, so just as today there is a great trade in reproductions, some famous statues by Greek sculptors were copied for the Roman market. Some of these copies have survived to our own time to provide testimony both to the genius of Greece and to the good taste of the Romans who admired it.

The Precious Metals. A true Roman of the heroic age despised riches. 'Nobody could overcome him, either by steel or with gold' was the high praise given to one early hero by Ennius, the poet of the time of the Second Punic War. Long before Romans deemed it right or proper for their fellow citizens to be seen wearing much jewellery, gold was lavishly used in beautifying temples, for there was little doubt that gold already occupied, in Roman eyes, the pride of place it has held from time immemorial as the metal most prized by man.

If the Romans of the early Republic did not gratify this 'accursed hunger for gold', as a later Roman described it, it was because they could not get it rather than because they did not want it. Italy has never had many gold deposits and what little there were soon became exhausted.

Silver was in much the same position. So scarce must it have been and so coveted towards the middle of the third century B.C., about ten years before the First Punic War, that a Roman patrician was expelled from the Senate for owning 10 lb of silver plates and dishes. This harsh action shows that, in their early Republican commonwealth, the Romans would not tolerate private ambitions thirsting for unusual social distinction. Energies now spent on 'keeping up with the neighbours' in clothes, furniture and accessories had to find other outlets in ancient Rome.

The story has been briefly told in Chapters 1 and 2 how, in the second century B.C., this small nation of warrior farmers rapidly overcame their neighbours in the Mediterranean so that within the lifetime of many a Roman they moved from a simple agricultural life with a few possessions to one relatively rich and, what is more important, one offering good chances of becoming far richer. Many of the first generation of Roman conquerors were set in their ways and did not suddenly change the habits of a lifetime. They boasted that they got more satisfaction out of ruling the men rich in gold and silver than in possessing the stuff themselves. Their wives and daughters may very likely have thought otherwise, for in time it soon became clear that Romans were becoming greedy for luxury and ostentation.

Scipio Aemilianus, who flourished in the middle of the second century B.C. and who married a sister of the Gracchi, owned about 32 lb of silver. His reforming brother-in-law Gaius Gracchus became a keen collector and is said to have spent 5,000 sesterces a pound for some of the silver he possessed. The same aesthetic feelings which today send rich collectors to Bond Street or Fifth Avenue for early Georgian silver then began to come into evidence in Republican Rome. Scipio Aemilianus and his circle were, however, daring pioneers. They gave themselves to Greek literature and civilization and were no more approved by their countrymen than were the 'Italianate Englishmen' who brought the Renaissance to England in the reign of the Tudors. Never before had the Romans had the means of gratifying such tastes on a truly lavish scale.

The result of a successful campaign was advertised in the most public manner possible by a grand procession along the Sacred Way to the heart of Rome, in which the triumphant general was followed by a motley throng of captives, and chariots piled high. with booty looted from the defeated land. The upper limits to the loot were usually only the amount of valuables possessed by. the vanquished and the means of transporting them to Rome. The booty was supposed to be public property, won not by a Roman general but by the Roman gods who had been the true architects of victory, and in the best days of the Republic much of it un-doubtedly was paid into the Treasury. Of one hero of the early Republic, M. Curius, it was said that 'after having subdued his enemies ... of all the booty and pillage taken from them he reserved nothing for himself except a little ewer of beechwood wherewith he might sacrifice to the Gods'.

Yet it is difficult to believe that the soldiers or their officers gave up all their winnings, including such things as gold rings, brace-lets, jewels and similar small articles of great value. They were of course given a share of the value of their haul, but it was not at first very large. As time went on the place of the gods in Roman campaigns became of small account and the generals began to set a bad example. Sulla and Lucullus returning from campaigns in the East when Cicero was in his early manhood became the richest men in Rome. When later on Lucullus threatened to make political trouble for Julius Caesar, the Dictator very soon reduced him to abject surrender by the blackmailing counter-threat of a legal inquiry into the origin of his fortune. No doubt Lucullus would not have emerged unscathed from such an inquiry. Caesar himself would have fared still worse under such investigation. Ill-gotten gains are supposed never to prosper, but, as the Nazis have since reminded the world, predatory nations rarely go to war except for what they can steal from their victims.

The first wealthy victims of the young Roman Republic were its former lords and masters, the Etruscans. At the looting of Veii in 396 B.C., the victorious Romans went nearly delirious with joy at the sight of the possessions of the slaughtered townsmen. But the wealth of the Etruscans was of small account compared with the riches of Carthage.

The cumulative economic effect of such piracy must clearly have been formidable. The impact of sudden riches would have been all the greater on a people living a relatively modest and simple life as the Romans were. In fact, it undermined that simple life. Covetousness and greed, restrained within the Roman community by ancient rules of behaviour, having once been let loose upon the foreigner, could no longer be chained up at home. Economic forces powerfully propelling every man to make the most of his opportunities gained increasing freedom. The results stimulated the industry and trade in precious metals and in turn reacted upon public finance and the money system.

War booty, however, was a windfall and it could not be picked up twice in the same area unless, like Asia Minor, that area had been very rich. Of more enduring value therefore were the gold and silver mines in newly won territories.

The capture of Spain from the Carthaginians after the Second Punic War gave Rome the richest source of precious metals in the ancient world. The amount of gold and silver taken from Spain will never be known. The partial record we have of some of it shows that Spain provided at least 5,000 lb of gold and 350,000 lb of silver between 206 B.C. and 168 B.C. This represented probably about one-twentieth of the entire income of the Republic at the beginning of the second century.

The occupation and control of the country was a long task for the Roman army, and it involved a lot of bloodshed. If all the cost and expense could be balanced throughout the first seventy years of occupation, it is doubtful whether Rome was able to show a worthwhile gain. Nevertheless this considerable new stock of gold and silver, although won at a high cost in men and supplies, was in circulation, and a new source of the precious metals had entered into the possession of Rome. It could not fail to give employment to the goldsmiths and silversmiths of Italy in general and of Rome in particular.

Their patrons would have been the rich, so this development did not mean much to the masses except in so far as they were able to benefit by the sight of gilded statues in the temples and public Forum. In the second century B.C. the goldsmiths were kept busy. Some of them were craftsmen making or re-making jewellery brought to them by their customers. Others were manufacturing jewellers owning sufficient capital to be able to buy their own stock of gold and gems which they worked up for sale in their shops. One way of making money was to buy a skilled slave and to set him up in business to make profits for his owner.

Greek slaves and freedmen especially were employed for highly skilled and artistic work as jewellers making cameos, brooches and other ornaments. One branch of the trade, engraving designs upon small gemstones, found a permanent market by providing the signet rings in widespread general use for sealing documents and other objects of value with an identifying design.

Building. The houses and buildings of Republican Rome had mostly disappeared long before the end of the Roman Empire and few relics of them are now extant. Archaeologists who have dug down through the foundations of later buildings have been able to unearth some remains of Republican Rome and thereby add to the knowledge provided by such structures as survive. From such evidence combined with scattered references in the writings of Roman authors of Republican days it is possible to glean some knowledge about the nature of the earlier city, although the few facts at our disposal make it impossible to picture it in any detail. Building is one of the earliest crafts and its traditional methods and materials have reigned uninterruptedly without any major change until the scientific revolution of our own times ushered in the age of concrete and of steel. Apart from their development of the use of a hard-setting lime mortar, the Romans invented no striking new methods but, in their practical way, used and improved those they had learnt from others. Thanks to the earlier discovery by the Etruscans, through their contact with the East, that heavy structural loads can be carried on arches of brick and stone, the Romans of the Republic were already able to build domed roofs and stone bridges. Already, while under Etruscan domination, the Romans had made their city one of the largest in Italy, (Plates 3a, 31).

By far the greatest building activity went into domestic architecture. The modest dwellings and more numerous hovels of the earlier Republican days were being replaced in the second century by the more ambitious mansions of the rich and the crowded blocks of many-storied apartments divided by narrow alleyways

which housed the vastly more numerous families of the poor.
alike were the work of Roman builders, free labourers and sla
mostly employed by contractors working for well-to-do clien
buying a home of their own or investing money as landlords of
some large apartment house. The Roman system of getting work
done at the lowest possible price by asking for competitive bids
from would-be contractors tended to keep costs down.

The materials used in Republican times were the local Roman
stone, tufa, squared in blocks which are characteristic of Roman
work wherever Roman remains exist. It is relatively soft and
weathers badly, so it was often faced with stucco. The harder
Travertine stone came into use before the end of the second
century B.C. and was used whenever great strength and resistance
to crushing was required as in the arches of bridges. Brick tiles
were in general use, but brick-making for house building was to
get its greatest development after Republican times. A good type
of lime mortar mixed with small stones (often mistakenly called
concrete) was widely used in and after the second century B.C.,
so making it possible for the first time to build houses of
more than one story without serious danger of collapse. Marble
was first used in building the temple of Jupiter and Juno in
146 B.C.

The Romans do not seem to have realized that their mortar
was more durable than the pieces of brick tiles which they often
used as an exterior to the mortar filling forming the core of their
walls. Local clays made good tiles and the industry was one of the
few open to Senators and patricians because it was regarded as an
agricultural occupation.

Characteristic of all Roman houses also was the low and almost
flat roof with flanged tiles held firmly by narrow semi-circular
ridge tiles. Glass was in general use for gems and urns but clear-
glass windows do not seem to have been introduced into Roman
houses until after the age of Cicero.

The normal Roman house of the well-to-do was square or
rectangular with a series of rooms opening upon an interior
courtyard. The roof sloped inwards to conduct the rainwater
into a sunken cistern in the middle of the courtyard. This central
opening to the sky also served to let the smoke of cooking out of
the house, a fact which perhaps explains its name, *atrium*: it was
a 'smoke-blackened' hole (*ater* meaning black). (Plate 5.)

As Greek influence spread, so the plan of the better Roman homes was enlarged to include a small courtyard at the back, usually in the form of a garden surrounded by a colonnade through which the rooms looked on to the garden. To this house-behind-the-house the Romans increasingly retired, for it was there that they found quiet, privacy and charm. Around the *peristylium*, as it was called by its Greek name, were the library, shrine, bedrooms, kitchen and dining-room. When the single-story 'bungalow' type of house was expanded to include a second story, the bedrooms would usually be on the upper floors. (Plate 4.)

The manual labourers, tilers, joiners, carpenters, lime-burners, stonemasons, painters, gardeners, marble and mosaic workers, whose labours created the capital city, remain, as their descendants in most ages have been, shadowy figures with no other memorials than the relics of their works.

Pottery. The average Roman home, in the most flourishing period of the Republic, contained a minimum amount of essential furniture, such as couches, tables, chairs and chests. In comparison with modern homes, it would have seemed half empty. The comparison with our household and kitchen ware would be less unequal, although in style, shape and decorations the differences are striking. The Roman kitchen and food store shows a variety of household utensils, especially lamps, jugs, jars, storage vessels, bowls, basins, ladles, plates and dishes, made for the most part from local clays. (Plate 9.)

Specialization led to improved skill in making the china-clay paste, and it also made possible the employment of skilled workers wherever designs were needed, as on glazed pottery and other decorated articles. Some concentration of the industry consequently developed. Pottery, of which the red glazed Arretine ware of Arretium was the most renowned, has been found all over the Roman world. (Plate 10.)

The annual production of pottery ware of all kinds must have amounted to many hundreds of tons. The Romans used earthenware for many purposes for which we now use enamel ware and metal. Breakages alone would keep the potters' wheels busy long before the spread of the power of Rome throughout the Mediterranean world created an overseas market for their wares.

City Industries. In the heroic age of the Republic food and
clothing were provided within the household. The tradition that
Roman women should themselves see to these essential tasks was
dignified by impressive examples provided by the proudest
patrician houses. It was a tradition by no means dead in Cicero's
day, although by then customs had changed and many fine ladies
found more interesting ways of spending their days than busying
themselves with spindle and loom. The poorer classes were often
unable to work for themselves even if they had wanted to because
they had neither the equipment nor the skill.

The wheat porridge on which Romans depended was made
simply. Here is a second-century recipe: 'Put half a pound of
clean wheat in a clean mortar. Wash it well, rub off the husk
thoroughly and rinse it clean. Then put in a pot with clean water
and cook. When done add milk by degrees until it is a thick
gruel.' 'Punic porridge' seems luxurious by comparison, for 3lb
of new cheese, half a pound of honey and one egg were added to
a pound of well-soaked spelt grits and the mixture was then
cooked. Bakers' shops were unknown in the time of the Second
Punic War. The first bakery was said to have been opened in
Rome in 172 B.C., but in the time of Cicero they had long been
well-patronized establishments. The bakers of the city also
ground wheat into flour. The word 'miller' (*pistor*) in Latin is also
used for 'baker'. Milling with hand-operated grinding-stones
was one of the earliest household duties to be given to slaves. It
was disgraceful for a Roman woman to have to work at grinding
corn. In large households, each with its own grindstones and
bakehouse, bread-making continued to be done at home. The
poor who had neither slaves, grindstones, nor ovens in their
cramped quarters, had the flour ground and baked for them by
the bakers, who had slaves or asses to grind wheat into flour.
'Factory'-baked loaves by the thousand were produced in the
large bakehouses of a man like Eurysaces the Roman baker whose
pride in his work, his advertising instincts, or both, led him to
have his large tomb built to resemble his bakehouse. The loaves
were flat and circular in shape like our English scones, often with
the baker's name imprinted on the dough. The Romans had no
yeast although they sometimes used a substitute. Usually their
bread must have been tough wholemeal. This is a recipe for
bread-making of the early second century B.C.: 'Wash the hands

and the kneading board well. Put flour on the kneading board, add water gradually and work it thoroughly. When you have worked it well, mould it and bake it under an earthenware cover.' (Plates 11, 12.)

The restaurant and catering trade seems never to have been run as it often is today by firms operating on a large scale through many branches. To judge from the later remains found at Pompeii there must have been scores of little booths and taverns where town and country folk could get a snack and a drink of cheap wine, but there was nothing to correspond to the multiple food shops of our large cities. (Plate 13.)

Retail trade in foodstuffs by butchers, market gardeners, olive-oil and wine vendors was also carried on by unorganized small-scale units and despised accordingly by the select and exclusive 'best people' of Roman society who would probably draw their supplies from their own estates. Many of the commonest articles now used in vast quantities every day were of course unknown to the Romans. Among them are potatoes, sugar, tea, coffee, beer, tobacco, and soap.

Tradition older than Rome itself gave the work of clothing the family to its women-folk. Roman wives gained social distinction and esteem by maintaining at least a show of this honourable custom, although in practice it was left more and more to the household slaves of the rich and to the new clothing industry which developed around the establishments of cleaners and dyers – the fullers.

Spinning wool or flax into yarn, is now done by machinery at amazing speed. Before Roman women could begin to make clothing they needed yarn and this they had to make themselves from raw wool by means of the distaff and spindle.

'With their hands according to custom they plied the eternal task. The left hand held the distaff charged with soft wool, then the right hand drew down the threads with up-turned fingers, shaped them, then with downward thumb twirled the spindle poised evenly on its rounded whorl, while at their feet wicker baskets held the soft skeins of snowy wool.' So did the poet Catullus, Cicero's contemporary, picture the three Fates spinning the threads of destiny and foretelling the fate of mankind. 'Run on ye spindles, run on, drawing out the threads' was the refrain of his song, as it must also have been the refrain running through the lives of countless thousands of Roman girls almost from the cradle to the grave.

The wool yarn thus patiently made by hand was next woven. The woollen cloth so produced was then made up into the simple and standard garments of the Roman; a tunic or vest as the only underclothes and a large semicircle of woollen cloth or toga as the only outer garment. Women wore a long tunic (*stola*) reaching to the feet, instead of a toga, secured by a girdle round the waist. The toga was the national costume of the Romans, who referred to themselves and their allies as 'men of the toga', in contrast with people like the Gauls, whom they called 'the men in breeches'. No country house, and few town houses of any size, would lack their vertical loom. While slave labour was to be had, and as long as Roman girls could be put to the task, there was small opportunity for a commercial clothing industry to develop. No guilds of spinners or weavers are heard of in Republican Rome. In Rome later on, however, the city crowds would have fewer facilities and many townspeople got their togas and tunics ready-made from the fullers. Exactly what part the fullers took in the clothing industry is not clear. Probably they did not undertake weaving and preparing clothes, but bought up what home-made articles domestic industry provided, and re-sold them. Other cloth-sellers provided a market for new or second-hand clothes, but Cato, who said that tunics, togas, blankets and smocks were to be bought at Rome, did not say by whom they were sold. (Plate 15.)

The cleaning business of the fullers was the nearest approach to the modern laundry and it must have been a busy trade because, lacking soap, no Roman had facilities for washing at home. The lack of soap made life in Republican Rome poorer than ours in a variety of ways hardly imaginable until in our own time a similar deficiency threatened wide areas of Europe as a result of war. Cleaning materials in Cicero's day were a few easily obtainable chemicals – potash, nitrum (natural carbonate of soda), fuller's earth (an alkaline clay) and – for the Romans in the poverty of their resources could not afford to be squeamish – human and animal urine derived from the street and lavatories of Rome. The clothes so treated were afterwards well washed and then hung out to dry in the Italian sun. They would then be brushed and carded to raise a soft surface. To bleach them white the clothes were hung over a wicker basket frame under which sulphur was burned or vaporized. (Plate 13b.)

No evidence remains to show how frequently Romans thought it necessary to send their togas and tunics to the cleaners nor do we know what it cost them to do so. To appear in public in a soiled and dirty toga was a common sign of mourning not merely on account of bereavement but on any other occasion demanding public sympathy. Citizens put on trial or those condemned to exile, as Cicero was in 58 B.C., would go about in a shabby state for this reason. Colour was never used except for ceremonial purposes, when it took the form of a purple band along the straight edge of the semicircular toga, which was then called a *toga praetexta*. It had religious associations, for the only Romans allowed to wear it were the priests, senior magistrates able to perform sacrifices, and young boys and girls. This public avowal of the sacred nature of childhood honours the ancient Romans by whom it was inspired. These purple bands of the toga and the flame-coloured veils of brides must have been all the more striking against the normal everyday sea of white clothes.

Lack of Information About Industrial Questions

It is clear that much busy trading and industrial activity made up the daily noise and bustle of the crowded city. Unfortunately there are answers to next to none of the many questions we are accustomed to asking about present-day industries: How many were employed? What were their earnings? How were they paid – by the hour or by piece rates? Were they concentrated in large-scale factories? Were many workers employed under one management? How was unemployment dealt with? What influence, if any, were the workers able to exert on the conditions of their employment? Was there anything corresponding to the modern trade union? or to the modern trust or cartel? Were the master manufacturers in agreement about prices and wages or did immemorial custom rule? How important was the export trade? What profits were made and what were the most profitable industries? One thing seems certain; strikes were unknown. All trades were, it is true, organized into guilds but for social purposes and not for collective bargaining as are the trade unions of today.

Public Works, Aqueducts and Water Supply

Temples, roads, sewers and aqueducts were among the earliest public works of the Republic. The need of the city of Rome for a purer water supply than that from the Tiber, yellow with sand and silt, is obvious and it was met in abundance. Conduits, partly underground and partly overground on a system of built-up arches, channelled a lavish supply of fresh water into the city from the hill country.

The two oldest aqueducts were mainly underground. They were the *Aqua Appia* constructed by the orders of Appius Claudius Caecus who was Censor in 312–308 B.C., and the *Anio Vetus* built between 279 and 269 B.C. They still furnished the main water supply of Rome in Cicero's day, pouring over 50 million gallons of water into Rome every 24 hours. They had been supplemented in 144 B.C. by a new supply from the Sabine hills thirty-five miles from Rome. (Plate 18.)

When the water got to Rome it was fed into a series of reservoirs arranged in threes one above the other. Water from the lowest supplied public fountains, the middle went to the public baths, while the uppermost, because it held less sediment, was reserved for private houses. (Plates 17a, 29.)

Stonemasons were busy building these water-channels and keeping them in repair. Plumbers had the job of connecting the supply to the houses of the well-to-do who could afford to buy the lead pipes, pay to have them laid and pay the annual water rate for the privilege. Those who did so owned the pipes, which were usually stamped with their names, partly as a proof of ownership, partly as evidence that water tax was due, and partly as a very necessary check upon the all too prevalent fraudulent diversion of water. The employees of the city water system, which was provided by the State and controlled by the Censor, were not above taking bribes from those who sought to get a water supply on the cheap by graft.

Land Drainage and Irrigation

Essential as it was to bring water to Rome it was just as necessary to take water away from parts of Campania and the Pontine marshes. Here the Romans benefited from the skill and experience of the Etruscans. Rome itself had been made habitable by the well-known main drain (*Cloaca Maxima*) which prevented the Forum from becoming a swamp by collecting and sending to the Tiber the waters from five of the city's famous seven hills (Capitol, Palatine, Viminal, Quirinal and Caelian). Later it became the main artery in the sewerage system of the city. (Plate 17b.)

The arid districts of Latium and Campania became abundantly fertile if they could be irrigated. It was not possible to do much in this way, but the Romans used what resources they had. The early exploit (around 396 B.C.) of tapping the overflow waters of the Alban lake for the benefit of the lands below was no mean achievement. On many Italian hills and mountains Rome's neighbours had constructed, with immense skill and labour, a great series of terraced plots of ground which they took infinite pains to protect against the fierce mountain rainstorms ever threatening their destruction. Many of these people were Samnites. A disastrous civil war between them and the Romans in Cicero's lifetime brought ruin to their lands from which they never recovered.

The Money System

The unit of reckoning used by Cicero and his friends in their accounts was the '*sestertius*' (literally a 'two-and-a-halfer'), a small silver coin about the same weight as the British silver threepenny piece. It was not often minted, so it was not much carried about. Bronze had been the metal traditionally used by the Romans for coinage, beginning in primitive times with bars of metal. These crude bars were later stamped with the device of a cow or other animal (*nota pecudum*) from whence comes the word for money, *pecunia* (*pecus* in Latin meaning 'a herd'). (Plate 20.)

Early in the third century B.C., around 289 B.C., a mint was set up, managed by three officials, and the bars were replaced by round coins which, although an improvement on the bars as money, were still very heavy and clumsy. These were:

   the round *as* weighing about 10 oz;
   the *semis* or half *as* weighing about 5 oz;
   the *uncia* or one-twelfth *as* weighing slightly less than three
      of our pennies.

These bronze coins were used in the country. For foreign trade and use in the cities, silver coins were minted in 269 B.C. Such Roman coins were merely one of many independent coinage systems of Italy. (Plate 19.)

In those far-off days money entered little into the life of the average Roman, who lived on the land and counted his riches by the extent of his holding, by the size of his crops, and by the numbers of his oxen, goats, pigs and other livestock.

It is important to trace the development of the Roman money system, for there is a world of difference between the settled routine of an agricultural people living in their traditional ways on the land, which is what the Romans of the heroic age were, and a modern, commercially-minded, money-using people in whose lives money-making can become a very real, serious, and all-absorbing end in itself. The Romans of the later age of Cicero had gone far along this road and they seem essentially modern in their use of money reckoning.

We have seen in our own time what havoc the sudden introduction of a money economy can wreak upon the lives and welfare of tradition-bound peoples in Africa and elsewhere. We know how the use of money can upset the age-long system of values of such peoples and so create a whole new range of bewildering problems for them. It is therefore plausible to believe that the relatively rapid spread of a developed money system had equally far-reaching effects upon the habits and outlook of the Roman citizen farmers of the third and second centuries B.C. They and their forefathers were accustomed to using money chiefly as a means of payment, not as a medium of exchange or as a way of accumulating treasure. These distinctions are important. As a means of payment, money would be required very occasionally, for such purposes as the payment of fines for damage done to a neighbour, or as part of a dowry and other ceremonial payments. As an accumulated treasure, money would be important chiefly in the State Treasury and to some extent in private ownership as evidence of personal prestige.

The use of money as a medium of exchange, instead of exchanging goods by barter, does not arise until foreign trade is developed, and not always then. The Carthaginians, although almost entirely a trading nation, got along without money, except as a means of paying their mercenary troops, until quite late in their history. Their extensive, wide-ranging trade was carried on, as that of traders with primitive peoples always has to be, by bartering one kind of goods against another, Tyrian purple against Cornish tin for example. The early Romans were an agricultural, not a trading people, and their lumps of copper and bronze were clearly unsuited for use as a medium of exchange.

Inconvenient enough for use in Rome and central Italy, these lumps of bronze possessed little attraction to the more civilized South and East, where Greek art and technical skill had long since introduced small silver coins as a medium of exchange and as an aid to Greek commerce. In alliance with the Carthaginians, who used silver in what money they had, Roman military power was soon extended from the mainland of Italy across the Adriatic. After the conflict, between 280 and 275 B.C., with the Greeks who had settled in Southern Italy, the Romans began to mint a silver coin (269 B.C.) which they called *nummus*. It was equivalent to the standard Greek coin *didrachma*, and it circulated in Rome but was most needed for trade in the new areas where Roman bronze was unknown. The Romans who at this time had expelled from the Senate no less a person than an ex-Consul because he owned some silver plate were clearly in no haste to adopt foreign customs in the use of the precious metals.

Shortly after this first silver coinage, the Romans began their deadly struggle with the Carthaginians for supremacy in the Mediterranean. The Roman coinage seems to have survived the First Punic War (264–241 B.C.) without alteration. The war was not fought on Italian soil and the relatively small demands upon domestic currency did not overtax the sources of supply of silver and copper. The Second Punic War (218–201 B.C.) was a very much more serious matter. Like all major wars, it involved expenditure which was huge in relation to the normal resources of Rome. Bronze was needed in large quantities to supply arms and armour, and one way of getting it quickly was to reduce the size of the bronze coins. This was not necessarily inflation, because the new smaller-size coins might still contain the same value in bronze since the metal itself was so greatly needed, in other words had become so much more valuable.

The *as* of the old bronze money was still the unit of account, but it suffered a rapid and steep decline from the original standard of about 10 oz to 6 oz (around 217 B.C.), then to about 3 oz (around 209 B.C.) and fell later to 2½ oz and 2 oz. It was still called an *as*. Later writers who had endured the deliberate robbery practised by unscrupulous rulers who debased the coinage for their own profit, naturally thought that this decline in the metal content of the coins represented a similar debasement by the earlier Republic. Their explanation is no longer believed. From the monetary point of view conditions at the two periods were worlds apart. As long as the old Roman bronze money was a means of payment, not a medium of exchange, it did not much matter what was the size of the coins. What had happened was that a great demand had arisen for bronze and silver for other uses besides the coinage. In other words, bronze and silver had become more valuable and their new values were reflected in the smaller amount of metal in the coins. The smaller coins were much more serviceable and no doubt helped along the more general use of money.

The currency suffered heavily during the Second Punic War, with its succession of severe crises, because it was a very much more desperate struggle than the first. Never since the Roman Republic emerged as an independent power was it in such peril as in the Second Punic War. Never, in the authentic as distinct from the legendary history of Rome, did the Roman people respond to the dangers which encompassed them with such bravery and resolution. All were ready to sacrifice their lives and fortunes in their city's cause. In 215 and 214 B.C. a Roman army was in dire peril in Spain. The Senate was unable to come to their rescue with fresh supplies because the Treasury was empty. There was only one solution. The supplies were obtained from the richer citizens and the army was saved. The bronze coinage also suffered when Hannibal cut off the copper zone of Etruria and Capua (until 211 B.C.).

About 205 B.C., shortly after the victory of the Metaurus, or perhaps earlier, a new silver coin was issued as a token of victory. This was the *victoriatus*. It was worth twice as much as the earlier *nummus*. Like the *nummus*, it was coined as a medium of exchange for foreign trade rather than for the home market, where bronze continued to be used. In 202 B.C. the Carthaginians were completely defeated and in the following year there was peace. It was not of long duration for, almost immediately, wars with Macedon and Syria followed, and in each the might of Rome prevailed. Heavy indemnities had been exacted from the defeated Carthaginians. After the First Punic War they were required to pay, over a period of 10 years, the sum of 3,200 talents. The second indemnity was 10,000 talents spread over 50 years. The talent was a Greek monetary unit not frequently used by the Romans. It is usually regarded as the equivalent of 6,000 *denarii* or 24,000 sesterces. This indemnity must have represented a vast amount of wealth to the all but ruined and impoverished Romans with their undeveloped monetary system, particularly as they were as yet little accustomed to the use of silver or precious metals.

Great as was the wealth of Carthage, it was of small account beside the riches of the Near East where the treasures of Persia brought back by Alexander the Great, were still intact. The Romans helped themselves to as much as they could carry. It is extremely difficult to frame any notion of the tremendous sudden accession of wealth which these vast hoards meant to a small, struggling City State of the ancient Mediterranean world. The power of gold and silver to stimulate the activities of men has had many illustrations in modern history. The sudden rise of Spain, the vigour of Elizabethan England, the great expansion in worldwide trade and commerce which followed the opening of the gold fields of California, of Australia and of South Africa in the nineteenth century, all conspire to suggest forcibly that, even if men cannot count on becoming civilized as soon as they become rich, nevertheless there is a very close connexion between much gold and great economic expansion. Consequently it is plausible to believe that the wealth of Persia which, as a result of Roman conquests, suddenly fertilized the Mediterranean world after the middle of the second century B.C., acted like a forced draught upon the slowly developing economic life of Rome and contributed powerfully to the wealth and urbanity of the civilization into which Cicero was born. It has indeed been suggested that this great store of riches, suddenly acquired and circulated by the Romans, alone maintained the Roman State until it was again slowly dissipated by being re-exported to those far Eastern lands whence it had originally come. It went back to pay for the silks and spices and the other exotic articles of luxury beloved of the Romans. A pound of silk by A.D. 301 was said to cost about three pounds of gold. This slow drain of precious metals, which was all

that the Romans could offer to Arabs, Persians, Indians and
Chinese in exchange for the products of the East, gradually, so it
has been said, sapped the vital principle by which the whole
economic system of the Roman Empire was maintained and thus
contributed as much as any other economic factor to the decline
and fall of Rome. However, the depreciation of the coinage by the
later Emperors as well as the drain of precious metals to the
East and the failure of the gold and silver mines were all factors in
the later breakdown. Yet if there were any truth in such a
theory, it would afford a better standard by which to value the
booty collected by Rome than any effort to put it into British
currency. On a rough valuation it probably more than doubled
the wealth owned by all the citizens of the Republic, which has
been guessed as about 1,000 million *denarii* at the beginning of
the second century B.C. Fifty years later (about 150 B.C.), Roman
national wealth had perhaps increased to about three times this
amount but it would still be a minute and insignificant sum compared with the estimated capital assets today of any British or
American community of the size of Rome.

Leaving such speculations and returning to the recorded state
of Rome in and after 200 B.C., there is no doubt that the Treasury
was again replenished. A settlement of accounts became possible.
The bronze coinage, reduced as it had been to an emergency
war issue of small metal content, called for attention merely in
order to meet the domestic needs of Rome. But more was now
required. Rome was no longer an Italian City State but was
supreme in the Mediterranean. Roman money for general circulation as a means of exchange throughout this expanded sphere of
influence was obviously needed as never before. Such a currency
could only be in silver. In or soon after 187 B.C. first appeared the
Roman *denarius*, a silver coin weighing slightly less than our
shilling, which was to become a household word not merely in the
Mediterranean but throughout the known world. (Its name still
survives as the '*d*' of our £ *s. d.*) The traditional account puts the
introduction of the *denarius* considerably earlier at 269 B.C., but
recent research in the light of the examination of many hoards of
coins, and other considerations, have suggested the later date of
around 187 B.C. as more probably true. The *denarius* was the
equivalent of 10 *asses* of bronze and bore the numeral X. Hence
its name 'tenner'. It had the great convenience at first of providing

the Romans with a simple decimal system: 10 *asses* – 5 *asses* – 2½ *asses*.

Half a *denarius* (five *asses*) was known as *quinarius* ('fiver'). It weighed roughly the same as a British sixpence. The fourth part of the *denarius* was the *sestertius* ('two-and-a-halfer') of about the same weight (18–15 grains) as a silver threepenny piece (22 grains). It was therefore inconveniently small. The *sestertius* of 2½ *asses* was already used as a unit of account. Of these three silver coins, the *denarius* alone was regularly minted. The *sestertius*, although seldom struck, remained the unit in which all values were currently reckoned.

Possibly very soon after the *denarius* and *sestertius* were introduced, the bronze coinage was reduced and put on a stable footing. The old *as* of about 10 oz was brought down to 2 oz and from about 123 B.C. was exchangeable with the *denarius* at 16 *asses* instead of at 10 *asses* except that until the time of Julius Caesar the pay of the soldiers was not subjected to this reduction, no doubt because they had to spend their pay abroad. They continued to get a *denarius* for 10 *asses*. The decimal system was given up by the people as a whole. The new rate of 16 *asses* to 1 *denarius* gave a value of silver in proportion to bronze of 112 to 1. The Romans thereby introduced a sensible economy in the use of metal as money. It was forced on them by the growing demand for metal for other purposes, so the bronze coinage never recovered its former bulky size and the *sestertius* took the place of the bronze *as* as the unit of account, because of all the Roman coins it was the easiest to reckon in after the decimal system represented by the *denarius* at its original value of 10 *asses* had been abandoned.

Probably at some time after 187 B.C. there were two temporary issues of gold coins, introduced, as the earlier silver didrachm and *victoriatus* had been, as an aid to Rome's foreign trade. The first issue was of three coins rated as 60, 40, and 20 *sestertii* each. The smallest was roughly the weight of the British threepenny silver piece, the medium one roughly the weight of a sixpence, and the largest was as heavy as a half-sovereign or as a sixpence and threepenny bit together. The best-known Roman gold coin, the *aureus*, was not struck regularly until the time of Julius Caesar. (Plate 19.)

During the remainder of the second century B.C. there was little serious disturbance of the currency. The *denarius* became established as a world coin. It replaced local Italian currencies as well as the earlier Roman silver coins (*nummus* and *victoriatus*), and the gold coins, all of which had been reserved for foreign trade. Such was the power and prestige of Rome that foreign countries could no longer scorn her coined money and demand a special coinage before consenting to trade with her.

During the period of three consecutive generations, Romans were therefore able to build their economic life around a simple and stable monetary standard in which the unit of reckoning was the *sestertius*, four of which went to make up a *denarius*, the coin they most frequently saw when they were fortunate enough, as vast masses of them were not, to be able to handle silver money regularly. For, to a greater extent than is possible in the economically developed states of today, the economic life of Rome, especially in the country districts, was still conducted without the need for many coins. The steady stream of coins from the mint and habits of buying and selling learned in the towns spread into these relatively backward areas where they stimulated trade and the desire to make money. As time went on, an expanding commerce and industry must have gradually made money transactions more general. Not enough is known to give any account of such increases as may have occurred in the money put into circulation. That the silver content of the *denarius* was maintained seems to prove, what may indeed be assumed, that there was no dearth of bullion. War indemnities from Carthage and the East were soon supplemented by the silver mines of Spain wrested from the Carthaginians and consolidated after many a bloody struggle. From these sources a flow of bullion was assured, but how much it amounted to and what effects it had on prices are merely matters of conjecture. In the absence of any sudden increase of population, for which there is no evidence, it might be assumed that all the elements of an inflationary condition were present. There would therefore have been the possibility of a slow, steady rise in prices and wages, in so far as there was a free market for goods and for labour.

Such a monetary development, at a time of growing wealth, should have helped enormously to build up confidence and to give powerful support to economic development. Through the elaboration of a banking system, Romans of Cicero's age were able to borrow money from silversmiths and goldsmiths, the *argentarii*, at interest, to maintain private accounts and to draw the equivalent of the modern cheque. Farmers, merchants, land-owners, craftsmen, free labourers, housewives, slave-dealers, and shipowners could all buy and sell without daily anxiety as to what their coins were worth. In Rome during the second century B.C., despite wars, none of which was as menacing as those of the previous century, and despite more serious civil discord, of which the attempted Gracchan reforms are the most striking symptoms, the money-making class of *equites* (knights) had a monetary foundation upon which they could and did build their fortunes.

In the troubled period from the birth of Cicero to the end of the Republic, this happy state of affairs gave way to a period of violent change. Cicero had barely attained his majority before the old bronze coinage had reached such a pitch of devaluation that it was abandoned. After 89 B.C. the conflict between the partisans of Sulla and Marius brought a 50 per cent drop in the value of the bronze coinage. Three years later repudiation of three-quarters of all outstanding debts proved a final blow and the Roman Republic issued no more bronze coins. The silver coinage also was alarmingly debased. The confusion reached such a point that no man knew what he was worth. Financial chaos on such a scale could hardly fail further to inflame unrest.

The party of Marius was out to maintain the value of the national money. The senatorial party supporting Sulla seemed willing to wreck it if thereby they could discomfit their enemies and secure the profits of inflation for themselves. In civil war a wrecked currency is usually one of the lesser evils, crippling though it naturally is. Amid all the cruel social and political miseries of this unhappy time there can be little doubt that the economic life of Rome received many rude shocks.

With the abandonment of the bronze coinage the silver *denarius* remained the chief prop of the Roman currency. Occasionally small quantities of the *sestertius* were again struck, as was the half *denarius* or *quinarius* for which the old name *victoriatus* was revived. In 89 B.C. the silver *sestertius* was struck for the first time for nearly a hundred years.

New complications arose in the first century B.C. from the

conflicts of the competing generals warring to seize control of the sources of power of the Roman State which, shrewd and ambitious, they saw that the Republican government was impotent to maintain. Power to issue coinage was one such means of control and it was usurped by harassed politicians who, at the risk of their lives and their fortunes, undertook the vast responsibilities of organizing and financing a civil war. Julius Caesar, Pompey, Antony, Brutus and Cassius, Octavian, all issued coins either in Rome or in the provinces with the double purpose of serving their cause with money and supporting it with propaganda. Every coin would advertise the leader by whom it was issued. The Republic bequeathed with its ruin a wrecked monetary system. When reconstruction became possible the state of the coinage was prominent among the political and administrative problems calling urgently for reform.

The money policy of Rome was controlled by the Senate. Three men were appointed at the beginning of the third century B.C. merely as mint officials with a purely executive task of obtaining metal, melting it and seeing that coins were properly made. What considerations influenced the Senate in deciding the quantities of money to put on the market is not known. There are grounds for supposing that a fall in the value of money relative to goods must have been a consequence of the sudden influx of gold and silver after the Roman victories over Carthage, Macedonia, and Syria. Was there a free market in the sense that anyone possessing precious metals could take his store to the mint and get money for it? The evidence does not seem clear. If therefore the Senate itself did not increase the supply of money considerably merely because silver could more readily be obtained, the supply of coinage would remain fairly constant and inflation would not occur. There were many other uses for the precious metals. The Romans of the heroic age believed in devoting much of their precious metals to the decoration of the temples of their gods and goddesses rather than to private use, but by Cicero's time the old prohibitions against the use of silver and gold for plates, dishes and household embellishment had long since been ignored.

It was not the practice of the Senate to allow the coins of the Republic to be used for the advertisement of any individual Roman, however distinguished, although the mint officials sometimes managed to choose types of coins related to their own family history. In the late Republic the heads of army commanders sometimes appeared on coins issued by their own authority during a campaign. The coins authorized by the Senate however usually bore religious emblems, such as the figure of Jupiter, chief God of the State. Other gods and goddesses were also depicted on coins: Minerva, Neptune, Janus, Mars, and Apollo. Sometimes the religious theme was varied by devices representing historical events: the foundation legend of Romulus and Remus, the Sabine women, the story of the traitress Tarpeia, the battle of Lake Regillus – an interesting illustration of the power and vitality of the legends of the early Republic. In the year before Cicero was assassinated this unbroken tradition suffered a rude interruption. The fact that the first representation of a living man on coins for everyday use from the official mint authorized by an obsequious Senate in 44 B.C. was the head of Julius Caesar is therefore of striking significance, pointing to a dramatic change in the traditions of old Rome. (Plate 28.)

Wages and Cost of Living

Scanty details have survived about the wages and cost of living of the Romans of the later Republic.

Cato in his memorandum book of hints on agriculture gives some few facts about the cost of maintaining slave labour in the first half of the second century B.C. One able-bodied slave employed on heavy farm work could be maintained for the equivalent of 78 *denarii* a year. This sum represents the cost of food and clothing alone and includes nothing for housing, but as the slaves were often little better sheltered than the farm animals, the omission is of little importance. Cato's calculation is valuable not merely as our sole source of information upon this very important question, but because it shows how, at an early period, the practical Romans were guiding their affairs by a careful calculation of costs. Such determination to control the daily affairs of life by precise arithmetic is a sign of a well-developed economic society. It shows the existence of a rational spirit which, after the fall of Rome, did not again develop in Europe until the beginning of what we now reckon to be the modern age in the Renaissance of the fifteenth and sixteenth centuries.

This is Cato's budget for a hard-working slave on the land:

48 *modii* (11½ bushels) wheat at 2½ sesterces	30 *denarii*
7 *amphorae* mixed wine (322½ pints, i.e. nearly 1 pint a day)	7 *denarii*
Vegetables, salt, figs, etc.	30 *denarii*
12 *sextarii* oil (11½ pints, i.e. nearly a pint a month)	2 *denarii*
Clothing and shoes	9 *denarii*

Annual cost of one slave 78 *denarii*

A bushel of English wheat is usually reckoned as about 60 lb Unless the best Italian wheat was very different, the slave's annual wheat supply would therefore amount to not less than 700 lb of wheat, or nearly 2 lb a day. Cato recommended a 25 per cent increase of this amount for the slaves in chains digging the vineyard. It would of course have been 'wholemeal', that is to say the valuable mineral and vitamin content of the wheat grain would not have been discarded for use as cattle food as it has been in order to produce the denatured white flour invented by our industrial age. Whether it was eaten in the old-fashioned style as a thick porridge or whether it was made into bread, it seems a heavy ration and a slave eating as much would certainly not starve (see the recipes on page 89). Cato in fact recommended for slaves a somewhat larger ration of wheat than that given to Roman soldiers, presumably because they always had a lot of hard work to do. Converted into bread by present-day methods, this wheat ration would yield about two loaves of bread a day. People not engaged on heavy manual labour would manage quite well on less than half this quantity, for 30 *modii* a year would provide about 1¼ lb of bread a day, an amount greater than that thought necessary for heavy manual workers under the British bread-rationing plan of July 1946.

Free labourers would naturally cost much more if only on account of house rent. A man and his wife might have the following budget:

60 *modii* wheat (14½ bushels) at 3 sesterces	45 *denarii*
Vegetables, oil, salt, wine, etc.	85 *denarii*
Dress	20 *denarii*
House and rent and extras	100 *denarii*

Annual cost of free labourer and wife 250 *denarii*

If the man and his wife consumed 60 *modii* of wheat a year, which seems unlikely, this total would rise to about 300 *denarii* a year.

These approximate figures give a rough idea of the cost of living in Rome on a bare subsistence standard. It would allow only the plainest and simplest diet. When fieldfares cost 3 *denarii* each and a peacock 50 *denarii* it is evident that free labourers would not see much poultry. Cato provided no meat for his slaves.

In comparing the cost of slave labour and free labour the purchase price of the slave must be taken into account. A capable slave might cost his owner 500 *denarii*. Supposing he lived for 20 years, this cost would average 25 *denarii* a year. It would still be necessary to add something for interest on the investment – at least 25 *denarii* a year. In other words, making allowance for the capital cost of a slave would add 50 *denarii* a year to the cost of keeping him alive of 78 *denarii* a year. With a total cost of 128 *denarii* a year a slave was therefore a good deal cheaper than a free labourer, who if he had a wife would need about 250 *denarii* a year. In other words the free labourer would need to be twice as efficient a workman as a slave to justify his employment in the eyes of a hard-fisted calculating Roman such as old Cato. But even if other Romans did not train their slaves as thoroughly as Cato trained his or insist as he did upon a full day's work from them, it still seems clear that for most ordinary jobs the free labourer could not hope to compete with the slave.

The sad fate of the free labourers of Rome and the enormous growth of the slave population of Italy after Cato's day suggests that most Romans did in fact either follow Cato's calculations and advice or else they arrived at the same conclusion themselves.

The Corn Dole

In 123 B.C. Gaius Gracchus, as part of his grand scheme of reforms for Rome, fixed the price of wheat by offering, to citizens only, a limited quantity (probably 5 *modii* a month or about 2 lb 6 oz a day) at 6⅓ *asses* a *modius*. It is thought that this was about half the market price. By this means a Roman citizen had the main element of his family's food requirements supplied for 380 *asses* a year or 23¾ *denarii*. Not all Roman citizens availed themselves of this opportunity, because no well-to-do Roman would join in a queue with the down-and-outs in order to save a couple of *denarii* a month on his bread bills. For this action Gaius Gracchus has been denounced as the man who began the vicious system of debauching the Roman people by a dole. It is plain that he did no such thing. Oversight of the corn supply had long been a recognized duty of government. The Romans in their earlier history had more than one experience of famine and they soon became very restive if the price of corn rose unduly high. The Aediles whose job it was to see that the corn reserves of the city were not allowed to drop too low were, it seems, sometimes reinforced by a special official (*praefectus annonae*) when there were signs of serious scarcity. Price stabilization was quite a logical development of such official responsibility.

Moralists of later days have said that Gracchus undermined people's readiness to work and made State paupers of them. This is plainly nonsense. During the Second World War and for long afterwards the British Treasury heavily subsidized bread so that it should be sold below cost price, but nobody feared that the British would show less enterprise or willingness to work as a result. The cheap corn is also said to have attracted an idle rabble to Rome, but as the supply was limited to Roman citizens this objection also is not very plausible.

To the political opponents of Gaius Gracchus, however, it seemed quite clear that the effect of his action if not its actual objective was to attract a mob of political supporters to Rome, and to the extent his action did this, it was no doubt politically a hazardous thing to have done. Nevertheless, the real troubles had other causes than cheap corn, and they therefore required other remedies. Anyway, the plan of Gaius Gracchus continued unchanged until the conservative revolution engineered with such ruthless authority by Sulla, who in 81 B.C. gave up State control of corn prices. Like the rest of his reforms, it was an attempt to put the clock back and it failed. In 73 B.C. about 40,000 Roman citizens again became entitled to buy 72 lb of wheat a month for about 2 *denarii*.

From 73 B.C. to 63 B.C. subsidized wheat cost the State about 8 million sesterces a year, no very formidable figure. It was not until after this date that State corn became a political football. In 62 B.C., after some dangerous riots stirred up by Metellus, a Tribune, M. Porcius Cato, great-grandson of the old Censor, in a bid to win support for the Senate, increased the numbers allowed to get cheap corn to 320,000. The cost thereupon jumped to 64 million sesterces a year. Caesar, when he was Consul in 59 B.C., met hisses in the theatre by threatening to restrict the privilege, but in the following year he allowed his tool the Tribune Clodius to take the revolutionary step of giving the corn free of charge. At first about 260,000 people benefited by being given wheat at the public expense. When a bribe of this sort has once been given it is difficult to limit it. Before long the numbers on the dole had risen to 320,000, or about one-third of the adult men citizens of the Republic. The State had to find over 120,000 tons of wheat a year and give it away. If every citizen drew 5 *modii* of wheat a month about 19¼ million *modii* a year would be required, more than six times the annual import of 3 million *modii* obtained as a free tithe from the Sicilians. The balance of over 16 million *modii* was an insupportable charge on the public revenue. With wheat at its normal price of around three-quarters of a *denarius* (3 sesterces) a *modius*, and with handling and distributing costs, the cost of the free wheat rose to about 18 million *denarii*, or 72 million sesterces, a year between 56 B.C. and 51 B.C.

As a political bribe in an age when bribery was barefaced, this free corn may have helped Caesar to win popularity. As soon as he had won complete power, he rapidly revised his free corn policy. Not a means test but a test of citizenship was soon applied to everyone on the dole. Many were found not to be Roman citizens and by striking off all but citizens he cut the list to 150,000 people (46 B.C.). Probably he also re-established the rule that some payment should be made for the corn – a rule from which none but the very poor were exempt. This conclusion is based on the fact that, later on, the distribution was made only to those holding a special ticket or voucher. At best, this reduction did not do much more than halve the formidable cost of the dole.

If the population of Rome can be regarded as a million in the age of Cicero and the average consumption per head as 30 *modii* or nearly 7½ bushels the city as a whole would have required over 190,000 tons a year or about 3,700 tons a week. Although wheat was the staple food of the Romans, the actual average consumption of every man, woman and child was probably not so high as 430 lb a head a year because the public corn of 5 *modii* for each citizen for one month undoubtedly fed more than two mouths and was very likely spread over a whole family. In modern Rome the figure was just under 180 kilos a head or about 395 lb, which gives an annual tonnage for 1 million people of about 176,466 tons. The British bread ration in July 1946 provided 4 million tons of bread (not wheat) for 47·1 million men, women and children, that is nearly 85,000 tons a year or 1,633 tons a week for every million of the population. Bread consumption per head tends to fall as living standards advance and as other more expensive foods become available, nevertheless the annual wheat requirement of the city in the time of Cicero seems high if, as the figures suggest, it was between 180,000 and 190,000 tons a year.

The formidable problem which the transport of so large a quantity of food presents has never had the study it deserves. It has been suggested that no city in antiquity could possibly cope with such a large food supply. Not wheat alone was involved, for there was an almost equal need for vegetables, fruit, cheese, oil and wine. A city of a million inhabitants obviously could not have come into existence without a very heavy commercial traffic. Thousands of ships, barges, carts and trucks must have been always on the move merely to keep the people fed. It would seem that merchants, dealers, clerks, book-keepers would have been busy superintending this vast supply problem in all its many details, but we know nothing of their offices or their equipment or of their methods of keeping records.

Some Comparative Incomes

The Roman way of life is not our way. We enjoy countless amenities, conveniences, tools, appliances, furnishings which they never knew. Their money system did not mean as much to them as ours does to us. Consequently any effort to compare their cost of living with ours is immensely difficult. We cannot grasp in our minds all that makes up each side of the comparison, still less fix values upon everything involved on each side. Our difficulties are all the greater because the facts about costs and prices in the whole 500 years of the Republic are extremely scanty. What few remain must therefore be treated with great caution since we are rarely able to compare them, as they ought to be compared, with series of others. It is for instance astonishing that no reliable figure remains to show the cost of a cow anywhere in Italy during the Republican period.

How modest Roman notions of wealth were in the great age of

the Republic is shown by the relatively small differences between the property owned by the five main classes into which the Roman public assembly was divided at about 269 B.C., when their property was valued in the old copper coin *as*, then weighing 9½ ounces, instead of in land as hitherto.

CLASS	SIZE OF FARM		MONEY ASSESSMENT
	iugera	acres	*asses*
I	20	12½	100,000
II	15	9⅜	75,000
III	10	6¼	50,000
IV	5	3⅛	25,000
V	2 to 2½	1¼	11,000

(The *iugerum* was exactly ⅝ of an acre.)

All these property-values would have seemed very modest in Cicero's time.

When we know that, in the second century B.C., 250 *denarii* or 1,000 sesterces would support a man and his wife for a year and that the bare necessities of a slave would cost about 80 *denarii* or 320 sesterces a year, we get two fairly clear and definite facts to give some meaning to the word '*denarius*' and to Roman money in general. The Romans usually reckoned in sesterces, four of which made one *denarius*.

What little we know about the incomes of the Roman upper classes stands in striking contrast to the low figures of the earnings of the common people. Cicero thought that an income of 600,000 sesterces would enable a Roman to live like a gentleman – perhaps because it is supposed to have been roughly his own income. At the end of his life he claimed that he had received more than 20 millions of sesterces in legacies alone. Taking his working lifetime as roughly forty years, he averaged half a million sesterces a year as the equivalent of his professional income. Crassus proudly said that a man was not wealthy unless he could support a legion on his income. To do so would have cost 4 million sesterces a year and not more than a handful of Rome's richest men could meet such a test. The remark itself is however very revealing. How few, if any, rich men in modern times would ever think of money incomes in relation to the number of armed retainers they enable their recipients to support?

In Roman society as in our own there were great inequalities in incomes. Then, as today, comparatively large sums were earned by entertainers. There is a story of a young actor making 100,000 sesterces in his first year, of a dancing girl getting 200,000 sesterces a year, while the veteran actor Roscius qualified for a gentleman's life with about 500,000 sesterces, earning as much as 16,000 sesterces at one performance. Having made enough money, he at length was able to refuse further payment and so to raise his social status to that of the *equites*. While farmers were lucky if they could make ends meet and realize such modest incomes as 10,000 sesterces from their country villas, more enterprising men were striking out on new lines.

We read of incomes of 50,000 sesterces a year secured from a Roman poultry farm. The 'poultry' included doves, cranes, storks and peacocks, as well as geese and hens. As a side-line, fishes, wild boars, and even dormice were raised. Romans did not acquire the taste for peacocks until Cicero's day, but it spread very rapidly until no banquet was complete without them. Cicero thought himself pretty independent and daring to have given one of Caesar's marshals, Hirtius, a dinner without a peacock.

The middle and lower classes also welcomed any occasion for a feast. More frequent than the public festivals at somebody's triumph were the club or trade-guild dinners which according to Cicero's old friend Varro 'now in endless number inflate the market price of provisions. ... More than that, modern luxury creates what one may call a daily banquet within the gates of Rome'. A single public feast or triumph might mean an order for 5,000 fieldfares at 3 *denarii* apiece which would yield 60,000 sesterces. Apart from the social advantage of going to such dinners they must have been the only opportunity the poorer workmen or tradesmen would have had of enjoying more expensive foods than they could themselves usually afford.

It was said that the first Roman to breed peacocks on a large scale (about 67 B.C.) made 60,000 sesterces a year. A farm of 200 *iugera* (125 acres) would not make more than half this sum.

Probably typical of the middle class is an otherwise unknown satirical poet who made 10,000 sesterces from his farm but more than twice as much from his birds and animals. Had he been possessed of sufficient capital to own a property near the sea with some fish ponds he thought he would have made 100,000 sesterces instead of his modest annual 30,000.

Bee-keeping did not pay so well but it needed less capital and was not such hard work as farming. Two brothers, not of the peasant class, who inherited a smallholding of only an acre were able to make 10,000 sesterces a year by selling honey.

There is a natural temptation to try to find some modern comparisons which might give a better understanding of the reality behind these figures of incomes, costs, and prices. In previous editions of this book the money paid to destitute people by the British Welfare State and the earnings of British people paying income tax were compared as an example of inequalities of resources between income-groups which may be less striking than the pronounced similar inequalities in Rome at the end of the Republic. At the same time it was emphasized that to put two such different economic and social systems side by side is dangerous because it might lead to comparisons which cannot fairly be made. There is no stable standard of measurement. Between 1955 and 1964 for example the minimum payments to destitute British subjects by the National Assistance Board almost doubled. Meagre as those payments may seem to those receiving them, they provide satisfactions of more human wants than any Roman slave or free labourer could have imagined.

The cost of maintaining a criminal in a State prison may be thought to provide a better base-line for comparison with the cost of a Roman slave. It is a calculation which can be made in any .country where official statistics on the subject are published. In England in 1964–5 for example, the food, clothing, bedding, and medicines alone provided for nearly 30,000 inmates of all penal and reformatory institutions cost roughly £58 15s. 0d. a head for the financial year, but it is an approximate figure. Some of the food was grown and some of the clothing and bedding were made by the prisoners, and an estimate of their cost is included. Many Roman slave households of course were also largely self-supporting in this way, and Cato's simple budget also omits such costs.

But apart from the approximate nature of the estimate and of Cato's budget also, the fact remains that rough as prison conditions are today, they are more humane than those of one of Cato's slaves. It seems best to give up any attempt to make any comparison, except in imagination. Money measures in a modern community cannot tell us accurately anything about the meaning of money measures two thousand years ago in a very different country. Roman money could not buy many staple things which can be bought today by British, American, Nigerian, or Indian money. Even if it were possible, which it is not, to relate Roman republican commodity prices to gold, and then to do the same for modern prices, the calculation would have to be re-made almost every year, so rapid has been the debauchery of modern money standards by the swindle of inflation. Moreover we have no justification for assuming that gold stood in the same relation to the ancient Roman economy as it does to our own today. When well-to-do Romans could be found in Cicero's day who thought nothing of spending from 200 to 1,000 sesterces on a pair of pigeons or 60,000 sesterces for a pedigree ass, there can be no doubt that there was money to burn in Rome. Cato himself thought that up to 400 sesterces a year was a justifiable expense for his toga, tunic, and shoes, yet he would not have spent more than this in maintaining a slave for a year. A well-to-do Roman lady would easily have spent ten times as much as Cato on her wardrobe in a year. Cato, when Censor (184–180 B.C.), imposed a heavy luxury tax on all property worth more than the very low amount of 6,000 sesterces.

How many wealthy Romans were there? The figure is not known. The Romans must have known however from their quinquennial census. The lowest estimate can be based upon the words of a reforming Tribune, L. Marcius Philippus, in 104 B.C., whom Cicero reports as saying that 'there are not in the State 2,000 persons who possess property'. Cicero greatly disapproved of this remark, which he said was made to win popular support. It was 'a pernicious speech aiming at a levelling of property and what can be more pestilential than that?' A lot depends on what Philippus regarded as property. As a guess at a round figure it is usually supposed that about 10,000 out of the million Romans were able to live what then passed for an easy and comfortable life although perhaps not 1,000 of them were outstandingly rich. In condemning Philippus in his last book (*De Officiis*) in 44 B.C. Cicero had forgotten a striking passage from his own speeches against Verres. In 70 B.C. he told Roman judges, 'We endure it and say nothing about it; but for years now we have been watching all the wealth of all the nations come into the possession of a handful of men.'

While the inequality of incomes is just as marked in modern days in England and especially in the United States, much more is done today by insurance schemes on a national scale and social services to safeguard the welfare of those too improvident or too poor to provide for themselves against all the more serious risks of ill-health, unemployment, disability and old age. No such generous view was ever held of the responsibility of the Roman Republic to any of its citizens in distress; consequently there was no elaborate system of taxation to provide for those public services which are accepted among us as almost part of the natural order of things – free education, medical and hospital care, unemployment pay, old-age pensions, war pensions, pensions for widows and orphans. Lacking all this the Romans had to swim or sink.

The Business Men

The business men of Rome were the *equites* or 'Knights'. Originally a military class, men rich enough to possess a horse (*equus*), they had always occupied a special place in Roman society. Before the Second Punic War there were about 2,000 of them out of a total of some 220,000 citizens. They first began to emerge as a separate force in Roman political, social and economic life around the middle of the second century B.C. By Cicero's time the old military character of the class had practically disappeared and there were probably around 10,000 men of equestrian status. Notwithstanding some serious setbacks, they as a class seem to have prospered materially during the second century B.C. A number of them founded families from which the political or senatorial class was later recruited, rather like the country squires of eighteenth-century England. Cicero's father was one of them. They usually stood outside politics. They might have entered the Senate but many were unwilling to pay the price. A Senator was forbidden to take public contracts or to engage in overseas trade. Many business men depended upon such activities for their profits. To get large public works undertaken as cheaply as possible the Romans, after the Second Punic War, increasingly relied upon the system of getting contractors to bid against each other for the work. To find the capital needed for such enterprises, the business men and their rich friends formed companies.

This development of a strong financial interest in Roman social life could not fail to have repercussions upon politics. While many business men did not aspire to political office, their prominence in society assured them of access to those in whose hands political power reposed. How, in the time of Gaius Gracchus, their interests began to receive special recognition, has already been described. They were not always so deeply identified with progressive policies, for they were loud in their opposition to allowing Rome's Italian neighbours a greater share in the privileges of citizenship and in the government or administration of the Republic, possibly because they did not want to let Italians into the management of public contracts, public lands or public offices. Whatever the reason, they were supported by the Roman rank and file who did not want to see more citizens with claims on cheap grain, war booty, or public land. Nor did they probably relish the idea of swelling the electorate, for then the bribes offered by the candidates whether in money, largesse or by public games would have to be spread more thinly and then everybody's share would be less.

Selfishness and exclusiveness brought fierce reprisals in the disastrous Social War of 90–88 B.C. when the Italians sought to gain by force the political rights they were unable to obtain by peaceful means (see p. 210). Economic influence in politics therefore could have some sinister results. On the whole, despite the tendency in recent years to see economic forces as the sole prime movers of politics, society and nearly everything else, it seems plain that at no time were the financial and economic leaders of Rome either able or allowed to take the place of the political leaders. The figure of Crassus (p. 247) may symbolize the failure of the business men to be more than business men. By contrast, the figure of Cicero's friend Atticus symbolizes the high degree of success a clever business man could achieve by remaining a business man. Foreign wars, civic wars, civic riot and commotion raged during his lifetime but nothing prevented him adding to his fortune. Steering his way with the utmost skill and caution he survived to die in his bed at the age of seventy-seven (32 B.C.) after having succeeded in marrying his only daughter to Agrippa, the right-hand man of the victorious Octavian who finally brought peace to Rome.

Atticus was exceptionally gifted, and by no means all his

business friends were able to weather the storms. The position they had succeeded in consolidating was seriously assailed when civil troubles grew. The warring political leaders needed money and an easy, quick way of getting it was to steal it from the rich. The victims were obvious enough. If they were not known opponents of one side or the other some charge could be trumped up against them. After they had been 'framed' in this way their proscription would follow. This meant assassination unless the victim preferred, as he often did, the simpler escape by voluntary exile or suicide.

This discreditable business was the surest sign that something was rotten within the Republic. It began under the supremacy of the 'popular' leader Marius when Cicero was in his twenties. Many of the most distinguished political families of Rome were butchered by this half-crazy old mob leader. His opponent Sulla came back to Rome from his campaigns in the East too late to save them but in time to avenge them in a renewed and cold-blooded slaughter. Despite his admiration for Sulla's political programme which he said 'was everything that was most eminent', Cicero realized very well that his methods were abominable. That generation had been cruel, he said, 'to an extent previously unknown in the history of the Republic'. Both parties were to blame and he looked back at that period (87–79 B.C.) as one from which all dignity and respect for law had departed.

The evil example of this cruelty survived. Cicero himself was one of the many hundreds to perish by it, but disastrous and hateful as it was then, political murder later became many times worse under some of the emperors. A guess at what may have been the deeper causes of this sudden outbreak of primitive passions in the otherwise apparently sane and civilized Romans is reserved for the last chapter of this book. Here the deplorable economic ruin caused by such disturbances is our main concern, and of this there can be no question.

Maritime Commerce and Communications

The heaviest tonnages of Rome's sea trade must have been the traffic in the necessities of life, above all wheat. A busy local trade with other ports than the capital went on in raw materials such as iron ore. During Republican times wheat for Rome was collected all over Italy but principally from Campania. The whole of Sicily's export surplus of wheat might be needed by Rome and additional cargoes were lifted from Africa, Sardinia, and Carthage, but Egypt, the famed granary of the Mediterranean, did not supply Rome with corn regularly until after the Republican days.

The 180,000–190,000 tons of wheat on which Rome depended each year represented a formidable transport problem when ships of 200 to 300 tons were large and when a total cargo of a mere 10,000 *modii*, about 64 tons, was by no means unusual. Up to 2,000 ships might well have been employed in this corn trade alone. On shore this tonnage had to be hauled in the two- or four-wheeled ox-carts, a still more formidable problem in the ancient world where good, serviceable roads were unknown until they were invented by the Romans.

More profitable but also more risky was the import trade of luxury articles for the market at Rome. Two or three men might pool their resources to fit out a few ships to bring glass from Syria, Tyrian purple cloth and cedar from Lebanon, cotton cloth, paper, and glass from the state factories of Egypt, and smaller consignments of spices, pearls, ivory, silk, and precious stones from the mysterious Orient brought by the northern overland caravan route or transshipped from the Red Sea.

The majority of the ships making for Italian ports would be manned not by Romans but by Greeks, Syrians or perhaps by South Italians. They were good ships, sometimes of two or three hundred tons and perfectly seaworthy, but they lacked one all-important instrument of navigation. The compass had not been invented. Except under very favourable conditions, therefore, it was impossible to strike boldly across the Mediterranean. Instead the ships were forced to hug the coast and to make their way through the many little islands of the Eastern Mediterranean.

Cicero spoke for all Romans when he said 'a sea voyage is a serious business'. A sudden squall of wind or rain or a mist might spring up and the ship would be in trouble. Not being able to determine any certain course the captain had to make a quick decision and it might turn out to be a bad one. Many a precious cargo went to the bottom after foundering on the treacherous rocks of the Aegean, and some have remained until modern times to yield treasures for the archaeologist and historian. Those who had chartered the ships then lost everything unless they had insured to protect themselves, as they were able to do with a Greek or Oriental banker at substantial premiums.

Shipping therefore was a hazardous business and the Romans mostly seem to have left it to the Greeks and Eastern races who had by force of circumstances taken to the sea just as the Romans stuck to agriculture. Ports such as Puteoli, the main port for Rome, had their foreign quarters just as the large ports of London and New York have today. Greeks, Syrians, and Lebanese of many towns and various religions had their own settlements, temples and cemeteries. The Romans seem to have been content to let them undertake most of their carrying trade. Not one protective tariff or preferential customs duty in favour of Roman citizens is known in Republican times. The scanty interest in and the physical limitations upon maritime commerce also explain the spasmodic use of naval power by the Romans. They won command of the sea from the land instead of controlling lands from the seas as the British learned to do.

Commerce employed many small traders, but conditions were against the rise of big commercial houses. There were no commercial travellers, no possibility of advertising and no mass markets. Life had to be simpler then than it is now. Many a Greek skipper found a livelihood plying his small craft up and down the coasts of Syria, Greece, and Italy, taking a cargo where he could find it or as it was offered him just as a modern tramp steamer does, perhaps speculating with his own or borrowed capital, buying consignments in one market and selling them at another, transporting anything and everything from merchandise to wild beasts for the public games at Rome, human slaves by the thousand and such private passengers as were willing to travel cheaply instead of going to the expense of hiring a private yacht. Regular services backwards and forwards, even on the most frequented routes, do not seem to have been arranged.

It was a traffic that could go on in spring, summer and early autumn. As winter came the boats made for their home ports where they were tied up until the sky cleared and the stars were again visible at night.

To the risk of shipwreck was added the still more formidable danger of falling a victim to pirates. It was a danger that had steadily increased since the end of the second Macedonian war (168 B.C.) when Rome selfishly broke the prosperity and naval strength of the island of Rhodes whose fleets until then had policed the Eastern Mediterranean. Anyone captured by pirates was lucky if he was merely held to ransom. His or her fate might easily be death, slavery, and in any case ruin. The seas were swarming with pirates, and the best evidence of Roman unconcern in maritime trade is the disgraceful way they allowed the pirates to prey upon traders until the corn supply of Rome itself was seriously threatened; when that happened (67 B.C.) the business men (*equites*) were able to force the Senate to appoint Pompey in supreme command of a huge force to clear the pirates off the seas. Ten years before this great clean-up Gaius Julius Caesar, then a young man of twenty-four, was captured by some of these pirates on his way to become a pupil of Molon, a famous teacher of the art of political oratory at Rhodes. He was held in captivity for thirty-eight days while some of his suite went off to raise the ransom demanded by the pirates as the price of his liberty. Caesar is said to have treated the pirates as though they were his body-guard instead of his captors, threatening to hang the lot of them when they did not applaud the speeches and literary efforts he had composed for their benefit. As soon as he was freed he is said to have collected some ships, returned, captured the pirates, and crucified them to a man. So early did he give proof of those qualities that were later to bring dismay to the loyal Republicans and to Cicero, who was to find him 'extraordinarily vigilant, extraordinarily bold. How clear-sighted! How alert! How well prepared!'

Despite all the difficulties and dangers from weather, rocks and pirates, there was a constant traffic along the Mediterranean shores from Spain to Alexandria. As the Republic grew, the traders increasingly turned to Italy and to Rome, the new centre of the world. By force of circumstances the cargoes carried to Rome were many times more bulky and valuable than the exports from Rome. Without imports, particularly without wheat, there would have been famine conditions in Rome. Sea traffic was therefore as important to Rome in Cicero's day as it is to London in our own time or as it was to the Hansa towns of the Renaissance whose device 'navigare necesse est, vivere non est necesse' ('seafaring is more important to us than life itself') was borrowed from a remark by Pompey. The one-way traffic resulted from no adverse balance of trade but represented the tribute exacted by Rome from its subject provinces whether as war booty, forced taxes, interest at exorbitant rates on loans made by Roman business men, or graft by Roman officials. All was grist to the mill.

The annual minimum shipment of nearly a million bushels of wheat from Sicily was an early staple shipment. Next in importance were the Eastern products, very largely of the highly-finished luxury goods already mentioned (p. 117). Useful raw materials came from the West. Gibbon, thinking no doubt of the great silver mines, said that Spain was the Mexico and Peru of the old world. At first its mineral wealth, already being tapped by the Phoenicians, was most celebrated. Tin, lead, iron, copper, silver and gold were extracted, so was rock salt of high quality and, later in the history of Rome, marble for building and decoration.

As the Romans established their hold on the country a more varied range of its products was exported. Shipbuilding timber, oak, pine, cork and pitch, olive oil, wheat, barley, honey, fruits and some vegetables were among the products of the land; horses, cattle, salt or smoked beef, hams, sheep, leather (raw material for Roman ropes as well as for footwear), wool, salt fish and 'garum' (a very popular flavoured paste, comparable perhaps to anchovy paste) were the principal animal and other food products. To these staple lines of commerce must be added the constant human cargoes of slaves.

Manufactured products were less evident, but already the fine steel of Northern Spain and the woollen and linen fabrics of the middle of the Peninsula were establishing their high reputation on the Roman market.

Somewhat similar cargoes were forthcoming from Marseilles, already the southern port for the trade of Western Europe. Fewer cargoes of precious metals, no doubt, were picked up there, but there were more animal products (including cheese). Thence also came amber brought all the way from Baltic and northern shores.

The Romans probably found it less difficult to get cargoes for return voyages to these western ports than they did on outward east-bound trips. Not merely were Roman manufactures required in Gaul and Spain, such as finished iron ware, copper and bronze containers, earthenware vases, lamps and utensils, but there was also a profitable market for the luxury goods and other articles from the East.

Freight charges and other shipping costs, such as port and

harbour dues, were low. Running costs were also small. Ships' crews were poorly paid and motive power was supplied by the wind. Apart from the risks the chief drawback about a long journey was the time it wasted. In 51 B.C. Cicero, much against his will, had to set out to become governor of Cilicia. He started from Rome early in May. On 10 May he told his friend Atticus that he was setting out from his villa at Pompeii. After a night with a friend he made a detour north to Beneventum. Five days later he was leaving Venusia where his consular dignity may have startled the eye of Quintus Horatius Flaccus, the fourteen-year-old son of a freedman, who later, like Cicero himself, was to share in the imperishable glory of the literature of Rome. He waited at Tarentum from 18 to 21 May, spending the time in political talks with Pompey. A day's journey took him across the heel of Italy to Brundisium which he reached on 22 May. There he remained recovering from a slight illness and waiting for a chance to sail in a private yacht across to Greece. Although it was midsummer, the voyage was sufficiently unpleasant to make Cicero decide to leave the ship at Actium on 15 June and to finish the journey by land as far as Athens. This took him until 24 June. He gladly spent a full ten days at this renowned city, his spiritual home, where, like so many politically ambitious young Romans, he had been a student. On 6 July he began his voyage through the islands of the Aegean: Ceos, Syros, Delos and Samos. A stiff wind took him along in an open boat a good deal faster than he wished, except for the last lap. He reached Ephesus on the main-land of Asia on 22 July. He was therefore longer than a fortnight making a sea voyage of less than 250 miles which a Greek steamer can now do in twenty-four hours and an aeroplane in an hour or less.

The return voyage from Ephesus to Athens in the following year (50 B.C.) took him from 1 to 14 October. He returned to Rome overland from Athens to Actium (7 November). He got north as far as the island of Corcyra by 9 November, but was kept there by bad weather until 22 November. This was a bad time of the year in which to make the shortest journey across the Adriatic.

Some of his fellow voyagers who would not wait with him paid the penalty for their haste to reach Italy by being shipwrecked. Not until 24 November 50 B.C. did he land on Italian soil at Tarentum.

However great the hurry there was no possibility of speeding up communications. An express letter by special messenger from Rome took forty-seven days to reach him in his province of Cilicia. 'Oh dear,' lamented Cicero when he got it, 'to think of the distance I am away.'

There was no public postal service. The Republic naturally employed messengers, as did financial and commercial groups having important interests in various parts of the world. The chance of sending a letter, therefore, depended upon the good will of friends travelling in the desired direction or on catching messengers journeying for their masters.

Well-to-do Romans must have found their letter-carriers among the most expensive of their personal servants.

Roman Roads

The practical intelligence of the Romans that made them concentrate upon developing an efficient army is seen also in the great care which they, above all peoples of antiquity, constantly gave to the creation and maintenance of a network of roads. The Romans, it may be said, invented long-distance roads. The consequences of their enterprise are now hard to grasp; so much do we take for granted of the technical progress of mankind. But in the ancient world it was the absence of the means of rapid communication that above all limited the expansion of States into Empires. It could not, of course, be maintained that it was because the Romans invented the road that they gained the mastery of the world, but it is difficult to see how they would have achieved it without their roads.

By their roads alone was it possible to ensure the rapid movement of the army with its supplies. Along the roads also travelled administrators and colonists and a regular communication service of letters and dispatches. The map (pp. 124, 125) shows the main network throughout Italy. Roman roads corresponded as far as possible to the ancient definition of a straight line as the shortest distance between two points. Nothing but serious obstacles of mountains and swamps were allowed to stand in the way of this ideal. Mere hills and marshes were often no deterrent.

Oversight of the public roads and highways within the territory of the Republic, was, along with the care of the temples, aqueducts, the Treasury and the taxes, an early duty of the Censors. Lesser

magistrates, the Aediles, were also given duties connected with
the roads of the city of Rome. Municipal officials had oversight of
the streets of their own towns, but both in Rome and elsewhere
the duty of keeping the streets in good shape was regarded as the
personal responsibility of the householders living on them. As
costs rose, and no doubt above all to get some uniformity and
order, the duty was increasingly taken over by public officials who
hired contractors for the actual work of construction and repair.

Some of the famous roads of Italy always bore the name of
the Censors by whose orders they had been planned. The oldest is
still renowned today, the *Via Appia*, or Appian Way, 'the Queen
of Roads'. Constructed by direction of Appius Claudius Caecus,
the celebrated blind Censor of 312 B.C., it crossed the Pontine
marshes on a solidly built viaduct. It connected Rome at first
with Capua, then with Beneventum, and was later extended to
Brundisium after that port had become a Roman colony in
244 B.C. Along this road, more than on any other, did the wealthy
Romans indulge their curious taste for building roadside tombs
and memorials to perpetuate the memory of their dead. By
Cicero's time the number and size of these funeral monuments
must have already reached large proportions. As the centuries
went on, such accretions, many of them no doubt tasteless and
ugly, must have created a formidable impression upon travellers
to the city. The well-known eighteenth-century Italian engraver,
Piranesi, has left a nightmare picture of the lengths to which this
particular form of Roman ancestor worship may ultimately have
degenerated. Cicero witnessed the earlier development of this
custom by which the Appian Way and the other main highways
on the borders of Rome and other Italian towns were transformed
into a monumental mason's paradise. The *Via Latina* was
another very old road south from Rome inland to Capua.

The 'Great North Road', the Flaminian Way from Rome to
Ariminum, the modern Rimini, perpetuates the name of the man
who completed it, the progressive Consul C. Flaminius, Censor in
220 B.C., who lost his life commanding the Roman army against
Hannibal at Lake Trasimene.

The first *Via Aemilia* (187 B.C.) was constructed by the Consul
M. Aemilius Lepidus during his campaign against the Ligurian
tribes of the north-west border lands of Italy. Running almost in a
straight line for 180 miles, it joined Ariminum to Placentia, cutting

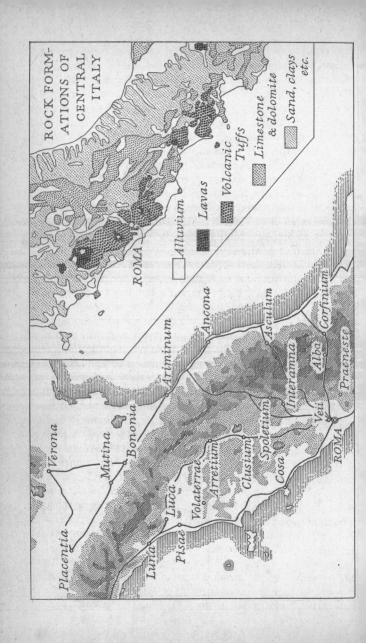

ROCK FORM-
ATIONS OF
CENTRAL
ITALY

Alluvium

Lavas

Volcanic
Tuffs

Limestone
& dolomite

Sand, clays
etc.

ROMA

Ariminum

Ancona

Asculum

Interamna

Alba

Corfinium

Praeneste

Veii

ROMA

Cosa

Spoletium

Clusium

Arretium

Volaterrae

Luca

Pisae

Luna

Bononia

Mutina

Verona

Placentia

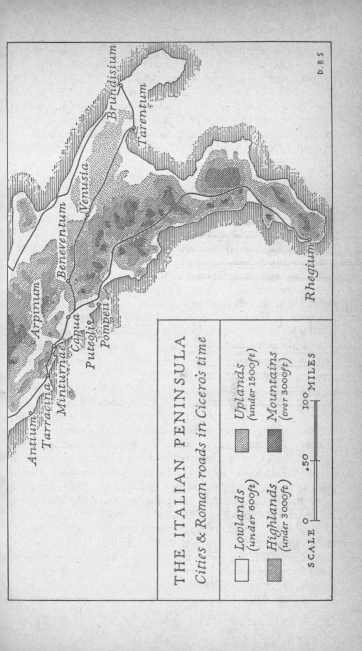

THE ITALIAN PENINSULA
Cities & Roman roads in Cicero's time

Lowlands (under 600ft)

Uplands (under 1500ft)

Highlands (under 3000ft)

Mountains (over 3000ft)

SCALE O   .50   100 MILES

D.B.S

through the heart of Cispadane Gaul. These road-making activities contributed powerfully to Rome's spread to the north.

Other well-known roads to the north from Rome included the *Via Aurelia* to Luna, and its continuation, the *Via Aemilia Scauri*. This second Aemilian road was planned by M. Aemilius Scaurus, Censor in 109 B.C., a popular figure, despite the shameful bribes he took from Jugurtha, the African enemy of Rome. He extended the road from Luna to Genoa along the sharp mountain sides of the Italian Riviera. The *Via Cassia* was an inland road to the north through Etruria. The Roman habit of naming roads after the men at whose instigation they were constructed has not been much imitated, although examples, such as the Bankhead Highway in the United States, exist to perpetuate it. There were of course many more roads and trackways than those here named.

To this day nobody can see the still surviving stretches of roads made by the Romans in many parts of Western Europe without admiring the engineering skill of the Roman road-makers. Many of these remains are later than the age of Cicero, but in Italy, at least, the main network had been filled in during his lifetime. In Republican Rome, as in the modern world, the existence of a good road stimulated economic development all along its route. Small towns along it grew in importance and new towns and villages sprang into existence to cater for the needs of travellers and to benefit by the new facility with which goods could be moved.

Travel by road was better organized in Italy in Cicero's day than it was in the England of Queen Anne eighteen hundred years later. Tradition has it that the Romans first learnt the art of constructing stone-paved or 'metalled' roads from the Carthaginians. The usual method was to construct the road surface in four layers of stones, coarse lime mortar and finer mortar in which the stone surface was embedded. The foundation for the surface stones was often nearly two feet thick. The top surface was slightly dome-shaped, or 'cambered', and the road itself, wherever the type of soil required it, would be supported by strengthening the ground each side of it by digging out the soft earth alongside the road and refilling the ditches so made with stones or rubble. In towns and cities there would be kerbs and, wherever there were drainage problems, as at Pompeii, stepping-stones across the road. (Plate 16.)

The aim of the Romans seems usually to have been a solid

construction requiring as little upkeep as possible. Hence their capital cost was no doubt high. That it was a good investment is proved by the survival of Roman roads during long centuries in which medieval dirt tracks, constantly needing repair and all too rarely getting it from the slovely and unskilful inheritors of the Roman Empire, alone had to suffice for the commerce and intercourse of mankind.

In Republican Rome, as today, road-making was regarded as a way of finding work for idle hands to do whether in the army or among the civilian population, although heavy navvying was done by slaves. Road-making was one of the activities included in the New Deal planned by the scheming brain of the younger Gracchus, who was always to be seen surrounded by contractors, engineers, soldiers and scholars. Milestones a thousand paces apart marked distances along some of the main roads, thanks largely to Gaius Gracchus. The Roman mile of 1,000 paces, each of 5 Roman feet, was 140 yards short of an English mile. The army made roads in the provinces, in Macedonia, Spain, and Gaul for example, and they conscripted local labour for much of the work. During the second half of the first century B.C., roughly the lifetime of Cicero's father, the Romans had begun their system of roads and fortified posts in the provinces. The *Via Egnatia* crossed the Balkan peninsula from Dyrrhachium to Thessalonica. The *Via Domitia* constructed by Domitius Ahenobarbus about 120 B.C. ran westwards from the Rhône through Southern France.

In Italy itself the work was normally let out to contractors by the Censors. With it went the construction of drainage canals, a particularly important public work in the Po valley, or Cisalpine Gaul, into which Roman power had been extended during the second century B.C.

It is not difficult to see the connexion between these roads and the process of romanization. By 89 B.C. all Cisalpine Gaul south of the Po (Cispadane Gaul), linked to the capital city by its road system, was given full citizenship.

A few scraps of information about the cost of some road work in Cicero's day have survived. Re-gravelling a twenty-mile stretch of the *Via Caecilia* cost 150,000 sesterces. Another stretch of about twenty-two miles in difficult country cost four times as much (600,000 sesterces).

Stone paving in the cities and great arterial roads was naturally much more expensive. A road surface of just over 2,000 feet in the town of Verulae cost nearly 86,000 sesterces, actually at the rate of about 225,000 sesterces a mile against the 75,000 sesterces a mile for gravel. Costs on these levels must have been a heavy burden on small communities.

Economic need, no less than military necessity, kept Romans on the roads. Some of the 180,000 or 190,000 tons of wheat alone required every year in Cicero's day to feed the city of Rome undoubtedly came down the Tiber and very much more, particularly of the Sicilian and overseas shipments, came up the river. Nevertheless there were wheat-growing districts unable to benefit by water carriage, and their supplies, together with the still greater tonnage of other supplies such as vegetables, fruit, cheese, olive oil, and wine, not to mention building materials and other heavy traffic, would fill hundreds of the heavy two- or four-wheeled drays tugged along Roman roads by slow and patient ox-teams. The vast size of Rome was made possible by the Roman roads, for Rome was the first great city of the ancient world to become independent of water transport for supplies to feed its huge population. Much of the carrying, including grain and wool, was done by pack mules, because wheeled transport was expensive. Mules were used in the army as beasts of burden. Sulla had 20,000 of them with his army in Athens. An ox-team was much slower, not being expected to cover more than eleven to twelve miles a day. It was also very much more expensive. Oxen eat more than mules and they need a team of men to manage them. When Cato, early in the second century B.C., was writing his notes on fitting up an olive mill he said that to transport the crusher weighing over a ton and a half required a team of six men and six boys. To bring it twenty-five miles and to return the ox-team took six days. The cost of transport on that short journey was already a sixth of the cost of the mill itself, so it is plain that for longer journeys the expense of haulage would reach formidable figures. Without a respectable road such a journey would have been still more difficult, if indeed it would have been possible at all except in dry weather. Compare a modern two-ton lorry at thirty miles an hour and more on a concrete road in order to see at a glance the difference in tempo between Cicero's age and our own. Yet the noise and bustle of Rome exhausted those who were not used to it just as today people not used to a large modern city are glad to escape to the slower, more even tempo of their countryside or small town.

Rome was not the only city in Italy to make strict rules to control traffic. Riding and driving in most towns, including Rome, were very carefully restricted and in some places were forbidden by day. In Rome under Julius Caesar all heavy transport had to be done at night, to the misery of the wretched Romans trying to sleep in the tenements near the main streets. Carriages in any case were available only to the very wealthy and they were often used to drive their owners to fashionable resorts such as Baiae and Pompeii. Cicero seems to have made many of his journeys, as most Romans did, at a walking pace, carried in a litter by slaves. Horses were much more expensive than oxen. The cost of an ox in Rome is not known. One very early price has been reported as about 300 sesterces, but a horse seems to have been valued at about 2,000 sesterces. These prices are not very reliable as they relate to different periods. However, Varro, a contemporary of Cicero, reports that a prize pedigree stallion ass might cost between 30,000 and 40,000 sesterces, so it is not apparent that the price of a really good animal mattered much to the well-to-do Roman. Varro at any rate makes less account of horses and mares than he does of cows and oxen, but he does not bother to refer to the price of either. It is an astonishing fact that in the whole of their remaining literature there are no reliable figures of the cost of these animals, so important to the Romans. The price of an ox has been guessed at 240 to 320 sesterces between 200 B.C. and 150 B.C. at a time when an unskilled farm slave cost between 1,200 and 2,000 sesterces.

The speed of man and horse fixed the upper limits of rapidity of communication on land in the Roman Republic and in the ancient world generally. Alarm signals in the form of fire-beacons were used, and the inventive genius of the Greeks seems to have come near to achieving a method of signalling by the reflection of the sun upon a flashing shield, but nothing like the Morse code seems to have occurred to them and their early promise of communication by heliography had no future until modern times. The manual labour of Roman craftsmen, aided by slaves and to some extent by animals, also fixed sharp limits to the productivity both of Roman industry and of agriculture. Some increase in general production may have been achieved in the last two centuries of the Republic, thanks as much to the reduction of negative forces such as war and piracy as to the increase of trade and the improvement of communications. But, in relation to what we understand by economic progress, based as it is now on mass production by machinery, the Roman advance must have been insignificantly small as far as the people as a whole were concerned. Neither in agriculture nor in industry could rapid improvement be expected.

From Economics to Politics

Such were the economic foundations of the Roman Republic as far as the very imperfect record allows us to see with any certainty. Beyond a few references to Senators, magistrates, tribunes of the people and governors of provinces, not much has so far been said about politics. It seems best not to follow the almost general practice of giving first place to Roman political organization, partly because political questions very often grow out of economic realities and cannot be fully understood without their economic background, but chiefly because politics played a small part in the lives of the 5 or 6 millions of ordinary work-a-day Italians and Romans.

But after allowance has been made for the lack of political activity on the part of the masses and when politics is seen in its proper perspective in the daily life of Rome, there need be no excuse for giving a considerable space to the Roman system of government and the Roman method of dealing with political affairs.

In agriculture, industrial production, trade, commerce and transport we have left the Romans so far behind that theirs is another world. But in politics we cannot claim the same progress. Everywhere men are still wrestling with the problem of the best form of government. The slow achievement of political freedom and constitutional government by Western Europe, the enduring political subordination and slavery of the Russians, the disaster in which the political life of Italy was involved by Mussolini in 1922, the still more tremendous catastrophe which allowed Hitler to begin the utter ruin of Germany in 1933 are all reminders, if such were needed, that the twentieth century cannot regard with scorn or contempt the Romans who let their politicians make away with their liberties 2,000 years ago.

Chapter Five

THE ROMAN REPUBLIC AND
THE SENATE

So great was the prestige of the men and institutions by which the destiny of Rome had been guided and so high was the pride it inspired in every well-born Roman that the stubborn, stolid and unimaginative Romans do not seem to have had serious doubts that the governing bodies of their City State would be equally able to manage the affairs of a world empire.

The feelings of respect, almost of awe, which Cicero, his contemporaries and successors felt for their ancestors of the heroic age extended also to the political organization of those early days. One followed from the other. In a single pithy line, one of the few remaining from the works of one of Rome's earliest poets, Ennius (239–169 B.C.), the matter was summed up by saying that the Roman State stood four-square upon the well-tried ways of life followed by the men of old,

> 'Moribus antiquis res stat Romana virisque.'

No Roman whose works have come down to us is more frequent or more discerning in his praise of the ancient Republican government than Cicero, and Cicero regarded that verse, both in its brevity and its truth, as the utterance of an oracle. It was a subject upon which he had thought long and deeply. Fragments survive of his most finished treatise upon the political organization of his country, *The Republic* or *The Commonwealth*, written towards the end of his busy life of public activity. In it Cicero put into the mouth of Scipio Aemilianus, one of the heroes of Rome, words which truly reflected his own opinion also. 'Of this I am fully conscious and certain, that of all forms of government, there is none which by constitution, in theory or in practice can be compared to that which our fathers left us and which had previously been left to them by their ancestors.' There was, he said furthermore in the same work, 'something peculiar in our form of government ... nothing better and nothing like it in any other State'.

With this ideal of the Roman Republic ever before his eyes it was his tragic fate to witness its ruin. At the age of fifty-two, after a stormy career in the course of which he had risen step by step from insignificance to the highest position in public life for which a Roman could hope, all his pride and satisfaction in his own achievements had turned sour.

Four years before Caesar delivered the final blow which extinguished the Republic, Cicero, writing to his best and most trusted friend, Atticus, already lamented, 'We have lost not only all the healthy sap and blood of our old constitution, but even its colour and outward show. There is no Republic to give a moment's pleasure or feeling of security.'

This momentous contrast between what Cicero thought of the Republic in its period of glory and what his actual experience of it was in his own day, plainly gives another clue to the decay of the Roman Republic. Something more than the mere form and organization of government is involved, because in a free State politics is a vital human activity, not a catalogue of offices, institutions, party programmes, bills and laws.

What then was the mystic political quality which enabled the old Republic to flourish and to what should the ruin of the later Republic be attributed? It is a natural question but to answer it would be to discover one of the deepest secrets of human society.

No form of government and no system of national political life readily yields the secrets of its inmost working, and the Roman government is no exception. Unlike the constitution of the United States, but more akin to that of England, it was the product of no definite time or year. Its growth and change was by no means rapid, simple or easy, for Rome was at first an agricultural centre, and as markedly conservative as agricultural communities, particularly in primitive times, invariably are.

It is worth while to glance back once more beyond the period which Cicero knew, beyond the time of his father and grandfather, to those far-off days when his own ancestors from the hill country round about sixty miles south of Rome had no love for the Romans, but on the contrary were often engaged in bitter fighting with them.

Throughout the earliest centuries of the Republic, politics had been a fairly simple business managed by a few officials called magistrates, given supreme power by the people who elected them afresh every year. The magistrates were guided by a strong advisory council called the Senate. Later in the history of the Republic, the arrangement was supposed to rest largely on popular support, because the people not merely elected the magistrates who became Senators after their first year of office, but also had the last word before any new law could come into force. In principle, therefore, the government of Rome had a thoroughly democratic foundation. Nevertheless a healthy democratic State did not emerge. Continually involved in war and exposed therefore to great peril, the people in their public assemblies could not provide for the continuity and co-ordination which war policy required. Inevitably the Senate, the only permanent source of advice, became also a source of authority. The willingness of the Senators to accept heavy responsibility and their success consolidated their power and influence. So it came about that 'the will of the people', untrained by education and political experience, was overlaid by sectional interests, particularly by those of the landowning classes.

From very early times the political life of Rome was warped and twisted by a class struggle in which the older and richer 'patrician' families resolutely sought to shut out from every political position of power and influence the unestablished newcomers and the poorer 'plebeian' families.

It remains difficult to say exactly what the origins of the patricians and plebeians were. In the time of the kings there had probably been no patriciate, and it seems likely that the oligarchy who overthrew the monarchy tried to mark themselves and their families off from the rest of the population, whence came a distinction between patrician and plebeian. In historical times at all events, the patricians seem to have been men able to trace descent from pure Roman citizens, the aristocrats, the men and families who, in the expressive American usage of the word, may be said to have 'belonged'. They alone, in the early Republic, were qualified to conduct religious ceremonies and largely because of that fact to share in the government of the city, for there was then a close connexion between religion and government. Apart from the slaves, who were not a 'social class' any more than were the domestic animals, there were two other classes of men in the city. One was made up of dependants or hangers-on of the aristocratic Romans or patricians. These were the 'clients', the men who listened with attentive ear. They 'half-belonged'. The third class did not 'belong' at all. These were the plebeians. The clients accepted their dependence. The plebeians resented their subordination, and the State of Rome was dangerously strained in their struggle to vindicate their social standing and to be allowed to take their fair share in the government of the Republic.

As there is nothing like clientship in modern Western society we are easily apt to underestimate the profound effect it had upon the whole development of Rome throughout its history. Clients came from the freed slaves and their descendants, immigrants, and poor citizens unable to stand on their own feet and therefore needing help and protection. The almost feudal dependence of clients upon their patrons tremendously reinforced the political and social influence of the leaders of society. The patron would help his client by giving him small parcels of land, a few animals, food or small sums of money. He would speak for him or tell him what to do in his rare encounters with public authority. In return the obsequious client often called to pay daily deference to his patron and was expected to rally to his support if necessary with whatever powers he possessed. That he should support his patron politically and vote the way the patron wanted in the public assemblies was one of the client's least burdensome duties. No doubt the more independent and energetic of the free citizens preferred to fend for themselves but in Rome as in every other community, such rare spirits would be in a minority. Clients remained clients because they had no ambition or ability to shoulder the responsibilities involved in striking out for themselves so they hung like a dead weight upon their leaders and more enterprising fellow-citizens.

The Roman Republic endured for nearly five centuries. Almost all the first half of this long period was dominated on the home front by the stubborn struggles of the plebeians against the patricians. Their first task, and it took sixty years, was to free themselves from systematic and often cruel exploitation. Then another century and a half were spent before the unprivileged plebeians won political and economic equality with the patricians. They never really succeeded in attaining complete social equality, for a certain snobbish aloofness from which Cicero also had to suffer remained characteristic of the patrician families, reduced though they were in numbers and in real influence by Cicero's day. Then and for many years afterwards they sought to mark themselves off from the crowd and to maintain that much-prized 'social distance' or prestige for which nearly everybody in a competitive society strives to a greater or lesser extent. One little habit of theirs long survived to puzzle later ages: patricians wore on their shoes little images of the crescent moon.

The class struggles of the early Republic left their mark upon the political framework of the State, the nature of its public offices and the manner in which elections were held. Before we can see Cicero, his friends and enemies as living human beings going to bed late at night after an exhausting day crowded with public and private business, it is necessary to know something about this framework of Roman politics and the levers and cogwheels by which it was set in motion.

The Senate

The machinery of government inherited by the Romans of Cicero's day from their forefathers had become a complex and unwieldy affair. In the far-off days of the early Republic it probably had the simplicity characteristic of a small-town government. The people of the town managed their own affairs, once they had driven off their alien king, and they acted through one or two officials whom they elected every year from their own number so that all had a chance to rule and were ruled in turn, which is one of Aristotle's principles of political liberty.

Except in times of war and other grave troubles these officials probably had routine duties, for a simple agricultural people is not fond of novelties. When a new problem cropped up the magistrates could look for advice in the first place to the council of city elders, the Roman Senate, but decisions upon major questions rested with the people. The ancient world knew nothing of coats of arms or heraldic badges, but there was one device which it was to learn and by which it was to be dominated for many centuries – S.P.Q.R., which stood for the Senate and the people of Rome, *Senatus Populusque Romanus*. The greatness of Rome was summed up in these words.

Origin of the Senate

The long history of the Roman Senate, its wide powers, its survival after disastrous crises, its close identification with the fortunes of the State, give it chief place among the clues to the special character of the Roman government for which Cicero was inquiring. The Senate had all Cicero's loyalty and devotion.

Ancient Roman tradition spoke of the Senate of the Republic as the successor to the council of one hundred advisers, city fathers (*patres*), chosen by their first king, Romulus, from among his people (plebeians). Owing perhaps to the ability, wisdom, and eminence of their forefathers, the Senators contrived for many generations to retain a position of great distinction in the Republic. The families of the leading Senators gained, through custom that hardened into something approaching a right, almost a monopoly of the succession to the chief offices in the Republic. These were the Consuls, Censors, Praetors, Aediles, and Quaestors who will be described in a succeeding chapter. The resentment of the plebeians excluded from these honours has already been indicated as the main theme of the political history of the early Republic.

Admission to the Senate was never to be had by direct election in the public assemblies of the Roman people. Consequently Senators had no constituencies as have American Senators and British Members of Parliament. There were no marked party divisions within the Senate although groups and cliques sometimes seem to have been formed. Towards the end of the fourth century B.C. (around 312 B.C.) the practice seems to have begun of admitting to its membership the senior magistrates of the Republic after their first year of office had expired. Thereafter any plebeians could become Senators if they had been elected to one of the senior magistracies, a right they had won a century before the Roman Republic emerged upon the scene as a Mediterranean world power during the First and Second Punic Wars (264 B.C. to 201 B.C.).

Powers of the Senate

The shattering defeats of the Roman Consuls and the Roman armies by Hannibal had thrown the fate of the Republic back upon the Senate as never before, and the Senators unquestionably proved equal to the demands made upon them. Their prestige rose naturally in consequence, and in this great age of the Republic they assumed powers and authority which, as a purely advisory body, they ought never to have possessed. The influence they so acquired was at the expense on the one hand of the independent authority and command of the annually elected magistrates and on the other hand of the popular assemblies of the supposedly sovereign Roman people.

In a real sense their pre-eminence had been forced upon them
to remedy the shortcomings of the Roman machinery of government. There was first the weakness of the chain of executive
authority whose links were new men elected afresh each year and
secondly the weakness of the popular element of the government,
the public assemblies, whose members had neither the knowledge
nor the wisdom to guide executive action in all its manifold and
complicated detail.

The Senate alone could provide the authority that everywhere
comes from ripe experience, wide knowledge, and constant attention to the affairs of State. The long catalogue of its activities included the all-important power of the purse, the weapon by which
the House of Commons won political supremacy in England.
It is true that as long as the Republic was sustained by revenue
raised from taxation within Italy the Roman people alone could
finally approve the taxes and tribute they should pay. After
167 B.C., however, no internal taxes were paid by Romans
resident in Italy, who alone voted in the public assemblies.
Management of the public revenue then devolved entirely upon
the Senate. At all times, moreover, it was the Senators and never
the people who decided how the money was to be spent and who
drew up the budgets of the various State officials. The Senators
could, if they chose, compel the officials to account for their
expenditure. They had oversight of the public property of the
Republic, the public land, mines, quarries and salt-works let out
to contractors by the Censors, the sale and distribution of war
booty and the management of the Mint.

In foreign affairs they were all-important save in one critical
respect. The Roman people in their public assembly alone had the
power of declaring war. But in this respect also the Senators were
in a pre-eminent position because of their knowledge of Rome's
treaties and agreements with other States and the fact that
diplomatic negotiations were entirely in their hands. It was a pre-
eminence supported also by the fact that Senators debated upon
terms of peace before they were submitted to the people for
ratification. Woe betide a Roman commander who accepted
conditions of peace that the Senate did not like! More than one
such unfortunate man was sent back to his enemies in chains with
a disavowal of his treaty. As a Foreign Ministry, the Senate
became involved, among other minor matters, in preventing

internal conflicts between cities, punishing the allied communities failing to make good their quota of men and money for Rome's wars, quelling slave insurrections, very occasionally relieving people stricken by flood, fire, pestilence or famine, resettling deserted colonies, and all too frequently, as time went on, listening to the sad laments of communities suffering under an unjust Roman governor. (See also pp. 39, 71.)

Until the last hundred years of the Republic the civil authority of the Senate was accepted without question as being superior to the military power of the senior magistrates and the army. It found money to equip and supply armies in the field and men to reinforce them. Whenever, in the great age of the Republic, it became necessary to maintain more armies in the provinces than the Consuls could control, the Senate assigned the additional commander to his post. It was to the Senate that the army commanders sent their reports and it was the Senate by whom they were reprimanded, recalled, or given the much coveted distinction of a public triumph through the streets of Rome. It was to the Senate that the troops looked for their share of booty and a grant of public land, the Roman equivalent of a military pension. Such were some of the many precautions the Romans took in their effort to solve the age-old problem, how to prevent men entrusted with military power from turning it against their employers.

In Italy, the Senate sought to preserve and enlarge peace at home. By its skilled judgement, able diplomacy, and wise resolution, the Senate directed the dealings of the Roman people with their neighbours so that, on the basis of leadership in Italy, Rome ultimately achieved world supremacy.

The supreme sanction in times of internal crisis, first used in 121 B.C., was the dread 'last decree', *Senatus consultum ultimum*, creating a kind of martial law and charging the chief magistrates to 'see to it that the State came to no harm'.

As the Roman Empire grew with the expansion of the Republic, in the second century B.C., a new field of State activities was opened. To the Roman provinces went more magistrates elected by the people of Rome: governors, judges, financial and supply officers. They had wide discretion in managing the affairs of their provinces. Nevertheless from these representatives of the *Senatus Populusque Romanus* came a stream of reports and requests for supplies of men, materials and money, although more money was expected to flow to Rome than the Romans were prepared to spend on their Empire. When the provincial official packed up after his year of office, handed over to his successor and hastened back to Rome, as he usually did with many more pleasurable anticipations than those with which he set out, he faced his fellow Senators once more. If they were not a court of inquiry into his conduct, they were at least the arbiters of praise and blame in the only important forum of public opinion in days when newspapers were unknown.

Nevertheless this long catalogue of senatorial powers and duties was subject to one all-important qualification. The Senate was supposed to be an advisory body. It could not meet unless it was called together by a senior magistrate and it did not deal with any business except that put to it by him. Yet from the very nature of the case, every magistrate in his senses would wish to be able to share the otherwise tremendous burden of sole responsibility for the destinies of the Republic with the City Fathers upon whose shoulders so much of it had rested from the earliest times.

However, in principle, executive and administrative decisions were the task of the public officials or magistrates chosen not by the Senate but by the Roman people.

Inevitably however the Senators acquired a powerful influence in the day-to-day conduct of public business. They got into the habit of appointing commissions of inquiry with very full powers to inquire and report. They did not stop at that but naturally went on to pass judgement also. The Senate never became a court of law, although at times it gave advice of quasi-judicial nature.

The Senate alone did not run the country, but it certainly took a large share of the work – a surprisingly large share of most important work when it is remembered that the Senate was not a popularly elected body. Moreover its share had increased greatly in the fourth and third centuries B.C.

To carry on administrative, executive and judicial work, however essential, is but half the task of government. The government must know *what* to do, it must have a policy, and be able to provide for adaptation and change to meet altering circumstances, natural growth, and external dangers. It was in this creative, originating work that the Assembly of the People was all-important, for as it has been said above, the People alone could make new laws. Unless some method of invalidating the laws could be found upon technical or religous grounds, that is to say usually by some form of trickery, there was no machinery for setting them aside by declaring them unconstitutional, as the Supreme Court of the United States can, for example, declare a Federal law unconstitutional in the United States of America. If a law had to be repealed, the People alone had the power, according to the theory of the Constitution, to repeal it.

When, therefore, it became a matter of adding to or altering the laws of Rome, the magistrates and Senate had to call the people into partnership. Here again, the partnership, although real, nevertheless in the best period of the Republic, in the third and second centuries B.C., left the Senate in the position of preponderance. Its leadership had been won on its sheer prestige. Largely on this ground alone it was able to influence, through the civic magistrates or executives, the manner in which the proposed new laws and other resolutions were put before the voting assembly of the electors, the people of Rome, the '*populus Romanus*'.

Towards the latter part of the second century B.C. senatorial prestige began steadily to decay. Senatorial influence had been long maintained by the ability of the well-to-do Senators to manipulate the voting in the Public Assembly by packing it with their own retainers and by bribery. When their authority and the authority of the Senate itself was openly challenged in the name of the Roman people, as it first decisively was by Tiberius Gracchus, the old constitutional peace and equilibrium was threatened and the political troubles of the Republic began their fatal course.

Procedure of the Senate

General statements attempting to collect together the occasional references to the work of the Roman Senate such as those given in the preceding paragraphs cannot do more than create a vague picture of a body of 300 men, labelled Senators, and summarize some of the reasons why they must be thought to have been important.

We see them dimly at various periods of Rome's history. In the early days of Rome they would leave their ploughs where they had perhaps been working stripped in the fields, throw on their rough tunics and togas which their women folk had spun and woven, and gather in one of the principal temples to plan the defence of the city against some local enemies or against the greatly feared Gaul. Generations of these men lived, worked, fought and died. Their successors, inheriting the fruits of their labours and their sacrifices, found the Senate and their own dignity a more imposing affair. In Cicero's day their privileges, their distinctive toga, with its broad purple stripe, their red sandals tied to the leg with leather thongs and fastened with a crescent-shaped buckle, their attentive band of clients, their crowded days, their power and influence were all on a scale of which their rude forefathers could have formed no imagination. We cannot follow the change in any detail because sufficient materials are lacking.

Not much is known about the procedure of the Roman Senate. Official records of every session were indeed made, but not one has survived. It is however known that the two highest magistracies of the Republic, the Consuls and Praetors, alone had the power of summoning the Senators. After 287 B.C. the people's representatives, any one of the ten Tribunes, was also able to call the Senate together and preside over the proceedings in the absence of a Consul or Praetor. The proceedings were opened by a religious ceremony including a sacrifice. Sons and grandsons of Senators who were of age could be admitted, but not the general public. The doors were left open.

The Consul, the chief magistrate, an elected official, usually presided. His duty was to lay the public business of the day before the Senators and to ask what course of action they would recommend. He had to follow a recognized order in asking for opinions. The Consuls-elect would be asked first and then other men who had been Consuls followed. The presiding magistrate could neither intervene in the debate, draft resolutions, nor vote. The Senate's decisions were determined by the weight of the opinions expressed by its senior members rather than by counting votes, but by Cicero's time members also left their places and ranged themselves by the speaker whose motion they approved. By such means the predominant view would be made clear.

The proceedings of the Senate seem to have been, if not secret, at least confidential, in the sense that they were not published in full as are the proceedings of the British Parliament or the United States Congress. The only record seems to have been a summary statement of the decisions at which the Senators had arrived and a list of completed business. It may have been on very much the same lines as the Votes and Proceedings of the British House of Commons in the late seventeenth and eighteenth centuries. The Roman record, like the British, was probably available only to the privileged few with easy access to the politically powerful class in Roman society. Cicero was able to get it when he was away from Rome, and very eager he was to have it.

To give publicity to all the proceedings of the Senate was a revolutionary thing to do. Julius Caesar took this step, not because he was concerned to improve the political education of the great mass of Roman citizens but because he wanted to discredit the Senators who spoke and voted against the policies he was trying to introduce when he was Consul or chief magistrate in 59 B.C. For the first time in that year the Romans were supplied with an official record of what was actually said in the Senate. Unfortunately there is no evidence of the effect, if any, of this new step. The Romans had nothing to correspond to our great national daily newspaper press. Moreover it seems unlikely that the great mass of the poorer Romans of the Republic were able to read. Very great caution must therefore be used in speaking of democracy and public partnership in political affairs in Rome where the conditions of life were in marked contrast to those of twentieth-century Great Britain or the United States.

News the official record did not supply, the personal reactions and assessments of public affairs, were sent by letters and passed on by word of mouth. If other Roman politicians put as much into their letters about the political scene at the capital of the world as Cicero and his friends put into theirs, there could be little lack of information about the main developments in the trend of public business from day to day.

Influence of the Senate

It is impossible, in a few lines, to sum up adequately the influence of the Senate throughout the long history of the Roman Republic.

The Senate throughout was in partnership with the People and the magistrates, so its influence was always the result of an interplay of forces, but it was undeniably great. With so many of the threads of policy in its hands and with so wide an opportunity to influence the activities of all other branches of government, it is not surprising that the history of the policy of the Roman Republic is largely a history of the Roman Senate.

A resolution of the Senate, *Senatus consultum*, was not a law, although Cicero, a loyal Senate man, thought it ought to have been. It was framed as a suggestion to the executive magistrates which, 'if they agreed', they would carry out or ask the citizen voters to accept as a law. It was advice the magistrates would not be likely to ignore. Moreover according to the traditions of the Republic no proposals for new laws should be submitted to the public before they had been approved by the Senate.

The magistrates, nearly always new to their single year of office, would be well aware that they were being closely watched in the Senate by a critical audience of Rome's leading citizens, many of whom had successfully administered the very offices they were struggling to run with credit. Naturally it was to the Senate rather than to the People who had elected them that the magistrates looked for support, instruction, and approval. The prestige of the Senate, already immense, was strengthened by this attitude and it would be sufficient to overawe any newly appointed magistrate, conscious that he did not know the ropes but that many Senators knew them very well indeed. The magistrates were therefore likely to advocate the Senate's policy in their dealings with the people.

During the first centuries of the history of the Republic the political 'centre of gravity' in Rome may be found more often in the Senate than anywhere else, especially during the central period from about 300 B.C. to 130 B.C. Thereafter senatorial influence was challenged in the name of the people of Rome, first by political reformers such as the Gracchi (p. 68) and lastly, with fatal results, by popular army commanders.

The history of the long struggle of the Senate, in the beginning against the enemies of the Roman people, later against the people, and of the ultimate subjection of both Senate and People to a third power which was not that Rule of Law for which Cicero pleaded, but that of a military despotism, is the main connecting link between the rise and grandeur of the Roman Republic and the decline and fall of the Roman Empire. It was Cicero's fate to be on the bridge when the Republican ship of State went down to irretrievable ruin. The question naturally arises, why the Roman people did not or could not save their government from disaster.

Chapter Six

THE ROMAN PEOPLE AND THE
POPULAR ASSEMBLIES

Patricians versus Plebeians

THE second part of the Roman State, the people (*Populus Romanus*), never succeeded in becoming the unified political force which the Senate, with its well-defined membership and common body of experience, had already become at an early period in the history of the Republic. The men of Cicero's day were all too ready to paint a glowing picture of the early Republic, but throughout a long period it seems to have been poisoned by the division between patricians and plebeians. Some of the stories about the divided state of Rome and the harshness and cruelty by which it was characterized in the first hundred years of the Republic have however been grossly overdrawn. It used for instance to be seriously asserted, until a more accurate interpretation was provided, that the Roman law of property allowed creditors to take the body of a debtor unable to meet his obligations and to carve him up into bits corresponding to the size of his debt to each.

It is difficult to imagine how a society organized on such a basis could have long survived. A considerably less spectacular view of the early Roman Republican constitution and government is now thought to be nearer the truth. It is believed, although certainty is unattainable, that in the legendary seventh and sixth centuries B.C., long before the historical period begins, the inhabitants of Rome were probably a closely knit community of many clans living, as somewhat primitive peoples often lived, a well-established family life according to a set and settled traditional and predominantly religious routine. The members of the clans, whether rich or poor, all formed one body of Roman citizens. The land they occupied belonged, not to individuals, but to the family. Just as it was through his family or clan that the primitive Roman had any rights in property, so it was through his clan that he obtained political rights. A newcomer from outside necessarily had neither property rights nor political rights. In time, the evident and growing prosperity of the Romans attracted neighbouring peoples who in increasing numbers came and settled with and around them. It was one thing to come to share in Rome's prosperity by working for Romans as craftsmen, traders, general workers and handymen, but another and very different thing in those early days to be allowed to share in the religious and political activity of the Roman clans. What at first was not a very serious matter, for the average Roman then had little say in the government which was in the hands of the kings and of the Etruscan overlords, later became a more serious exclusion. When the historical period begins the Roman community had already progressed beyond the ownership of land in common by the clans to ownership in severalty by private persons. Land became, as a result of this early development, something capable of transfer from man to man, or, as the Romans put it, 'something which could be taken with the hand' (res mancipi) like slaves, cattle, and other negotiable property.

The legendary King Servius Tullius (578–534 B.C.) is said to have laid the basis upon which subsequently the unity of the Roman people, early settlers and immigrants, whether freemen or freed slaves, was slowly to be achieved.

Semi-legendary tradition regards the main feature of the 'Servian reforms', as they are called after the King, as a decisive break with the old organization as it had been shaped by Romulus, the founder of the city. The early organization formed groups of Roman families into curiae and these in turn into three 'tribes'. Such had been the growth of the city, that by the sixth century some way had to be found to bring into its service the many men who did not belong to the family groups of curiae. So Servius Tullius increased the number of tribes within the city from three to four and created sixteen new tribes outside the city. Next the army was enlarged by drawing into military service all the men of Rome whether they were members of the original clans or merely newcomers who had made their home in Rome. The army was organized into classes, each class subdivided into centuries. There were said to be five classes, into which men were drafted according to the amount of their possessions, since their wealth determined their ability to provide themselves with arms, armour and equipment. The richest men, able to bring a horse (*equus*), called therefore *equites*, stood above the five classes of foot soldiers. The poorest men unable to equip themselves were all put into a group by themselves outside the classes. Men in the first class were the best equipped for war with bronze helmet, round shield, cuirass and greaves or shin-guards, sword and spear. The other classes were less well equipped, the fifth class, it was said by Livy, had only slings and stones. The poorest class of *proletarii* were only called upon in a serious emergency. The older clan or family arrangement by *curiae* lumped the rich and poor together but there was much to be said for this new arrangement. Newcomers, allowed to share in the prosperity of the nation, were also expected to take full part in its defence and to contribute their share of taxation to its support. The well-to-do, in the first three classes, best able to provide their own equipment, bore the brunt of the wars. They had most to lose, and most therefore to defend. The adoption of a property qualification in recruiting the army, dictated by the strictly practical question of military efficiency, also satisfied a sense of social justice. Practical expediency also dictated the very different arrangement of the citizens on a residential classification by 'tribes' for taxation and government. In these very early days of the Republic the tribes made possible orderly gatherings for public purposes such as the choice of a king. Their 'political' functions would be about as rudimentary as those of the medieval Scottish clans. 'The Tribes', said the Roman historian Livy, 'had nothing to do with the distribution and number of the centuries.' The army reorganization was, in short, undertaken for strictly military reasons. It was not until later, when the kings had disappeared, that the 'centuries' of the army began to acquire political importance. Then the emphasis upon property in its composition naturally became evident in its political decisions. The early 'Servian' organization of the Roman abled-bodied men was probably as follows (see also p. 110):

Equites or cavalry	18 centuries
Class I	80
II	20
III	20
IV	20
V	30
All men outside the classes	5
	Total 193 centuries

No doubt because tax-collecting and recruiting for the army demanded it, Servius Tullius is also credited with beginning the first census of Romans and their property which tradition reported as revealing a total of 80,000 male citizens, which means, as a rough guess, a total population of the Roman State of 300,000 to 400,000. This is a high figure in relation to the roughly 340 square miles of land on which they depended for a living. It does not seem possible, from the scanty evidence remaining, to say when the centuries of the army organization began to take part in political matters, although it seems plausible to believe that the creation of the Republic and the expulsion of the kings may well have been a critical time favouring such a development.

Such, in rough outline, seems to have been the extent to which the people began to share in the government of the small and primitive Roman State which it was the task of the Republic to develop. For the long ensuing story it is not possible to do more than to attempt to draw attention to some of the main problems and to the efforts the Romans made to solve them.

The principal trouble was undoubtedly the division of society between patricians and plebeians which seems to have grown after the creation of the Republic (509 B.C.). For when all allowances have been made for errors, imperfect knowledge and the different environment of more primitive times, it seems undoubtedly true that the split in early Roman society was wide, deep, and dangerous. It lasted for too long, and it was resolved not by cordial co-operation but in the sullen defeat of the declining and weakened patricians or aristocrats. Of the many factors which have been brought forward to account for it, the contrast between the privileges of the rich patricians and the lack of opportunities of the poor plebeians has usually had most emphasis. In a simple agricultural community differences arose naturally from the possession of land and the law of debt. The two hung together. The patrician class, who were probably descendants from some specially gifted natural leaders of men, were not merely the wealthier landlords, but they alone, at first, were allowed to lend money at interest. They controlled the government, which meant that theirs was the heavy responsibility for the welfare of the State. Naturally, like most politicians in power, they made the laws to suit themselves. They were able to do so at first with the easy connivance of men of their own class who were the effective part of the popular assembly. Later, when after 287 B.C. their control of the popular assembly was no longer automatically assured, they succeeded in prolonging it by their prestige, influence, and money power.

With all the grasping tenacity of the small hardworking landowner, the patricians saw every movement of the plebeians towards emancipation as a threat to their own property and security. As long as they possessed bands of clients and money with which to equip and reward them they were not likely to forgo the advantages they could get by keeping the plebeians in a subordinate position. Small wonder, therefore, that the whole internal history of Rome in the first 200 years of the Republic was dominated by the bitter opposition of patrician and plebeian. If the story had ended there, it would not have any very special claim to the subsequent attention of mankind. But when the two contending parties had achieved some working understanding and mutual concord the memory of their divisions lingered on to animate new antagonisms between rich and poor and to create political strife every bit as fierce as that which sprang from divisions in a more primitive state of society. Later Roman historians seized upon the story of the struggle of patrician and plebeian, because it seemed to afford a parallel to discords they could not help observing among their own contemporaries. And indeed they well might, for the hard-faced selfishness of the Roman landowners remained as one of their principal characteristics, and the social divisions to which it contributed were symptomatic of cleavages in Roman society which the Roman Republic proved unable to repair.

Cicero had to deal with their descendants, that is to say with those of their descendants who had survived the catastrophic civil wars by which Italy was cursed in his youth. Many of the leading Roman families then lost their best men who might otherwise have survived to help, with Cicero, to save the Republic. His fate, he clearly realized, was bound up with theirs, but few of them seem to have had any sense of political reality or of the danger they were in. Cicero called these survivors of a heroic race 'the fish-breeders' because their pride was not in sustaining the Republic, but in their fish ponds. 'Our leading men,' he said, 'think themselves in the seventh heaven if they have bearded mullets in their fish ponds that will come to hand for food.' When affairs moved to a crisis they were no use at all. It was the old story which we have seen repeated in the face of Nazi and Fascist aggression. Cicero saw that he could expect no help from them. 'They are such fools that they seem to expect that, though the Republic is lost, their fish ponds will be safe.' How similar to the naïve stupidity of a few of the well-to-do who, in 1938 and 1939, thought that their investments and other possessions would remain intact even if the Nazis did take over their country. The story of the Roman Republic provides in a relatively simple form an excellent illustration of the complex and disastrous interaction between private interests narrowly conceived and political privileges irresponsibly exploited.

The Political Organizations of the Roman People: The Comitia

The mass of the common people of Rome never became a democracy if by that word it is meant that their opinions should have been the chief influence in shaping the political destiny of their country. It would be unhistorical and misleading to believe that the Roman people were struggling to develop a democratic form of government such as that imagined by the political theorists of the nineteenth century. Conditions in Italy created special difficulties. The spread of Rome's territories over central Italy meant that a citizen in Ancona would need about four days over difficult mountainous country if he were to come to Rome to vote in the public assembly. Three so-called assemblies of the people were developed as Rome grew in size and influence, each bringing some increase in the political influence of the common man, but the old were never entirely superseded by the new. The Romans did not like giving up old institutions created by their forefathers.

The first assembly of the Roman people, based upon the old Roman family and religious groupings or *curiae* and known in consequence as the *comitia curiata*, consisting of both patricians and plebeians, very early lost any political significance it may once have possessed.

The assembly of Roman men of military age in the army 'centuries' formed a more enduring public assembly (the *comitia centuriata*) by which laws were agreed (down to 287 B.C.) and by which the chief magistrates were elected throughout the Republic. It rested however upon a class distinction, since the army of the early Republic down almost to Cicero's day continued to be grouped into five classes according to the amount of property owned by each soldier. It was this assembly of Roman centuries which, in addition to electing the chief magistrates, used to approve declarations of war and to ratify treaties of peace. To it also a Roman citizen could appeal against sentence of death if convicted in Rome.

The political struggles arising from the inferior position of the plebeians culminated in 287 B.C. in a reform which finally eclipsed the *comitia centuriata* as a law-making body. It was then overshadowed by the body in which the plebeians had long since joined together in defence of their rights and in pursuit of their claim to a greater share in the management of the State.

To achieve such a victory had cost the plebeians a hard struggle. The first step had been the political 'general strike' or exodus from Rome of the discontented plebeians about 494 B.C. That decisive move won for the plebeians the appointment of two special officials chosen by themselves to safeguard their interests. From the beginning of the fifth century B.C. thus dates the extraordinary office of Tribune of the People, protector of the common man of Rome from oppression. The Tribune was not an executive magistrate responsible for positive action. He was a negative force having power to forbid, by his veto, action taken by a magistrate which he considered opposed to the interests of the plebeians. The Tribunes and two men to assist them called Aediles were elected in an assembly of plebeians, the *concilium plebis*. Besides electing these representatives the plebeians went on to talk about other matters of common concern as well. In this way began the public assembly which was to grow until, already 200 years before Cicero's day, it became the body everyone had in mind when they spoke of the People of Rome as a political force.

Very early in the Republic, about 471 B.C., the plebeians were recorded as voting upon a new basis, by 'tribes', that is to say, not upon any division by family or clan (as in the *comitia curiata*) or by wealth (as in the *comitia centuriata*) but according to the district of the city (tribe) in which the voter resided. This system gave a better cross-section of the people, was simpler to organize than the 193 voting centuries of the army centuriate assembly, and unlike the army it could be called together within the city walls without breaking with the law and custom of the Republic.

Summoned under the presidency of a Tribune, the plebeian assembly expressed its view upon the various problems of the day put to it by the Tribune in the form of a *plebiscitum*, from which the modern 'plebiscite' is derived.

Such resolutions of the assembled plebeians had not at first the force of law. They had not been arrived at under the presidency of a magistrate competent to observe the religious ceremonies (the *auspicia*) deemed necessary on all such public occasions. Consequently before a plebiscite could acquire legal force it had to be confirmed with due religious precautions, both by 'the people', that is to say the *comitia centuriata*, and by the Senate. In the early years of the Republic these two bodies like the magistrates also could usually be relied upon to support the patricians. Unless a magistrate proposed a law to the *comitia centuriata*, it was impossible for it to come before them.

Nevertheless plebiscites would express opinions shared by all or nearly all the plebeians and perhaps make rules which they would themselves obey. They were analogous to the rules made by a self-governing association, brotherhood or trade union. The fact that the plebeians, who formed already a majority of the inhabitants of Rome in the fourth century B.C., had declared their wishes through a plebiscite must have strengthened the hands of the Tribunes immensely in their negotiations with Authority represented by the magistrates and the Senate. It became an obvious ambition for the plebeians to ensure that their resolutions should become part of the laws of Rome.

During the consulship of Valerius and Horatius in 449 B.C. the plebeians are said to have achieved this aim and, in addition, to have obtained legal recognition of the sacred character of the Tribunes' office. Their victory was apparent rather than real because it seems to have been subject to the rule that no bills or proposed plebiscites could be put before the tribal assembly of the plebeians without the consent of the Senate. The struggle was prolonged for another 160 years before the plebeians were able to set aside this form of Senate control.

Comitia Tributa

This third assembly of the Roman people as a whole grew out of
the meetings of the plebeians in their *concilium plebis*. There a
man did not have a greater influence if he belonged to an old
Roman family or was a soldier in the army, whether a well-to-do
equestrian or from one of the five army classes of men of property,
so it became more truly representative of the City State.

The area of the Roman State at the end of the fourth century
B.C. covered the Latin and Campanian plains and by 241 B.C. had
spread over the Apennines to the Adriatic shore, thus including
a large part of Central Italy. In that year its organization into
thirty-five local districts or 'tribes' was completed, thereby giving
full voting rights to many dependants on Rome hitherto *cives sine
suffragio*. 'Tribe' was the name given to the men entitled to a
vote in one of these districts or, as we might now call them,
electorates (see diagram, pp. 22, 23).

The urban part of the city of Rome itself was however still
represented by the four districts into which it was traditionally
said to have been divided by King Servius Tullius some 300
years earlier in the sixth century B.C. He had probably made no
distinction between the landowners and the landless in distributing citizens among the tribes, but in 304 B.C. the consul,
Q. Fabius Maximus, a renowned army commander, sorted the
urban residents out of the rustic tribes and lumped them into the
four tribes covering the city area. No matter how many people
filled the city tribes, they could not get more than their four votes
in the popular assembly. This arrangement lasted throughout the
history of the Republic. Even when Roman citizenship was
granted to the whole adult male population of Italy, as it was, in
theory, after the fierce civil war which occurred when Cicero was
a young man (90–89 B.C.), the new voters were allocated among
the thirty-five tribes. By that time membership of a tribe had no
necessary connexion with place of residence, and by that time
also the old rule of 304 B.C. had long been neglected so that the
landowners had included their freedmen and clients, who mostly
drifted to Rome, in their own rural tribes. No development
did more than this to undermine the Republican system of
government.

Now decisions in the Roman assemblies were not arrived at by counting the vote of every voter in a straight fight but by counting the votes of groups, that is to say by *curiae* in the oldest assembly, by centuries in the army assembly, and by tribes in the plebeian assembly. The result was that each of the thirty-five tribes or wards had one vote irrespective of the number of voters who swelled their ranks. The four city wards or tribes were therefore in a permanent minority and the whole voting strength of the citizens went at first to the large class of small landowning farmers spread out over Central Italy.

Frequent wars, a growing population, and a diminishing fertility of the soil had meanwhile been provoking indebtedness and discontent which customary reverence for authority became progressively less able to control. Symptomatic of such troubles was the law of 367 B.C. forbidding any Roman to lease more than 500 *iugera* (312½ acres) of public land and the new rules restricting the right to pasture cattle upon it. In 357 B.C. a tax was put upon masters freeing slaves. The ex-slave was likely to remain under the political influence of his former master as one of his band of 'clients', or subservient hangers-on, free in theory but economically and above all socially dependent upon their patron (p. 134).

The internal state of the city got no better with the turn of the century. The severity of the third Samnite war (p. 12) and the poverty and distress it caused were aggravated by an outbreak of an epidemic or plague. The early years of the third century B.C. were a depressing time for the citizens of Rome.

Their troubles came to a head in 287 B.C. in the last serious civic upheaval before the days of Cicero. Exasperated by long years of stubborn opposition to their demands for greater influence in the affairs of their City State, the plebeians adopted the old device of leaving Rome in a body at the very time when the Greeks in the south of Italy were building up a grand alliance against Rome.

The patricians appointed a Dictator, Q. Hortensius, to effect a settlement. He took the only possible course of accepting the demands of the discontented plebeians. In a law of 287 B.C. which has since borne his name, the centuriate assembly recognized that an assembly organized on a tribal basis was more satisfactory as a law-approving body. For it was agreed that in future plebiscites passed by the tribal assembly were to have the full force of law guaranteed by the Valerian-Horatian law of 449 B.C. without it being necessary for the presiding officer, a Tribune, first to obtain the consent of the Senate. The *comitia centuriata* had been freed from this dependence on the Senate in 339 B.C.

The result of this new legislative independence of the tribal assembly was to strengthen the power and prestige of the Tribunes. Their powers were already great for they could veto any act of the Government, a power backed up by the right to prosecute any magistrate, except a Dictator, who sought to ignore their veto. Probably the Tribunes were then first admitted to the Senate where later, in 261 B.C., they acquired the right to summon it and to preside over its deliberations if the Consuls and Praetors were absent. They thus merged into the political aristocracy.

It seems to have been by this Hortensian law also that the practice arose of forbidding elections and assemblies of the people on market days in Rome. It is true that the country folk were thereby set free to go about their urgent private affairs, including for instance their law-suits, but it also meant that the one really good opportunity of getting something like a representative political assembly of the Roman people was lost. The men from the country could rarely afford to journey specially to Rome to vote.

Democracy in the Roman Republic

It has been rashly and inaccurately said that the *Lex Hortensia* of 287 B.C. marks the final triumph of democracy in Rome. If the fact that there was no general strike or exodus of the plebeians from Rome after that date can be taken as an indication of the satisfaction of the political ambitions of the average Roman, then there is some good reason to suppose that the settlement was indeed a most important landmark; but it was no real democratic triumph, for the Romans never achieved self-government in our modern sense.

The constitutional reform achieved by the *Lex Hortensia* was the nearest approach made by the Roman Republic towards granting adult manhood suffrage to Roman citizens. Not to all the citizens of Italy, despite the fact that their destinies were henceforward to be controlled from Rome. It is true that in Cicero's lifetime many more Italians were given the right to vote, but they were unable to use it effectively. Early hopes of a fruitful partnership between the Senate, the chief magistrates, and the people failed and faded as one generation of Romans succeeded another.

The system of voting by centuries in the *comitia centuriata* did not attempt to give equal weight to the opinions of all citizens, since from the earliest times the landowners and property owners with upwards of 88 votes out of 193 votes were nearly always able to have things their own way. The assembly of tribes marked a distinct improvement from this point of view because within the thirty-five tribes each citizen had an equal vote whether he was rich or poor. It is true that the numbers voting in some of the rustic tribes might be mere fractions of those voting in the four urban tribes but such inequality was incidental to the effort to give representation to all the citizen voters scattered throughout Italy.

After the passage of the *Lex Hortensia* by the *comitia centuriata* that body is not known to have passed another law for 200 years. All legislation was henceforth carried through the tribal assembly, the *comitia tributa*. All that the centuriate assembly was thereafter summoned to do was to elect the chief officers of the State, the Consuls, Praetors and Censors, and to act as a court of appeal in cases where Roman citizens had been condemned to death within the city area. The centuries therefore remained an important influence in the government of Rome despite their loss of legislative power, because great authority in day-to-day matters was left to the chief officers or magistrates. The profound respect which the Romans felt for traditional authority made them quite content to obey their leaders.

The division of the Roman people on a family or 'snob' basis between patrician and plebeian had been very much a division on the basis of rich men against poor men. As time went on the patricians declined in numbers while the plebeians were increasing in numbers and wealth. Wealth was not an automatic passport to political influence in Rome any more than it has been in England. But in the long run it was easier and more natural for the sons of the well-to-do to enter politics and to achieve high office than it was for the sons of poor men to emerge from that obscurity to which society generally relegates the impecunious. When a man had once achieved fame by winning election to one of the chief political offices of the State, his sons and grandsons stood a much better chance of following in his footsteps to become themselves political leaders, than if he had never succeeded in political life. The 'struggle of the orders' as the strife between the plebeians and patricians has been called, had, by the third century B.C., become merely a distant memory. It was succeeded by a new division of society, that between the governing classes or nobility, *nobiles*, and the rest. It was a division that endured as long as the Republic. The task of a 'new man', such as Cicero, trying to make his way to the highest office of State without the memory of distinguished ancestors to help him, was extraordinarily difficult.

How did the Romans manage their popular elective and legislative assemblies? No contemporary, accurate description has survived. There have been many guesses how the centuriate assembly worked after it had been revised and brought into relation with the tribal assembly as it was after 241 B.C. It seems clear that there must have been some close connexion between the two because it would have been no light matter to summon a public assembly and there would be a natural tendency to get as much business done at one meeting as possible. If that is so, then elections to high public office and the passage of laws as well as appeals to the people against sentences imposing fines or the death penalty must have taken place on the same day. An assembly of the people by tribes could have been turned into an assembly by centuries. It is doubtful whether the presiding magistrate ordered any plebeians not strictly entitled to vote in the classes of the centuriate assembly to depart. The important fact seems to be that the basis of the whole political organization of the Roman State was now the tribes. Within each tribe the centuries could be formed into their five classes, according to their wealth. Each of the five classes could in turn be divided into juniors and seniors. In theory therefore it would have been possible in each of the five classes of the *comitia centuriata* to form seventy voting centuries instead of there being merely the thirty-five voting groups of the tribal assembly. The complication did not end there, because in addition to the five main classes there were two standing outside them. The first was that of the *equites* (or 'knights'), every bit as wealthy and distinguished as the first class, and the second was the very much larger class, in fact the largest of all, the poorer, plebeian citizens. There were eighteen centuries of *equites* and but one century of plebeians. Four more centuries, including the trumpeters and horn-blowers, completed the centuriate assembly. The probable arrangement of the assembly has long been a subject of controversy. By some writers it is assumed to have consisted of 373 centuries but it is more probable that the Romans kept to the traditional number of 193 centuries. At the end of the First Punic War in 241 B.C. the 'tribal' organization of the Roman Republic was completed by the addition of two new tribes bringing the total to thirty-five. At the same time it is believed that the *comitia centuriata* was revised and brought into relationship with the tribes. The first class was reduced from eighty to seventy centuries, thirty-five centuries of seniors and thirty-five of juniors.

The numbers in the classes of the first and second class now matched those of the tribes.

Misled it seems by a tendency to view the history of Roman politics as a struggle to achieve a democratic society, many scholars in the last 150 years have regarded the reform of the *comitia centuriata* of 241 B.C. as a milestone in the battle for the political emancipation of the masses. It seems truer to say that it was a change designed to reaffirm and to consolidate the hold of the property-owning classes upon that *comitia* which had the privilege of electing the chief magistrates. Not that the landowners were in any great danger. There was, as yet, no 'popular' movement of poor men led by demagogues against the rich. Rome's victories by the third century B.C. had assured land, slaves and the possibility of increasing wealth to most of its citizens. But this expansion of Rome's territories had the effect of taking more and more of the wealthy classes enrolled in the first and second classes of the *comitia centuriata* farther and farther away from the city. The assembly by tribes, *comitia tributa,* had been enlarged to take account of this development and as a result thirty-one country tribes could always prevail against the four urban tribes into which (since 304 B.C.) all the landless city dwellers were grouped. What more natural than to seek to apply this same new arrangement to the centuries of the *comitia centuriata*? It was in all probability done by summoning the members of the first and second classes of the *comitia centuriata* from their places in the tribal formation and getting their vote by centuries together with that of the eighteen centuries of *equites.* In most elections of magistrates, which was the main work of the *comitia centuriata,* it would not be necessary to ask the third,

fourth and fifth classes to vote at all because the voting strength
of the *equites* and first and second classes together would give a
clear majority, as the following table shows.

REFORMED COMITIA CENTURIATA AFTER 241 B.C.

Equites	18 centuries	
Class I	70 centuries	co-ordinated with
II	35 centuries	the tribes
III	20 centuries	
IV	20 centuries	
V	25 centuries	
	188	
Proletariat, etc.	5 centuries	
	Total 193 centuries	

Although the *equites* and the first and second class had 123
votes out of the total of 193 voting centuries, the numbers of
citizens in those centuries was far less than the numbers making
up the less well-to-do third, fourth and fifth centuries who
together would muster fewer citizens than the largest class of all,
the proletariat in a single century.

The marked bias in favour of wealth and age in the centuriate
assembly is therefore evident. In the earlier period when the centuriate assembly was the sole or the chief law-making body of the
Republic this political bias in favour of the well-to-do had been
more strongly marked. Such had been its position from the foundation of the Republic (509 B.C.) despite the Valerian-Horatian law
(449 B.C.), when the plebiscites of the plebeian council were recognized, and until the Hortensian law (287 B.C.), when it was at last
subordinated to the tribal assembly, an outgrowth of the plebeian
council, and superseded as a legislative body. In the far-off early
years of the Republic the *equites* ('knights') and the first class
alone had an absolute majority over all the rest with 98 out of a
total of 193 votes. If the rearrangement outlined above occurred,
as some writers suppose, at about the end of the First Punic War,
these two groups of the leading centuries had only 88 out of a total
of 193 votes. But with the help of the thirty-five centuries of the
second class they were still in control. Cicero thought this was the
best way to organize a public assembly, 'for when the people are

divided according to wealth, rank and age, their decisions are wiser', he said, in his book on *The Laws*, 'than when they meet without classification in the assembly of tribes'. He, like Plato before him, did not trust the political wisdom of the masses or believe that the largest numbers ought to carry, as an automatic right, the greatest weight in public affairs.

A system which gave eighteen votes to 1,800 rich men and not more than five to some 130,000 poor plebeians is not democracy as the word is understood today. It was a disproportion which grew more pronounced as time went on. Although it does not seem to have been felt as a grievance in the third century B.C., it was liable, in later periods, to provide plausible arguments for demagogues trying to sharpen the division of the poor against the rich, politically powerful Romans. So disproportionate a share of influence invited further evils. When public morality and standards of political conduct had sunk low, unscrupulous men found that they could get themselves elected to office by bribing the members of a relatively few centuries. They had the money and with it they seemed to have everything else. That the whole of Rome was for sale to the highest bidder was the conclusion of Rome's enemy, Jugurtha, an African prince, just before the age of Cicero.

Was the position any better in the assembly of tribes by which all the laws were passed? There again a small number of property owners were able to exert a much greater influence in the affairs of state than could the far larger number of impoverished Romans herded together in the city. This state of affairs arose also from the peculiar nature of the system of assembling the people to vote which the Romans had inherited from their forefathers and had never bothered to change. Their conservatism served them ill.

By Cicero's day the old division of the Roman republic into its thirty-five electoral divisions or tribes had long since lost its original significance. The numbers entitled to vote as Roman citizens had increased from less than 200,000 to nearly a million, a figure which should have been two or three times larger, as a result of the grant of full citizenship rights to the Italian peoples who had revolted against Rome in the Social War (90 B.C. to 89 B.C.) (see p. 210). To vote they had still to be enrolled in one of the thirty-five tribes. The tribes had by this time lost their close connexion with the districts after which some of them had been named and from which they had sprung. From time immemorial Romans had got used to being herded into thirty-five divisions or compartments to vote and they found it convenient to continue to run their electoral machinery that way. Each tribe had its own division of the place at which the meeting was held and the tribes were divided from each other by ropes or temporary fences rather like sheep runs. In order to vote, the electors filed along to a raised exit where stood a 'returning officer' or man to count the votes. After 131 B.C., when oral voting in legislation was discontinued, he counted ballot tablets instead. The secret ballot had first been introduced for elections in 139 B.C. As the people were only asked to approve or reject a new law they either presented a tablet saying they approved the proposal made to them or one that declared that they preferred the existing order of things. When the people voted in centuries the same arrangement was used except that at least seventy divisions were needed for the first class instead of thirty-five to accommodate the two 'half-tribes' of seniors and juniors. The machinery was complicated and it took a good deal of time to operate. To get a decision from the centuriate assembly would take at least five hours, because at least ninety-seven centuries had to vote instead of eighteen tribes before an absolute majority could be achieved. The simpler arrangements for the tribal assembly allowed a vote of the Roman people to be taken in about one hour.

Of these thirty-five tribes, four only represented the city of Rome. The majority vote in the tribal assembly therefore was always in the hands of the thirty-one 'rustic' tribes, at first the small landowners of Central Italy. The city-dwellers and urban proletariat were therefore always swamped by the agricultural middle class. Any plebeian or freedman who was not a freeholder was lumped into the four urban tribes. It did not matter how much the population of the city grew, the city masses got no more than these four votes because the voting was by tribes and not by heads. When therefore the assembly by tribes became the chief law-making authority, and this had been its pre-eminent position for 200 years before Cicero's time, everything depended upon maintaining a stalwart band of prosperous freeholders, alive to their responsibilities, aware of their opportunities and determined to keep Rome the free, just and prosperous State they all believed it to have been in the brave days of old. How all hope of seeing this happy result gradually disappeared is part of the story of the decay and extinction of Roman democracy. To that story many elements contribute. The failure of the small Roman farmer to survive the economic pressure (or 'greed' as reforming Romans called it) of the large cattle-ranchers is one (Chapter 3). Another was the influx into the city of freed slaves and the increase in the numbers of clients dependent upon the rich and the politically powerful who had these subservient dependants enrolled in rustic tribes where they swamped the rural voters who could not leave their farms. Had anything been done to help the dregs of the population in the city to improve their lot in life by land-settlement schemes or by education or by the other means used in social-service schemes today, the results might have been less disastrous. As it was, the character of the citizen voters of Rome had already deteriorated so seriously that by Cicero's day the Republic was finally ruined.

With the expansion of the Roman State, the tribal assembly had become as unrepresentative of the people in whose name it spoke as the centuriate assembly had been at the end of the fourth century B.C.

The influence and future development of the tribal assembly suffered moreover from two other limitations, neither of which might be thought of very great significance, but both of which had profound and unfortunate effects. The first, which has already been emphasized, was that every voter had to come to Rome to vote. It was just as though every British or American voter was required to vote in a General Election in London or Washington. Now it was a settled rule that public assemblies might not be held on market days (p. 154). As the small farmers, who formed the majority of the voters, could not spare time or transport to come often to Rome merely to vote, the roots of the assembly were not sufficiently vigorous. Unless some question of vital concern to themselves arose, the country electors therefore would tend to become merely the farmers able to afford a horse and to leave a bailiff in charge of their farms while they were away. It has been recorded (Chapter 3) how farming around Rome was becoming less profitable because of soil erosion and exhaustion. The growth in wealth of the leading citizens of Rome, all of whom shared directly or indirectly in the plunder and profits which came from Rome's rule of the Mediterranean, was meanwhile producing a boom in real estate all round the capital city. A fashionable country seat had to be at a reasonable distance from the capital. Farming land was consequently being bought up for luxury building and many small farmer voters were either forced to seek land at a greater distance from the *comitia* wherein they should have voted, or to swell the ranks of the unemployed at Rome where the one asset they could sell was their vote. The Italians who were admitted to the citizenship after the Social War had also to come greater distances if they wished to use their vote. Not many of them could afford to do so.

The second weakness of the electoral machinery made this first weakness all the more serious. Legally it made no difference to the results of the voting whether many or few voters came to Rome at election times. Nothing in the laws or constitution of Rome laid down a minimum number of voters, or quorum, necessary to make up a voting tribe or century. Ten men could cast a vote as a tribe and their vote would count just as much as if ten thousand men had voted. This curious fact no doubt owed its justification to the difficulty, recorded above, that the farmers had in attending the public assemblies. Merely a handful of farmers could 'hold the fort' for their tribe as long as no quorum was required. The great utility of this device was that in theory, and very often no doubt in practice also, it prevented the countryman always being swamped by the townsman. At times however, such a state of affairs was an open invitation to bribery and still more to intimidation. The surging urban mobs, for whom the *comitia* was a welcome diversion in a life of poverty and boredom, might be relied upon, in their huge ward groupings, to make life dangerous as well as unpleasant for a few rural voters who might venture to oppose their will. For, despite the fact that the voting in the *comitia centuriata* after 139 B.C. and in the *comitia tributa* after 131 B.C. was by ballot, the small attendance at any one tribe or ward would leave little doubt about the identity of the voters and of their opinions.

The cost of bribing was of small account to the wealthy or reckless candidate for high office, so the *Populus Romanus* fell a prey to a gang of paid nominees of scheming men who did not find it very difficult to rig the political machine and to get the stamp of public approval for their own designs. Bribes were used to swing elections in the *comitia centuriata* and bribes secured the approval or rejection of bills presented to the *comitia tributa*.

Unless we are to disbelieve some very confident assertions made by Cicero to Roman audiences, the people as a whole were not willing supporters of this caricature of democracy. There were, said Cicero, three places where the judgement and the will of the Roman people was made known. First the public meeting summoned by a magistrate (the *contio*, see p. 169), secondly the voting assemblies (*comitia tributa* and *comitia centuriata*) and thirdly the audiences at the gladiatorial combats and public shows. It was easy in all three, he said, to distinguish genuine expressions of opinion from those bought and paid for by agitators. The demagogues, the ambitious schemers, whom we may in the modern idiom translate as gangsters; and their hired gangs, whom we may call thugs, became able to tyrannize over the rest. Cicero claimed, in 56 B.C., that 'apart from the thugs and gangsters everybody in the Republic seems to be of the same opinion'. And so they should have been, for 'at present', he said, 'there is no subject on which the people should disagree with their chosen magistrates and leaders'. In his view the bulk of the people would not respond to bribes and they valued peace and security far more than perpetual brawls, so they did not rally to the gangsters. Cicero contrasted the so-called 'popular' party of his day with truly popular leaders of the past. Tiberius and Gaius Gracchus won their great popular following by the attractiveness of their political programme. They did not owe their fame to a gang of hired fellows. It was different now. Not merely was there no popular movement behind the agitators but they were, he said, 'the object of hatred of the Roman people'.

Why, then, did they prevail?

The answer cannot be found on political grounds, still less upon constitutional grounds alone. The whole temper and condition of Roman social life is involved, as Chapter 18 of this work will try to show. Meanwhile it seems evident that the will of the people never really possessed the force that the Roman constitution assumed it to possess. Dominated at first by the stolid Roman farmers in the thirty-one rural tribes, they had for generations been content on the whole to accept the Senate's lead. When ready consent was not forthcoming, the Senators were often able to carry the day with the votes of the many small men dependent upon them, their families and their friends. If necessary the Senators were ready to bribe sufficient of the remainder to ensure a favourable vote. In the first century B.C., the Senators were finding it more and more difficult to maintain their hold on the assemblies by these means. Many of their humble dependants had been driven off the land to live in idleness in the city and to sell their vote to the highest bidder. It was often a useful vote because unemployed farmers living in Rome still voted with their rural tribe. The Senators now had to compete for it with the business men (*equites*) who, since the second century B.C., were taking an increasingly independent line in politics and who often had very much longer purses than the Senators. Senatorial control was weakened by this disturbance of the old balance of power but the business men gained nothing by upsetting it. In the confusion caused by their quarrels, both they and the Senators, deaf to Cicero's insistent plea for harmony between them, *concordia ordinum*, fell a prey to a third power based upon the political strength of a popular army commander.

This was the breakdown of public life. If every country gets the government it deserves, then Rome by Cicero's time was going downhill. As political morality and politics decayed, bad practices increasingly drove out good.

In Rome it was not so much an example of the political failure of a developed system of democratic government. The state had been prosperous and strong as an oligarchy. It was rather a case of true political democracy failing to develop from a system which offered some good promise of developing it. Above all it was not defects in the machinery of government, but rather deficiencies in the men in charge of it that caused the breakdown.

At length bribery, one of the evils here mentioned, had alone become so great that no laws could restrain it. According to Cicero's brother, it was the chief plague-spot of the State. Men do not resort to such extreme measures for nothing, and the question naturally arises, what were the prizes of political life that drove men to such lengths to win them?

Chapter Seven

THE MAGISTRATES

CIVILIAN officials or Magistrates took the place of the kings who had ruled Rome until about 509 B.C. At first, like the kings before them, they were the centre of gravity in the Republic, but a century or more before Cicero was born they had become the third force in the State, in command for their year of office, it is true, but in fact subject to the controlling influence of the Senate and the People of Rome. The most venerable office of them all was that of the two *Consules* who inherited at first all the civil and some of the religious power of the former kings. The executive power of Rome was then highly concentrated, but very soon, in the first hundred years of the Republic, growth in business and in responsibilities made it necessary to provide the Consuls with helpers and subordinates.

The Consuls did not choose these lesser magistrates. They were elected by the people, just as the Consuls were, and so had an independent standing which meant that the Consuls could not dismiss them. The government of Rome therefore, unlike that of England, did not have a unified or hierarchical administration. The power of the executives, or the magistrates, was at first very great. In the first 150 years of the Republic, the magistrates overshadowed the Senate and commanded the people.

In early times the Consuls had to be relieved of some of the heavy burden of presiding over the day-to-day business of the State. First of all, two *Quaestores* were given the work of looking after the public accounts and dealing with all the miscellaneous details of financial administration. Later the more important office of *Censor* was set up (about 443 B.C.) to discover how many citizens there were and how much property they owned, all information which the government wanted in levying taxes and in mobilizing the army. The Censors also chose new members to fill vacancies in the Senate. Then (367 B.C.) a *Praetor* relieved the Consuls of the complicated and growing legal business of the State by presiding, instead of a Consul, in the law courts. The Praetor and Censors were given powers which made them very nearly equal to the Consuls. This was largely for political reasons. The patricians hoped to keep the offices of Censor and Praetor for themselves. Nevertheless the Consuls could give instructions both to Quaestors and Praetors, although they could not dismiss them, and to hold the consular office remained the chief ambition of every politically-minded Roman. 'The Consul', said Cicero in his book on *The Laws*, repeating what Polybius said about a hundred years earlier, 'has the legal right to enforce obedience from all other officials except the Tribunes.' Other subordinate officers were also created as the growth of public business involved ever-growing business for the State. The *Aediles* (at first plebeian assistants to the Tribunes), whose main job was to supervise the city, its streets, sewers, temples and market-places, and to arrange public shows and festivals, were more important than the Quaestors but less important than the Praetors.

Ancestral custom and the immemorial practice of Rome required that the magistrates of the early Republic should all be drawn from the patrician class. They were unpaid. In the early days of the City State of Rome there was nothing odd in the fact that the leader of the State had to earn the income to support his dignity from his farm. What was of small consequence when the State was small, became of very much greater consequence when Rome grew to be a world Empire and when nobody, save a very exceptional personality, could hope to become a magistrate unless he was rich enough to be able to buy his way into public favour if not by direct bribery, then by providing, as part of his election campaign, lavish public spectacles in which men fought and killed wild beasts or each other in revolting gladiatorial combats. Cicero is one of the rare examples in the later Republic of a relatively poor man who was able to make his way without paying for ruinously expensive large-scale entertainments for the people. He was also exceptional in despising such exhibitions, which, he said, were disgusting.

The Consuls

Two Consuls were elected together by the army assembly of the centuries (*comitia centuriata*). In a succeeding ceremony a special act of the ancient clan assembly (*comitia curiata*) conferred upon them the power of command (*imperium*). It was the nearest thing to absolute power and unified command or to being made a king that the Romans were prepared to consider, except in times of mortal danger when everything was put into the hands of one *Dictator* whose authority was never given for more than a strictly limited period. The two Consuls were each elected for a year's term of office. If for any reason the election could not be held or if both Consuls had died, the emergency period was bridged for five days at a time by a 'temporary king', an *interrex*. Unless he was a plebeian, any Senator might be an *interrex*, for all were thought equal to a king. Public life could not however go on in the same way under the rule of constantly changing *interreges*. The law courts, for example, were then unable to sit and much of the ordinary political life of Rome was suspended. Cicero was to see one such period lasting for seven months in 53 B.C. Clearly no settled administration could then be devised except by the Senate because the chief executive officer was in power for too short a time.

Throughout the Republic, Consular dignity remained the summit of any Roman's political and social ambition. There was no other career offering anything like a similar reward to energy, ability and enterprise. Politics was the one supremely honourable profession and to be Consul was its highest prize. In essence it was a link between Senate and People, responsible to both, an unenviable situation between an upper and a nether millstone. The Consul met the Senate because he was its presiding officer (unless away from Rome with the army, when the Praetor would preside). The Senate could not meet for public business unless summoned by a Consul or Praetor. After 287 B.C. a Tribune might also convene the Senate in the absence of these senior magistrates. The Consul was in the Senate but not, as the British Prime Minister with his Cabinet is in the House of Commons, actively steering and guiding the business of the legislature. The Consul was there quite as much to ask advice and to listen, as to express his own opinion. He could not suggest to the Senators what line of action they should approve, far less could he try to force any line of action upon them by demanding a vote of confidence with its implied promise or threat of resignation or by dissolving the assembly if he met with a refusal.

Nevertheless the Consul was the figure upon whom all the business of the State centred. He received ambassadors and conducted them to the Senate. Letters, reports and dispatches from allies and foreign powers, from Roman generals and governors, would be transmitted to the Senate through the Consul. Throughout the Republic the Romans remembered past happenings less by the date on which they occurred after the founding of the City, A.U.C. I, or 753 B.C. in our chronology, than by the names of the Consuls who were in office at the time in question.

But the Consul's authority was cramped not merely because all important decisions were taken by the Senate, but because he did not rule alone. Two Consuls were appointed together at the same time with the same powers. Judged by modern ideas of government and organization, this is an almost incredible state of affairs. Both Consuls obviously could not rule together, but this practical difficulty was met by their alternating one after the other. The senior Consul is supposed to have taken the first month of duty. Since their powers were equal and in theory supreme, each could stop the other taking any action he did not like. If a Consul cherished ideas of his own with a determination to get things done or to spend money in ways which found no favour among the Senators, it was not very difficult for them to stop him. Simply to realize that he had the Senate against him would normally be enough. Hardy spirits prepared to defy the Senate would soon find other obstacles in their path – opposition from their colleague, from other magistrates, or from the religious officials.

So much for the upper millstone. It was weighty enough. Below were the people. To them the Consul appeared a highly dignified figure. In Republican Rome where it was a settled rule that everyone should dress plainly and in the same style of white toga, the Consul stood out from the crowd in his distinctive toga with its broad purple band, his scarlet shoes and his escort of twelve lictors each bearing the emblem of State, the axe bound with rods. These were the celebrated *fasces*, symbolic of the power once held to beat and behead Roman citizens without trial, and fittingly therefore revived by Mussolini in the twentieth century as both the label and the emblem of Imperial Italy.

No public assembly of the *comitia centuriata* to elect magistrates or to agree to laws could lawfully be held in the early days of the Republic unless summoned by the Consul (or the Praetor). The proceedings began with ceremonial observances which the

Consul conducted by virtue of religious power inherited by him from the kings. The Consul could also, if he wished, bring the people together less formally to hear his report on affairs of State, to prepare them for the decisions to be requested from them a little later in their formal voting assembly, to explain administrative tasks to them and to get their help in taking the census, for instance. Such an informal meeting was called a *contio* to distinguish it from the formal assembly or *comitia*. In those days, long before the development of newspapers and radio, the *contio* was the only direct method of political education and enlightenment at the disposal of the Roman people. They were able, in a *contio*, to ask questions.

The public assemblies summoned to consider proposed changes in the law were much more in the Consul's hands. The citizens were summoned to hear his proposals and to say 'yes' or 'no' to them without debate. The Consul would previously have got the Senate's agreement to the way in which the matter was to be laid before the public, so his own part in the proceedings was fairly well determined for him in advance. Nevertheless his must have been an exacting and strenuous duty. It was no light task to mediate between a supposedly sovereign people and a supreme deliberative assembly, particularly when that assembly, the Roman Senate, did not depend upon popular votes for its existence.

If the people took a violent dislike to a Consul they could attack him through their Tribunes. He could not be put on trial before the people while still in office, but he could be compelled to abdicate and then be tried. If he came to trial his judges would have been Senators until 122 B.C., when Gaius Gracchus gave the business men judicial privileges. There was no regular method of calling him to give an account of his year's work, although it was customary for the retiring Consul to address the people on laying down his office. Cicero was very grieved, and rightly so, when his political opponents put up a Tribune to forbid him to speak to the people after his momentous year as Consul in 63 B.C.

Consuls possessed very much greater powers outside Rome, especially in time of war. For the Consuls were the Commanders-in-Chief and in the many wars of the Republic they were in the field at the head of the Roman army. Wars were frequent and they immensely strengthened the Consuls' power. 'Men do not rashly resist the powers of the Consuls,' said the Greek historian Polybius at the time of the Third Punic War, 'because one and all may become subject to their absolute authority on a campaign.' The Romans certainly could not be accused of any lack of faith in the democratic principle of choosing their leaders by election. They committed supreme command, for the short space of a year at a time, to two men who were supposed to combine the gift of political leadership with the skill in war on land or sea of the Combined Chiefs of Staff. The surprising thing is not the failure which this apparently rash proceeding involved, but the extent of its success. The failures were serious enough.

The principle of alternate rule still held good in war as in peace. When the two Consuls were both with the army, unless they could agree between themselves which should be Commander-in-Chief, the almost farcical situation developed in which one Consul commanded on one day and the other the next day. It seems highly probable that the battle of Cannae (216 B.C.), a defeat which very nearly brought the State to ruin, was lost mainly because of this divided command. Later, Rome had sufficient armies in the field to provide each Consul with an independent command of his own, so that particular difficulty ceased to occur.

Supreme though they were in the field, they did not themselves raise troops or lead them out to fight without the authority of the Senate. 'Without a decree of the Senate,' said Polybius, 'they can be supplied neither with corn nor clothes nor pay, so that all the plans of a Commander must be futile if the Senate is resolved either to shrink from danger or hamper his plans.'

Leaders of Rome, the Consuls were at first necessarily chosen exclusively from patrician families. To break down this tradition and to secure election to the consulship was an obvious ambition for every plebeian as their class gained in wealth. Before they could succeed, however, they had to overcome deep-rooted jealousy founded on established customs and rights. Religious scruples which the patricians either felt or imagined that they felt on the subject of plebeians performing State ceremonies seem also to have been made an obstacle. The gods, it was argued, would either not respond or else react vindictively towards any pollution of Roman religious observances by plebeians. The second team of *decemvirs* in 450 B.C. (p. 197) no doubt on this ground forbade marriage between patrician and plebeian, because a plebeian could not meddle with the religious ceremonies carried out every day before the domestic altar in the home of every Roman patrician.

The plebeians attacked both their exclusion from the consulship and the marriage bar. The patricians put up a determined fight and gave way piecemeal only when they saw that resistance was hopeless. In 445 B.C. they yielded on the marriage question. It was the least dangerous concession, because Roman law gave patrician fathers absolute power over their sons and daughters. Their exclusiveness served them ill and was the main cause of their steady decline in numbers.

After accepting the possibility of acquiring plebeian sons-in-law or daughters-in-law, the patricians strove in vain to preserve their monopoly of the consulship, but they were forced to a compromise. Sooner than allow a plebeian to sit in a Consul's seat they changed the name of the office whenever there were plebeians to fill it.

Instead of the two Consuls, the Senate was to decide that a varying number of three to eight mixed patrician and plebeian 'military tribunes with consular powers' were to serve (444 B.C.). This arrangement lasted for seventy-seven years (until 367 B.C.). Very few plebeians enjoyed this honour. The patricians gave away as little as they could and some of the Consuls' powers were taken away to create the new office of Censor to which patricians alone were admissible.

The Censors

Taking the census, or numbering the people, was one of the chief duties of the Consuls, but it was one they had tended to neglect in the many other preoccupations of their office. From early times some strong superstitions seem to have been attached in the public mind to any form of census, each of which had to be followed by a solemn 'purification'. Being of a religious nature it would have been a ceremony which plebeians could not conduct. When therefore the patricians agreed to a change in the Consul's office in 445 B.C., they sought at the same time to create a new monopoly for themselves in the office of Censor. Two Censors were appointed in 444 B.C. and thereafter. Their main duty was to take a census every five years, and to use its results to reshape the political organization of the Roman Republic. The task did not take them five years, but about eighteen months, the length of ti.ne for which they themselves held office. However, there was no need for a more frequent census, so there was no point in holding more frequent elections for Censors. Their duties, like the duties of the other magistrates, must have required a staff of clerks and assistants, but of them we know nothing. It seems that the Censors, like the other magistrates, were expected to find their own clerks and assistants from their household slaves and freedmen. So there was no real civil service in the Roman Republic. The practical results of the census were of obvious and immediate importance to every Roman. It discovered when he was of military age. It found out what he owned and that helped to decide the army 'century' in which he should serve and vote (in the *comitia centuriata*). It did not automatically decide the matter because the Romans had no compunction about refusing to allow criminals or unworthy men to vote. It was easier to pick out and exclude such men in a small City State, which Rome originally was, where the character of the citizens would be more easily and generally known, than it would be in the huge cities and States today.

The Censors were also responsible after about 312 B.C. for keeping the register of the Senators. They were able to strike off the register any Senators who had broken the law or had been guilty of an offence against morality. The censors also had the powers formerly exercised by the kings and later by the Consuls of nominating men to fill vacancies in the Senate. This tremendous power of saying whether a man was fit to be a Senator had consequences which influenced all the subsequent history of the Republic. For the Censors seem early to have given preference to men who had held a magistracy. This not unnatural method of selection had the effect, however, of creating a new social class made up of the families of the men who had been magistrates. These families later were to take the place of the old patrician families in the class divisions of the Roman State. Except in matters of finance, where they let out State contracts for tax-collecting, for public works such as building and repairing aqueducts and for the use of national resources, the Censors did not intervene in shaping the policy of the State. In Cicero's day the office was suspended by the Dictator Sulla and Censors were no longer regularly elected between 82 and 70 B.C. Sulla saw to it that the number of ex-magistrates was then automatically sufficient to fill any vacancies which occurred in the Senate.

The Quaestors

The Consuls were early provided with junior magistrates bearing the same title as military paymasters (Quaestors) to help with detailed administrative work. Election to the office of Quaestor was the first stepping-stone in a political career. As their title suggests, their duties were principally the business of supervising the collection of taxes and of making payments. In addition to being custodians of the State's Treasury they kept many of the official records which were stored in it – copies of laws, decisions of the Senate, and other State documents. They also had clerks and assistants, but if, as seems probable, they were provided by the State, we do not know how they were recruited or paid. Possessing no *imperium* or military powers, Quaestors did not have an escort of lictors. Neither were they elected by the same body of voters as the Consuls, but by the *comitia tributa*. Plebeians were not eligible for the office until 421 B.C. and none seem in fact to have been elected until 409 B.C.

There were at first two Quaestors, but four were appointed after 421 B.C. and the number was later increased again. Sulla raised the number to twenty each year and provided them with an automatic entry into the Senate. By this means the Senate was kept up to strength.

The Praetors and the Development of Roman Law

The Praetor was mainly, but not entirely, engaged in legal business. The patricians created this new office in 367 B.C., the year in which they were forced to agree to admitting plebeians to one of the two consular offices. They sought to counter-balance that new plebeian gain by setting up a new and influential magistracy reserved for members of their own class. Their case was largely based upon plebeian ignorance of the law, a subject with which at first none but patrician priests and Consuls might meddle. It was a thin pretext because there was no such thing as a legal profession in those early days, and the men elected as Praetors were not chosen specially on account of their knowledge of the law. After 367 B.C., when the Consuls ceased to preside in the law courts, the Praetors took over most of that work. After election by the assembly of the centuries for their year of office the Praetors began at some later period to declare the rules of law which they intended to follow. During their year's service they would naturally have to make decisions upon disputed points of legal principle and practice. In these two ways the Praetors laid down the law and so began the slow building of that great body of Roman law and Roman legal practice to which many countries today owe the core of their legal system. Then also began the system of trial by judge and jury which has since done so much to guarantee the lives, liberty and property of Englishmen in particular and much of the rest of mankind in general.

A more remarkable testimony to the Roman faith in law and due legal process as the right remedy for disputes was the creation in 242 B.C. of the office of second Praetor to deal with cases in which foreign residents and visitors to Rome were involved. His title was *Praetor peregrinus*. With the establishment of this new judge, the Romans laid the foundations for a new view of justice. Instead of regarding their law as applicable only to Roman citizens, they extended it to protect private persons as such. By recognizing the need to allow for the rights as well as the different customs of foreign peoples the Romans paid tribute to that Rule of Law, the elaboration of which is their greatest, because their most enduring, contribution to human civilization. The fact that the United Nations of the twentieth century have had to rally all their forces in defence of this great principle of human progress against tyrannical totalitarian prison-states, is the best measure of its meaning for human society.

The Praetor, like the Consul, stood above all the other regular magistrates because the *imperium* was conferred upon him. He was more than a judge. He could, if necessary, owing to the absence of a Consul, take the Consul's place as convener and presiding officer of the Senate or assembly of the people. He had an escort of two lictors, each carrying the axe and rods symbolic of the power of life and death. He could, therefore, take a military command as no other magistrate except the Consul was empowered to do without special appointment. Consequently

Praetors were sent to administer law in the provinces. After their first year's service they could be sent to serve in another province as propraetor. In 227 B.C. an additional Praetor was appointed to go to Sicily and another to Sardinia, both won from the Carthaginians. The growth of business abroad and at home required more administrators and after 199 B.C. six Praetors were usually elected. Two Praetors went to Spain to govern the two provinces of 'Nearer' and 'Further' Spain into which the Peninsula was divided after it had been won from Carthage in the Second Punic War. The continued expansion of Rome meant that more Praetors were needed. In or around 80 B.C. there were eight. Julius Caesar created twelve and later sixteen, but he did it to swamp the Senate with new men rather than to provide urgently needed public officials.

The Dictator

The Dictator and his Master of Horse, who naturally possessed the *imperium*, were never appointed except in times of grave national crisis resulting from war on Italian soil and then only for six months at a time. Over forty Dictators are recorded between 363 and 300 B.C., very few thereafter.

The supreme power of the Dictator was shown by his escort of twenty-four lictors, double the number allowed to a Consul. They bore the *fasces*, the axe projecting from a bundle of rods. Curiously however no Dictator was allowed on horseback in Rome. He would then have seemed too like a king. Moreover he was not allowed to go outside Italy. No military Dictator was appointed after 202 B.C., after the battle of Zama, although in Cicero's time dictatorial powers were assumed by Sulla and by Julius Caesar.

The Curule Aediles

The compromise solution of 367 B.C. creating a plebeian Consul and a patrician Praetor was said to have brought such relief that to celebrate it another day was added to the Great Games, until then three days of public holiday and rejoicing.

The story goes, but it sounds suspiciously like patrician propaganda, that the two assistants of the Tribunes of the People, the Aediles, who should have supervised this new event, would not do so, whereupon young men of patrician rank volunteered for the work and were elected as Aediles with a dignity superior to that of their plebeian colleagues. They were promoted to a special chair of office, the Curule chair, or chariot seat, in which none but Consuls, Praetors or Dictators could sit. They also had the privilege of being allowed a special mark of rank on their toga, the purple stripe of a magistrate on the *toga praetexta*. They did not possess *imperium* and were not therefore provided with any lictors as escort. Their main duties were to aid the Consul in executing the law on such questions as prosecuting offenders against the money-lending laws, profiteers in the grain trade, and those guilty of damage to public property. They pursued non-political offenders and exercised police powers in matters such as market control. They had nothing like a regular police force under their command. Republican Rome knew neither police nor firemen. Upon the Aediles also rested the responsibility of preserving Rome from famine by ensuring the grain supply.

The difference in grade between these patrician Curule Aediles and the plebeian Aediles was naturally unwelcome to the plebeians, and it presented them with another exclusive and privileged position for which they were bound to fight. Their victory was rapid, for it was soon agreed that plebeians should be eligible for the office every other year. Except for their more dignified trappings, the Curule Aediles differed little from their plebeian colleagues.

Tribunes of the People

The Tribunes of the People, whose political history reached back almost to the first years of the Republic, were not magistrates, but their peculiar authority to intervene in the name of the people against the executive power of the State entitles them to be regarded as a kind of 'counter-magistrate' (see p. 150).

In the light of later developments in the Roman Republic and from what we know of the general problem of organization and administration, the office of Tribune might have been expected to lead at once to chaos. 'How much will you give me for withholding my veto?' seems on the face of it to be a form of blackmail which the inviolable Tribunes would always have been able to apply with success.

In fact matters rarely worked out that way. After about 457 B.C. there were ten Tribunes spread over the city so that their ever-open doors could be easy of access to citizens in trouble. Any one of the ten could veto the acts of the remainder, so one way of countering their influence was to try to play off one Tribune against another. The religious sanction possessed by the Consuls and Praetors might also be invoked against the Tribunes in the early days of the Republic, for the Tribunes could not take the auspices.

Later, about 150 B.C., two laws known as the Aelian and Fufian laws seem to have given the senior magistrates the right to dismiss plebeian assemblies and, simply by declaring unfavourable omens, to nullify much of the powers of the Tribunes. Cicero regarded these laws as 'a most holy means of weakening and repressing the fury of the Tribunes'. He was to see them swept away in 58 B.C. by his enemy Clodius after they had been shamefully misused by the governing classes. For over 300 years before Cicero's troubled times the Tribunes seem to have worked without any very serious friction. Ancestral custom, a genuine will to co-operate in sustaining the State, may have brought about this satisfactory state of affairs quite as much as the ingenuity of the governing classes in thwarting the Tribunes. Social harmony cannot have been a complete illusion during the centuries in which the Senate trusted the Tribunes of the People to propose new legislation to the *comitia tributa*.

The Tribunes helped to maintain social harmony because they acted as a kind of safety-valve. Cicero recognized this when in his book on *The Laws* he said that 'by having a leader such as a Tribune, the people sometimes behave more temperately than if they had none at all'. His words show that the Tribunes were by no means exclusively negative forces. Conscientious Tribunes helped the magistrates by indicating sore spots and points of friction in the body politic and they were able to explain complicated state policies to the people and to get their support for them. Their membership of the Senate and important position there (p. 154) tended to make them more aristocratic in outlook.

There is no official in modern England or in the United States comparable to the ancient Tribunes of Rome. The present-day powers of trade-union leaders may both in their positive aspect as responsible leaders of the workers co-operating with the management of industries and in their negative aspect as strike-leaders appear as a superficial analogy. But they have no legal right whatever to veto the actions of public officials, which is what the Tribunes could do, although they have often created embarrassments for the governments of their countries by inflicting loss and hardship on their fellow countrymen by strike action holding up commercial, industrial and transport undertakings.

Nowadays Her Majesty's Inspectors of Factories and Workshops, Ships, Schools, Mines, and Quarries and other administrative officials of the Welfare State, acting under Acts of Parliament and backed therefore by the police and the law courts, provide a protective network shielding the British public from wrongs and oppression far more effectively and completely than the Tribunes were ever able to help the Romans.

With the creation of the Praetor and the Curule Aediles the ranks of the chief magistrates of the Roman State as they existed in Cicero's day were complete. Except for some increase in their number to cope with the great growth of State business, no new rivals to them were created. The framework of the Republican constitution which Cicero so loyally sought to preserve at the cost of his life had therefore been determined in all its essentials by 367 B.C., at a time when Rome was a very small power in Italy. Cicero therefore was born into a stable political society whose chief officials had a continuous history of over two and a half centuries, considerably longer that is to say than that of the office of British Prime Minister, and longer still than the office of President and Secretary of State of the United States.*

Politics and elections in Rome did not merely revolve around the election of senior magistrates and the passing of laws. Although by Cicero's time the chief religious officials and members of the high priestly organizations no longer possessed the outstanding position they had once occupied in the public life of Rome, their power and influence were by no means negligible. Cicero himself was ambitious to be among their number and proud indeed he was of the distinction when at last he succeeded in achieving it.

* The various grades of the more important magistrates and their relationships are shown on Chart XIII in the first edition of this book.

Chapter Eight

RELIGIOUS OFFICIALS

Priestly 'Colleges'

JUST as the two Consuls who took over the government of Rome from the kings did not long remain the only important magistrates or rulers of Rome, so the chief religious official (*Rex Sacrorum* or King for Sacrifices), who was then given religious powers formerly in the hands of the kings, also soon lost them to priests organized as colleagues in bodies known as 'colleges'. These were the Pontiffs, the Augurs, and the keepers of the Sibylline Books, all of them men able to exert a very considerable influence in political affairs by playing upon the superstitious fears by which the simple Roman agriculturists were so easily to be swayed.

Of all the arguments used against the political ambitions of the plebeians, none was more frequent or more effective than that to grant them would endanger religion. Consequently the patricians retained their monopoly of the religious offices with the utmost tenacity, soon to be matched by the equal determination of the plebeians never to admit their own inferiority in the sight of the gods of Rome.

The Sibylline Books

The promise of one consulship, secured in 367 B.C., was more than a political victory for the plebeians. As one argument against their becoming full Consuls had been the religious argument, the plebeians could claim that their victory not only gave them the Consulate, but gave them entry to other places also where hitherto religion had been the only barrier. In this way they began to share equally with patricians in the college of ten men responsible for the guardianship of the Sibylline books. A Sibyl was a maiden supposed to be inspired by the gods with the power of foretelling fate. Great regard was therefore paid to her utterances. At Cumae in Italy, so the legend reports, dwelt a Sibyl of great renown. It was from her, so it was said, that the last king of Rome bought the Sibylline books, an ancient collection of Greek oracular utterances. The well-known legend, with acute and perennial testimony to the reluctance and the consequent cost with which mankind chooses the path of wisdom, records how the king refused to buy the books when they were first offered because he hoped to get them cheaper. The Sibyl thereupon burned three of the books and demanded the same price for the six remaining; this also was refused, whereupon three more were burned, and then the original price was paid by the King for the remaining three. The books became treasured possessions, because they were supposed to contain the key to the Fate of Rome. Very much might depend upon the interpretation placed upon texts selected at a critical juncture, and it was to this fact that the political importance of the office of Keeper of the Sibylline books was due. The books were reverently guarded and consulted in all emergencies of the Roman State and the practice had not ceased in Cicero's day. In the fateful year 83 B.C., the year that Sulla returned from the East to wreak vengeance on the popular party of Marius (see p. 214), the Roman Capitol was struck by lightning. The venerable temple of Jupiter, which had stood as an impressive symbol of the might of Rome from the earliest years of the Republic, caught fire and was consumed. With it perished the Sibylline books. They were replaced and the substitutes went on serving the old purpose, although the attention paid to them gradually diminished. It was just as well, because they seem to have been a hotch-potch of nonsense and the fact could not be concealed. 'Whoever was the author of these Sibylline oracles,' said Cicero, making it pretty plain that he did not believe the hoary legend about the inspired Sibyl, 'they are very ingeniously composed, since as all specific definition of person and place is omitted, they in some way or other appear to predict everything that happens. Besides, the Sibylline oracles are involved in such profound obscurity that the same verses might seem at times to refer to different subjects.'

Religion, for the average Roman, was above all a personal affair, centring round his own family, fields, and fireside. There were no churches, no regular weekly services, no ethical or moral teaching through sermons, and no scriptures. The organized, official or State aspect of Roman religion was not therefore of great significance for the daily lives of the masses, as will be explained in Chapter 17. Its political importance was nevertheless considerable. None of the religious offices or colleges at Rome was of greater account than that of the Pontiffs (*Pontifices*). With the Chief Pontiff (*Pontifex Maximus*) at their head they exercised great influence in all departments of Roman life. They were the highest priestly college in the State and theirs was the awesome and responsible duty of ensuring both that the gods were not offended and that their will was made known.

Everything that amongst an ignorant and superstitious people could be supposed to depend upon supernatural powers came under their control. This priestly order had an unknown origin of immemorable antiquity. Modern scholars have detected among the recorded practices of the Roman priests survivals of pagan rites from the successive ages of stone, of bronze, and of iron. The priestly order was at first self-perpetuating, appointments to it being made by the Chief Pontiff. Needless to say, membership was confined to patricians.

After the manner of such bodies they clung tenaciously to their rules, forms of prayer and all the rest of the ritual to which they had devoted their lives. Along with their records, all were closely guarded secrets which they would divulge to nobody, least of all, in the early days of the Republic, to the despised plebeian. If the Pontiffs had exercised none but strictly priestly functions, the plebeians might not have felt a resentment greater than that which exclusion and its presumption of inferiority would naturally inspire. But the early supremacy of ritual law over private law had left the Pontiffs in control of marriages, adoptions, burials and other events of life having ceremonial aspects. More than this, they were invested with wide powers over customary law, powers which survived from primitive times when the very greatest importance was attached to the choice and order of words and phrases. Cicero had often heard his old teacher, Quintus Mucius Scaevola, say that no one could be a good Pontiff without a knowledge of the civil law. The practical, relatively unemotional character of the early Romans is seen in the great attention they gave to the formal side of religion, particularly in the correct employment of formulas sanctioned by long usage. Not religious observances alone and forms of prayer, sacrifice, and celebration, but dedications, consecrations, and solemn vows could not be undertaken without priestly aid. Such no doubt was the origin of the traditional and unquestioned monopoly of legal forms and the rules of law still enjoyed in historic times by the Pontiffs. The possession of property usually involved the performance of some religious rites. The law of property therefore resulted from the authority of the Pontiffs, as Cicero said in his book on *The Laws*, 'in order that the performance of the rites may be imposed upon those to whom the property passes, so that the memory of them may not die out at the death of the father of the family'. The Pontiffs consequently had attempted 'to fix with exactness the persons who are bound to perform the rites'.

When therefore the plebeians first secured a statement of the law of Rome in the celebrated Twelve Tables in 451 B.C. (see p. 194) they certainly won a victory over the patricians, but above all it was a victory over the priestly class. In the same year as that in which plebeians won the right to become Consuls and joined the keepers of the Sibylline Books (367 B.C.), the creation of a civil Praetor further weakened the hold of the Pontiffs by striking at the tradition that none but priests could be trusted with public law. There was nothing to prevent Pontiffs becoming Senators and some of them were to be found in that august body. They ruled over the calendar and had the task of adjusting the number of days in a month and of deciding whether there should be an additional month in any one year. The duty had been given them by law in 191 B.C. They do not seem to have been particularly successful. Indeed it was alleged that their errors had sinister motives and that 'either from hatred or from favour to cut short or to extend the tenure of office, or that a farmer of the public revenue might gain or lose by the length of the year ... they deliberately made worse what had been entrusted to them to set right'. The Roman year consisted of merely 355 days, so constant adjustment in the calendar was inevitable. Sometimes it was not undertaken, with the result that it was midwinter in the month which should have been spring. Julius Caesar finally put matters to rights in 46 B.C. when he was Dictator by introducing the new calendar of 365 days to the year, since known after him as the Julian calendar. To do so the year had to be extended by three whole months to adjust the calendar to the sun. Julius Caesar's calendar remained unaltered in Europe until A.D. 1582 and in Great Britain until A.D. 1752. The first day, or Kalends, of January A.U.C. 709 in Caesar's new calendar is the 1st January 45 B.C. in our chronology.

Before the Julian calendar, nobody knew for certain how many days there would be in the year, when the public festivals would fall, what days were of good omen and what of bad omen for the conduct of business. To a people so bound by religious observances as the Roman farmers, it was most disconcerting to find that festivals and ceremonies connected with the harvests and other events of the farming year came at the wrong time. The effect of such uncertainty upon public and private affairs and the manner in which that uncertainty could be exploited to check plebeian ambitions and activities was another natural source of complaint. The plebeians had therefore strong motives for wishing to gain admission to the college of Pontiffs.

The Augurs

Plebeians also wanted to become Augurs. This college, which was as ancient as that of the Pontiffs, specialized in what was thought to be the science of interpreting signs given by the gods for the guidance of mankind in such natural phenomena as thunder, lightning, and the flight of birds. These were the auspices. Every Roman used to believe in the deep significance of such events. There were degrees of knowledge, and when it was a question of interpreting omens before holding elections, fighting battles or conducting other forms of public business, the task of taking the auspices was reserved for the chief magistrate in charge who might call upon the Augurs for their expert aid. If the magistrates wished to suspend any proposed course of business all they had to do was to find and declare that the omens were unfavourable. Omens were not hard to find or to invent.

Roman history is full of portents and manifestations from the heavens. At all times of distress and danger the signs and wonders became more extravagant and the means of averting the disasters they were supposed to threaten grew more elaborate. Flaming torches and phantom navies would be seen in the sky. Statues and oxen were reported to have spoken. Showers of blood, of stones, of flesh which was seized by an enormous number of birds, were said to have rained down from heaven. Unnatural births, strange defects in the sacrificial animals, caused great alarm. Other mysterious occurrences excited still greater dismay. Automatic movements of the statues of gods and goddesses, Mars shaking his spear, shields sweating blood, blood in sacred streams, blood from newly harvested corn, double moons, sudden shrinkage in the sacred books and votive tablets, all these and many more were reported and widely circulated at various times. Not all were believed but sufficient bewildered folk were found, particularly in a dangerous crisis, to create conditions threatening panic. In that state it was not difficult to secure the submission of the common man and to involve him in eager contribution to those propitiatory sacrifices which, so the priests declared, were alone able to avert the disasters so obviously threatening the State.

The notion, widespread in free-thinking and Jacobin circles in the eighteenth and nineteenth centuries, that the priesthood is a means of keeping the people in subjection, was no novelty to some shrewd observers in ancient Rome. The intelligent Greek, Polybius, who had witnessed the effect of wild rumours during his enforced residence in Rome in the first half of the second century B.C. (167–151 B.C.), came to the conclusion that superstition maintained the cohesion of the Roman State, and he agreed that it was necessary because the multitude had to be kept in submission by invisible terrors and their accompanying pageantry. 'The greatest advantage which the Roman system has over others', he wrote, 'seems to me to be in their grasp of religious questions. What the rest of the world condemns, I mean superstition, is a cementing force with them. This side of Religion has reached such a state of melodramatic pomp with them, both in private and in civic life, that further exaggeration is out of the question. ... I regard it as an instrument of government. ... Every democracy is fickle, full of irrational passion, anarchical greed and violence. Your only means of holding it together are the fears of the unseen world and suchlike melodramatic show.' In addition to religious practices having to do with the gods and goddesses and with the unseen forces of nature, magic rites conferring occult powers on human beings without any intervention by the gods also strongly influenced religious behaviour.

In time the people of Rome learned to distrust many of the so-called manifestations from on high. The plebeians in particular had only too often seen how these real or pretended religious phenomena could be used to prevent them getting what they wanted. The patricians when faced with the obstinate claims of the plebeians 'called to their aid, not men alone, but gods'. They made a religious question of elections. If a severe winter had been a divine warning, a succeeding pestilence had been a judgement. They would declare that it had been found in the Book of Fate that the gods must be appeased. So the plebeians would be told before an election that the auspices showed that the gods deemed it an insult that the highest offices should be made common and the distinction of classes thrown into confusion.

Before long such devices proved fatal to the religious claims on which they were founded. After the Roman State had survived numerous plebeian Consuls, Censors and other magistrates who had helped to conduct religious ceremonies, it was no longer easy to pretend that they could not become Pontiffs and Augurs. The plebeians asked their patrician rivals, 'Who has ever had occasion to regret the vows which have been made on behalf of the State by so many plebeian Consuls and Dictators before taking command of their armies or engaging in battle?' They could and did claim that if a count was made of the commanders since war was first waged under the auspices of plebeians, there would be found to be as many triumphs as commanders. The patrician opposition stuck to their old line, but it was no longer pressed with any intense conviction or hope of success.

Tradition relates that one of the last political monopolies of the Pontiffs had already been broken (304 B.C.) through the persevering efforts of the son of a former slave. With the aid or connivance of his patron, the far-seeing would-be reformer Appius Claudius, he made it his business to attend court proceedings long enough to note down and publish the procedural forms and language used there by the Pontiffs. The game was up, their secrets were out, and the patricians soon had to give way. After 300 B.C., five out of nine Pontiffs and four out of eight Augurs were thenceforward drawn from the ranks of the plebeians. In the third century, about 230 B.C., the *Pontifex Maximus* became a public official elected by seventeen tribes chosen by lot from the thirty-five. Other priestly offices before long were filled in the same way. It is difficult to believe that much of the mysterious side of public religion could long have survived this change.

Other Religious Offices

Patricians retained their monopoly of some religious posts, possessing no political influence – that of the *Rex Sacrorum* (King for Sacrifices), the *Flamines* (each dedicated to the service of one god) and the *Salii* (a college of priests maintaining old rites, which included an elaborate procession through the city and ceremonial war dances in March, month of Mars, God of War, and the traditional time for beginning spring campaigns).

By Cicero's time, the decay of the State religion of Rome in the sophisticated society circles, as well as among the mixed population of the city, had gone so far that priestly influence in politics was almost at an end. Almost, but not quite. It may be thought that so cultivated, philosophic and commonsense a man of the world as Cicero would not waste much time upon the Sibylline books and the science of augury, but on the contrary he and his fellow Senators had to spend a good deal of time in January 56 B.C. considering whether a quotation from the Sibylline books should prevent a Roman army going to Egypt.

In the spring of 59 B.C., when Caesar, Pompey, and Crassus by joining forces had removed all possibility of Cicero or anyone else taking an independent line in Roman politics, Cicero declared his disgust with politics. 'I have determined not to think about politics', he wrote. He retired to Antium. In April, that month of beauty in Italy, he said, 'I either enjoy myself with books of which I have a delightful stock at Antium, or I just count the waves.' But his busy scheming brain, still eager for personal distinction, could not rest.

There was one prize which might lure him back. 'Who is to have the augurship?' he inquires from his friend Atticus still in Rome listening to the political gossip of the city. He clearly hoped that the answer to his question might be 'Cicero'. It was, he said, 'the one bait by which those personages could catch me', adding, 'You see what a big price I put on myself.' There were obviously many Romans who thought the same way, and it will be worth while now to turn to an account of some reasons why they thought so; for brief generalized descriptions of the chief parts of the machinery of government in Rome, Senate public assemblies, senior magistrates (Quaestor, Aedile, Praetor Censor, Consul) and priestly colleges, necessary as they are to an understanding of the busy life of political Rome, can hardly possess much living interest until they are seen in relation to the life of Roman politicians and their constant competitive struggles with each other.

Chapter Nine

THE GOVERNMENT OF THE
ROMAN REPUBLIC AS A WORKING
CONCERN

To give a picture of the Roman system of government merely by taking the machine to pieces, as it were, labelling and describing some of the chief parts, does not take us very far towards finding how the machine actually worked. That discovery can never be easy because relatively few people, apart from those actually engaged in politics, public administration, journalism and one or two other specialized occupations, have clear and definite ideas how any system of government works.

The essential facts about the Roman system may perhaps emerge by comparing it with the very different British system. Like the Roman, it also was the unplanned product of centuries of growth and adaptation. The government of the United Kingdom is in the hands of an executive committee called the Cabinet, responsible to the House of Commons, which is another name for the elected representatives of the people. There is nothing Parliament cannot do, because the United Kingdom is ruled by laws which everybody must obey and which nobody but Parliament can alter. It is a very closely-knit system linking together people and government. The word 'people' is used to mean every man and woman of British nationality over twenty-one years of age.*

The electors at the base of the Roman system were not, as in Great Britain, every man and woman over twenty-one years of age. Women did not vote at all, and the men voted on new laws or on the election of Tribunes and junior magistrates only if they were in Rome and available at the time when their thirty-one country wards (tribes) and four city wards were called together by a

---

* Three coloured charts (XIII, XIV and XV), included in the first edition of this book, attempted to illustrate diagrammatically the machinery of government in Rome in 150 B.C. and under Julius Caesar 45 B.C. and to compare both with the machinery of government in Britain A.D. 1948.

Consul, Praetor or Tribune. Rearranged in 193 centuries, most but not all of these men elected every year the senior magistrates, Consuls, Praetors, Curule Aediles and, every five years, the two Censors. They did not elect a representative assembly, like the British House of Commons, from the majority party of whose members a parliamentary executive or Cabinet is created to assume responsibility for all executive action taken in the name of the State.

Political action in the Roman Republic had many sources. It might issue from any one of the elected magistrates. It might be taken by the Senate, on its own initiative, or it might result from new laws voted directly by the people themselves. It was however subjected to impediments from which British government activity is free. Since no man ruled alone but each had a colleague with equal powers, each magistrate could block or veto activity by a colleague that he did not like. The Consuls could block all other magistrates, but otherwise there seems to have been no hierarchical or 'scalar' organization of the executive administration able to provide effective co-ordinated activity all along the line. But assuming that any one set of magistrates had decided upon a line of action, they might nevertheless find themselves blocked completely by any one of the ten Tribunes, with, however, the proviso that none of the other nine Tribunes disagreed with their colleague's veto. For one Tribune could veto the act of another. From about 150 B.C. to 58 B.C. the Aelian and Fufian laws subjected the Tribunes to control on religious grounds by the State officials wielding the powers of the ancient priestly offices.

The bad thing about the interference of either Tribunes or religious officials was that it was completely arbitrary. There is nothing like it in any modern democratic State. In the United States of America today the Supreme Court is able to veto executive action and to rule that laws passed by Congress are unconstitutional and cannot therefore be enforced. It cannot do so on arbitrary grounds but only to safeguard the Rule of Law. The strength and solidity of public support for the Supreme Court if it is thought to be under attack demonstrates the deep attachment of the American public to the vital principle of the Rule of Law. The Romans had no similar constitutional safeguard to ensure that true law and right reason should prevail.

The Roman Senate was in an anomalous position both in relation to legislative and administrative action and in respect of its power to sustain the Rule of Law. It was but weakly related to the executive machinery and it stood in no such essential relationship to the whole machinery of government as does the British Parliament. As long as the prestige of the Senate was high, as it was in the heroic age of the Republic down to about 130 B.C., it was able to exert an all-pervading influence throughout the entire Roman system of government. Like the pull of the sun, it influenced the actions of every magistrate, the source of all executive political action, and it also determined the choice of questions submitted for the decision of the supposedly sovereign Roman people. Apart from the Senate, there was no other political force in the republic sufficiently strong to produce order out of what would otherwise have been, and did in fact become, a dangerous confusion. But the Senators were fatally divorced from the people. In Cicero's time many of them owed their position to the fact that their ancestors had held high office, so making it easy for them to follow in their footsteps. But they commanded no army. They controlled no police force. It is true that they each had their private band of slaves, ex-slaves, hired men and hangers-on, but for the most part this motley crew hung on for what they could get and were in no mood to stand by their patron if the cold steel of a few legionaries or troops of armed gangsters threatened his life. Senators lacked the unfailing support and loyalty of the only force that mattered in the long run, that which sprang from the will and purpose of the private citizen.

As time went on their political skill was exercised less in co-operating with the people in a genuine partnership than in managing the popular assemblies by packing them with their own nominees, by bribing the rest and by obstructing them when these devices failed. They stood in this respect in a very different position from that of a British Member of Parliament with his direct links with the electors. A threat of insult or violence to their M.P. awakens echoes in a British constituency which soon show that there are more than formal bonds between British electors and their representatives. Trouble or injustice in any corner of the British Isles is very soon ventilated in Parliament by the M.P. for the constituency concerned. To safeguard their cause the people in Rome had to rely upon their Tribunes, who developed a sort of vested interest in opposition. Citizens of the Republic outside Rome lacked such resource. The Tribunes were, apart from remarkable men like the Gracchi, usually unable to withstand the powerful forces which the governing classes were able to bring to bear upon the political scene by means of their well-organized machinery of influence and control.

Worse was to come, as the subsequent story of the political development of the Republic in the age of Cicero will show, when the Senate was no longer able to control the situation. Great public duties such as those arising inevitably from the need to run an Empire cannot be successfully discharged on a basis of political jobbery, which became about all that the Senate had to offer. The Romans muddled on with their government. It had no sustaining support in public determination and it muddled to disaster.

British political evolution has been just as unplanned as was the Roman. It has been just as misunderstood by intelligent foreigners. Montesquieu, analysing the British constitution as he found it in the mid eighteenth century, thought he detected in it the same mystic 'balance of powers' that he read about in the description Polybius gave of the Roman constitution nineteen hundred years earlier. The Senate, Magistrates, and People of Rome may have achieved for a time the balanced partnership in political action described by Polybius, but the record shows that they were unable to maintain it. The plain fact is that if political power in a State is divided and balanced, there is grave danger that occasions may arise when it may be difficult if not nearly impossible to get anything done. It may always take a disappointingly long time to get action upon many minor, but important matters, as the Americans, whose ancestors were influenced by the Montesquieu tradition, have on occasion discovered. In Great Britain the Parliamentary executive is a more flexible and efficient source of political action than the complicated mechanism of the Roman Republic ever became.

It is always dangerous to oversimplify arguments of this sort in the attempt to grasp the complicated notion of the working of the political machinery of a State. Yet the broad contrast between Rome and Great Britain is plain enough to show that the Roman system was not capable of the same continuous efficient action in one direction with all the united force of the State that the British not only can, but must, mobilize if it is to work at all. In the Roman system, in fact, common action by all parts of the Republic was not enforced by the organization of the government. There was instead, as a result of the creation of the ten Tribunes and their leadership of the Assembly of the People, almost a State within a State. It seems as though the 'opposition', to use a modern parliamentary term with no Roman equivalent, had been allowed to set up a rival system of government instead of being integrated, however grumblingly and imperfectly, in a law-making process. When unity was achieved it was almost despite the system which was fundamentally defective and bad, from the standpoint of political and administrative organization.

To believe this is not necessarily to regard the Republic as doomed. A bad system of government and a clumsy administration will not ruin a nation endowed with vitality and resilience. Embarrassing, inconvenient and expensive as such defects may prove to be, they can be overcome. Many States in the U.S.A. found in our own times that they had inherited from the horse-and-buggy era a clumsy, inefficient system of government. But Massachusetts, Virginia and New York and other States did not fail to prosper and progress for that reason. On the contrary, their progress was very real and before long it included a reform of their governmental machine as well.

Republican Rome failed to take this step forward, but its failure must be explained on broader grounds than that of its government machinery alone. It was the spirit to drive the machine that was at fault.

Chapter Ten

THE SUBSTANCE OF ROMAN POLITICS

In brief outline the main framework of the Roman State has now been described. But *what* did it do? What were the problems to which Roman politicians devoted their days and what caused the political strife of which Roman history is full?

The story of unrest and commotion within the Republic provides the easiest answer because it points to the problems on which there was fierce disagreement. Such a record of disturbance and struggle should not be allowed to blind our eyes to the very much greater amount of public business which roused little controversy, which went on quietly day by day and kept the Republic an active, going concern. There would not be space to recount all the petty business and small adjustments in the administration of the Republic even if we had a record of them. We know that hundreds of Consuls, thousands of Quaestors, Aediles and Praetors succeeded each other down the ages, many of them now mere names and many more totally unknown even by name. Hundreds of election meetings were held to listen to proposals for laws of which we have no knowledge whatever. Such lack of knowledge is neither surprising nor very disappointing. The twentieth century cannot be expected to follow with eager interest all that happened in a small Italian city over 2,000 years ago. Consequently we need try to do no more than to look at some of the main problems, since it is from them that the distinctive character of the Roman people emerges and through them that we may perhaps gain some insight into the slow growth of human liberties.

The first task of the early generations of the Republic was clearly to hammer out some general rules and principles to govern the dealings of the patricians and the plebeians with each other. The process was very different from that with which we are familiar in a modern city and still more unlike that employed in national governments today. For centuries the Romans had been able to assemble all the citizens together in one big meeting or *comitia* to decide upon all important new questions. But for centuries also the new questions were a small part of their lives, which for the most part were governed by habit, tradition, and unquestioning obedience to the properly constituted authority of their magistrates and priests.

First Statement of the Laws of Rome: The Twelve Tables

One very necessary task facing the plebeians and their Tribunes, before they could begin to make any political progress, was to get some clear understanding about the laws by which Rome was supposed to be governed. In the first years of the Republic very few if any of the laws were written; some more were in the memory of men who had agreed to them in the public assembly of the *comitia centuriata*. But by far the largest and most important body of law was known only by the priests of the Roman religion, the high Pontiffs, who alone were competent to declare it. Customary law has normally governed slowly evolving agricultural societies and Rome was no exception. The 'ways of our ancestors' (*mos maiorum*) were expected to be a complete guide to behaviour on most occasions of life and it was sufficient to accuse anyone of disregarding them in order to put him in the position of a defendant in serious danger of moral reprobation if not of complete condemnation. So hidebound a way of life may seem very cramped and limited to a freer age, but it was correspondingly tough and strong. At the beginning of the Republic the Pontiffs shared their knowledge of the law to some extent with the Consuls. An aura of mystery remained about the whole subject. There was still something divine about a lawgiver. Between breaking the law and insulting religion it was not easy to draw a line, and few Romans doubted that the gods would visit terrible penalties upon the sacrilegious.

Both Consuls and Pontiffs were patricians. Indeed it was widely believed by patricians that dreadful disasters would fall upon the State if so mean a person as a plebeian was allowed to meddle in any matters of religion.

In seeking to weaken this tremendous weapon of patrician political monopoly, the plebeians and their Tribunes clearly faced a very difficult task. The struggle was prolonged, bitter but determined. Year after year the plebeians re-elected their Tribunes to carry afresh to the magistrates and Senate their demand for a clear statement of the laws. Year after year it was refused. The wrangling went on until 455 B.C. when, according to the traditional account which some scholars now regard with considerable scepticism, a commission of inquiry of three men was dispatched to Greece to study the Greek codes of law.

The interest of the story lies not alone in the light it might throw upon the origins of early Roman laws, but in the grand question when Greek civilization first began to exercise its profound influence on the Roman mind. The great age of Greece had not then reached its full splendour. Plato was not born and Socrates had not attained manhood. Nevertheless, if the story is true, the Romans may be supposed to have felt that they had much to learn, and the mission was said to have been absent for three years. Its return was the signal for the struggle to break out afresh. There seems little doubt that there was a grave crisis which was finally resolved by a drastic change in the Roman constitution. The plebeians gave up their Tribunes; the patricians resigned the power of the Consuls in favour of a commission of ten men with consular powers, who were to govern the country so justly that the Tribunes would no longer be needed. Among their first duties would be to declare the fundamental law of Rome.

The task was performed, and it is said to have resulted in a code of law accepted by the people and posted on twelve tablets (451–450 B.C.). These were the famous Twelve Tables. Despite the fact that in the succeeding history of Rome their contents were honoured and constantly referred to, no complete copy of them survived. The Romans themselves, when they began to write about law, depended for their knowledge of the Twelve Tables upon a collection of rules made at the beginning of the second century B.C. which was said to contain all that was known of them at that early date. Some modern scholars have thrown grave doubt upon the tradition, reported by the Roman historians, of so early a development of a Roman code. The Twelve Tables were indeed referred to not long ago as a 'school book of 190 B.C.' It has been confidently maintained that at so early a time as 450 B.C., before Romans generally had acquired the art of reading or writing, the laws themselves would be handed on from generation to generation chiefly by word of mouth and that the priests, who took special care of the business, were therefore naturally the chief authorities. That a concise statement of the main principles of the laws of Rome had been put together at a very early time and that it had been recorded upon bronze tablets and exhibited in the Forum is not, however, seriously doubted.

The Romans may have thought about the Twelve Tables rather as the average Englishman or American, untrained in medieval constitutional law and practice, has regarded Magna Charta, as a respectable historical guarantee which he can invoke to justify his own desires and political objectives.

From the fragments which have been preserved some idea of their importance from this point of view can be obtained. As to their scope as a whole, opinions seem to differ. It has been said that their purpose was not to declare general rights of all Romans but to serve the more practical need of providing a close and minute statement of the procedure to be followed in civil and criminal cases.

Yet the Twelve Tables were generally referred to by Roman writers as the first complete statement of the whole body of Roman Law, public, criminal and private. They probably summarized the best rules and practices of village life as they had grown up and been slowly established over the centuries. As such they were never entirely superseded. If what survived of them had merely been a technical guide to lawyers, they would hardly have been learned by heart by Roman children, as Cicero said he had to learn them, although he added that the practice had ceased to be general after his own boyhood.

Much of the contents of the Twelve Tables seems to have referred to religious observances and the rules of private law. Among the many benefits they were supposed to have conferred were the recognition of the plebeian form of marriage by simple consent of both parties, the equal division of intestate inheritances between sons and daughters, the easier emancipation of slaves, freedom of contract between Romans, freedom of association in guilds and 'colleges' for religious and other observances, provided that they respected the law, and above all some amendment to the law of debt. Lending money at interest was not forbidden, but its profits were limited to 10 per cent, under severe penalties, including a rule that anyone who charged more could be made to restore four times as much money as he had illegally squeezed from his victim. Such a provision has been held to be a later addition to the Twelve Tables, for money transactions were by no means general until long after the fifth century B.C. However, it is known that under Etruscan domination Rome was a trading centre. The treaty of alliance with Carthage concluded immediately after the expulsion of the Etruscan king also refers to trade practices.

The political and constitutional parts of the Twelve Tables were also said to have been fundamental and far-reaching. Provision was made for the death penalty against traitors, against judges who accepted bribes, and also against anyone convicted of indulging in incantations against a citizen. At the same time a fair trial and the right of appeal was guaranteed. In particular the old right of a citizen condemned to death to appeal to the greatest assembly of the people (the *comitia centuriata*) was confirmed by the Twelve Tables. Cicero had cause to rue the day when, as Consul, he acted so as to give his enemies a chance of accusing him of being neglectful of this ancient rule. Finally the sovereignty of the popular assembly was asserted by the rule that its enactments were to be the last word, which meant that they could not be subject to arbitrary change by Senate or magistrates.

To have extracted such a charter of rights and liberties in times when the law was both undeclared and an engine of oppression, would have been so great an achievement that its very scope and range excites some scepticism, but whatever the truth about the actual date of all their various clauses may be, the Twelve Tables remain an impressive monument to the early development of Roman Law.

Social Cleavage in the Roman Republic

Not the least important thing about the Twelve Tables was that for the first time a declaration had been secured limiting the power of the patricians to say through their priests what the law was. The authority of the Twelve Tables is therefore one aspect of the struggle of the Romans to establish the Rule of Law at the foundation of civil society. After the appointment of the Tribunes, this was the second major victory of the plebeians. But the experiment of appointing ten men to supersede Consuls and Tribunes in order to introduce the reform was not a success. The Consuls and the Tribunes were brought back in their stead.

Legend records the harshness and villainy of the second team of ten men (*Decemviri*) and the recovery of the earlier Republican constitution after an attempt by Appius Claudius, the leading *Decemvir*, to enslave a beautiful plebeian girl, Verginia. The girl's soldier father, who preferred to see her dead rather than a slave to one of the minions of Appius Claudius, stabbed her as she was about to be led away, rushed back to the camp and raised a mutiny which overturned the *Decemviri*. The parallel between the pathetic story of Verginia, whose death removed a hateful tyranny, and the earlier story of the dishonour and death of Lucretia, by which Rome was freed from the tyranny of a foreign king, has been cited as evidence of their legendary nature. Both stories were kept alive because they drove home lessons in constitutional, political and social right and wrong, which the ancient historians of Rome wished to enforce. The tales have, it has been said, another message. They show the power of the Roman woman and the respect which was felt to be her due, whether patrician or plebeian.

With the passage of years many of the descendants of plebeian families acquired a lineage little inferior to that of the patricians. Some of them also became as wealthy, but very many of them no doubt remained poor, with all the poverty of a primitive agricultural people struggling for food, shelter and clothing for themselves and their families, either on their own smallholdings or as hired men working with the owners of plots often considerably less than five or ten acres in extent.

Slow Progress by the Plebeians

Every effort made by the plebeians to improve their chance of becoming magistrates seems to have encountered opposition, difficulty and resentment from the patricians. The struggle lasted over 200 years (494–287 B.C.). For at least the first fifty years (494–445 B.C.) the plebeians' main task seems to have been to protect themselves from arbitrary rule and to rescue their bodies and souls from the worst effects of irresponsible patrician domination. They were, at this early period, no violent revolutionaries, prepared if need be to wreck the State so as to ruin their masters. In fact Rome is most remarkable for the absence from its annals of violent revolutionary outbreaks. Few other Republican states can show so long a reign of internal order and respect for the law.

Despite the 'consular compromise' of 445 B.C. (p. 171), patrician candidates continued to be elected to the office of military Tribune with consular powers. Later Roman historians plausibly explained the fact by saying that the plebeians recognized their own political inferiority and put the welfare of the State before their ambitions for their own class.

The compromise lasted over seventy years, when it was finally ended after five paralysing years of political crisis by the plebiscites carried through the plebeian assembly by two Tribunes, Licinius and Sextius, and known thereafter as the Licinian-Sextian Rogations, of 368–367 B.C. They provided for the compulsory election of one plebeian as Consul. The new law was bitterly resented by the patricians but they were bought off by the creation of the new office of Praetor (p. 173), who was almost a deputy Consul.

Thereafter plebeian progress was more rapid. The first record of a plebeian in the Senate is in 401 B.C., although there may have been some at an earlier date. Despite plebeian ambitions, it seems that it was not until 172 B.C. that both Consuls were men of plebeian origin.

The traditional story shows the patricians as bad losers. When their own weakness and the growing strength of the plebeians forced them to give way, their frustration and annoyance broke out in all manner of mean and petty devices. As long as they had power they surrendered nothing. When surrender was inevitable they engaged in any kind of delaying action that their malice could suggest and their ingenuity contrive. Yet the animosity never rose, as it had often risen in Greece, to the point where one of the parties decided to go off to live elsewhere. Until the days of Tiberius Gracchus towards the end of the second century B.C. the struggle never caused loss of life.

Rise of a New Élite – the 'Optimates'

During the course of this long, obstinate, wasteful and, as it seems to us, lamentably perverse struggle, the two classes by whom it was waged had greatly changed. By Cicero's time the aristocratic patricians had greatly declined in numbers. The famous first families of Rome, the Valerii, Fabii, Cornelii, Aemilii, Furii and Manlii were weakened, politically obscure or extinct. The plebeians had not merely increased, they had absorbed the State and had created an *élite* or aristocracy of their own. Yet some of their famous families were also in decay – the Sempronii, Fulvii and Claudii Marcelli. But the Marcii, Junii, Domitii and especially the Metelli were outstanding and were linked by many marriage ties to the survivors of more ancient patrician houses. Two hundred years is a long time in the history of an average family and even today, with vastly better public and private records, relatively few families are conscious of so long a continuous descent. The natural result was that the surviving descendants of plebeian aristocrats stepped into the places of patrician aristocrats to form a new nobility distinguished not so much by the length of their family tree as by the number of magistrates among their ancestors. They became known as *optimates*.

The special favour shown to all elected to high office as Praetor, Censor or Consul has already been emphasized. To have become a senior magistrate was a passport to the Senate valid for life. Once in the Senate a 'consular', as former Consuls were called, was listened to before lesser men were asked to speak.

There was a natural expectancy that one at least of the sons of the great man would follow in his father's footsteps. Thirty or forty noble families, said Cicero, passed on the consulship from hand to hand between each other. Their sons, as Cicero remarked with the bitterness of one who had to make his own way by great energy joined with great ability, were marked out for the consulship while still in their cradles.

The badge and sign of nobility were not, as with us, survivals of feudal titles of honour, but knowledge of the part played by ancestors in the historic past. Their names would be associated with critical events, and they would be remembered for their part in wars and triumphs or in civic affairs as Consuls, judges, governors and law-makers.

The central hall of the residences of the distinguished families of Rome would be decorated with a collection of death masks and portrait busts of those of their forefathers who had held a senior magistracy or 'Curule' office. These likenesses, suspended in a place of honour in the family home, were a constant daily reminder to all members of the family and to all visitors of the dignity and historic glory of the house. They powerfully sustained the strong Roman tradition that the sole but sure way to social distinction lay through political and military service to the State. To reinforce their message publicly such likenesses were borne in state, by men in the costume and insignia of the departed, on ceremonial family occasions, especially at funerals. Such displays must have created a formidable impression. The cool and intelligent mind of Polybius confessed to their power to stir human emotions. 'There could not', he said, 'easily be a more inspiring spectacle than this for a young man of noble ambitions and virtuous aspirations. For can we conceive anyone to be un-moved at the sight of all the likenesses collected together of the men who have earned glory, all as it were living and breathing? What could be a more glorious spectacle?' It seems that many Roman families yielded on such occasions to the strong tempta-tion to accompany such displays with boastful orations, many of which, as Cicero complained, had perverted and falsified the history of Rome. Cicero himself could make no such impressive display in his house, for he was a 'new man', without ancestors distinguished in the service of the Republic.

Insensibly, therefore, a mixed new nobility of office holders arose to take the place of the old nobility who had in the past been office holders mainly because they were aristocrats, members of a patrician clan. Such was the origin of a number of the best citizens, or 'Nobiles', as they were described in Cicero's Rome.

The result was the rule of a powerful and dignified aristocracy. Their manners and habit of life, their devotion to public service, their scant regard for social pretensions founded upon mere wealth, their high sense of honour in their dealings with each other all set the tone and formed the spirit of a society that was to rule the State without serious challenge for upwards of 400 years. Inevitably also a class division was perpetuated in Roman society. The average citizen who had no political ambitions gave more or less willing obedience to the men who ruled him, without as far as we know feeling any strong resentment or frustration at his own exclusion. Exceptionally, a very few able men without magisterial ancestry, 'new men' as they were called, might, if their abilities were outstanding, make their way by their own merit. Cicero was one of them and, fully aware and proud as he was of his own great abilities, he never forgot that to the men around him in the Senate he was an outsider, an upstart and a man from the countryside, accepted by the best families, it is true, but accepted the more graciously in proportion as he remembered the real, if invisible, gulf by which they and he were divided.

The Recorded Legislation of the Roman Republic

So far, it has not been possible to refer to more than the central themes of Roman politics. Taken alone they would give an inadequate picture, which it is desirable to supplement by setting out as completely as possible the general framework of Roman legislative activity. Unfortunately nothing has survived from the lost literature of Republican Rome to make possible the publication of a Roman code of law during the age of Cicero, such as the Federal Code provides for the United States of America or the Chronological Table and Index to the Statutes outlines for Great Britain. Few modern historians of ancient Rome have troubled to collect together all the known references to laws or projected laws. An attempt is made below to give them regrouped under their main subject-headings to show the date of the first known law or legislative measure on each separate subject and the number of Bills and enactments throughout the history of the Republic. The numbers of the laws passed, or Bills considered, have been rearranged below in two periods. The first 400 years of the Republic form the first period. The second is that from 100 B.C. to 30 B.C., covering Cicero's active life and extending to the close of the Republican era.

SUBJECT	DATE OF FIRST KNOWN LEGISLATIVE ACTION	TOTAL LAWS AND BILLS RECORDED TO	
		100 B.C.	100–30 B.C.
Comitia: constitution, procedure and powers	449 B.C.	9	4
Appeals: limitation of penalties	509 B.C.	13	1
Magistrates: general rules	509 B.C.	7	4
Prolonging commands, assignment of provinces	327 B.C.	14	16
Deprivation of command	217 B.C.	6	8
Magistrates: rules for normal offices			
Consuls	449 B.C.	4	–
Praetors	367 B.C.	6	3

SUBJECT	DATE OF FIRST KNOWN LEGISLATIVE ACTION	TOTAL LAWS AND BILLS RECORDED TO	
		100 B.C.	100–30 B.C.
Magistrates: rules for normal offices—*cont.*			
Dictator	499 B.C.?	6	6
Censors	443 B.C.?	5	4
Curule Aediles	367 B.C.	1	–
Quaestors	509 B.C.	3	2
Military Tribune, and Military Tribune with consular powers	445 B.C.	7	–
Tribunes and plebeian Aediles	494 B.C.	10	8
Special magistrates, creation, powers, duties, confirmation	462 B.C.	13	10
Exemption from laws	298 B.C.	9	3
Senate	449 B.C.	5	3
Priesthood	367 B.C.	5	6
Cults, Calendar, Festivals, Games	472 B.C.?	11	8
Social Classes, admission to patrician or to plebeian status	383 B.C.	4	6
Award of extraordinary honours	509 B.C.	5	12
Citizenship: grant or deprivavation		11	13
forbidding usurpation of	332 B.C.	2	2
Voting: electoral rules	189 B.C.	4	6
Army	390 B.C.	9	1
Triumphs and ovations: general rules and special awards	449 B.C.	9	5
Declarations of war	505 B.C.	27	–
International relations generally	273 B.C.	6	6
Treaties of Peace and Alliance	446 B.C.	20	2
Municipal and Provincial ordinances	189 B.C.	5	10
Public Revenue and Expenditure	509 B.C.	9	10
Colonies: Foundation of, and emigration schemes	395 B.C.	15	6
Land Laws	486 B.C.	32	13
Food Supply, mainly corn supply	440 B.C.	6	10

SUBJECT	DATE OF FIRST KNOWN LEGISLATIVE ACTION	TOTAL LAWS AND BILLS RECORDED TO 100 B.C.	100–30 B.C.
Roads and Water	123 B.C.	1	4
Weights, Measures, Currency	269 B.C.	3	2
Workers' Associations	58 B.C.	–	1
Social Behaviour: sumptuary laws	217 B.C.	10	6
Debt: Interest on loans	367 B.C.	13	14
Gambling and wagers	241 B.C.	? 10	?
Private Law:			
Guardianship or wardship	136 B.C.	2	1
Gifts and Dowries	204 B.C.	2	–
Marriage	445 B.C.	3?	–
Inheritance	204 B.C.	2	2
Slaves, manumission of	357 B.C.	1	–
Acquisition of ownership	149 B.C.	2	–
Various: Damage; Wrongs	286 B.C.	6?	–
Legal Procedure	204 B.C.	5	–
Pains and penalties against various individuals	510 B.C.	12	4
Pardons and Amnesties	449 B.C.	5	15
Trials by special commission	413 B.C.	14	7
Relating to the Judiciary	133 B.C.	6	11
Criminal Law:			
Bribery	432 B.C.	4	10
Treason	103 B.C.	1	3
Violence	81 B.C.	–	4
Extortion	149 B.C.	4	4
Embezzlement	81 B.C.	–	1
Sexual offences	331 B.C.?	3	1
Murder	123 B.C.	1	2
Unlawful assembly	139 B.C.	1	–
Slander	80 B.C.	–	1
Kidnapping	209 B.C.?	1	–
Forgery	81 B.C.	–	1
Private wrongs	81 B.C.	–	2

This bare list of the main subject-matter of not quite 700 laws and a few proposed laws, inaccurate as it necessarily is, must be a most inadequate summing-up of the legislative activity of nearly 500 years of a vigorous and growing State. Moreover we do not possess the text or anything like an accurate summary of the actual content of most of the measures listed above. Nevertheless the fact that these laws have proved worthy of some mention in what remains of Latin literature may be taken as a rough assurance that we have here an index to the character of the legislation of Republican Rome. It shows a normal society actively engaged in shaping the framework of its political life. Allowance must be made of course for the fact that the material remaining relating to the last century of the Republic, is fuller and more reliable than that relating to earlier ages. Bearing this fact in mind, it is still possible to read special significance into some entries in the preceding table.

Such, for example, is the evidence of the relatively large number of laws in Cicero's day compared with the number in the previous four hundred years on such subjects as prolonging commands and assigning provinces (16 against 14); awards of extraordinary honours (12 against 5); pardons and amnesties (15 against 5); bribery (10 against 4); food supply (10 against 6) and debt (14 against 13).

On the other hand most of the constitutional legislation relating to the public assemblies, *comitia*, the magistrates, Tribunes, Senate and the Army had been shaped before Cicero's time. The list also brings out the fact that the era of foreign wars by vote of the people was over by Cicero's day, as was also the practice of concluding treaties of peace by a public law.

The chief and most controversial public problems of the Romans in the formative years of their national life, during roughly the first half of the political history of the Roman Republic beginning in 509 B.C., undoubtedly centred around the struggle of the plebeians to free themselves from oppression and to win political equality with the patricians. The striking thing about this early epoch was that the political contests engaged the activity of the majority of the people of Rome. They were not merely battles between politicians. The people were stirred by them to such an extent that unless they had been satisfied they would have refused to continue to belong to the Roman Republic.

Chapter Eleven

PUBLIC WELFARE AND PRIVATE
AMBITIONS

LOOKING back upon the achievements of the Roman people we
can see how between 509 B.C. and 287 B.C. a stable system, carefully maintaining its ancestral models intact from one generation
to another, was gradually being broken up under the impact of
social injustices which stimulated first a private and class consciousness of wrongs and then an insistent demand for remedies.
The search for a remedy inevitably led the oppressed to take
from their oppressors, for their own use, as much power and
authority as seemed necessary for safety. A public assembly was
organized to counter-balance the authority of the Senate and
magistrates. The powers of the priests and magistrates were
further checked first by the appointment of 'counter-magistrates'
(as the Tribunes may be described) and next by allowing the unprivileged plebeian himself to become a candidate for high office
in the State.

An effort was made (451 B.C.) to establish a just body of law by
the Twelve Tables and to ensure that the people and not the
Senators heard the appeals of citizens condemned by a magistrate.
Nevertheless these changes did little to shake the power of the
magistrates and Senate, who continued to have almost everything
their own way for about another hundred years (451-367 B.C.).
Thereafter the political activity of the people gained increasing
strength until in 287 B.C. the plebeians or poor commons had won
what seemed to be a complete victory. The struggle had been long
and persistent. The people had numbers on their side and a sense
of being the victims of very unjust discrimination. But their
ability and their opportunities to stand up for themselves in the
political arena were limited and they were furthermore distracted
by the constant wars they had to fight. The senatorial aristocrats
on the other hand started the contest with the immense advantage
of having all the levers of power in their hands and the knowledge
how to use them. From their ranks moreover came all the men

who were able to devote continuous attention to political problems and who were driven by the compelling necessity to get things done. Naturally they wanted to get things done in their own way and for their own advantage, or at least not to their disadvantage. Consequently they could not be too scrupulous about ways and means. Yet it must never be forgotten that the patricians contributed a great and indispensable service in accepting responsibility for the welfare and even for the survival of the State. Such heavy public responsibility is the last thing the average man is willing to shoulder.

The complicated nature of the Roman political machinery, with its elaborate balancing of powers and above all its early subservience to religious influence, provided many opportunities for those in control to play off one force against another. One or other of the ten Tribunes, and almost certainly the religious officials, could be relied upon to support the serried ranks of the chief men in the Senate and the leading magistrates against untimely and uncomfortable efforts on the part of the masses, their leaders and those who, for private political ambition, set themselves up as the champions of the poor.

Era of Political Stability

After 287 B.C. when the hectic period of internal strife for participation in the political control of Rome finally ended with the decision in favour of the majority of Roman citizens organized in the *comitia tributa*, no golden period of vigorous democratic rule at once followed. The next fifty years were politically stagnant. The public assembly, despite its newly won freedom from senatorial control, signally failed to make further use of its victory. It can only be concluded that the responsibility, power, prestige, authority and determination of the governing classes in the Senate and among the magistrates were still so high that they were able to retain much of the influence that long-established custom had always allowed them. Supreme danger does not provoke revolutionary political innovations and the deadly battles with the Carthaginians after 264 B.C. postponed political evolution until the immediate peril had passed. Then victory proved a powerful solvent of custom, habit, political behaviour and of the opinions in the minds of men. In 232 B.C. new energies were

Inscribed Bust of Cicero. 1st cent. A.D.

1

(a) Plough and Cart with Oxen, Sheep, Goats, and Pigs. 1st cent. B.C.

(b) Marble Relief showing Bronze Bucket

(c) Bronze Bucket

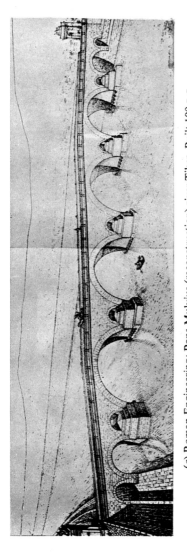

(a) Roman Engineering: Pons Mulvius (reconstruction) river Tiber. Built 109 B.C.

(b) Roman Warships. Fresco painted between A.D. 63 and 79. Pompeii

Graeco-Roman Villas on a Waterfront. Fresco *c*. A.D. 63–79. Pompeii

(a) View from Atrium into Peristylium.
Middle of 1st cent. B.C. Pompeii

(b) Atrium with Impluvium in the Foreground.
Early 1st cent. A.D. Pompeii

5

(a) 'Cave Canem' (Beware of the Dog). Pompeii

(b) Bronze Table on Mosaic Floor. Middle of 1st cent. A.D. Pompeii

(a) Mules' Heads cast in Bronze. *c.* 40 B.C.

(b) Iron Chest Studded with Bronze Nails. Before A.D. 79. Pompeii

7

Bronze Portable Stove or Water-Heater. *c.* 150 B.C. Pompeii

(a) Lamp for Seven Lights. Baked clay. Probably 1st cent. B.C.

(b) Clay Storage Jars. 1st cent. A.D. Pompeii

(a) Mould for Glazed Red Pottery Bowl. c. 25–10 B.C.

(b) Clay Stamp used to produce relief
work as shown in plate (a) above

10

(a) Work in a Roman Bakery. Relief on the tomb shown on plate 12

(b) Grain Mills and Baking Stove. Before A.D. 79. Pompeii

Tomb of the Baker M. Vergilius Eurysaces.
1st cent. B.C. to 1st cent. A.D. Rome

12

(a) Public Tavern. Before A.D. 79. Pompeii

(b) A Fuller's Workshop. Before A.D. 79. Pompeii

13

(*a*) Soldiers Receiving Release

(*b*) and (*c*) Sacrifice of the Suovetaurilia. From an Altar in memory of
the First Battle of Philippi, 42 B.C.

(a) Roman Draper's Shop: Selling Cushions. Middle of 1st cent. B.C.

(b) Roman Draper's Shop: Selling Cloth. Middle of 1st cent. B.C.

(a) Paved Street with Fountains. Before A.D. 79. Pompeii

(b) Stepping Stones and Carriage Ruts. Before A.D. 79. Pompeii

(*a*) Fountain at Entrance to the Market.
Middle of 1st cent. A.D. Pompeii

(*b*) Cloaca Maxima. after 200 B.C. Rome

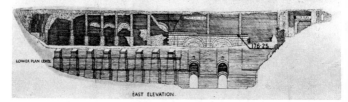

(*a*) Roman Aqueduct: Aqua Marcia. Built 272 B.C.

(*b*) Arches of the Aqueduct of Claudius. 1st cent. A.D.

(a)–(h) Bronze Coinage of the Roman Republic, 268–240 B.C.
(i)–(k) Silver Coinage of the Roman Republic, c. 88 B.C.
(l) Gold Coin of the Roman Republic, c. 81 B.C.

19

Aes Grave: Bronze Bar with Figure of Bull. 3rd cent. B.C. (much reduced in scale)

20

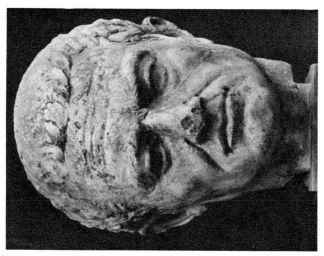

(a) A Young Roman

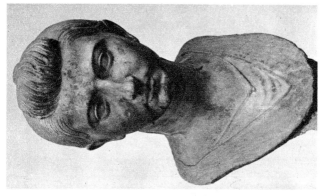

(b) A Young Roman Lady

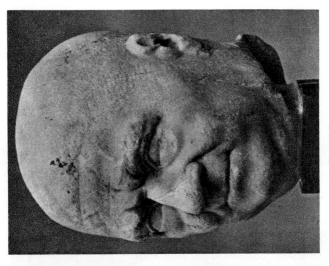

(b) Old Roman

(a) Elderly Roman Lady

Roman Citizen with Busts of his Ancestors. Augustan era

(a) Tombstone of the Butcher Aurelius Hermia. 1st cent. B.C.

(b) Ancestor Worship: Altar of the Parentes. Before A.D. 79. Pompeii

(a) Lar, God of the House. 1st cent. A.D.

(b) Ceremonial Mourning of a Lady. 1st cent. A.D. Rome

(a) A Roman Account Book from Pompeii. Before A.D. 79

(b) Surgical Instruments from Pompeii. Before A.D. 79

Pompey the Great

(*b*) *Obverse:* Junius Brutus,
44–43 B.C.
Reverse: Cap of Liberty

(*a*) *Obverse:* Caesar, 44 B.C.
Reverse: Venus Victrix

(*c*) *Obverse:* Pompey, 46–44 B.C.
Reverse: Spanish cities greeting
Pompeii

(*d*) *Obverse:* Apollo.
Reverse: Horsemen
c. 68 B.C.

Four Silver Denarii of Cicero's time

Roman Garden with Fountain. 1st cent. B.C. Pompeii

Painting in Cicero's time. Dionysiac Mysteries. 1st cent. B.C.

A Roman Temple, probably dedicated to Mater Matuta. Middle 1st cent. B.C. Rome

31

(a) Racing Chariot. Bronze Statuette. 1st cent. B.C.–1st cent. A.D.

(b) Amphitheatre for Gladiators and Animal Fights.
Begun 70 B.C. Pompeii

devoted to political purposes. C. Flaminius, as a Tribune, carried a land settlement law through the *comitia tributa* in the teeth of senatorial opposition. The *comitia* revived and approved some new measures for civic and political improvements. Then came the Second Punic War, which wrecked and ruined the Roman countryside and left a heritage of misfortune so bewildering that it paralysed rather than stimulated men to constructive political action.

The disasters of the Second Punic War may have obscured for the time being the memory of the seemingly radical programme of C. Flaminius, but those disasters themselves set the scene for programmes of more far-reaching scope.

Gradually, as the economic consequences of the war and of the changing fortunes of Roman agriculture and land-tenure worked themselves out, a new approach to public problems began to develop. Two generations were to elapse before, in 134 B.C., another tribune, Tiberius Gracchus, took up the challenge presented by the lives of the men of his time and sought by political means to find a remedy for the troubles around him. During those two generations the power of the ruling classes, despite the principle of democratic partnership, to put it no higher, for which Romans had striven until 287 B.C., had made considerable inroads upon the field assigned by the constitution to the popular assembly. Permanent courts manned by Senators took over judicial powers; the Senate took upon itself to extend for a second year, without election by the people, the period of office of magistrates going to rule Rome's newly won provinces and dependencies; the Senate quietly assumed all responsibility for the public finances of the Republic after 167 B.C., when Romans resident in Italy ceased to pay direct taxation; and lastly the Senate undertook to determine the strength of the armed forces of the State.

Era of Stress and Growing Tension

The buoyancy and tension of the well balanced political forces of magistrates, Senate, and popular assembly which the curious and observant Greek political writer and historian Polybius had noted as one of the excellences of Rome in the period of the Second Punic War, to which in turn Cicero among others also was to look back as to a golden age, had evidently proved unable to survive. Probably the energies of many men of those two generations less attracted by public affairs, went increasingly into the more absorbing, more exciting and, for many, more rewarding outlets in making their fortunes from the world empire they had begun to build. It was a race to wealth the like of which had not previously been seen. The competitors were unevenly matched and many started with heavy handicaps. Thousands won great prizes but tens of thousands failed.

Meanwhile a profound change seems to have taken place in the attitude of the Romans to their public problems. The people who, according to the traditional account, in their serried ranks had insisted in the past upon guarantees for their rights and liberties through their own public assembly and their own Tribunes; the people who had curbed the arbitrary power of magistrates and priests and had established in their place a rule of law symbolized by the Twelve Tables, no longer occupy the front rank in the political battles of the new age of Rome, the modern age of Cicero, Caesar, Pompey, and Augustus. It seems as though that unsleeping vigilance, upon which political and all other liberty has so often been found to depend, was lulled until vested interests had grown with such strength and tenacity of purpose that a revolution was required to break them. Not being accustomed to revolutions, the Romans managed theirs very badly, although in fairness to them it must be admitted that other folk from other lands had come to their capital city to complicate the problem they had to face. They hacked and hewed at it until in the end the vitality of their Republic was all but drained away.

By the beginning of the first century B.C. the old struggles between plebeian and patrician for access to the seats of authority were long since dead. Fiercer and more deadly struggles then broke out between active, ambitious politicians for control of the government. In these struggles the people as a whole were the victims, never, except in the Social War, the protagonists by whom the battles were begun. The people, to be sure, had troubles enough. They arose naturally from the restricted economic conditions of the time and were those of every predominantly agricultural community before the days of mechanized farming: land, food, and debt. They were nothing new. By Cicero's time life was indeed more complicated and economic interests were more diversified, but ways of earning a living and the prospect of becoming wealthy were little better for the common man than they had been in more primitive times. Economic conditions throughout Italy as a whole do not seem to have changed sufficiently to explain the civic strife and commotion that darkened the last century of the Republic.

Reformers and Demagogues

The source of the troubles must therefore be sought elsewhere. The new factor was not the mounting resentment and indignation of an oppressed and poverty-stricken people, but the hopes aroused by one or two men who had plans for improving the lot of their fellow citizens and who came forward as political leaders with the aim of getting their plans put into force.

It might have been thought that the fate of the brothers Tiberius and Gaius Gracchus, who made the boldest attempt to grapple with the land question, would have discouraged imitators, because it became clear that they had been unable to evoke or to create a popular following strong enough to carry through their carefully devised policy (see Chapter 3).

Meanwhile the poverty-stricken masses of Rome were becoming men of a different stamp from the stalwart farmers of old. Excitable and unsteady, they were ready to back almost any man who would offer them land and bread. They were therefore a standing temptation to political adventurers who had only to turn demagogue in order to be carried forward on a wave of popular enthusiasm. More than one hardy, unscrupulous Roman, overconfident of his skill, suffered shipwreck in trying to ride that wave. Such were Glaucia, a Praetor, and Saturninus, a Tribune, who sought to use the bait of cheap wheat and more land to strengthen their hands in an effort to break the power of the Senate. Both perished in the upheaval they provoked in 100 B.C. M. Livius Drusus, a reformer from the ranks of the senatorial party, who was the son of the enemy of Gaius Gracchus, met a similar fate after having revived the Gracchan proposal to grant citizenship to the Italians in 91 B.C. His failure was the immediate cause of the Social War of 90–89 B.C.

The Social War, 90–89 B.C.

The public questions decided at Rome were of vital importance not merely to Romans but to the other people of Italy as well.

The 'Italians' as distinct from the Romans wanted the same rights and privileges as the Romans possessed, and they were no longer content, after they had to fight Rome's wars, to be regarded as inferior people whom the Romans might refuse to treat as their equals in such matters as rights to public land, trading privileges, and other indications of their social standing and position in the State.

Gaius Gracchus had excited their hopes in the generation before Cicero when he drew up the plans, which lost him his popular following in Rome, to give full citizenship to all Latins and Latin rights to all other Italians. The Romans wanted no Italians sharing their cheap corn, free circus shows, distributions of land, or the occasional bribes given for their votes in the public assemblies.

We lack detailed knowledge of this confused and discreditable period. It culminated in that bitter Social War in which Rome had to fight again for supremacy in Italy. The Italians formed a confederacy, without however at first being able to include the Etruscans and Umbrians. They set up a Senate with Consuls of their own and waged war on Rome in which at least 300,000 men lost their lives. After one or two defeats, Rome saw that no peace could be permanent that refused civic rights to Italians. Citizenship was therefore promised in 90 B.C. to all the allies willing to lay down their arms. Many accepted and a similar offer in the following year meant that at heavy cost most of the Italians had won the right to become citizens of Rome. But no more than a mere half million actually became full citizens with voting rights in Rome's elections instead of the two or three millions who should have been given the privilege. Moreover, by a shabby trick most of the new voters were confined at first to a minority of the thirty-five electoral tribes or wards. But the right to vote at Rome, although valuable, was only one of the privileges desired by the Italians. Now at last able to call themselves by the proud title of Roman Citizen, they were no longer at the mercy of any Roman army officer or magistrate. Henceforth Rome was no longer a City State but the capital of Italy (88 B.C.). That Rome was still the paramount power is seen in the fact that it was the Roman Empire and not an Italian Empire that ruled the world. Thereafter the Oscan and other Italian cultures sank to mere provincial peculiarities.

These few lines upon a grim struggle cannot now open our eyes to the savagery and slaughter by which Italy was then torn to pieces. We can but dimly imagine the loss and ruin, but the memory of it must be carried forward to deepen the impression of gloom and impoverishment of the political scene in which Cicero and his contemporaries had to act.

The Social War was the last spontaneous mass movement in the history of the Roman Republic, but it was not the Romans who took the initiative. It was a struggle that overlaid a civil war in Rome itself, provoked by no mass movement and serving not public so much as private and personal ambitions nourished upon the power of supreme military command.

This new force in the State was created by the practice of allowing the people in their public assembly to vote for a law conferring a high command upon a popular general. The Senate then lost its age-old right of saying who should conduct a particular war or who should be sent to rule in the provinces, how many legions they were to have and how much money they were to be allowed. On very rare occasions the Senate had been compelled in the past to yield such powers to the people. Scipio Africanus in 205 B.C. practically forced the Senate to give him the command in Africa against the Carthaginians in the Second Punic War. Sixty years later another Scipio by adoption (Aemilianus) was entrusted with the third and final war against Carthage by the vote of the people in a plebiscite (147 B.C.). These were very exceptional appointments. In the year before Cicero was born his distinguished townsman Marius succeeded in being elected as Consul for 107 B.C. He had been serving in North Africa under Metellus, Consul for 109 B.C., who had been sent there with inadequate forces by the Senate against Jugurtha, a fierce, unscrupulous barbarian prince who had secured the Kingdom of Numidia by murdering his cousins, the two brothers, Adherbal and Hiempsal, co-heirs with him to this domain of their grandfather, Masinissa. The war had not gone well. Some ugly stories alleged that heavy bribes, paid by Jugurtha to some influential Romans, were responsible for the failure of the legions. Jugurtha had already learned the power of bribery in his dealings with the Romans. He regarded Rome as 'a city up for sale and destined to perish, if it finds a buyer.'

Disloyal to his commander, Marius was able, in this poisoned political atmosphere, to get a Tribune to propose to the public assembly that he should replace Metellus. The manoeuvre succeeded and, aided by the dash and brilliance of his young staff officer L. Cornelius Sulla, Marius soon brought the war to a close, returning with Jugurtha a prisoner who was to be killed in the Roman prison.

Marius and Sulla

This tough old man then added to the laurels earned for him in Africa by Sulla, by saving Rome from a threatened invasion by huge armies of two barbaric peoples of the North. These were the Teutoni allied with the Cimbri from the Baltic. The Cimbri had been on the move since 113 B.C. and Rome had lost several battles against them before Marius reorganized the Roman army (p. 49) and succeeded in destroying first the Teutoni at Aquae Sextiae near Marseilles (102 B.C.) and next the Cimbri at Vercellae near Turin (101 B.C.). These two tremendous victories removed for centuries any new threat by barbarians to the Roman people. Great as had been the glory then earned by Marius, he lost it all by becoming involved in the internal politics of the city on the side of Glaucia and Saturninus. As a politician, he was as unskilful as they, for he ended by being the agent by whom they were suppressed in 100 B.C. He then went into retirement, from which he did not emerge until he thought he saw, in the confusion of the Social War, an opportunity to return to the scene of his former triumphs. To regain his lost prestige, he wanted the command in the war in the East against Mithridates which the Senate had entrusted to Sulla. He had no difficulty in getting it by a resolution passed in the popular assembly.

But his 'direct action' tactics failed. Sulla refused to obey and declined to hand over his troops. Instead he marched at their head to settle the matter his own way in Rome. Marius, who had no army, fled. Sulla had the law repealed, and legally retained his command against Mithridates. Although he met with no serious opposition, his action was civil war, a war to control the Roman army that had conquered and could control the whole world. It was not a fight to decide whether the people or the Senate should control the army. The people had no means of control. The army is part of the executive machinery of government and should have remained in the hands of those responsible for executive action.

The people should never have been allowed to say who was to command because it was a decision they were powerless to enforce, as Sulla proved when he refused to obey them. The political system that until then had controlled military power broke down with the sudden emergence of a new third independent power in the State. Sulla proved for everybody to see that whatever the constitutional rights and wrongs of the situation might be, any man having military supremacy, that is to say, a sufficiently large force of Roman soldiers willing to follow him through thick and thin, could easily have political supremacy also if he wanted it. Before he went off with his army to the Eastern wars he had no time to do more than to make one or two changes in the government of Rome. One was to require the approval of the Senate before any new law could be put before the citizen body. No longer should this be the plebeian assembly; that lost all its law-making powers and was only allowed to elect Tribunes. They too were shorn of their powers of proposing new laws and rules. All such legislative business was henceforth to be taken before the *comitia centuriata* (p. 158) where voting power was weighted in favour of the owners of property. Sulla thought to secure this conservative revolution by making the new consul of 87 B.C., L. Cornelius Cinna, swear a mighty oath of loyalty to him and his cause. But Sulla had hardly left Rome before Cinna began to propose changes. He revived the plans to give the new Italian citizens fair voting rights which had been proposed by P. Sulpicius Rufus the year before. He was the Tribune who had tried to get Sulla's Eastern command transferred to Marius and he lost his life in the riots his schemes provoked. Cinna was opposed by his colleague, the Consul Cn. Octavius. Forced to withdraw from Rome, he set about collecting troops. Old Marius saw his opportunity and speedily recruited an army of his veterans. Converging upon Rome they easily overcame the flabby resistance of Octavius and the Senate, and, with a cold brutality new in Roman public life, they murdered the leading men of the Senate and of the governing class. From this appalling slaughter the Senate never recovered. The oldest, most eminent and most experienced of the traditional rulers of Rome disappeared in a blood-bath of revolting horror, the like of which had never been seen in Rome before. The consul Octavius was slain with some ceremony and Marius set his slaves to butcher his enemies right and left until it was too much even for Cinna who had all these slaves killed by his soldiers. Cinna got himself re-elected as Consul in the following year, 86 B.C., with Marius as his colleague. For the seventh time the old man became Consul, but his triumph was very short, for he soon died. Sulla meanwhile was campaigning in the East. Cinna, with Carbo as his consular colleague in 85 B.C., was preparing for the inevitable civil war against him which Cinna decided to fight in Greece. Early in the following year however his own troops killed him as he was preparing to sail. Carbo resolved to wait for Sulla to return and to fight it out in Italy. For three years both sides had prepared for the clash which was inevitably fierce and bloody. In 82 B.C. Carbo had the son of old Marius as his consular colleague. Following in his father's footsteps, he slaughtered more prominent men and Senators likely to sympathize with Sulla. Among them was Q. Mucius Scaevola, *Pontifex Maximus* and holder therefore of a most sacred office. It was from him that young Cicero had received his first lessons in statesmanship. None but the lesser men, with some fortunate exceptions, remained. The weakness of the Senate as a political force in Cicero's lifetime must be attributed in part to the work of the butcher Marius, his son and his accomplices.

If Sulla had not made plain in 88 B.C. the lesson that a resolute army commander could snap his fingers at Senate and people alike, there was no doubt about it when he returned victorious from the East five years later. Cold, hard, inflexible of purpose but willing to stoop to any treachery and deceit to get his own way, Sulla determined to make the demagogues pay for their crimes. He gave fair warning of his intentions. Civil war began as soon as he had landed. In 82 B.C. a Roman army under Sulla fought desperate battles against the armies of the Roman Consuls and discontented Italians, especially the Samnites, who were finally broken and overcome in a fierce fight outside the walls of Rome. The slaughter at the battle of the Colline Gate was followed by another reign of terror which, in numbers slain, outdid the butchery of Marius. Samnite captives were slaughtered to a man in a massacre which soon extended not merely to all Sulla's enemies but to those against whom any of his minions cherished a grudge. Their political and personal enmity was sharpened by their greed for gain and many of their victims perished so that their property might pass to their slayers. Nearly 5,000 names were said to have appeared on Sulla's dread proscription lists that sealed the doom of many a prominent Roman and deprived many families and children of their inheritance and of their political rights. Many rich business men who had rashly opposed the Senate then perished. One young relative of Marius, deeply implicated in the 'democratic' cause, curiously escaped. He was, it was said, too dissolute and wild to be taken seriously. His name was Gaius Julius Caesar. This was the first truly Roman civil war and the Romans, among them Cicero, then in his twenties, never forgot the tragedy of that terrible time. The bloodshed of the Social and civil wars in the ten years between 90 B.C. and 81 B.C. is thought to have caused the death of about half a million Romans and Italians. With them perished the best and most active citizens of Italy.

Sulla's Reforms

After such an experience, Roman politicians could never feel that they were standing upon firm ground, despite the fact that Sulla had used his absolute power after being elected as Dictator by the *comitia centuriata* in 82 B.C. to enforce a series of changes in the machinery of government that would, so he hoped, make it impossible for irresponsible Tribunes or soldiers again to use the ward-assembly of the People (*comitia tributa*) to defeat the Senate and the constitutional authority of the magistrates.

Sulla, fiercely proud, had known what it was to be a poor man. Yet he did not choose the easy path to fame of becoming a mob leader, trading upon the poverty of the masses and buying their support with rash and illusory promises. He favoured firm government by the established leaders whose ancestors had run the country from the earliest times. This meant strengthening the Senate. He increased its numbers, then probably down to about 150 men, to about 600, probably with the approval of the public assembly, if not by actual popular election. Many of the new Senators came from the ranks of the business men. Sulla may have counted upon harnessing the political activity of the business and commercial class, for the new Senators would, he no doubt hoped, give their support and that of their many dependants to the Senate.

Gaius Gracchus had replaced senators as judges or assessors in the Court of Claims by businessmen to whom he also gave the management of the taxation of the Asiatic provinces. Not without great justification, for they had shamefully abused their powers, Sulla deprived them of both these privileges. To keep the enlarged Senate up to strength, Sulla gave the Quaestors automatic entry to it on their election by the public assembly, the *comitia centuriata*. No longer should the Censors be allowed to appoint Senators. The venerable office of Censor was discontinued so there was no means whereby the new electors from Italy could be registered. The graded advancement in the magistracies, now increased in numbers, was again made the rule, as it first seems to have been in 180 B.C. No man could henceforth become a Consul until he was at least 42 years old, Praetor before he was 39, or Quaestor before 30. To prevent re-elections to the consular office such as Marius had secured, Sulla reinforced an old rule that no man could be re-elected as Consul within ten years of holding that office. By making it necessary for a man to remain in the Senate for eight years before he could rise to the responsible position of Praetor, Sulla hoped to ensure that none but men loyal to the Senate should reach positions of real power, which of course included the command of Roman armies.

Having strengthened the Senate, which had been dangerously diminished in talent and experience by the Social War, the civil war and the subsequent murders, Sulla's next task was to ensure that it should henceforth remain in full control of the political activity of the Republic, which meant in particular in control of the public assembly of the people. He therefore re-established the rule that no measures should be proposed to the people for their assent that had not previously received the approval of the Senate.

Besides weighting the scales heavily in favour of responsible government, he struck at the safety valves of popular unrest. The office of Tribune was the first and special object of his attack. Its power was blunted by the rule that a Tribune could never hold any other office and should not moreover serve again as Tribune until ten years had elapsed since his first year of office. By making it plain in this way that there was no political future for a Tribune, Sulla sought to discourage active and ambitious men from seeking the office. The powers of the office itself were notably diminished. Probably the Tribunes lost their ancient power of proposing new legislation to the people. Limits were put upon their right to prosecute and to intervene in the business of the State.

It is not known whether Sulla interfered with the composition of the public assembly, which probably continued to meet in the tribal organization that had been the rule for the previous 200 years.

Control of the army was a problem that Sulla failed to solve. To discourage the ambitious army commanders he did, it is true, favour a tendency to limit their period of service to one year and he made them guilty of treason if they did not give up their command to their successor or if they left their province at the head of their army without authority. Such rules, as he himself had proved, were not worth the paper on which they were written. The real problem, now that the army was recruited on a voluntary basis and no longer depended upon conscription, was how to enlist an army and to secure its loyalty to the Senate and the Republic. The recruits joined for what they could get. A successful general would provide them with booty and see that they got allotments of land as soon as they were demobilized after the campaign was over. Naturally the troops would stick to their general in the hope of these benefits. In comparison with such solid advantages the Republic was but a name and before long a successful general, so it is said, uttered those very words. How might the Republic have been saved? Not by a respectable constitutional general. For he would obey the Senate, give the Treasury all the loot his men could gather and refer them to the Senate when they asked for their share and for an additional reward in the shape of allotments of land. The Senate had usually a deaf ear for such requests. They could not or would not contemplate the only possible remedies, which plainly were attractive forms of reward for army service, guaranteed and justly administered. To provide for the troops in this way would have been beyond the limited powers of the Senate, which possessed no civil service or executive machinery.

Sulla at any rate did not solve the problem. As long as he lived his new rules were no doubt obeyed. The Senate and the traditional party of law and order had everything their own way. The machinery was there, but would there always be men to work it as Sulla apparently expected? In 79 B.C. he retired and in the following year, after a brief period of exotic luxury amid his vast wealth, he died. He wrote an inscription for his own monument. It said 'No friend has ever done me a kindness and no enemy a wrong without being fully repaid.' It is a boast that every gangster would like to make his own.

Such was the condition of public affairs in the Republic of Rome when Cicero embarked upon his political career.

Chapter Twelve

THE LADDER OF FAME IN ROME

The Prestige of Politics

To win election as a magistrate and to become a Senator, or to be admitted to one of the priestly colleges, had long been the height of ambition for any active, able young man of Rome. No other profession in which nowadays men can rise to public fame yielded rewards so substantial as those to be earned in politics in the Roman Republic. Authors, scientists, professors, industrialists, business men, bankers and journalists, whose names are more widely known in contemporary England or America than those of many Cabinet Ministers, either did not exist or were little regarded by the men and women around Cicero. Their houses were not thronged every morning by assiduous crowds of friends, supporters and clients such as those who flocked to pay court to the leading men in public life. Their names were not on everybody's lips.

In the world of entertainment and of sport the difference between Rome and more recent times is not so pronounced. The Roman actor Roscius seems to have enjoyed rewards such as those given to David Garrick or to Sir Henry Irving. Many a Roman gladiator and charioteer must have been as great a hero to city crowds as a star player in a British football team and to have had a following as enthusiastic as any of the renowned figures of American baseball. But these men did not make history and their day was brief. The laurels of the eminent politicians and statesmen did not wither so soon and they knew it. Cicero once professed that his main concern was with what people would be saying about him in 600 years' time. 'I am much more afraid of that', he said, 'than of the petty gossip of the men of today.'

Throughout the history of the Republic the best families of Rome sent their most gifted sons into political life. When Cicero was murdered the last of the great independent Roman politicians disappeared and they were to have no successors. Until the governing classes of Rome lost their freedom, politics was a good career for the few able to enjoy it. It found responsible jobs and gratifying dignity for the *élite* of the educated and socially active men of Rome. But competition was keen and the successful were numbered by tens, not by hundreds.

Gifted much above the ordinary run of his countrymen in wit, humour, quick insight, intelligence, and emotional sensibility, Cicero did not find it difficult to achieve personal distinction in the highest social circles of Rome. What lay behind the brief record of his career with which this book began and how is it to be translated into understandable terms of human activity and achievement?

That he should have been able to adopt such a life at all is the first surprise, because he did not come from a family whose menfolk had already achieved political distinction. His father was of the equestrian order, and none of his ancestors had succeeded in ennobling the family by having served as one of the chief magistrates of Rome. They seem, on the contrary, to have been hard-working farmers occupying a farmhouse by no means large or impressive. Cicero started life therefore under a heavy handicap. He was a 'new man' and he had to break into a jealously guarded circle wherein 'new men' were by no means welcome. His father, although a retired country gentleman, had intellectual interests. He seems to have done his best to find opportunities for his son, Marcus, who had already shown signs of great promise, to make a start in life in the great city. Marcus and his younger brother, Quintus, accordingly went with their father to Rome where they were fortunate in being able to profit by his friendship with two venerable figures in the politics of the Republic, Quintus Mucius Scaevola, an Augur, and his nephew of the same name who was *Pontifex Maximus*, the head of the priestly class. Between his sixteenth and eighteenth birthdays, young Marcus lived with the distinguished Augur, learning eagerly from his example and his conversation how a Roman might succeed in public life. Profiting by this experience he was able to some extent to make up for the great disadvantage of coming from a non-political family. Scaevola was not his only teacher, for he gave grateful recognition to other men who had influenced his early development, particularly three Greeks, Archias, a poet and man of letters, Philo, a philosopher, and Molon of Rhodes, a pleader in the law courts. Through them, he declared, he had gained that abiding

interest in books and the life of the mind which were to be
throughout life his unfailing source of support and consolation.

After his brief military service he gave himself up entirely to
study and to private practice in speaking and writing. He
reached early manhood at a time when Rome was torn by fierce
political struggles between Marius and Sulla. The behaviour
of these two ambitious and ruthless men must have contrasted
strangely with the picture of orderly political life and the tradition
of loyalty to the institutions of the Republic which young Cicero
had received not only from the aged Pontifex Scaevola, soon to be
slain in the civic strife, but from all the many people who looked
back to the grand story of Rome and her rise to fame.

Cicero's Early Political Career

When Cicero was training himself for a political career, inspired
by his old friends the Scaevolas, Augur and Pontifex, and by the
praise and encouragement of his Greek tutors, his first ambition
was to persuade the assembly of the people, the *comitia tributa*,
to elect him to one of the twenty posts of junior Treasury officials,
or *Quaestors*, which fell vacant every year. Before he could stand
any chance in this contest he had to become a familiar figure to
the city electors. There was only one way for a 'new man' to win
such distinction and that was by constant activity in the crowded
Forum, pleading cases before the Roman courts with the idle city
populace listening to the proceedings. Although there was no
formal legal profession and anyone might volunteer to defend or
prosecute, yet then as always people liable to lose heavily by an
unfavourable judgement naturally sought a skilful advocate to
plead their cause. This is where Cicero's great natural gifts of
fluent, graceful and impressive speech, developed as they had been
by his heavy investment in legal study and by long practice,
stood him in very good stead. But a young man had to work very
hard to gain his laurels. Cicero took a bold course by suddenly
attracting attention by undertaking the defence of a wretched
victim of the greed and insolence of a favourite of Sulla, then the
all-powerful Dictator of Rome (80 B.C.). This was sufficient in
itself to excite interest, particularly as Cicero won the case. He
continued to act as defending counsel in other lawsuits, despite
the evident danger of crossing Sulla, until 79 B.C., when for

reasons of health, safety and further study he went on a two years' tour in Athens, among the famous cities of Asia and in Rhodes. When he returned, with renewed vigour, the great Sulla was no more. The dread he had inspired was slowly abating and there was some hope that the traditional routine of Republican government might continue.

Cicero re-entered ardently the legal battleground where in a short time he achieved such success that veteran orators of the Forum, ripe for election to the consulate, found themselves outdistanced by this almost unknown young man from the country. As soon as he reached the age of thirty, he was able to seek election as Quaestor and his candidature was at once successful (76 B.C.). Quaestors had to serve not in Rome alone and Cicero found himself posted to Sicily. Throughout 75 B.C. he gave himself up to his new public duties and he obviously thought he had done well in supervising the export of corn to feed Rome and keeping a watchful eye upon that part of the administrative work of governing Sicily which it fell to him to undertake under his chief, the Praetor or Roman governor of the island. Returning to Rome full of his exploits he found not only that nobody felt grateful to him for his devotion to duty but that hardly anyone remembered where he had been. So much for the fame of a Quaestor. But thanks to Sulla's reforms, it brought one enduring reward – life-membership of the Roman Senate. It is true that as a new recruit and a backbencher, it was most unlikely that Cicero would be called upon to speak. However he had a vote and he now belonged to the most exclusive, dignified and influential club in the world.

For four more years he toiled and slaved in the courts. Each year twenty new Quaestors were elected, all his potential rivals for political distinction.

Pompey and Crassus

Meanwhile political developments were undermining the Roman constitution as it had been reshaped by Sulla. In 70 B.C. despite all the rules, a young man, son of the Consul under whom Cicero had served in his one campaign during the Social War, Gnaeus Pompeius, already and prematurely nicknamed by Sulla 'the Great', had become Consul. Yet he possessed none of the qualifications earned by service as junior magistrate and by slow advancement in the routine of politics, the *cursus honorum*. The story of his rise to power was to become familiar and indeed it was no longer new. The Senate had wanted a capable commander to defend the Sullan constitution against no less a man than the Consul for the year 78 B.C., Lepidus, who had so soon taken upon himself to undo the work of the Dictator. Pompey, who had shown ability against Sulla's enemies in the civil war, was a necessary choice for the Senate, who by no means trusted him. But he had a powerful influence in the important recruiting-ground of Picenum, where his father's reputation stood high. Successful against the rebels under Lepidus whom he defeated and put to flight, he was immediately afterwards sent to Spain at his own request where Sertorius, who, like Sulla, had been one of the most able of all the officers of Marius, still had the country under his control. Hardly had Pompey succeeded in bringing such aid to the Roman commander, Metellus, in Spain that the forces of Sertorius were broken, when new alarms disturbed the peace in Italy. In 73 B.C. some gladiators, accustomed to dangerous fighting, began to organize a formidable slave revolt under an able leader, Spartacus. They defeated both the Consuls in 72 B.C. and a new Roman army, recruited by another of Sulla's lieutenants, M. Licinius Crassus, was also unable to defeat the rebels at his first encounter with them. The fate of thousands of Italian homes, at the mercy of great gangs of desperate and maddened slaves led by cut-throats and gladiators, was pitiable indeed. The Senate, who had no reason to feel confident of Crassus, summoned Pompey back to help subdue the Spartacists. By the time he arrived, however, Crassus had just about completed the task and Pompey's men had little more to do than destroy the fugitives from the slave army defeated by Crassus in a pitched battle. (Plates 27, 28.)

The Senate's enemies had been overcome, but there were two generals made powerful by victories, Pompey and Crassus, both at the head of their loyal armies. The Senators disliked them both; Sulla had mistrusted Pompey because of his effort to capitalize some military successes in Africa, and Crassus because of his sharp practices in profiting from the many large fortunes confiscated during the proscriptions. With no love for each other, they nevertheless were not such fools as to fall for the ingenious plan cherished, it seems, by some Senators, according to which they should fight each other and let the Senate dispose of the victor. A simpler plan from their point of view was to sink their personal feelings and to combine against the Senate. Accordingly, at the head of their armies they marched on Rome demanding that they celebrate their triumphs and become Consuls for the year 70 B.C. The Senate was powerless and they were both elected despite the fact that neither had the necessary legal qualifications. They were an ill-assorted pair, deeply suspicious of each other and with no regard for the policy and plans of Sulla whom they had so powerfully helped. Together they struck heavy blows at Sulla's constitution. They restored the power of the Tribunes and they deprived the Senate of the right to approve all new measures before they were submitted to the public assembly. The main bulwark of the Senators' defence against ill-advised and irresponsible legislation was removed only ten years after it had first been won back for them by the great Dictator. The people were pleased. In the same year the Censors were restored, their authority over the Senate was again affirmed, and a purge of the senatorial ranks began. The Censors were able to begin enrolling the new Italian citizens as voters, an empty gesture, for ballot boxes were still not provided in the municipalities. It remained to satisfy the business men, who were again admitted to share jury service with the Senators on such terms that the Senators were no longer able to control the Court of Claims.

Popular as these acts no doubt were outside senatorial circles they cannot be described as a reform. Merely to undo Sulla's work and to leave matters at that was to restore a threat of chaos that Sulla had at least sought to remove. Pompey does not seem to have realized the fact. He never seems to have reached a true understanding of the forces at work shaping the political destiny of the Republic. Cicero had not yet reached a position from which he could intervene in these matters of high constitutional principle.

Cicero as Aedile and Praetor

He was fully occupied in making his career in the courts. His fame seems to have been rising steadily. When in 70 B.C he sought election as Aedile to serve in the following year, he was triumphantly elected by a greater number of votes than any of his three competitors. His triumph was the greater because he was not a rich man and the main duty of an Aedile from the point of view of the man in the street was that he should spend lavishly on public shows and festivals. Unlike Caesar five years later, who borrowed money on a ruinously extravagant scale in order to buy the favours of the mobs of Rome, Cicero managed this business cleverly and honestly and he further added to his laurels by his successful prosecution of Verres, a corrupt governor of Sicily, who had almost bled white the wretched Sicilians whom Cicero had done his best to serve five years earlier.

After his year of office as Aedile Cicero was thirty-eight. He was half-way on in his effort to climb the ladder of fame. He had still to strive for the greatest prizes and they were the most difficult to grasp. One of the two consular posts was the ultimate summit of ambition, but for that Cicero would not be able to compete until his forty-second year. Before he could even hope to become a candidate he had to get himself elected as one of the eight Praetors. Except for political complications which made it necessary for the elections to be held three times, Cicero had little difficulty in becoming the First Praetor of the city in 66 B.C. In this office he presided in the highest civil court of Rome and was also a commissioner in extortion trials such as the one he had led against Verres. These high judicial duties did not prevent him, as they would now prevent British or American judges, from continuing to appear as advocate in the courts. Neither was it thought unseemly when he made a political speech appealing to the people to vote supreme powers and large forces to Pompey. In continuing disregard of Sulla's Constitution which, as Consul, he had already undermined, Pompey wanted to take the command of the war in the East against Rome's old enemy, King Mithridates, who had murdered tens of thousands of Italian traders over twenty years earlier, had never been completely subdued by Sulla and was again threatening the security of Rome's eastern frontiers in Asia Minor and in Greece. The Senate had appointed Lucullus to this command and he had already been in the field since 74 B.C. Pompey had already vast force under his command, given to him by a law of 67 B.C. to wipe out piracy in the Mediterranean. Fresh from his complete victory over the pirates, Pompey got the command and went to the East with a force so huge that there was nothing to prevent him returning as another Sulla if he had the mind to do so.

No sooner had Cicero completed his year as Praetor, given up his *imperium*, and dismissed the two lictors who accompanied his ceremonious journeys through the city, than he began to scheme and plan to become one of the two Consuls. If he had chosen to take a province he could have gone off at once to rule as governor (*propraetor*) in one of Rome's dependencies. He preferred to remain in Rome and to work hard for the consulship. Two years had to elapse before he could legally take the office, should he be fortunate enough to be elected. When Praetors were elected at the rate of eight a year it is clear that the number of possible candidates for the consulate might be large. There was no upper age limit for a Consul and in theory therefore at any one time there might be anything from fifty to a hundred Roman politicians of eminence and considerable experience fully quali-fied for the office. The power of family influence was so important that ordinary men had to possess it in full measure if they were to stand a chance of success. Great self-confidence joined with unusual ability was naturally required in any man who lacked such influence, and many ex-Praetors would not choose to run, either because they knew that they could not 'make the grade', or because they preferred a quiet life to the harassing duties and grave responsibilities of a co-President of the Roman Republic.

How to Win an Election in Rome

As it turned out, Cicero had six competitors. Something of the tense excitement of his struggle survives in his letters, but it remains still more vividly on record in a little electioneering manual generally thought to have been written for his benefit by his brother Quintus. Full of sound sense, it is not likely that it contained anything of importance Cicero himself would not know full well. In any case it shows how anxious his brother was for him to succeed. His anxiety was well founded. He begged Marcus to remember how difficult it was to succeed in Rome with its confused jumble of people, amidst so many traps and pitfalls and so much vice and where arrogance, stupidity, ill-will, snobbishness, evil tempers and worse manners all created so many more difficulties and dangers for the unfortunate candidate. Cicero also must never forget, said his brother, that he was a 'new man'. That in itself was a bad enough handicap and Quintus could do little more than try to prove that it need not be an insuperable bar. Had not a 'new man', Gaius Coelius, become Consul? It is true that it was thirty years ago, but he had two very distinguished aristocrats against him and yet he had managed to beat one of them.

The great thing, said Quintus, was for Cicero not to be dismayed by the undoubted difficulty of his task. He should count up his advantages and resources and see that all were energetically employed in his cause. Nothing should be neglected. That all his friends should be enlisted in his support went without saying. Everyone whom Cicero had helped in the law courts should be reminded that the time had now come when they could show their gratitude. An elastic meaning should be given to the word 'friends' which 'has a wider application during a canvass than in other times'. It should cover all the many callers at Cicero's house. Every art must be used to induce as many as possible to make a habit of calling, Marcus must become able to greet all those people by name: 'Make the faculty you possess of recognizing people conspicuous and go on increasing and improving it every day. I don't think there is anything so popular or so conciliatory.' Still more important was it for Marcus always to be accompanied by a large throng in his daily visit to the Forum. Quintus recommended his brother to go down to the Forum at fixed times because 'the daily escort by its numbers produces a great impression and confers great personal distinction'. We can believe this the better when we remember that there were no newspapers or other publicity devices open to Roman statesmen.

Outside the circle of friends were the 'neighbours, clients, freedmen and even your slaves, for nearly all the talk which forms one's public reputation comes from domestic sources'. Then came the broad social classes about whom Quintus encouraged Cicero to believe that he could count upon 'all the business men, nearly the whole of the equestrian order, many municipal towns' and 'a large number of the rising generation who have become attached to you in their enthusiasm for rhetoric'. The most tricky of all to win over would be the aristocrats, the *optimates*, the men into whose exclusive circles Cicero was hoping to enter. 'All these men must be canvassed with care. Agents must be sent to them and they must be convinced that we have always been at one politically with the *optimates* and that we have never been demagogues.' The Roman *equites* ('Knights') along with the loyalists and wealthy must also be brought to believe that Cicero was 'eager for peace and quiet times'. To talk like this and at the same time to tell Marcus that he had 'already won the city populace' and that 'the people think of you as not likely to be hostile to their interests from the fact that in your style of speaking and in your declared convictions you have been on the popular side' shows how a politician can delude himself into believing that he could reconcile the irreconcilable and make the best of all worlds. But Quintus had not lost all powers of distinguishing between honesty and lack of principle. He excused himself by saying 'There is great need of a flattering manner which, however faulty and discreditable in other transactions of life, is yet necessary during a candidature.' Combined with flattery of friends went the opposite treatment for the enemies: 'See if possible that some new scandal is started against our competitors for crime or looseness of life or corruption, such as is in harmony with their characters.'

Quintus Cicero was evidently a man of few illusions; he knew what won and lost elections. No nonsense from him about the supreme importance of a programme full of high ideals for the betterment of the human race, of campaign pledges, or of fervid professions of faith in this or that remedy for public troubles. Instead, a set of severely practical suggestions on the supremely important problem, 'how to win more votes than the other fellow'. Cicero, although a moralist and philosopher, was sufficiently a politician to realize the need for votes and he accordingly bent all his energies to winning them. One weapon he seems to have disdained. He does not seem to have sought to buy votes by outright bribery, neither did Quintus recommend that he should do so. Their joint plan of action seems to have been to try to prevent their opponents giving bribes by threatening their agents with all the penalties of the law. Men who took bribes could not be punished as they would be under English law, but those who offered bribes were liable to severe penalties.

Cicero as Consul: 63 B.C.

Fortunately for Cicero the other candidates were less acceptable to the governing class than he was. So in 63 B.C. he became Consul together with a political nonentity named C. Antonius Hybrida.

This man, 'afraid of his own shadow' to use the description by Cicero's brother Quintus, was only too glad to lie low and do nothing provided that he could make sure of a rich province after his year of office. Cicero, who did not want a province, easily satisfied him with the promise of Macedonia. 63 B.C. was therefore Cicero's year. He never forgot it and did his best to ensure that nobody else forgot it either. For it turned out to be a year of crisis. The foundations of political life in Rome had not been stable since the times of Sulla and Marius thirty years earlier. It was as though the political world had become volcanic, liable at any moment to violent eruptions. Unlike the Consuls of more settled times, Cicero found that winning his election was merely the beginning of his troubles.

What above all alarmed the men active in public affairs was the tremendous power of Pompey. Those with much to lose were the least happy, and of them all, Pompey's former colleague, Crassus, now immensely rich, was most uneasy. By outward appearance he had not done badly. After being Consul in 70 B.C., he became Censor in 65 B.C. But the highest political offices were now somewhat of a sham if the occupant had no legions to pit against a rival like Pompey, at the head of an army. Crassus had reason to be nervous. His father and his brother had been killed for opposing Marius and Cinna. He had himself seen how strong was a dictator's urge to put rich men's names on proscription lists merely in order to be able to steal their property, and he had given all his energy and enthusiasm to the supreme task of becoming rich. He was himself therefore ripe for a proscription list and he had no assurance, when Pompey returned with his army and fleet from the East, that one would not be compiled. Consequently he bent his energies to building himself up politically. His weapons were his money, his skill as an advocate, and the energy and intelligence with which he studied political tactics. By defending wealthy clients, by lending money to influential Senators and rising young politicians and by buying votes in the *comitia*, he slowly fortified his position. He needed helpers and he was shrewd enough to enlist the aid of a young, daring and supremely able aristocrat, Gaius Julius Caesar, then beginning to make his way in political life. After serving as Quaestor in Spain in 68 B.C., he became Aedile in Rome in 65 B.C., when he astonished the populace by the incredible magnificence of the games and free banquets he lavished upon them. His aristocratic indifference to the huge cost of these celebrations was no doubt based upon his confidence that the bills would be underwritten by Crassus while he himself would reap in full the benefits from the immense publicity value of the proceedings. The bills were certainly stupendous. In time Caesar met them by finding over 19 million sesterces, nearly one-tenth of the public revenue of the Republic, an enormous sum to come out of the pocket of one individual. About this time (69–68 B.C.), he lost his second wife, who had been a daughter of Cinna, and his aunt, the widow of Marius. At their funerals he forcibly reminded the city mob of his connexions with these two popular heroes, both hateful to the Senators.

Crassus and Caesar, with little love for each other and still less genuine enthusiasm for the mob, were forced, when they combined, to align themselves against Pompey and to play the game of the 'popular' party in opposition to the Senate. Had the Senators been intelligent enough to give their support to Pompey, whom they need not have feared as much as the schemes of Crassus and Caesar, it is unlikely that the pair would have long survived as a dangerous opposition. Instead, the preliminary skirmishes in what was to be a long and disastrous political war took place in the year when Cicero was Consul.

His first big task was indeed the unpleasant duty of opposing a bill proposing vast measures of confiscation and resettlement as part of a plan for the redistribution of land among the poorer landless Romans. The bill stood in the name of Rullus, an obscure Tribune of the People, but its author was Caesar and its motives were political rather than economic. We know no more about the actual text of the bill than Cicero has preserved in his speeches against it, and he was concerned to inflame popular opposition, not to discuss it on its merits. Ten men, armed with very wide power, 'ten kings' Cicero called them, were to administer its provisions. The measure seems to have been so loosely drafted that Cicero was able to argue that it virtually empowered these commissioners to sell the whole of the possessions of the Roman people beyond the seas, all lands, palaces, buildings, and other property in order to create a fund for the purchase of land in Italy for redistribution. Rullus did not stop at that. Egypt was not yet a Roman province, but that did not prevent him including on the basis of a forged will purporting to convey the country to

Rome, the incorporation of Egypt in the Roman domain as part of his plan. There could be only one conclusion. His real aim was to put the fabulous wealth of the Pharaohs and their Greek successors, the Ptolemies, at the disposal of Caesar and Crassus in their struggle against Pompey.

There was small chance of Pompey and his friends overlooking such a threat, but the failure of the bill did not exhaust its utility. It was designed not so much to aid the poor as to make the poor hate the conservative politicians who were bound to oppose it. One of Caesar's aims seems to have been to hasten a show-down with the slow-moving conservatives who ruled Rome. The immediate effect of the new bill was to put Cicero 'on the spot' by facing him with the choice of incurring like the Gracchi the remorseless hatred of all influential Romans if he supported a bill more drastic and far-reaching than the Gracchan laws, or of losing popularity among the masses if he opposed it. Cicero, whose idea of justice included unquestioning belief in the sacred rights of private property, had to oppose the bill and he needed all his skill to secure its rejection.

Three times did he have to speak against it with all the authority of his consular position. Three times therefore he was in grave danger of being pilloried as the man who stood between the masses and their hopes of sudden gain. Caesar had struck a blow not merely at Cicero but at other more distinguished Romans upon whom Cicero had to depend, Pompey for instance. In other words Caesar was 'playing politics' while pretending to serve his fellow-men.

From this time onwards Cicero had to throw in his lot with the conservative classes, the *optimates*. He was soon to cement the ties with the blood of his opponents. Among his competitors for the Consulate, the one he feared most was a seedy aristocrat, Lucius Sergius Catilina. In low water financially, this man had tried to restore his fortunes on the usual lines by misgoverning the province of Africa as propraetor in 67 B.C. Accusations of corruption on his return made it impossible for him to run for the consulship of 65 B.C., but he succeeded by bribery in securing an acquittal which left him free to challenge Cicero in the following year. Cicero may well have felt the need for extreme caution because Catiline had the support of Julius Caesar, Crassus, the demagogues and the masses or 'the popular party'. Catiline's

failure by a few votes stirred him to more desperate moves. He
was understandably goaded and enraged by Cicero's denuncia-
tions of him as unprincipled, ill-tempered and of reckless audacity.
Evidently Cicero did not neglect the advice of his brother's
electioneering manual, for he collected all the scandals and slanders
he could find about Catiline, which were plenty, and flung them
in his face. Cicero became Consul and left Catiline licking his
wounds, nursing a heavy bill for election expenses and thirsting
for revenge. Catiline tried to murder Cicero then, so Cicero said,
but he was doubly determined to do so after he had again run
for the consulship for the following year (62 B.C.) and had again
been defeated in July 63 B.C. Like a bankrupt gambler, he had
doubled the stakes on borrowed money only to plunge to final
ruin.

The Treason of Catiline: 63 B.C.

The steadily declining state of public morale in Rome had
already produced scores of desperate men who surrounded
Catiline as their leader, sharing his dissolute way of life and
sponging on him for gifts and money. Crippled with debts and
cursed with lavish tastes, they all, like Catiline, could see no
solution for their troubles save in drastic measures of debt-repudi-
ation and confiscation. Catiline's problem seems to have been
that faced by decadent landowning aristocracies everywhere.
Their capital was in their estates. In the early days of the Republic
the Romans had been content to live on their estates. Now their
fashionable descendants had to have money to burn in the gay
city.   How could they get it except by borrowing on the security
of their landed property? This way was the road to ruin, for
their income in money from their estates was soon unable to pay
the interest on their debts. Thus did the development of a money
economy combined with a sophisticated city life contribute to the
downfall of the descendants of the stern and simple Roman
fathers of the Republic. Many lesser men were equally involved
in debt and equally therefore exposed to the harsh laws permitting
the imprisonment and slavery of insolvent debtors. By making
their cause his own, Catiline was perhaps able to confer upon his
private ambitions some semblance of a respectable public policy.
If so he was a singularly poor politician, because the alarm he
caused among timid business men and financiers by his tactics

had in itself provoked an economic crisis in which men with money became exceedingly loth to part with it. They wanted their loans repaid and they refused to lend more. Their attitude reduced many more people to the same straits as Catiline and his friends who sought political power in order to apply their revolutionary remedy of debt-reduction. Being unable to succeed by fair means they resolved upon foul. The story of the Catilinian conspiracy has long been one of the staple topics of Roman history. The traditional account says that after being twice defeated as a candidate for the consulship Catiline planned to raise a private army from any riff-raff he could find, including Gauls if necessary, to occupy Rome, to murder Cicero and other prominent men, and to increase the general panic by setting fire to their houses and threatening the whole city with conflagration. Cicero at length began to get more circumstantial evidence of what was being plotted. Crassus and Caesar seem to have realized that their former protégé Catiline was becoming too dangerous and they are thought to have taken steps to make Cicero aware of the fact.

By some means Cicero learned enough to be able to make things so hot that Catiline, who at first tried to bluff his way out of the business, was forced to leave Rome. Cicero still lacked firm proof of the full extent of the conspiracy, but the alarm already aroused had been sufficient to induce the Senate, on 21 October 63 B.C., to pass the extreme emergency decree 'Let the Consuls see to it that the Republic incurs no injury.' Rather like our martial law, this decree could not set aside established laws but it powerfully increased the Consul's discretionary authority. By a great stroke of good fortune a few days later, some Gauls on a mission to Rome revealed an approach from some of Catiline's men who had remained in Rome, offering them immense bribes at the expense of the constitution and the finances of the Republic if they would get their fellow tribesmen, the Allobroges, to join the armed rising then being planned. The news was brought to Cicero. It gave him his opportunity. He at once got the Gauls to send a reply to Catiline's men requiring the leading conspirators to give a written oath, signed and sealed, solemnly guaranteeing that they meant business when they sought help from the tribes of Gaul to enable Catiline to overturn the Roman Republic. To such depths had these violent men descended that four at once gave their written guarantees. They did not scruple to truckle to the age-long enemies of Rome.

The envoys were allowed to set out from Rome on their way back to their own country on the night of 2 December 63 B.C. carrying upon them their damning evidence of Roman treason. They had not gone far before they were intercepted and were brought, with their document, to Cicero. By these means Cicero was clearly able to prove the guilt of the four conspirators. He had them arrested, summoned the Senate, and so was able to prove that his suspicions of Catiline had been fully justified. Striving to remain constitutionally correct he consulted the Senate about the next step. The offence of the conspirators was great and it richly merited the death penalty. So thought the Senators until Caesar recommended life imprisonment instead. Unable to carry the Senators with him Caesar nevertheless caused opinion to wobble until Cato vigorously demanded the death penalty. Cicero called for a vote and the Senate agreed with Cato. Cicero thereupon had the men strangled in the City prison. They were Roman citizens. They had not been tried, neither had an appeal to the people of Rome against the death sentence been allowed.

Five years later Cicero was to suffer bitterly for his neglect of an elementary principle of the Roman constitution, but for the time being he had reached a pinnacle of fame which few Consuls in ordinary years would hope to attain. For nipping civil war in the bud he was acclaimed Father of his Country and became the proud recipient of an amount of fulsome praise almost sufficient to satisfy his own vanity in his achievement.

Catiline himself presented little serious difficulty. After he had been forced out of Rome he tried to organize his few thousand followers and to march to join the Gauls. His army was not properly organized and it was half-armed. The disciplined, well-trained Roman forces which Cicero sent against him were easily able to prevent any such move. Catiline and his motley gang were wiped out after turning at bay with the courage of desperation upon a Roman force of three legions (January 62 B.C.).

So ended the Conspiracy of Catiline. There could have been no other solution. Nevertheless writers of our day, determined at all costs to find in history something to give reality to their own dreams of eternal class warfare, have not hesitated to suggest that

Catiline has been unfairly treated, firstly by Cicero as the base tool of a degenerate oligarchy and later by biased plutocratic historians. They ask if he was not really a champion of the poor against the owners of the money-bags. Such an interpretation will not stand examination, although we only have the official version of his exploits, not his own. Neither do we know what Caesar and Crassus were really up to, but despite such uncertainties it is very difficult to regard Catiline as otherwise than reckless of national welfare. It is hard to believe that he really cared for the poor. He was out for himself. The poor were merely pawns in the all-engrossing game of personal political ambitions; a situation in which they have not seldom figured since the last century of the Roman Republic.

Chapter Thirteen

THE DUEL OF POMPEY AND CAESAR
AND THE DOWNFALL OF THE
ROMAN REPUBLIC

Manoeuvring for Position

BEFORE long the sudden collapse of Catiline's sorry crew made the whole business something of a nine days' wonder, except to Cicero who frequently re-lived in memory his days of triumph. There were some Romans who were probably quite content that all memory of it should disappear as soon as possible. Caesar and Crassus, in particular, the leaders of the 'Popular Party', as they are often misleadingly described, had every motive to wish it forgotten. Their earlier association with Catiline had given rise to some dark suspicions which they had not been able entirely to allay. Sorting out the skeletons in the cupboards of Julius Caesar has never been a popular task amongst his many hero-worshippers. If it had been, more attention would no doubt have been given to his relations with Catiline. Compromised as he seems to have been, Caesar with his usual skill cut the connexion before Catiline became too dangerous. He had no doubt realized that he could not get the influence he wanted in the government of Rome by the indirect method of having a nominee elected as Consul. He must also have lost any illusions he may have had upon the ease and safety with which power could be won by revolution and armed rebellion. Yet he had at all costs to strengthen his personal political position. When Cicero was Consul, Caesar caused a sensation by getting himself elected, in spite of the fact that some venerable old gentlemen were also candidates, at the early age of thirty-seven as Rome's chief religious official, the *Pontifex Maximus*. His scanty interest in religious questions is the best measure of Caesar's political opportunism and still more of the frivolity of the Roman electorate. Caesar must have found many of the duties a bore although they immensely increased his personal prestige. For this exalted position was given for life. It provided him with an official residence and no doubt a con-

siderable measure of personal security. His enemies would have
to think twice before murdering so distinguished a religious
figure, although this sacred office had not saved the life of
Cicero's old friend and tutor Q. Mucius Scaevola, who had been
slain by the son of Marius.

To be *Pontifex Maximus* moreover did not pay Caesar's debts
nor, what was really serious, did it get him far in the competitive
struggle against Pompey, then easily the most powerful citizen of
the Republic thanks to his vast command and large forces in
Asia. When did Caesar first get the idea that his best way of
getting political power for himself would be through an alliance
with the all-powerful Pompey? Some sort of understanding or
bargain, of which Cicero was ignorant, may have been negotiated
while Pompey was still in the East, for Cicero failed to get the
enthusiastic praise for his conduct as Consul which he clearly
expected from Pompey. In December 62 B.C., Pompey had
returned to celebrate his triumph after the final conquest of the
East. He had created or reorganized four Roman provinces
there – Asia, Bithynia, Cilicia, and Syria. He had almost doubled
the annual revenue of Rome. He had organized the Eastern
Mediterranean under Roman supervision and sent back a vast
hoard of slaves and booty. With such tremendous power and
resources he could have taken anything he wanted in the way
of power and influence. Yet he amazed the Roman world by
dismissing his army. All that he asked was to be allowed to
celebrate his triumph, which he did, on 28 September 61 B.C.,
with the most immense spectacular show, befitting the last large-
scale looting expedition which Romans were able to make against
the East. After the stupendous parade of his amassed booty of
gold, jewels, precious stones, and works of art he discarded
Alexander the Great's tunic which he had worn in the procession
and became once more a private citizen of the Roman Republic.

Had he so chosen, he could very easily have defied the law and
custom of Rome just as Sulla did, keeping his army and using it if
necessary to compel his fellow citizens to obey him as the uncrowned king of Rome. Many Romans fully expected him to do
so. Some, including perhaps Cicero, secretly hoped he would do so.
Not of course for any special love of Pompey, still less for any
desire for a military dictatorship, but because they could see no
other way of preventing the breakdown of effective government.

If Pompey does not seize power, they may well have thought, somebody else will, and who could tell but that it might be left to the wild men, the self-appointed champions of the masses of the people? Pompey might not be very good but anyone else, Crassus or Caesar, for example, might be very much worse.

Whether Pompey failed to take the plunge into one-man rule because the idea was too new and too stained by the examples of Marius and Sulla, whether he was disgusted with politics and with the narrow, self-seeking yet unruly political schemers, whether he lacked sufficient energy and drive, or whether he just did not know what to do and had no far-reaching political plans at all, as his puzzle-headed face suggests, will probably never be known. It has even been suggested that he had already struck a bargain with Caesar and was merely biding his time, but this seems most improbable. It was not for such a reason that he would not congratulate Cicero on his exploits against Catiline. He would, so one theory goes, have been more pleased if Catiline had defeated the Consul so that he, Pompey, might have had the glory of coming to the rescue of the Republic. The probable explanation of his attitude is rather his good opinion of himself and the complacency with which he regarded all the smaller men who had never possessed a command such as his, who could not, as he was certain he could, quickly recruit a new force just as big merely by the magic of his name. The vast fortune he had made in the East no longer left Crassus in the unique position he had formerly occupied. What alone seems certain is that any Roman politicians who believed that Pompey's failure to seize power was a true testimony to the vitality of Roman Republican traditions were deluding themselves.

Pompey was the last great Roman commander of the Republic voluntarily to renounce supreme power. His example merely proved to others, particularly to Julius Caesar, what a fool he had been. The behaviour of the Senate showed little gratitude for, or understanding of, Pompey's undoubtedly great achievements in stamping out tens of thousands of pirates, releasing the prisoners and the plunder they had taken, and in bringing what seems to have been a wise and statesmanlike order into the vast confusion of Asiatic politics. So badly did the Senators behave that Pompey himself must have realized the folly of his self-denial. For the Senators would not, as he asked, approve his settlement of the

East as a whole. They insisted upon examining it in detail, country by country and point by point, and they began to offer criticisms of this matter and that. What was worse, they refused to provide land settlements for his demobilized soldiers. The irony of the situation lay in the fact that Pompey had filled the Roman Treasury with part of the proceeds of his Eastern campaigns, so the Senators had little justification for pretending, as they did, that the State could not afford the rewards for which Pompey asked.

Self-help with or without the Senate was clearly the only path for a politician to take if he meant business and did not intend to suffer frustration at the hands of feeble opponents who had no plans of their own but would prevent action by others. Henceforward the political struggles of Rome were less over laws designed to bring economic and social reform than over measures contrived by clever politicians to embarrass their opponents and to advance their own fortunes. Such was Julius Caesar's land bill presented by Rullus and defeated by Cicero in 63 B.C. Political tactics designed on these lines have been common enough in our own times. In a swift revealing phrase, Napoleon summed up the tremendous cataclysm of the French Revolution by saying that 'Vanity made the Revolution; Liberty was only the pretext'. So also, in our own day, the totalitarian revolutionary programmes to win power at all costs and by any manoeuvre, concealing entirely selfish motives under specious plans for the public good find many parallels in the degenerate latter days of the Roman Republic.

The First Triumvirate and the First Consulship of Julius Caesar

In 60 B.C. Pompey made another unsuccessful effort to get a land bill passed providing land for his veterans. The Senators, who succeeded in obstructing him, had won a barren victory, for they drove Pompey finally into an alliance with Caesar. The two most powerful men in Rome combined forces and there was nobody to oppose them, particularly as they were very soon joined by Crassus, king of the money-makers of the city. The alliance of these three men, known to later ages as the First Triumvirate, relegated the old Republican machinery of government to the scrap heap. The alliance between Caesar and Pompey was cemented by a strong personal tie. Pompey married Julia, the charming daughter of Julius Caesar, in the following year, when Caesar became Consul for the first time (59 B.C.).

As soon as Caesar, as Consul, had to accept full responsibility for his own measures, nothing more was heard of the grandiose scheme for land-resettlement proposed by Rullus to embarrass Cicero. Instead Caesar did little more than create, from the wealth of the Near East, a fund from which to buy land in Italy to provide for some of Pompey's demobilized men and to find a few allotments for the Roman poor. The plan, modest as it was, excited violent animosity in the Senate. Caesar therefore took it direct to the people and 'rail-roaded' it through in the teeth of senatorial opposition and despite the pathetic attempts of his fellow-Consul, Bibulus, to rule him out of order on religious grounds. Caesar's action was illegal and everyone knew it. The high-handed way in which he proceeded led the wits to describe the year 59 B.C. as the Consulate of Julius and Caesar instead of Bibulus and Caesar. To teach the opposition a lesson he next proceeded to seize the last fertile land in Italy belonging to the Roman people, the Campanian land taken from the city of Capua as punishment for its aid to Hannibal. Such a move was inevitably clumsy and unjust, for it drove many smallholders from their plots to make room for newcomers, or, if the occupiers were allowed to stay, it made them pay rent to the new owners. In either case the Treasury suffered a total loss because rents for the land were no longer public property.

The opposition was fierce and every constitutional method was tried in order to prevent Caesar's plans being adopted. Caesar had an answer. He had, it is true, been deprived of an army command because the Senators saw to it when his election seemed likely that his 'province' after his year of office should be supervision of the cattle tracks and forests of Italy. In the first few months of his year as Consul, Caesar got one of the Tribunes, P. Vatinius, to propose and carry through the public assembly a law giving him the province of Cisalpine Gaul for five years with an army of three legions. When the newly-appointed governor of Transalpine Gaul suddenly died, the Senators, as though despairing of further resistance, gave his province also to Caesar, with another legion. Caesar soon set about recruiting his forces and by stationing them near Rome he completely overawed his opponents. The Senate, as a constitutional force, simply collapsed. Caesar was Dictator in all but name.

The same shameless illegality and tough political bargaining is seen in another political deal put through by the Triumvirate during Caesar's consulship. Crassus, one of the trio, with his business friends found that they had made a bad bargain by offering the State too high a sum for the right of collecting public revenues in the Eastern province of Asia. They had been trying to get relief for some time. Cicero, who rarely refused to help the business men, promised his support but privately he was outspoken. 'The case is scandalous, the demand a disgraceful one and a confession of rash speculation.' He excused his support for the swindle by the need for harmony between the social classes. 'There was a very great risk that if they got no concession they would be alienated from the Senate.' Caesar, who did not want them alienated from Julius Caesar, obligingly had a law passed, despite the opposition of many Senators, reducing by one-third the sum they had contracted to pay. Up went the price of the stock of the lucky company and some respectable fortunes were soon made at public expense.

Finally Pompey's Eastern conquests and provincial arrangements, which had not yet been legally accepted by the Roman Government, were formally ratified. Both Crassus and Pompey thus had their rewards from the partnership.

Caesar's year as Consul in 59 B.C. was given up almost entirely to political manoeuvres and shady deals of this sort, many of them driven through by strong-arm tactics and in complete defiance of established constitutional rules and practices. Caesar heeded neither the protests of the Senate nor that of his consular colleague. All opposition was ignored or silenced. To be sure the opposition was not very enlightened, but Caesar's way of meeting it was that of a political gangster.

Moreover, he emerged from his year of office with a term of power as proconsul in Gaul of over four years, with unusual powers to select his own chiefs of staff and to found colonies at his own discretion, and an army large enough to protect him from any attack that his enemies might seek to mount against him in revenge for the high-handed treatment he had meted out to them as Consul. Beyond Gaul might be unpredictable possibilities of conquest and of enrichment. Caesar was thus set up with a powerful command in much the same way as Pompey had been against the pirates and against Mithridates nine years earlier.

Apart from such personal self-seeking, what had Caesar to show in the way of laws for strictly public purposes? He collected and improved previous laws attempting to safeguard the provinces against plundering Roman governors, and he arranged to publish a public gazette giving the text of resolutions of the Senate, of the new laws of the people as well as important public news. That was about all. The publicity for the activities of the Senate was however mainly designed to discredit it in the eyes of the Roman masses. For a few minor improvements such as these, the Romans paid the supreme sacrifice of their constitution and traditional form of government. Such was Caesar's enduring influence and example that five years later Cicero said that since Caesar's consulship there had been 'no genuine Consuls, but mere hucksters of provinces, mere agents and slaves of sedition'.

Political Gangsters and Riots in Rome

When Caesar left Rome for his new command in 58 B.C. he left the troublemaker P. Clodius behind. Clodius was a Claudius, one of the proudest patrician houses of Rome. His family was as old as the Republic. Twelve generations of Claudii, all of consular rank, lay between him and the founder of his house, Appius Claudius Sabinus, who had been Consul in 495 B.C. Clodius was therefore unable to become a Tribune of the People as he wished to be. Caesar, as Consul and *Pontifex Maximus*, had sanctioned the formalities by which Clodius was adopted as the son of a plebeian lad of nineteen years, many years younger than Clodius.

Caesar rightly judged that Clodius would be able to keep the political cauldron simmering, a task at which he succeeded only too well. Clodius struck at established authority by diminishing the power of the Censors to expel Senators (Clodius was a Senator) and abolishing the power of magistrates and priests to interfere in public business on religious grounds (Caesar had suffered from these powers at the hands of Bibulus, his colleague as Consul in 59 B.C.). Clodius became the darling of the mob by giving corn away as a free dole to all applicants and by abolishing the law which forbade working men to unite in their clubs or societies (*collegia*). The conservative and well-to-do classes were fools enough to believe his assurances that he meant them no harm and he was able to get these laws passed. As soon as he had reduced the power of his opponents and had been able to create organized groups bound to support him by the bribes of free wheat provided at the public expense, Clodius revealed himself as a political gangster operating on a grand scale. He could not have become the head of these gangs unaided and he was not the man for whom the whole plot was to work. When Caesar helped Clodius to become first a plebeian and then a Tribune he knew what he was about. In this he no doubt had the active support of Caesar's partner in the Triumvirate, Crassus, who hated Cicero for having defeated his tool, Catiline, and for his successful opposition to the land bill of Rullus through which Crassus and Caesar had hoped to gain resources against Pompey.

But Clodius was not without some private ambitions of his own, and the one to which he was most devoted was to revenge himself upon Cicero. He was still smarting from the disgrace in which he had been involved in the year 62 B.C. when, disguised as a woman (not a very difficult disguise for his girlish features), he got into the house of the *Pontifex Maximus* at night during a state function, the chief festival of the Bona Dea, at which women only were allowed to be present. The *Pontifex Maximus* was of course Julius Caesar, and his wife Pompeia was in charge of the ceremonies. She was a granddaughter of Sulla, not a relation of Pompey. Clodius was already suspected of an intrigue with her and the whole affair caused an immense scandal. Caesar, whose own morals were the jest of the town, took advantage of the occasion to divorce his wife on the grounds that 'Caesar's wife must be above suspicion'. The more sober-minded citizens probably relished this cynicism as little as they approved the sacrilege of Clodius, who was duly brought to trial. He tried to get off on an alibi, swearing that he was at Interamna, ninety miles away from the city, during the festival, but Cicero testified that he had seen him in Rome three hours before the crime. Had the trial been honestly conducted Clodius would certainly have been condemned. But he managed to pack the jury. Describing them in a letter to his friend Atticus, Cicero said 'There was never a seedier lot round a table in a gambling hell. Senators under a cloud, *equites* out at elbow, Tribunes who were not so much guardians of public treasure as seekers of treasure on their own account' (a play on their official title, i.e. 'bribe takers' instead of 'tax collectors'). Clodius was saved by the gold of Crassus, who 'in two days' time, by the agency of a single slave, and one too from a school of gladiators, settled the whole business – he summoned the jurors to an interview, made a promise, offered security, paid money down. Still further, good heavens, what a scandal! even favours from certain ladies, and introductions to young men of rank were thrown in as a kind of tip to some of the jurors'. Despite these precautions twenty-five of the fifty-six jurors, risking death at the hands of the gang, voted Clodius guilty, but the thirty-one in favour of his acquittal carried the day. 'A perfectly notorious fact has been hushed up by bribing the jury' was Cicero's comment. He did not spare Clodius himself. 'I overwhelmed Clodius in the Senate to his face, both in a set speech, very weighty and serious, and also in an interchange of repartee.' Clodius had taunted Cicero with his country origin in Arpinum, accusing him of being seen at the fashionable sea resort of Baiae where the bourgeois were out of place and asking 'What business has an Arpinate with hot baths?' Cicero retorted, 'It is as though you were to say I had been in disguise.' Not relishing this reference to his own escapade, Clodius went on to jeer at Cicero about his new house: '"You have bought a house," says he. "You would think that he said", I answered, "'You have bought a jury.'" "They didn't trust you on your oath," said he. "Yes," said I, "twenty-five jurors did trust me, thirty-one didn't trust you, for they took care to get their money beforehand." Here he was overpowered by a burst of applause and broke down without a word to say.'

The whole wretched business alarmed Cicero, as well it might. A year later he said that it had first brought home to him 'the insecurity and rotten state of the law courts'. It also earned him the undying hatred of Clodius. Cicero did not spare Clodius and would not let him forget his disgrace. When Clodius had become a candidate for the tribuneship and 'when the matter was mooted in the Senate, I cut the fellow to pieces', wrote Cicero. 'On his saying that he had completed the journey from the Sicilian Straits in seven days, and that it was impossible for anyone to have gone out to meet him, and that he had entered the city by night, and making a great parade of this in a public meeting, I remarked that that was nothing new for him. Seven days from Sicily to Rome,

three hours from Rome to Interamna. Entered by night, did he?
So he did before. No one went to meet him? Neither did anyone
on the other occasion.' And so on. Three years after the scandal
Clodius, now a Tribune thanks to Caesar's influence and the
money of Crassus, was able to strike. As soon as he had established himself he proposed a law making exile or death the
penalty for anyone who should condemn or had already condemned a Roman citizen to death without giving him the right to
appeal to the vote of the people. This was no new doctrine, for
the right was said to have been guaranteed by the Twelve Tables.

Cicero Exiled

Cicero was thoroughly frightened. He had been too impressed
by his own achievements as Consul to see the need to safeguard his
position. He flattered himself that 'Ever since I won what I may
call the splendid and immortal glory of the famous fifth of
December [the day on which he had Catiline's conspirators
executed] I have never ceased to play my part in the Republic in
the same lofty spirit.' But he had no party of his own behind him
and he had disdained to make himself indispensable to those who
had secured that power in the State which the Senate and magistrates no longer really controlled. Too vain and too irresolute, he
had failed to take precautions to meet the political hurricane
which he had the intelligence to see was on its way. When it broke
he was swept before it. Clodius got his law passed and Cicero was
an obvious victim for its retrospective penalty. Nobody would
act to save him although very many were genuinely distressed to
see him go. He appealed in vain to Caesar, Pompey, and Crassus.
Caesar wished to weaken the Senate and Cicero was the most
powerful influence on the side of the Senate in Roman politics.
So Cicero had to be taught a lesson. Crassus hated him, and
Pompey, put out by Cicero's vainglorious boasting of his achievements as Consul and by his presumption in regarding himself as
Pompey's equal, would not risk opposing his two partners in
order to save him. A broken man, he fled to Greece in March
58 B.C. Clodius at once had his lavish town house destroyed. But
when he came to putting Cicero's property up to auction there
were no bidders. Clodius got one of his creatures to acquire the
site of Cicero's town house, on which he thereupon put a small

temple of Liberty so that Cicero would not again be able to build on dedicated soil.

Encouraged by his success and intoxicated by such exhibitions of his power, Clodius seems to have forgotten the men to whom he owed his position. Before his year of office was up he was violently attacking Pompey, who at length consented to act on behalf of the strong public opinion demanding Cicero's recall. With his armed gang of toughs, Clodius broke up any opposition. He threatened to burn down Pompey's house and to kill him. Pompey, not long since the most powerful man in the world, locked himself up in his house as in a besieged fortress.

The expense of maintaining the mob on free wheat was meanwhile mounting and to pay for it Clodius began to use the treasure brought back by Pompey from the East. Stung to action, Pompey set about organizing an opposition. He got Caesar to agree to Cicero's recall on condition that he made no further trouble for the three rulers of Rome, and for Caesar in particular, but Clodius was too much for him. He madly turned against Caesar and sought an alliance with Caesar's opponents with a promise that he would declare Caesar's land laws null and void. At length his year of office as Tribune came to an end but not before he had thoroughly confused and alarmed the whole city. Although his legal power had lapsed he kept his gang of blackguards and endeavoured through them to maintain his position. When a law for Cicero's return was proposed in January 57 B.C., he and his gang broke up the meeting and left the Forum running with blood.

In the absence of any police or armed force to keep order, Clodius seems to have been able to do as he liked. It was not until another Tribune, Milo, took matters into his own hands, bought a band of gladiators and faced Clodius with a rival gang of cutthroats that, seven months later, at the cost of another riot and more bloodshed, a law was eventually passed on 4 August 57 B.C. recalling Cicero.

Chaos and Confusion in Rome

Politics in the city had gone from bad to worse during Cicero's absence. Caesar was away in his province of Gaul darting hither and thither in search of a success which would serve to build up his reputation in Rome. Failing to make any impression upon them by the news of his victories he announced the conquest and annexation of Gaul. He was far from having overrun the whole country but his bluff succeeded and it caused a wave of excitement and enthusiasm throughout Italy sufficiently intense to get him all the political support he needed. He journeyed as far as Luca to meet his two uneasy partners in power, Pompey and Crassus, succeeded in re-cementing their crumbling alliance and at once returned to try to make his conquests the reality he had pretended them to be (April 56 B.C.).

Pompey had already had his fill of military glory and he had made his pile in foreign conquests. Crassus, the third member of the Triumvirate, had no need of money. This ageing banker had inherited 300 talents from his father, itself a fortune, and had increased it to 7,000 talents (168 million sesterces) by a mixture of skill and sharp practice at the expense of his less fortunate fellow Romans. His wealth and his ability as a political 'fixer' had given him his political power, but he was not content. He hankered after an army of his own, perhaps to make himself independent and truly the equal of his more powerful partners. Perhaps also he longed for military glory. At all events he became ambitious to attack Parthia, the only country now remaining on the borders of the Roman Empire likely to yield an immense store of booty. Rome had no quarrel with the Parthians but nothing would content the old man until he was entrusted with an expedition against them. At the conference with Caesar he got agreement for his plans and at once set about organizing his expedition. His energy and vigour, which would have been honourable in a better cause, met the just reward of purely aggressive warfare. His campaign failed after his defeat at Carrhae, May 53 B.C.

Crassus failed because he exposed his troops to the swiftly mounted Parthian bowmen on the desert wastes where they had no natural cover. It was not that the Romans had never faced arrows before. What was new was the almost unending hail of them. The Parthians had brought up ammunition trains in the shape of camels loaded with arrows and the Romans could never get to grips with them. Their own cavalry was inadequate and the result was that they were shot to pieces. Crassus lost his son in a skirmish and, a brave but pathetic figure, he was forced to retreat, pursued by the harassing fire of the Parthian archers. Driven by his men to discuss terms with the Parthians, he and his staff were treacherously slain by the enemy so that the Roman army was in worse plight than before. Scarcely a quarter of them managed, after great hardship, to struggle back to Syria.

When the news of this disaster reached Rome in July 53 B.C., it was not counterbalanced by more encouraging reports from Gaul. Despite his boasted conquest of Gaul and then of Britain in 55 and 54 B.C., Caesar was still up to his neck in difficulties. His struggles against the stubborn tribes seemed never to end. The fighting got fiercer and more bloodthirsty. Year after year Caesar was faced with one danger after another and nothing but his energy, his amazing genius and the loyalty he had inspired among his troops saw him through. The sufferings of the wretched Gauls must have been appalling as Caesar murdered and exterminated whole tribes of men, women and children by the hundred thousand, looted and burned their habitations. The climax came in the grisly scenes at the siege of Alesia in 52 B.C., when, after each side had endured hardships beyond breaking-point, Roman discipline carried the day and Vercingetorix, the redoubtable leader of the Gauls, was finally captured. With Roman brutality Caesar kept this warrior chief, whose crime was to have sought to defend his people, for six years in captivity, then paraded him through Rome in his triumphant victory march and afterwards had him murdered in the Roman gaol. Yet, by the standards of the time, Caesar could claim, with general consent, that clemency was one of his outstanding qualities.

Pompey, who now with Caesar alone controlled the fate of the Republic, remained in Rome. He had been given command in Spain (54 B.C.) but he left the work to his staff officers and did not leave the vicinity of Rome. He had not made the most of his opportunities. He would not even bestir himself to keep order in the capital city of the world. Cicero, who got an immense ovation from the public when he returned, nevertheless found his enemy Clodius as much of a menace as ever. He had succeeded in getting back the site of his house with an inadequate sum of money to enable him to rebuild. But Clodius would not leave him alone. 'On the third of November,' wrote Cicero in 57 B.C., 'the workmen were driven from the site of my house by armed ruffians; the house of my brother Quintus was first smashed with volleys of stones thrown from my site, and then set on fire by order of

Clodius, firebrands having been thrown into it in the sight of the whole town, amidst loud exclamations of indignation and sorrow, I will not say of the *loyalists*, for I rather think there are none, but of simply every human being. That madman [i.e. Clodius] runs riot, thinks after this mad prank of nothing short of murdering his opponents, canvasses the city street by street, makes open offers of freedom to slaves.' A week later, 'on the eleventh of November, as I was going down the Sacred Way, he followed me with his gang. There were shouts, stone-throwing, brandishing of clubs and swords, and all this without a moment's warning. I and my party stepped aside into Tettius Damio's vestibule; those accompanying me easily prevented his roughs from getting in.'

Why was nothing done about such lawlessness? The havoc wrought by gang warfare in a city without a police force may have been a hazard which the wealthy with their private bands of armed retainers were prepared to run, but for most people it must have been a frightful menace. They may well have been ready to pay almost any price to be freed from their chronic sense of insecurity. Cicero and his friends did little except talk, as a brief account of a debate in the Senate in December 57 B.C. will show. The Consul-designate, Marcellinus, complained in 'serious tones of the Clodian incendiarism, massacres and stonings'. Cicero was called upon for his opinion. Describing the scene to his brother Quintus, he said 'I made a long speech upon the whole story of P. Clodius's mad proceedings and murderous violence. I impeached him as though he were on his trial, amidst frequent murmurs of approbation from the whole Senate.' Cicero was not lacking in courage. Clodius was in his seat in the Senate and his roughs were outside crowding on the steps of the Senate House, shouting and yelling.

The incident typifies the impotence of the Senate, for the gang warfare of Clodius and his opponent Milo went on until January 52 B.C., when Clodius was at last caught with an insufficient escort and was murdered by Milo's gang. For five years he had been at large, a terror to the city. Cicero defended Milo, on trial for his life, but his crime was flagrant and he sought to escape inevitable condemnation by going into exile. Pompey, still proconsul commanding Spain from Rome, was summoned by the Senate to restore public order as sole Consul, a task which he rapidly completed. But his sudden show of energy in bringing to an end a disgraceful state of confusion, which he or Caesar might earlier have arrested, was no sign that constitutional government was returning to Rome.

Writing to his brother then serving under Caesar in Gaul in the autumn of 54 B.C., Cicero had already summed up the position when he said 'You must see that the Republic, the Senate, the law courts are mere ciphers and that not one of us has any constitutional position at all.' He was right. The Republic was at an end. The long-drawn-out uncertainty and lack of security must have made hundreds of sober, substantial but non-political Romans long for settled, orderly government. It was difficult to see how it was to be provided unless a properly constituted administrative authority were given supreme power and left undisturbed to use it.

The situation had become desperate through the incompetence of the oligarchy, the unrestrained ambition of lawless men, and the failure to create an efficient executive machinery of government and to link it with and subordinate it to the policy-making authorities (Senate and People). Unless one man could be given a free hand to set up the authority to make the rules and ensure that they were obeyed, it seemed impossible to make any progress. Yet nobody could bring himself to accept the idea, still less to say who that one man should be. There were only two possible candidates, Pompey and Caesar. Relations between the two had steadily worsened. Pompey's wife, Julia, to whom he was devoted, was well able to keep the peace between her husband and her father, but she died in September 54 B.C. The disappearance of Crassus in the following year left Caesar and Pompey face to face. Caesar was still in Gaul, hardened by five years' exhausting campaigns and protected from the consequences of his many illegal actions while Consul only as long as he stayed there or obtained an equally powerful position elsewhere. He therefore wished to become Consul again when his term of service in Gaul finally ended in 49 B.C. From afar he played a very clever game in the politics of Rome. He was well and secretly served during the year 50 B.C. by a young member of the aristocracy, C. Scribonius Curio, who posed as the champion of the Senate against Caesar. With great ingenuity he pointed all the arguments against Caesar so that they really attacked Pompey. The arguments were all designed to make the world believe that Curio's one aim was to restore full power to the Senate. Consequently he assumed senatorial support for the demand that Pompey should disband his forces if Caesar was asked to relinquish his command and he resolutely vetoed the appointment of a successor to Caesar. The fact that he had been heavily bribed by Caesar does not seem at first to have leaked out, so he was able thoroughly to confuse the situation and to gain precious time for Caesar while steadily undermining Pompey's position.

Caesar Crosses the Rubicon

The situation had become thoroughly unstable. The lack of trust of the two chief actors in each other, the deep suspicions with which both were regarded by the Senate, produced a situation so inflammable that the least thing might suffice to start a conflagration. Rumours began to circulate that Caesar was on the march. A strong party of appeasement in the Senate was silenced by fear of the power of Pompey who had some troops near the city. So when the Consuls called upon Pompey to save the State against Caesar there was nothing left but to fight it out. Caesar had behaved with studious correctness, making the minimum demands and asking for nothing beyond the essential guarantee that he should not be expected to return unarmed to fall into the hands of his enemies. But when the Consuls commissioned Pompey against him he no longer needed a pretext but with his usual dash and energy he marched at once. On the night of 10 January 49 B.C., with only one legion, he crossed the Rubicon, the little stream which separated his province from Italy, and quickly occupied Ariminum. Pompey was caught unprepared. He had not mobilized an army when Caesar overran his recruiting-ground of Picenum and began to enlist the very men upon whom Pompey had counted to join him. To the clear-sighted it was already plain that in backing Pompey against Caesar the Consuls had made the Senate run a desperate hazard. It was too late to draw back. So swift was the advance of Caesar that Pompey could not maintain himself in Italy and was forced to leave for the East in the hope of being able to build up a force there. Caesar nearly caught him at Brundisium but was unable to prevent his escape on 17 March 49 B.C.

The conflict was no longer one between the Republic and an

autocrat as it had been in the days of the kings but between two would-be autocrats. Whichever won, the Republic was lost.

It was the culminating tragedy not only in the life of Cicero and the men around him, but of all hopes of political democracy in the Roman Republic. Cicero saw well enough what was coming and in 49 B.C., when there could be little doubt that a fierce civil war between Caesar and Pompey was imminent, he was heartbroken. 'It is not a proscription that is so much to be feared, as a general destruction; so vast are the forces which I see will take part in the conflict on both sides. ... Nothing can exceed the misery, ruin and disgrace. ... The sun seems to me to have disappeared from the universe.'

Yet when the conflict had become a reality he was stunned. He had to tell himself the facts, they were so unbelievable: 'An army of the Roman people is actually surrounding Gnaeus Pompeius; it has enclosed him with fosse and palisade; it is preventing his escape. Are we alive? Is our City still intact? Are the Praetors presiding in the Courts, the Aediles making preparations for their games, the *optimates* entering their investments, myself quietly looking on?' He did not know what to do. 'Troubles', he said, 'have made me stupid.'

Old nightmares from the past must have risen up to shatter his peace. The Social War between Italians and Romans and the civil war of Sulla and Marius during his youth and early manhood seemed to have been fought in vain. The ghosts of Catiline and his conspirators walked again. The crowds Caesar collected were the same crowds who followed Catiline. 'What a crew! What an inferno! ... What a gang of bankrupts and desperadoes! ... Don't imagine that there is a single scoundrel in Italy who is not to be found among them. I saw them *en masse* at Formiae. I never, by Hercules! believed them to be human beings, and I knew them all, but had never seen them collected in one place.'

Despite Caesar's friendly entreaty, Cicero resolved in June to leave Italy and to depart to Greece to join Pompey, not from any high opinion of Pompey's ability and not believing that the inevitable trend of events could be arrested. 'The worst', he said, 'has come to the worst', and he left not for the sake of the Republic, 'which I regard as completely abolished', but 'because I cannot endure the sight of what is happening or of what is certain to happen.'

He was right. The Republic was dead. The Roman people had travelled a long way in their political development since the heroic age to which Cicero, from the tragedy, strife and disasters of his own time, looked back with such vain longing.

Caesar the Dictator

Caesar seems to have thought with good reason that his choice was the unenviable alternative 'slay or be slain'. In what followed he seems to have been led on to supreme power rather than to have achieved it as a long-premeditated purpose. His enemies in after years, Cicero among them, spoke as though Caesar had all along determined to become supreme in the State. But when Pompey eluded him and left Italy with many of the Senators to raise an army in the scene of his former triumphs in the East, what could Caesar do but accept the challenge? Before following Pompey, however, he had to make sure of Rome, his base, and the West. After a few days in Rome, where he emptied the Treasury, he went to Pompey's province of Spain early in April 49 B.C. to remove the threat of the hostile army there. Victorious at Ilerda in a lightning campaign, he then joined one of his lieutenants, Decimus Brutus, and reduced Marseilles which had declared for Pompey. He then returned to Rome and in January 48 B.C., with seven legions, he went to settle accounts with Pompey who was doing his best to collect an army and by a blockade to starve Italy. His power seemed formidable, but Caesar, after being forced to retreat at Dyrrhachium, whither he had pursued Pompey with a small force, defeated him decisively, although outnumbered two to one, at Pharsalus on 9 August 48 B.C. Pompey escaped to Egypt where he was murdered by the wily Egyptians who did not want other people's wars brought within their own borders. They had their own troubles. Their young King Ptolemy and his sister Cleopatra had been jointly left as co-rulers of the country by their father, but neither the ministers nor the army would recognize Cleopatra's right to share the throne.

When Caesar arrived in Alexandria to make sure that Egypt would not become a stronghold of his enemies, his intervention was not welcomed. He was in fact blockaded in Alexandria and for about six months was in deadly peril. Reinforced at last, he fought his way out of the trap. King Ptolemy XII was drowned

in flight with his defeated forces, so Caesar had the task of placing
Cleopatra firmly on her throne and winning her support for his
cause. He succeeded so well that their names have ever since been
linked in one of the grand romances of history, to be rivalled
by her later and fatal attachment to Marcus Antonius, one of
Caesar's staff officers, the Mark Antony of English literature.
What truth there may be in the story involving her with Caesar
rests upon few facts. Caesar did not leave Egypt for three months
after his rescue and his settlement of Egypt. Shortly after his
departure Cleopatra had a son who was given the name of
Caesarion. Later on, in 46 B.C., probably with this infant, she
came to Rome where she lived in royal state to the disgust
of many Romans, Cicero included. Thoroughly spoilt by the
servility, adulation and snobbery of her Egyptian subjects, she
was not to know that there was no glamour attached to the royal
title in the eyes of Romans of the old school, Cicero included. He
called her 'The Queen' and could never remember without a
twinge the insolent airs she gave herself while she was living in
Caesar's villa across the Tiber. She sought to make some amends
later on, possibly when she had found her bearings in the new
and, to her, strange social life of Rome, by promising Cicero some
presents. He hastened to explain that they would be 'all things of
the learned sort and suitable to my character'. They were prob
ably books.

After having been often in great peril but saved by a combina
tion of great energy and greater good luck, Caesar had at las
removed all the serious dangers threatening him from Italy
Spain, Marseilles and Egypt. The Near East threatened trouble
stirred up by Pharnaces, son of Mithridates (p. 225). Thithe
Caesar went from Alexandria to write, so the story goes, from th
battlefield of Zela early in August 47 B.C. his famous dispatch
'I came, I saw, I conquered' (*Veni, vidi, vici*).

Africa alone was able to cause trouble, for there were th
remnants of Pompey's followers and the supporters of th
Senate's cause. Before going on to eliminate this last centre o
opposition, Caesar returned to Rome. On the way he met Cicer
for the first time since he had tried in vain to dissuade him fro
joining Pompey. Caesar must have heard the treacherous tales o
Cicero's brother Quintus and his unpleasant son. Cicero ha
been languishing in Brundisium from July 48 B.C. to Septemb

47 B.C., miserable, bored, uncertain of his fate, and beset by family troubles. His only daughter, his darling Tullia, could not bring herself to part from her scoundrel husband, Dolabella, and he was planning his own divorce from Terentia. Life in Pompey's camp had been a second exile more hopeless and more depressing than his banishment from Rome; his stay in the dull and dismal port of Brundisium was a third. The utter defeat and ruin of the Republican constitution, and with it the shattering of his own way of life, was the crowning misery. What would Caesar do with him? At last Caesar came, after first sending a friendly letter. Nothing could have been more cordial than his greeting. Cicero, again a free man, with one huge load off his mind but many remaining, set off at once for Rome, his villas and what was left of civilization. But no independent place of political honour or distinction remained for him or anyone else in public life as long as Caesar lived.

Meanwhile Caesar had still to deal with the diehard Republicans who, under leaders bearing the renowned names of Scipio and Cato, had for nearly a year and a half been collecting an army against him. Caesar landed in North Africa, devoted three months to building up his forces and on 6 April 46 B.C. decisively defeated Scipio at Thapsus. The slaughter of Caesar's enemies on that occasion was formidable. Cato fled to Utica and committed suicide. The gods, it was said, favoured the winning side but to Cato the losing side seemed the best. A certain theatrical eccentricity characterized Cato's last action just as it had marked his whole life. Yet it was an historic suicide, remembered and imitated in after years as being in accordance with the best traditions of the ancient Republic, of which indeed it soon became a part. Caesar feared Cato's stern spirit and wrote an 'anti-Cato' pamphlet against his ideas, but it has not survived. The defeated fugitives made their way to Spain, where in one last desperate encounter, they were overcome by Caesar at Munda, 17 March 45 B.C. Again there were sickening losses. Caesar's vow of death to all opponents had been no idle threat. Surveying his slaughtered foes at Pharsalus he remarked grimly 'They asked for it'.

Whether, as he said later, Caesar had always been 'ambitious to be king of the Roman people and master of the whole world', Cicero was undoubtedly right when he added 'and he achieved it'. The achievement was due as much to the obstinacy of his enemies as to his own implacable nature, for he showed on many occasions that he wished to spare Roman lives whenever he could. Circumstances had, however, made it inevitable that he should wade through slaughter to his throne. It would be as odd to blame the Republicans for trying to save what they could of the Republic as to blame Caesar for refusing to put his neck into the noose they had tied ready for him. From the head-on clash of irreconcilable wills there could be no issue save in complete victory for one side. The tragedy lay in the fact that matters had been allowed to drift into so disastrous a position.

The Failure of Julius Caesar

In contrast to the less resolute and less ambitious defenders of senatorial privileges and power, Caesar seems to have earned his victory. He was not afraid to grasp the wheel as the ship of state floundered in the hurricane. He was not merely Dictator (October 48 B.C.) but was reappointed as such for ten years in the summer of 46 B.C. with the proconsular power giving him command of all armies and the Censor's power controlling the lists of Senators, *equites* and citizens generally. He was given the great distinction of always being the first to vote in the Senate. A Dictator he was immune from the veto of the Tribunes, which meant that the common people lost their one defence, such as it was, against the arbitrary power of the magistrates. His power was tripled by reason of his full control over all public money and his authority to issue edicts which relieved him of the duty of consulting the Public Assembly. Elected *Pontifex Maximus* in 63 B.C. (p. 181), he added to his other powers as Dictator by being elected to all the priestly colleges as well. He became Dictator for life early in February 44 B.C. He dominated and 'streamlined' the lumbering old government machinery of the Roman Republic, controlling all the magistrates who were still nominally elected. But it was Caesar who nominated most of them for 'election' and he controlled the public assembly where the elections took place and where new laws were passed.

Never before had a Roman citizen allowed himself to receive honours and marks of distinction normally reserved for the gods. But Caesar hinted at the divine origin of his family. The fifth month in the Roman calendar, Quinctilis, was renamed Julius and the face of Caesar appeared upon the national coinage from the official Mint of the Republic where hitherto had figured the effigies of the gods. These seemed like the acts of Eastern monarchs anxious for the blind adulation of their subjects. (Plate 28.)

Yet what was the alternative? The Republicans had no man to match against Caesar. Their sorry champion Pompey, lacking almost all the qualities that made Caesar great, except ambition, certainly had neither the energy nor the skill demanded by the supreme task of directing the destinies of the Roman world.

Cicero had no trust in Caesar's skill. 'While we are his slaves,' he said, as preparations were being made in Rome for Caesar's fourfold triumph over Gaul, Egypt, Pontus and Africa in his third consulate (46 B.C.), 'he is a slave to circumstance. ... He is unable to say what is going to happen.' But as time went on Caesar's conduct surprised and impressed Cicero, who confessed himself 'struck with astonishment at Caesar's sobriety, fairness and wisdom'. He was amazed to find that 'every day something is done in a spirit of greater clemency and liberality than we feared would be the case'. Caesar had no complete reform programme for Rome worked out in advance but he developed one as time went on. Cicero's old friendship with Caesar seemed to be taking new roots. On Caesar's side there was certainly no greater obstacle to the pleasures of society than the crushing demands made by public business upon his time. Cicero and other consulars had to wait when they called on Caesar, so great was the work of ruling the world single-handed. Cicero did not resent this so much as Caesar sympathetically feared he would. What really poisoned life for Cicero was the realization that he was no longer free to live his old life of strenuous activity in the stimulating, exciting rough and tumble of politics in the Senate and in the crowded Forum. No longer was there a free course for political talent and ambition. There were no longer laurels and applause for practised old hands at the game of political oratory. A feeling of unreality had come upon the scenes of Cicero's former triumphs; 'the men, the Forum and the Senate House', he wrote, 'are all utterly repulsive to me.' Many old familiar faces were no longer there, for there had been a formidable blood-letting in that most disastrous civil war. He could not resist a bitter jest. 'Really? Does Brutus say that Caesar is going to join the *optimates*? That's good news! But where will he find them?

Unless by chance he should hang himself' – and seek them, that is to say, in the other world whither his soldiers had dispatched so many *optimates* in the battles of those ruinous past five years (49–45 B.C.).

In spite of the best intentions, to which Cicero grudgingly bore witness, such efforts as Caesar was able to make during his short supremacy at Rome seem in the main opportunist and unplanned. From his policy of giving Roman citizenship to the inhabitants of northern Cisalpine Gaul in 49 B.C. he may be thought to have wished to facilitate the rule of the people. In fact he did nothing to transfer power to the people although it was under colour of promoting their interests that he had himself won supremacy. Similarly his changes in the Senate, whose membership he enlarged, had no deep significance because he did not intend to treat the Senate with more than an empty politeness. Complete concentration of all important decisions in his own hands was his policy. With his trained and loyal army behind him, it was a policy he could easily enforce. Although such despotism might serve the immediate interests of internal peace, as Tacitus, the bitter, incisive critic of the Caesars, later grudgingly admitted, it soured and embittered the old political aristocracy, and consequently could give no guarantee that the peace would last longer than the Dictator's life, as indeed events soon proved it could not. The peace itself was a fragile affair.

The social fabric of Rome had been shaken to its foundations. An economic collapse was a natural accompaniment of war between the citizens. To retain their armies in being, it had been necessary for the warring generals not merely to guarantee the pay of the troops but to outbid each other with additional bribes. Caesar himself had set the example when he doubled the pay of the common soldier, making it 900 sesterces a year.

To fight the civil war, larger Roman armies were assembled than had ever faced the enemies of Rome. Caesar left forces to garrison Gaul, Spain, and Italy and pursued Pompey to Greece with seven legions. Pompey had eleven under his command. After the clash at Pharsalus had eliminated Pompey in 48 B.C. Caesar absorbed what remained of the defeated army and collected about forty legions.

When he returned to Rome to celebrate his fourfold triumph won mainly against Romans, there was no distinction between

Caesar's income and the revenue of the Roman Republic. The calls upon him were tremendous. Every legionary soldier was rewarded during the triumph with 20,000 sesterces. Each centurion had 40,000 sesterces and each military tribune 80,000 sesterces. Nearly double the annual revenue of the Republic was needed to pay such rewards. Their magnitude in relation to the normal pay of the troops is a revealing indication of the links between Caesar and the armed men whose support gave him supreme power.

Faced with demands for liquid resources on such a scale, what could Caesar do except lay his hands on every source of wealth that he could find? Rich men and communities in Asia, Spain, and Egypt were forced to pay under every kind of pretext. The property of his enemies, especially those slain in battle, became Caesar's property, although with the gallantry of a gentleman burglar he usually let widows keep their dowry. Lands, houses, furniture, temple treasures were confiscated either to be divided up amongst his supporters or to be thrown on the market, which naturally could no longer absorb so much business. Immensely valuable properties changed hands at ridiculous prices. The lack of community spirit and the free scope given to inflated personal ambitions make this story of social disintegration a sad commentary upon the mass of enthusiastic writing in which men have sought to glorify the Roman character in general and that of Julius Caesar in particular. To the men who had to live through this period it must have seemed one of appalling ruin produced by gangsterdom on the grand scale.

After the civil war, Caesar's economic programme was on conventional lines set by the problems of the age and by previous efforts to deal with them. There was the debt question, to be met by reducing money-lenders' rates of interest, and the land question, to be met by settling capable citizens on allotments of land that had become 'public' because it was owned by the enemies of Caesar or by their heirs. Economies were obviously necessary after the great expense of the civil wars. The free corn dole was reduced for that reason rather than for any desire to offend the mob. But Caesar also abolished all the newer working men's clubs which Clodius had so industriously fostered when building up his political power. Now that the mob, like the Senate, was under firm control, Caesar could draw in the reins. New constructive schemes of real promise were not conspicuous. Some useful reforms such as tidying up the calendar and beginning a restatement of the laws of Rome and some large-scale public works such as draining the Pontine marshes and constructing a ship canal at Corinth were among his contributions to, or his unfulfilled plans for, the New Deal the Romans needed.

He has sometimes been credited with beginning that permanent civil service for the lack of which the executive power of Rome was always notably less effective than it might have been. But he did no more than to provide his own party, which Cicero no doubt thought of as his gang, with efficient staff officers. His project of extending Roman citizenship widely to include Rome's subject races, such as those he had lived among for nearly ten years in Gaul, with his other plans, remained visionary schemes reserved for a later age to pursue.

Useful and important as were some of his ideas, they did not amount to a New Deal, still less did they offer any hope of enlarging the lives of the masses and so of filling the vacuum of Roman social life with a new moral spirit. We have seen dictators fail in our own day, despite their tremendous propaganda machines which for a time seemed likely to wield an influence over the minds of their victims at once more permanent and more pernicious than the physical force so savagely and so sadistically applied to their bodies. Caesar had a rudimentary propaganda machine, made up of a few agents and political jackals in addition to his personal friends and the very much greater body of his legionaries who, no doubt, could be expected to 'back up the boss'. For all his genius, he also would have been unable to stay the course. He lacked adequate means of swaying or controlling men at a greater distance than his personal prestige and influence could reach, but even had he possessed a developed propaganda machine, he had no grand new idea, no *mystique*, by which he could guide, enchant, or bemuse the population of Italy. His power, arising from his own outstanding character and genius, had to be built upon the personal followers he was able to get together by every means then known to an energetic, unscrupulous and ambitious man. Some were attracted by bribes in the crude form of outright gifts of cash from Caesar's enormous funds provided by ten years' pillage in Gaul and the Low Countries; others were eager for remunerative jobs on his staff, while many were content to bask in reflected glory when the great man turned his smiles and flattery upon them. There was no doubt about Caesar's consummate ability to succeed with men on any of these lines. Yet even so his recruits, apart from the solid ranks of his legions and his relatively few personal friends, came from the disaffected classes, from the needy debtors, the failures and misfits who always have a vested interest in social unrest. A few more solid and respectable figures were no doubt also attracted, such as Italians smarting from wounds inflicted by Rome in the Social War, together with a few bankers and financiers concerned only to preserve their fortunes and led by their gambler's instinct to back Caesar to win. We have seen how such classes in Germany backed Hitler to restore firm rule and to guarantee their fortunes and their profits. It is most important, therefore, to remember that Caesar did no more than to recruit a gang. He formed no political party. Not one of his eager followers contributed anything of value to the Roman State. Those of them who were active at all completed its ruin. Some of the better Romans serving under him in Gaul left him before his final triumph.

The proud Roman governing class as a whole naturally did not fall before his wiles. They had a natural contempt for the riff-raff who flocked to Caesar. Their families had not been supreme throughout the recorded history of Rome for them to bargain away their birthright for such comparative trifles as Caesar could offer, particularly when it never occurred to them to look upon any one member of their charmed circle otherwise than as an equal. Why, when many of them had ample fortunes, should they take bribes from Caesar? Why, when the Roman people had constantly been willing in the past to make them Consuls, which to their way of thinking was all that Caesar should have been, need they depend upon him for a position of dignity in the State? No wonder, then, that Caesarism spelt uncompensated frustration to the haughty aristocrats of Rome. Incompetent as many of them were, they had not all sunk so low that they were willing to compete with thugs and bullies for Caesar's favour or tamely to submit to a political impotence leading quite obviously to political extinction. With them it was a matter of pride, so there was little point in appealing to their pockets. Not till their ranks had been still further thinned by civil war, which again broke out after Caesar had been assassinated by the Republican 'Old Guard', were their necks sufficiently bent for the yoke, but even then the yoke had to be designed and laid on with a gentler hand and with more tactful care than Caesar, for all his great personal charm, was able to command.

Cicero had no formula to facilitate that operation. He and many of his friends could not endure the thought that one man should have more power than the Republic. Did not the history of the Republic begin with a lesson upon the Roman's duty to assassinate a tyrant king? It was a Brutus who slew Tarquin. There was still a Brutus in Roman public life. He and one or two like-minded Senators, Cassius (probably the ringleader), Casca and Tillius Cimber, resolved to remove the tyrant. Cicero was not let into their conspiracy. How, with twenty-three daggers, they struck Caesar down in the Senate remains one of the most dramatic tragedies of Roman history.

The daggers of the assassins of the Ides of March 44 B.C. prevented Julius Caesar showing whether he could make a success of his programme, and ever since his countless hero-worshippers have been guessing that he would have proved the saviour of Rome. A more careful judgement suggests doubts. The task was tremendous, even for a man of Caesar's genius. He was always in a hurry. He never had time to spare to try to conciliate opposition. His unconcealed intention to retain absolute authority naturally antagonized everybody of any importance. Never before had Rome endured a Dictator who set no limit to the period of his dictatorship.

Cicero's Last Stand

The murder of Julius Caesar on 15 March 44 B.C. did not at first bring Cicero back into active politics. He spoke in the Senate on 17 March, but from then until the end of August he kept away from Rome and continued his philosophical writing. His books on the *Nature of the Gods*, on *Divination*, on *Fate*, on *Old Age*, on *Friendship*, and his best-known philosophical manual on *Duty* (*De Officiis*) were all written before the end of that year. In this last work he answers the many critics of his retired and scholarly way of life, still apparently strange to the majority of his countrymen. 'If the man lives who would belittle the study of philosophy, he wrote, 'I quite fail to see what in the world he would see fit to praise.' A perfect retort to the low-brows of all time. It was addressed to his boy who, as a student in Athens, was following in his father's footsteps, but not with his father's eager interest. Cicero resolved to visit him and to find in the studious calm of Athens the peace that eluded him at home. Bad weather held him back. Meanwhile the political situation in Rome in the months following the murder of Julius Caesar was increasingly ominous. Cicero, misled by hopes that Caesar's assassins would succeed in giving the Republic renewed life and vigour, again threw himself into public affairs, in one last grand effort to give reality to his dreams of what the Roman Republic might be. Had he known, said Lord Macaulay, what was necessary to his peace, he would never have left his library again for the maelstrom of Roman politics. But Cicero could not rest among his manuscripts at a time when every political principle for which he had stood was in jeopardy and when honesty and public liberty were at stake. There was indeed a desperate need for a firm lead and a clear policy.

The confusion of the times was tremendous. Already a bare three weeks after the fatal Ides of March 44 B.C., Cicero spoke to a friend who said to him, 'The state of things is perfectly shocking. There is no way out of the mess; for if a man with Caesar's genius failed, who can hope to succeed?' Cicero, reporting these words, added, 'I am not sure he is wrong.' Six or seven weeks later he saw that the man was right. 'I was a fool, I now see, to be consoled by the Ides of March. The fact is we showed the courage of men, the prudence of children.' Their lack of prudence was of course the failure of Caesar's assassins to plan their way through to making full use of the power they had knocked out of Caesar's grasp. They acted as though the enfeebled form of the Roman Republic possessed a vitality of its own. They seemed to think that, left to itself, its ancient glories would return. There could have been no greater delusion. The directing, executive task had been too much for Julius Caesar, well-equipped and fully supported as he was by a more efficient, obedient and well-organized body of subordinates than any Roman Consul had ever possessed. This vast concentration of power, influence, and wealth, got together by a man who alone knew how to use it, now awaited a new master.

The folly of the assassins of 15 March is shown by the fact

that they did nothing to ensure the transfer of these huge resources to their own hands. The money available alone was a tremendous asset. Caesar's private estate was estimated at about 100 million sesterces. He left 700 million sesterces in the Treasury. More important than the money by far was Caesar's army, bound to him by gratitude, by oaths of allegiance, by a supreme confidence in their great commander and by a sense of their immense importance as the men who had decided the fate of the Republic.

Instead of being ready with plans to use these sources of power themselves, Caesar's murderers were so concerned to observe the proper constitutional rules that they practically handed them over to the surviving Consul, who was none other than Caesar's own henchman, Mark Antony. Some of the more clear-sighted of the senatorial party among the conspirators had been in favour of sending Antony to his doom along with Caesar, but they had been overruled by the sticklers for principle. Within two months Cicero, who had not been let into the plot, with many others bitterly regretted the failure to eliminate Antony, as well he might. For Antony, who must have been surprised to find himself alive, kept his head and soon saw that with Caesar's resources behind him he had a very good chance of standing up to the Senators. The people of Rome, who had been panic-stricken by Caesar's murder, were easily enraged against those who had so wantonly disturbed their hard-won tranquillity. In vain did Cicero trust his 'one hope, that the Roman people will at last show themselves worthy of their ancestors'. Opinion hardened against the assassins as, all too late in the day, they gathered their forces against Antony.

Cicero's gloomiest expectations which Caesar had shown to have been unjustified, as far as he was concerned, were fulfilled by the new civil war that thereupon broke out. Proscription, murder, and confiscation soon became the order of the day. At first there was a manoeuvring for position and a struggle for provinces that would provide an army and resources. Antony, with a bodyguard of armed men allowed him by the Senate on the pretence that it was needed to suppress the rioting by Caesar's followers that Antony himself did much to excite, was able to secure the great recruiting-round of Cisalpine Gaul together with four of Caesar's legions. The province had already been assigned by Caesar to one of the assassins, Decimus Brutus, who was gathering an army there. Antony saw that he would have to fight.

A month after the assassination the situation was further upset by the arrival of Julius Caesar's lawful heir, his great-nephew C. Octavius, then a young man of only nineteen years (44 B.C.). He wanted his share of Caesar's possessions, that is to say his private fortune as well as his name. Antony, who had spent the money already, did his best to obstruct him, but Octavius anticipated legal justification and assumed the name of C. Julius Caesar Octavianus and proceeded to set about raising an army of his own, to which he had no shadow of a claim. He was successful, 'and no wonder', said Cicero, 'for he gives each man 500 *denarii*'. This was more than two years' pay of a legionary.

Ignoring him with some contempt, Antony closed upon Decimus Brutus and seemed likely to eliminate him by besieging him in Mutina. It proved beyond the power of the senatorial forces under the command of Hirtius and Pansa, who had succeeded Antony as Consuls for the year 43 B.C., to raise the siege alone. In their desperate plight the Senators accepted Octavian as an ally upon the strong advice of Cicero who had much contact with the young man and who was above all desperately anxious to save Decimus Brutus. With this new force and their own army the Consuls at length defeated Antony although they both lost their lives in the ensuing actions. Octavian was then left in command of their armies.

The alliance between Caesar's heir and the Senate on behalf of Caesar's murderers, never cordial on either side, broke down as soon as the Senate thought itself strong enough to dispense with him. Unfortunately their attitude became clear to Octavian. The Senate overestimated the extent of Antony's defeat, declared his men, who were Caesar's veterans, to be outlaws and nominated Decimus Brutus, who had been designated by Caesar as Consul for 42 B.C., to lead the armies of the Republic. No longer were Roman armies content to be mere pawns in the political game. They saw no reason for killing each other to oblige rival Roman politicians and they took the initiative, or were reported to have done so, demanding that Octavian should become Consul. Cicero, who saw the advantages of maintaining friendly relations with Octavian, worked hard for a complete understanding with the young man, but he was not listened to by the over-confident Senators.

While Octavian was negotiating in Rome, Antony was in Gaul. He was there confronted by two armies of the Republic under the provincial governors, Lepidus and Plancus. Had they decided to stand by the Senate, as Cicero begged them to do, they might have eliminated Antony. Again the legionaries seem to have taken charge of the situation. Lepidus, who had been Caesar's Master of Horse while his chief had been Dictator, joined Antony and gave as his excuse to the Senate that his men fraternized with Antony's army and would not fight. Plancus did not wait for that to happen but joined Antony as soon as he saw what had happened to Lepidus. Decimus Brutus lost his troops to the enemy in the same way and was caught and killed by Antony's orders. Although Octavian had forced the Senate to agree to his becoming Consul (19 August 43 B.C.), Antony was now more than match for him, and he must have known it, and therefore did not want a battle. Antony could not be sure that his troops would not desert him for Caesar's heir. The way was ready for Antony and Octavian to do a deal between themselves. With Lepidus, a political lightweight, they combined early in November 43 B.C. in the Second Triumvirate and carried all before them.

Antony meanwhile had carried Caesarism to its logical conclusion. He and his fellow thugs cast aside any disguise and appeared as the gangsters they were, determined to run things their own way, to take what they wanted, to have a roaring good time and to murder out of hand anybody who stood in their path. Cicero attacked them in most outspoken terms, saying that the Senate should brand with their severest censure, for the guidance of posterity, the action of Antony who, said Cicero, was 'the first man who has openly taken armed men about with him in this city, a thing which the Kings never did nor those men who, since the Kings have been banished, have endeavoured to seize on kingly power. I can recall Cinna; I have seen Sulla, and lately Caesar. For these three men are the only ones, since the city was delivered by Lucius Brutus, who have had more power than the entire Republic. I cannot assert that no man in their retinue had weapons. This I do say, that they had not many and that they concealed them.' To be at the mercy of armed violence was new and it was hateful. 'Is it not better to perish a thousand times than to be unable to live in one's own city without a guard of armed men?' asked Cicero, and he knew the answer. 'Believe me, there is no protection in that; a man must be defended by the affection and good will of his fellow citizens, not by arms.'

Cicero saw Antony for the unscrupulous adventurer he was and, with tremendous force and courage, denounced him (between September 44 B.C. and April 43 B.C.) before the Senate and the people in speeches of such eloquence that they recalled the classic invectives of Demosthenes against Philip of Macedon, and have always been known as Cicero's *Philippic Orations* in consequence.

The Second Triumvirate and the Murder of Cicero

Violent in his scorn of and contempt for Antony, an irascible army commander who was using Caesar's inheritance to gratify his own base desires and worthless way of life, Cicero unfortunately misjudged the extent to which he could rely upon Caesar's great-nephew and heir to take the same line. As long as young Octavian was opposed to Antony, Cicero and the Republic had a fair chance of surviving. It is improbable that Octavian would have remained long in partnership with Caesar's murderers. But the Senators played a most unskilful game. Such was their ineptitude that Octavian was driven to conclude that he might better secure his own position by becoming the ally instead of the opponent of Antony. When that happened, on 27 November 43 B.C., Antony's enemies in Italy were without support and there was no hope for the Senators, including the Ciceros, save in flight. Their names were on the first proscription lists sent post-haste to Rome. Quintus and his son, now completely united with Cicero against Antony, were the first to be slain. They had gone to Rome to get money for their journey to Greece where remnants of Caesar's assassins still had some forces. They were caught and killed. Antony sent a squad to look for his arch-enemy. Octavian, to his eternal shame, made no effort to spare the old man whom he had so recently consulted and flattered. Cicero had been on board the ship which might have taken him to a temporary refuge but bad winter weather and sea-sickness forced him ashore. Before he could regain the vessel the litter in which his slaves were carrying him back to the shore was intercepted and the great orator and spokesman of the liberties of the Roman people was silenced by one stroke of a centurion's sword (7 December 43 B.C.). His head and hands were cut off and sent back to Rome for Antony and his wife. While they gloated over the bloody spectacle, many an honest man who had heard Cicero describing the fate which awaited Rome if Antony was victorious must have shuddered as he recalled those words and realized, now that it was too late, that Cicero had spoken truly and their ancient liberties were no more.

The greatest disaster ever to befall the Romans in all their long history mounted to its climax amid bloodshed and degradation. Three hundred Senators and 2,000 *equites*, doomed by Antony's proscription lists, were slaughtered by his thugs. Life in Rome was shattered. So great a catastrophe defies measurement. It certainly cannot be reckoned in money although the formidable economic losses reveal something of its results.

Antony had soon run through the funds left by Caesar. He needed more. After he was joined by Caesar's heir, Octavian, and by Lepidus in a second 'Triumvirate' they stole the property of the men they had proscribed and of 400 rich women. In addition they demanded a forced loan of one year's income and a capital levy of two per cent on all fortunes greater than 400,000 sesterces. By these means they gained a flying start. Caesar's assassins were less successful.

The Senate also tried to raise a capital levy of four per cent and a curious and surely very clumsy tax of $2\frac{1}{2}$ sesterces on every tile on the roofs of the houses within its jurisdiction. So for the first time for 120 years the citizens of Rome were again made to pay taxes, with the difference that it was to finance a civil war, not a foreign war.

Although the Republican cause had collapsed in Italy, hopes were brighter in the East. Cassius, by prompt action, had secured Syria, where he collected twelve legions. Marcus Brutus, 'the noblest Roman of them all', had gone to Athens, where he was joined by young students such as Cicero's son, and Quintus Horatius Flaccus, then beginning to store an experience of life which in mellower years he was to distil in verses that have never lost their charm. At the end of 43 B.C. Brutus and Cassius joined forces and began to raise the large sums needed to maintain their troops. They increased normal revenues by forced loans. Rhodes made difficulties about paying. It was sacked without mercy and the plunder came to about 19 million sesterces. Such an example was convincing, and altogether they collected about 400 million sesterces. By the autumn of 42 B.C. Antony and Octavian had transported an army to Macedonia, where they met almost equal numbers of the Republican forces at Philippi, not far from the point where the *Via Egnatia* reached the sea. Antony's dash and energy won the first encounter, whereupon Cassius committed suicide. About a month later, Brutus led his men against Antony and Octavian but was defeated. He also committed suicide. The second battle of Philippi on 23 October 42 B.C. and the defeat and death of Brutus and Cassius finally crushed and ruined the Republic.

Chapter Fourteen

THE REPUBLICAN TRADITION IN
CICERO'S DAY

It is not difficult to picture a Roman house, its furniture and household utensils, the clothes and shoes the Romans wore, the carriages, travelling-chairs, ships and conveyances in which they rode, their pens and ink-pots, the rolls of parchment which formed their books, and many more such objects of antiquarian interest; sufficient has been discovered in the ruins of Pompeii and Herculaneum to enable us to get a fair idea of these merely external things in the Roman scene. They are interesting, but their interest is limited and can soon be exhausted, as many a weary museum visitor has discovered.

What we should really like to know about social life in Rome must include a great deal more. We want to be able to imagine the Roman busy at his farm, in politics, trade, or industry, so that we may fill more of the bare framework of previous chapters with living human beings. To achieve so huge a task is next to impossible. Few possess this degree of penetrating insight into our own society. It is painfully evident in the troubled and tangled lives around us how rarely people are able to transcend their personal experience and to grasp in imagination the life of a person of different sex, age, class or group in society, whether it be that of housewife, shop assistant, miner, cotton-spinner, bank clerk, diplomat, Member of Parliament, agricultural labourer, Negro bootblack, elevator boy or railway servant or any other of the thousands of different walks of life in a modern society.

When we fail to understand each other in this modern machine age, how much more difficult it is to see the Roman world through Roman eyes! Nevertheless, resources are not entirely lacking. Enough remains from the largely vanished literature of Rome to give a general picture of the main features of the busy life that went on there. Indeed, some of the Roman classics seem to reveal a living society startlingly real and by no means utterly foreign in spirit to our own. There are sufficient letters, speeches and other works of Cicero himself and of other Romans to prove that these impressions of vivid reality are by no means an illusion. On closer examination, however, some wide gaps in our knowledge begin to become evident. The ways of life of the great mass of Romans and Italians are inadequately known.

Cato the Censor and the Parting of the Ways

Imperfect as our real, deep knowledge is and in all probability must remain, there is one critical period in Roman history to which we can point with some certainty as a very definite turning point. Around the time of the Second Punic War a momentous change began which made the Rome of the time of Cicero and Caesar a very different place from the Rome of the heroic age. It was a change that nothing could arrest. Before it began the Romans found all their interest in cultivating their farms in their age-old customary way, in defending their city, in managing its politics and observing their religious practices hallowed by immemorial tradition. Within a hundred years this way of life counted for little in Rome. Instead there was a mad race for luxury and enjoyment. Religion lost any vital hold on life. Romans were content to let a professional army, recruited naturally from the poorest classes, replace the army in which every citizen had been proud to serve. Politics had become a matter of personal ambition rather than of devotion to public welfare. The old race of Roman citizens proper was not maintained. Their numbers began in fact to decline after the Second Punic War and, when they again began to increase, their growth was slow. Small families of two to three children were the rule. Rome and Italy were swarming with slaves and the descendants of slaves.

No record of their numbers has been preserved, but it has been estimated that as early as 170 B.C. free Romans were already outnumbered by residents of alien folk. They multiplied in the land like the rabbits of Australia and they devoured the patrimony of the free citizen. Because rich men found it easier to turn the small plots of the free citizens into large cattle ranches, their slaves drove the small farmer off the land. Skilled slaves from Greece and the East took the bread out of the mouths of the free artisans and craftsmen. Brawny slaves from Gaul and Spain robbed free Italians of the chance of developing their muscles and their self-respect in hard manual work. Rome became an amalgam of mixed peoples, ragtag and bobtail, and their ways were not the traditional ways of Rome. Enslavement had made such a drastic break in the lives of these miserable folk that they could preserve few traditions of their own upon which to guide their lives. A seething mass of crushed, humiliated and certainly bewildered folk was faced with the tremendous task of somehow finding its own bearings and of rebuilding a sane habit of life after the meaningless tragedy of slavery in a foreign land had over-whelmed it. In this heartbreaking work they had few if any helpers, little or no consolation or guide. Naturally they stumbled and floundered, ready to follow anyone offering them any material inducement or attraction to improve their miserable lot. Their situation demands more than a momentary thought, for in it lay the possibility of a mighty change. When men and women are abjectly wretched, nothing but hope can sustain their lives. To hope is to have faith. Upon this fertile soil, not very long after Cicero and his contemporaries had passed away, the new Christian doctrine of humility, sympathy, love and belief in a world to come was to awaken responses in Roman hearts that were to create a new order of society. In glaring contrast to the lot of the slaves and the poor in Rome was the rapidly growing wealth, luxury and ostentation of the wealthy and governing classes, many of whom were giving themselves up to the frank enjoyment of their unprecedented abundance of material pos-sessions. For the first time in Roman history, after the Second Punic War, coined money was getting into general and rapid circulation. This new instrument, facilitating the exchange of goods and serving as a store of wealth and value, enormously stimulated the economic activity of the Roman people. Men could now become rich and influential although they did not possess land, flocks and herds. These new possibilities still further widened the unmistakable divergence of interests between the rich and poor which boded ill for the Republic.

Could these troubles have been foreseen and if so would it have been possible to prevent them? A pointless question, judged by the sequel. Warning voices were, however, to be heard almost as soon as the change was beginning. One was that of the Greek hostage and historian Polybius who could not help noticing the beginnings of weaknesses which had been the fatal symptoms of decline in his own land. 'Some Romans', he said, 'were all out for women, others for unnatural vice and many for shows and drink and all the extravagance which shows and drink occasion. These were all vices for which the Greeks had a weakness and the Romans had immediately caught this contagion from them during the third Macedonian War.'

A Roman voice vainly calling upon his countrymen to halt was that of Cato the Censor. His long life spanned this momentous epoch during which Roman ways underwent a radical change. As a boy before the Second Punic War he had been brought up in the strict old way. Before he died as an old man, in the days of Cicero's grandfather, his countrymen had already turned their faces towards the full realization of their new opportunities, and Cato himself seems to have tried to combine something of the grasping greed of the new times with the stricter morality of former days. The picture of Cato that has come down to us may not be completely trustworthy but it reveals an upright, harsh, puritanical and bigoted character completely foreign to the more easy-going, cultivated, urbane and civilized friends of Cicero. As a young man, Cato was content to work hard in the fields with his slaves and to live upon rough country fare, boiling his own dish of vegetables while his young wife baked the bread. The hard life he led on the land he was equally content to live on the field of battle where his tough constitution carried him into the thickest of many a battle: in Italy against Hannibal, and later in Greece against Antiochus.

The wars at length were over and new wealth with new ideas of luxury, refinement and culture began to reach Rome. Cato stubbornly opposed the new ways of life to which they led. Tough on the field of battle, he was equally tough in the Forum of Rome. He secured many verdicts against his political opponents, for he was no mean orator. He successfully defended himself on over forty occasions. He did not spare the great Scipio Africanus who retired from Rome in disgust after being arraigned by Cato, to whom his liking for Greek civilization ('that race of babblers', snorted Cato) was anathema. Cato's oratory was much admired. Except for one or two scraps it has all been lost. For one piece of advice he certainly deserves to be for ever remembered: 'Stick to the point and the words will come' (*rem tene, verba sequentur*).

He rose to be Consul in 195 B.C. and achieved the high honour of becoming Censor in 184 B.C. He was then fifty years old. By this time Rome was tasting the sweets of triumph and of peace. Wealth and refinement were growing at a pace which greatly alarmed Cato. To interfere with private life, and to repress what were considered to be dangerous departures from the time-honoured customs of Rome, had always been the special province of the Censor. As the old scheme of social values died and the new age of luxury dawned, such matters were no longer taken very seriously, except by Cato, who had already been active enough in a private capacity to merit the title of Censor before he sought election to that high office. His enemies tried to kill his chances by telling the voters that they would be making a heavy rod for their own backs if they chose Cato. But choose him they did, and he soon got to work. He clapped a heavy tax on luxuries, and from his own manner of life it can be imagined that his definition of a luxury was nothing if not comprehensive. There was a great outburst of luxury, especially after the war with Macedon. Growing interest in material well-being was beginning to have disruptive effects. Cato thought it an outrage for Romans to spend more for handsome boy slaves than they were prepared to invest in landed estate, and to give more money for a single jar of caviare than they would for livestock. But he did not stop at that. Fine clothes, carriages, jewellery and other adornments beloved by women, silver utensils and any such possession valued above the low amount of 1,500 *denarii* or 6,000 sesterces were all on his list of luxuries to be heavily taxed. To a materialistic age such a rule seems at best folly, at worst the sadism of a thwarted personality. But Cato seems sincerely to have felt that the old ways were best and that it was up to him to see that they were honoured.

The Censor had power to appoint and dismiss Senators. Cato had his own ideas upon behaviour not permitted to a Senator, among which apparently was the crime of kissing your wife in the daytime. The story goes that a Senator, Manilius, committed this offence, which was aggravated by the circumstance that his daughter witnessed the deed. Cato expelled him from the Senate. Again, if Cato can be given the credit due to high principles, he struck a blow against popular laxity and against behaviour formerly thought inconsistent with the gravity, poise, seriousness and dignity of conspicuous public characters. Nevertheless it is not easy to credit Cato with such high-mindedness. Let us remember however, that to so human a person as Dorothy Osborne in late seventeenth-century England, a husband kissing his wife in public seemed 'as ill a sight as one would wish to see'.

The public treasury benefited from Cato's strict regard for the external proprieties. The lash with which he smote the luxurious did not spare fraudulent contractors or the financiers who were normally allowed to make a good thing out of collecting taxes for the State.

His voice was not the last, but it was certainly the most vigorous to be raised by any of the foremost officers of State against the tide of change which was surging against the foundations of Rome, but the social forces at work were far too strong for a lone Cato. He was one of the last of the old Republican Censors, and none who succeeded him in the office seems to have been able, supposing they had been willing, to try to follow his example. Lip-service continued to be paid to the ideals he championed. Laws were passed to check bribery, to restrain private luxury, to control provincial governors, to drive out Greek philosophers, and to favour or restrain different classes of society. By Cicero's time efforts on these lines by a would-be reforming Censor were merely funny.

It might be thought that such a man as Cato would have scorned to seek a livelihood otherwise than on the traditional Roman farm. He had a farm, to be sure, and, if anyone could have made farming pay, Cato should have been able to do so. In his later years he fell in with the prevailing tide and became a money-maker to the extent that candour compelled him to recommend anyone in need of a good income not to rely upon farming, for he tapped many other sources of gain himself. He bought and sold estates, bought slaves whom he trained and sold at a profit, invested in fullers' establishments (the Roman equivalent of a laundry and dye-works) and, despite the prohibition, secretly had shares in overseas trading enterprises. What he thought truly wonderful and godlike was for a man to be able to double his inheritance before he died. Yet despite such concessions to the new currents sweeping away the world of his boyhood he was not completely engulfed. His measure of success was not merely wealth, nor the number of statues erected to him. He would rather have people asking why there was no statue to Cato, than for them to have opportunities to see many such. Cato fought hard all his life, and after his death left treatises on military discipline, Roman history, farming, and other subjects to admonish and instruct his successors. Severely practical manuals, to judge by the sole specimen which has survived (his handbook on farming which has already been quoted above), they made no pretence of literary grace for which, indeed, Cato had scant regard.

Cato seems a survival into Rome's age of prosperity of a typical product of the earlier period of narrow resources. At the best his example represented a resolute determination to subordinate material conditions to an ideal way of living. But it no longer had a vital message for the new age. If Cato was unwilling to face change or to conceive standards of value other than those traditionally given high regard in the past, the intensity of his feeling burned with a purer flame by being concentrated upon limited purposes, redeeming his whole character because they centred around love of country, of home, and of family. A man inapt to awaken respect, still less affection, in a later and very different age, but one at least deserving high regard as a product of his own age, as a Roman who sought to acquit himself according to the right as he had learned it from his father and as he was determined to pass it on to his son.

Typical of this man must have been his undying distrust and hatred of the beaten Carthaginians. He had not lived through the Second Punic War without forming the fixed determination that there should never be another. As Carthage revived and her trading voyages again began to bring her some measure of prosperity, Cato's disquiet grew. He openly advocated the complete obliteration of the power which he had seen so nearly destroy Rome. He never made a speech in the Senate without concluding with the words 'Carthage must be destroyed'. Cato's slogan, long ridiculed in Rome, probably as the ravings of a bloodthirsty old dotard, eventually triumphed. Three years after Cato's death Carthage was destroyed (146 B.C.) as completely as the Nazis in our own day have wiped out Lidice and many other innocent settlements in Europe. Its inhabitants were massacred, its site was ploughed over by the victorious Romans after a desperate resistance by the wretched Carthaginians who were offered what amounted to death by slow starvation or by the sword.

Cato's fears were probably groundless. It is difficult to believe

that Rome had any real reason to fear the re-establishment of
the military power of Carthage. An attempt has been made to
explain Rome's action as masking a determination to kill Carthaginian competition with the rising olive-oil and wine industry
in Italy in which Cato and his like were investing, but purely
economic worries would not have excited the fierce animosity
which the Romans exhibited. A protective tariff would have been
a simpler weapon than war, but it was never the policy of the
Roman Republic to devise such aids for its business men.

Although he had no permanent successes, Cato's spirit lived on
to influence the lives of many Romans. He become a tradition for
Rome and he remains a tradition in European civilization. He
may be recognized in many a pillar of Victorian society in
England, and still more in Scotland.

There were men alive when Cicero was a boy who had seen
Cato in the streets of Rome and heard him in the Forum. His
belief in nostrums and his cures for ill health had been fatal to his
family, but his constitution was proof against his remedies as well
as against diseases until his eighty-sixth year when he died
(149 B.C.). Cicero's grandfather may well have seen him and more
often listened to the stories he inspired. Cicero himself, who had a
nostalgic longing for the ordered security and unity of the heroic
age of the Republic, makes Cato the principal speaker in his
dialogue study *On Old Age*. In Cicero's idealized picture the old
man, mellowed by age and experience after his active life in what
he thought the service of his country, is by no means the un-
sympathetic figure which the few remaining anecdotes about his
earlier years must have made him seem to his younger contemporaries.

Breakdown of the Old Order

Less than a hundred years after the death of Cato, Cicero was
going about lamenting the death of that Republic of which Cato
had been a typical product and one of the chief ornaments. Would
not Cato, had he survived, have said 'I told you so'? He was dead
but his great-grandson was alive, bearing his name and doing his
best to copy the strange old man, already old-fashioned a hundred
years before him. But to provide a mirror of such antique pattern
did not help the vision of his contemporaries. The unswerving

virtues of the younger Cato were a source of confusion rather than of light.

Much obviously must have gone wrong. Some obvious sources of weakness have already been thrown up by the brief review in the preceding pages of the involved and clumsy system of government, of the social cleavage between rich and poor, of the arrogance of the office-holding nobility, of the rigid insistence of money-lenders upon their bond, of the fearsome growth of slavery and of the greed with which opportunities to make away with public land were seized by the well-to-do.

There is, as a wise Scot once said, 'a great deal of ruin in a nation'. Knowing that the ultimate fate of the Roman Republic was ruin, it is tempting, when giving some account of its history, to throw all the emphasis upon facts which seem related, or to point directly, to the final catastrophe. But for the hundreds whose personal tragedies loom so grimly in the histories of war, slaughter, debt, slavery, and disaster, there were thousands, in town and country, contriving somehow to make do, on however poor a level. From provincial families as yet little affected by the habits of Rome, clever country boys came to seek their fortunes in Rome, and they did not all succumb to the temptations of the city. Cicero was one of them. Without new recruits from the un-spoiled healthy country homes, the decay of Rome might well have been more rapid and very much more difficult to heal. Millions living in the Italian peninsula under Roman rule had their land to till, their farm animals to care for, their round of religious ceremonies to observe and their periodical visits to nearby markets. All that humdrum daily life went on.

But it did not go on with the serene regularity that had once been the rule. Conservative and peaceful as the Italian farmers no doubt wished to be, they could not escape the consequences of the storms which raged at Rome. The sickness from which Roman society was suffering spread throughout the peninsula. When civil war broke out, as it did in Cicero's lifetime, it was accompanied by a frightening amount of lawlessness. Slave in-surrections made many an isolated farmstead as unsafe as it had been when Hannibal was ravaging Italy. Bandits infesting the land would attack any stray traveller they came across and, after robbing him, were as likely as not to sell him to a slave-owner to end his days chained in a slave gang. Hence no doubt the stress laid by writers such as Cicero on the importance of devoting money given in charity not merely to relieving the poor but also to ransoming prisoners.

The tragedy gradually worked up to a climax in the period roughly represented by the lives of Cicero's father and Cicero himself. The extent of the disasters which had overtaken the Romans can best be realized from the fact that civil wars did not occur in Rome until the days of Marius and Sulla, and of Caesar, Antony, Pompey and Octavius. All manner of explanations of the reason for the unrest have been suggested. If they had been merely political it should not have proved impossible to so practical-minded, commonsense a race as the Romans to have devised a political remedy. If economic troubles alone had been involved, the Roman spirit of compromise might have satisfied the worst discontents as it had succeeded in doing before, unless of course it is argued that greed, ambition, envy and the fears which they occasioned had reached such a pitch that they could no longer be controlled. That would merely be to charge the Romans with a specially large extra dose of original sin without offering any reason why it should suddenly have developed.

Should not a comprehensive explanation be sought in the general temper of Roman social behaviour and the changed way in which the Romans regarded life in society? Such an explanation of the new state of affairs points to the changed Roman outlook on life after they had cast themselves adrift from their old moorings and had forgotten or despised their simple ancestral mode of life and its ancient set of values, to embark instead upon new and uncharted seas.

The various grades of society with which Cicero was familiar in Rome differed from those of the early Republic and none had changed more in outlook and interests than the leaders of Roman society. They may therefore be looked at more closely, for although they were relatively few in numbers, it was upon them that the fate of Rome depended. Their mode of life, their education, their intellectual interests and their scientific achievements may all throw some light upon the inner nature of the social life of Rome. (Plates 21–6.)

Chapter Fifteen

THE ROMAN ARISTOCRACY

Cicero and the Party of 'the Best People'

CICERO and his noblemen friends lived in a lordly style. Their houses were large and spacious. Their household staff were so numerous that they could not have recognized them all or known their names. Certainly they never had to bother themselves with the detail of domestic worries. There were slaves to do everything from simple menial jobs such as opening the door up to confidential secretarial work and the general management of the whole complicated household under the direct orders of the master and his wife.

The head of the house, the father of the household, *pater-familias*, was, in theory at least, still the supreme dictator of the entire family organization. Immemorial custom of the Romans had made him the sole judge of right and wrong within the walls of his own property. He could do what he liked with his own. His decision was final. He could torture or kill his slaves, he could decide whether any infant newly born to him should be reared or exposed and left to perish. He could pass sentence of death on his wife, his sons and daughters. In practice matters had progressed very much since the primitive days in which the early Roman fathers were supposed not merely to have possessed, but actually to have exercised such powers. Legally they had them still and the sadists and criminals who exist in every society were able freely to indulge themselves with no more serious results than the disapproval of their neighbours, about whom they were most unlikely to concern themselves very deeply.

The general atmosphere of family life in Cicero's day was as far removed from such primitive brutalities as the England of George III was from the feudal tyrannies of the Norman Barons. Roman wives and mothers in particular had attained a degree of equality and independence which left them with little fear of their domineering men-folk. The meek and henpecked Roman husband was already a stock comedy figure in the great days of the Second Punic War, and that was about the time when Cato the Censor invented, or repeated, the hoary saying that 'we rule the world but our women-folk rule us'. It is true that Romans were able to divorce their wives with little formality, provided that they repaid their dowry, which might often be inconvenient because Romans liked marrying wealthy women. But wives seem to have been able to divorce their husbands almost as easily.

By Cicero's time the ancient religious aspect of the marriage ceremony seems to have lost its meaning for sophisticated Romans. No longer was it felt to be so tremendous a thing for a woman to leave the protecting household spirits of her father's house and to come under the sway of those of another abode. So the elaborate ritual and emotional ceremonies of earlier marriage festivals had given way to much more matter-of-fact unions, just as the Registry Office has replaced the altar for many people in our own time. All that was necessary was for the man to ask the woman before witnesses whether she wished to become *materfamilias*. She answered 'yes' and in turn asked the man if he wished to become *paterfamilias*, to which he also answered 'yes', whereupon they would be considered to be legally married. Yet the old ceremonies probably survived in country districts and among conservative households. That the poetry and the religion of marriage was by no means extinct in Cicero's day is evident for instance from a vivid marriage song of his young contemporary Catullus, the freshest and most vigorous lyric poet of all surviving Roman literature.

In the active and ambitious social and political circles in which Cicero moved, women played an important even if a secondary role. This was new in the history of Western civilization. They had long ruled the domestic scene, but in the last century of the Republic they had a wider influence over the arts and the business of life, politics included. The traditional view of woman was still that of a discreet and mostly silent helpmate in the home, busy with her slave girls, winding, spinning, and weaving the wool on which the household depended for its clothing. In the aristocratic society by which Rome was governed, her responsibilities were much heavier. When, as often, her husband was absent in the service of the State, she had to assume control over the household and the estate. Great care therefore was taken to ensure suitable matches for the sons and daughters of Rome's governing class. Girls were able to retain their own property on marriage so they

were not wholly within their husband's power. By the end of the
Republic they did not always take their husband's name. We need
not regard the beautiful and notorious Clodia, sister of P. Clodius,
the enemy of Cicero, as typical of an emancipated Roman woman
in order to believe that they then all enjoyed a life of remarkable
freedom and independence.

The round of social visits began early in the day. Prominent
men like Cicero had to give over their morning to a host of callers,
most of whom they found a great bore but few or none of whom
they discouraged. A thronged levee bore comforting evidence of
the great man's standing and importance in the eyes of public
opinion. He had to be equally alert and attentive at nights, for his
evenings were occupied in a succession of small, select and highly
luxurious dinner parties in elegant patrician homes. These events
in the crowded social calendar of Rome alternated with similar
functions in hardly less elegant villas in the fresher country air of
Baiae, Capua, Pompeii and other fashionable resorts within
fairly easy reach of the capital.

The Roman day was divided into a fixed number of hours,
beginning at sunrise. The length of the hour accordingly varied
with the seasons, being forty-four minutes in midwinter and
seventy-five minutes in midsummer. The Romans had no clocks
or watches; sundials were a comparatively recent invention
dating from the First Punic War. Sociable Romans consequently
could not rely upon their guests arriving at the right time for
dinner, so a slave was sent out to the home of each guest at a
suitable time in advance of the meal to conduct him to the feast.
The dinner had to be very carefully planned. The couches on
which the men guests reclined at the meal had to be allotted
according to strict rules of precedence, and most well-to-do
Romans employed a special social secretary to help them on such
occasions. None but an abandoned woman reclined during meals.
The ladies sat upright at the table. Cicero was an inveterate diner-
out and he was hospitable in return. Social gatherings at dinner
then, as now, exercised their subtle influence, shaping and
moulding the curious amalgam of high society and acting as a
security market or exchange on which the personal reputations of
the members of society were always being reassessed and re-
valued. In the relatively small and highly compact social life of
Cicero's Rome such parties were all the more influential because

there were no newspapers and no effective public opinion except that made by Roman society itself. The leaders of that society were the *optimates*, the 'best people' descended from the great families of mixed patrician and plebeian descent. They were prominently represented among the 600 Senators and their families and they could be sure of the respect if not the deference of those of the Senators, Cicero, for example, who could not boast patrician descent.

The social force represented by the lesser gentry, the financiers, bankers, traders and money-making class of *equites* (or 'knights') could at times become substantial, but after the manner of their kind in all ages they accepted the domination of the political class which was at the same time the class of their social superiors. The families of these upper classes may have numbered about 10,000 of Rome's entire population which, in Cicero's time, has generally been estimated at about a million, of whom perhaps over 200,000 were slaves. Several hundred thousands of the remainder would be freedmen or the descendants of slaves.

The senatorial aristocracy were, for Cicero, the party of 'the best people'. As he grew older, he had no other social ambitions than to live and move among them and to be accepted by them as a man of distinction. Politically, they were maddening. Cicero had a right to be enraged with them. He gave his talent and his life to their service, but won in return small response, little gratitude, and no help.

Aiding the moneymakers, most of whom were of the equestrian order, was not a very rewarding occupation. The trouble about them was that in their devotion to the all-absorbing task of filling their money-bags they had no time for the niceties of political principle. Cicero had to be prepared for some pretty drastic compromises if he wanted their support. Some of his friends were not so accommodating, particularly Cato, great-grandson of old Cato the Censor and Caesar's stern critic. This is how Cicero reacted to Cato's principles in the heat of a political crisis. 'As for our friend Cato, you do not love him more than I do: but after all, with the very best intentions and the most absolute honesty, he sometimes does harm to the Republic. He speaks and votes as though he were in the Republic of Plato, not among the scum of Romulus' (by which Cicero meant his contemporaries).

In a more deliberate and reflective mood Cicero took much the same line. In his long letter of advice to his brother who, in March 61 B.C., had become propraetor of Asia, he faced up again to the problem of the greed and lack of morality of the business men. Urging his brother 'to take care of the interests of all, to remedy men's misfortunes, to provide for their safety, to resolve that you will be both called and believed to be the "father of Asia"', he candidly admitted: 'However, to such a resolution and deliberate policy on your part the great obstacle is the business men [*publicani*].' The dilemma with which Cicero found himself faced was that although the political support of the business men was essential to his programme of 'harmony between the social classes' it was forthcoming only at the price of making no resistance to their greedy demands.

'If we oppose them,' he told his brother, 'we shall alienate from ourselves and from the Republic an order which has done us excellent service. If on the other hand we comply with them in every case, we shall allow the complete ruin of those whose interests, to say nothing of their preservation, we are bound to consult.' That is to say, the business men would not support anyone who tried to stop them fleecing the subject races in the provinces. Cicero had not forgotten Verres. He had seen enough of the money-lenders' and tax-gatherers' behaviour in his province of Cilicia and at home, to know what he was talking about. 'After hearing the grievances of citizens of Italy, I can comprehend what happens to allies in distant lands.' Well might he ruefully conclude that 'to conduct oneself in this matter in such a way as to satisfy the business men, especially when contracts have been taken at a loss, and yet to preserve the allies from ruin, seems to demand a virtue with something divine in it'.

The godlike ruler of Cicero's dreams did not emerge during his lifetime and where Cicero failed no other Roman succeeded in creating wise, public-spirited citizens from among the self-seeking business classes. How far Romans had gone in two generations! When, in the days of Cicero's grandfather, old Cato had been asked 'How about money-lending?' as a way of making a living, his blunt answer had been 'How about murder?'

The Profits of Empire

The balance sheet of Rome's gains when the Republic became an imperial world power cannot be drawn in any detail. It is however possible to make a rough guess at the probable order of magnitude of the main items in the revenue of the self-supporting Republic in the heroic days of the Second Punic War and of the later Republic of Cicero's time.

The contrast is striking, as the following estimates by Professor Tenney Frank reveal:

ESTIMATED TOTAL EXPENSES AND REVENUE OF ROME IN
THE SECOND PUNIC WAR

in millions of sesterces. 217 B.C. to 201 B.C.

EXPENDITURE		REVENUE	
Army pay	720	Property tax on citizens (*tributum*)	260
Food for allied troops	144	Loans, contributions, exceptional taxes	468
Land transport	60	Port dues, rentals, etc.	40
Arms and equipment	80	Tithes on public land	96
Navy and sea transport	140	Booty	260
		Sacred treasury	20
Total, 17 years' expenditure: 1,144 millions		Total, 17 years' revenue: 1,144 millions	

The average annual amount was a mere 67½ million sesterces or about 17 million *denarii* a year for the seventeen years of war.

During the Punic War, as these figures show, the citizens of Rome paid their way despite the desperate crisis in which they were so nearly engulfed. Little more than one-fifth of the State revenue came from foreign sources and that was an exceptional result of war.

By Cicero's day, on the other hand, the Romans had long been accustomed to having most of their bills paid for them by dependent territories. Sources of revenue inside Italy did not provide more than about one-fifth of all the income needed by the Republic, and this small amount was not taxation so much as rent for the use of land and property which would have been paid in any case, whether the Republic or a private citizen had been the owner. The Republic possessed other income-earning assets such as public forests, public aqueducts, a salt monopoly, public fisheries, iron, copper, silver, gold and other metal mines. Such

State and industrial trading enterprises were not run by public officials, but were handed over to any company who would make the highest bid for the right to operate them. As with so many of its public responsibilities, the State preferred to farm out administrative tasks rather than to have them carried out by its own officials. The growth of business partnerships on the lines of joint-stock companies was no doubt stimulated by these opportunities for profit-making, and their activities spread into many branches of economic life unconnected with public administration, such as foreign trade and house-building.

During Cicero's active life, the revenue of the Republic was more than doubled as a result of the organization of the tribute-paying dependencies which then made up the Roman Empire. Contrast the following estimate with that given above of the revenue of the Republic in the heroic age of the Second Punic War:

ESTIMATED ANNUAL REVENUE OF ROME IN THE AGE
OF CICERO (ABOUT 63 B.C.)

Sicily	16 million sesterces
Sardinia and Corsica	6 million sesterces
Macedonia	8 million sesterces
Asia and Islands	60 million sesterces
Spain	34 million sesterces
Gallia Narbonensis (the Provence and Cévennes district of modern France)	14 million sesterces
Africa and Cyrene	24 million sesterces
All other rates, rents and taxes	40 million sesterces

Estimated total average annual revenue: 202 million sesterce

Such revenue was spent almost entirely upon the army, navy and military equipment, food and stores. Public works and the corn subsidy together with administration costs were the main items in the civil as opposed to the military expenditure. Civil administration was not expensive. The aim had always been to run the Republic and to govern Rome on the cheap. The chief magistrates were paid no salaries. It is true that each was provided at the public expense with a small office staff and that those who, like the Aediles, had practical work to supervise, probably had a labour force of public slaves to help in the repair of wate and sewerage systems. But this aid was negligible in comparison with the huge expense of those very lavish public games and spectacles and other forms of ostentation which the great officials had to provide in return or as a bribe for the honour of being elected. The need to find money to pay for these extravagances powerfully stimulated the ruling classes to look for funds from the provinces now at their mercy.

These sketchy estimates of the public finances of the Republic support the view that war must be ranked with agriculture as a major industry of the Roman people and they show that, in the end, war turned out to be a highly profitable enterprise. To provide the sinews of war had always been the main reason why the Romans had to pay taxes.

The chief war tax was the ancient *tributum*, a capital levy traditionally imposed at the rate of one-thousandth part of the property of every citizen. In times of special need it was increased two or three times. The strain of the Second Punic War, for example, led to its being doubled in 215 B.C. and many heavier sacrifices were demanded before the war was over. When the final victory had been won the Republic repaid from the Carthaginian indemnity some of these exactions. For the first thirty years of the second century B.C., the *tributum* continued to be levied. In 184 B.C. Cato who was then Censor demanded a triple levy.

As long as the old traditions of Rome were still honoured, wars were not declared for the sake of the loot they might provide. Rome had no territorial ambitions to be satisfied at the expense of her Mediterranean neighbours. But as the power of Rome grew, new relationships with foreign territories began to be formed. When Rome replaced the former rulers of territories like Sicily and Macedonia it automatically acquired the revenues which those rulers used to enjoy. Foreign tribute was then received which went to enrich the Treasury of the Republic. The year 167 B.C. was memorable for Roman citizens, for then it was decided that the wealth coming from Macedonia by way of tribute was sufficient to make it no longer necessary to demand payment of the *tributum* by the Romans living in Italy.

By Cicero's time there was scarcely a Roman living who remembered paying the tax which had financed the growth of the Republic. Taxation in Cicero's eyes was a great evil. 'Care should be taken', he said, 'lest, as was often the case among our ancestors, on account of the poverty of the Treasury and the continuity of wars, it may be necessary to impose taxation.' Like Mr Gladstone, he evidently believed that money should 'fructify in the pockets of the people'. His countrymen had long been of the same mind. And no wonder. In an age when money was by no means so widely spread throughout the community as it is today, it was no light burden suddenly to be called upon to find ready cash equivalent to a one- or two-thousandth part of all one's possessions. On such occasions money-lenders with ready cash were able to reap a rich harvest. Then, as in later ages, they were a race of men singularly immune from tenderness and charitable emotions towards their victims and their resolute insistence upon at least twelve per cent interest on their loans had every guarantee of State support should it be needed, as indeed it often was. Romans could be harder to each other than to a vanquished enemy.

During the first hundred years of the Republic the citizen soldiers had to serve in the army at their own expense. They were first paid after 406 B.C., but the cost of their food and equipment was deducted from their pay. Army needs accounted for by far the largest expenditure of the State and it was a rising cost because the expense of maintaining the legion of 4,000 to 4,200 men grew as the Republic developed.

Between 200 B.C. and 150 B.C., it has been estimated that one legion would have cost about 2,400,000 sesterces a year. It rose to about 3,200,000 sesterces between 150 B.C. and 90 B.C., when the rank and file were paid 480 sesterces a year, centurions 960 sesterces and cavalry 1,440 sesterces. After that, in Cicero's lifetime, it grew to 4,000,000 sesterces a year.

The increased cost of the army during the break-up of the Republican constitution was not so much an index of the increased cost of living or of the growing wealth of Rome as of the need to bribe the legionaries in order to be assured of their loyalty and devotion. The official army rates of pay then became less important than the shares of booty divided by a victorious general among his troops. A fair share of booty was one of the oldest traditional rights of the Roman soldier, but never in the history of the Republic did the distribution of booty carry with it political influence on so large a scale as it did in the time of Cicero.

Opportunities of collecting loot had existed at earlier times and the Romans had not neglected them. But neither had they exploited them as they might have done and as they later did on a vast and comprehensive scale. When in 196 B.C. Flamininus announced the freedom of Greece 'without garrison or tribute', the Greeks were not merely astounded but, said Polybius, who was a boy of about eight years when the words were spoken and who must have often discussed them with his elders if he had not heard them himself, they were filled with admiration that 'the Romans and their leader Flamininus should have deliberately incurred unlimited expense and danger for the sole purpose of freeing Greece', a generous tribute of gratitude that an Englishman of the twentieth century may perhaps be pardoned for associating with the activities of his own countrymen, from the days of Lord Byron to those of Sir Winston Churchill, who have sought with some success to be not less generous to Greece than were Flamininus and the Senate of Rome.

The wars with Antiochus from 192 B.C. to 189 B.C. proved more lucrative and were traditionally regarded as a powerful stimulus to luxury and sophisticated ways of life in Rome, so great was the loot brought back by the victorious legions.

Despite great diplomatic activity, the opportunities of collecting booty on a large scale were infrequent during the second half of the second century B.C. because there were no large-scale operations by the Roman army against countries possessing much wealth. But already by the middle of the second century Roman power was being used for self-advancement by younger members of the Roman governing class. Their fathers and forefathers had become famous at a high cost in personal endeavour against the enemies of the Republic, but they had not become rich. Scipio, Paulus, Cato and the father of the Gracchi left no great fortunes and it was with difficulty that their daughters were provided with dowries. Now, however, the new generation wanted the fame of successful generalship in the field and they did not object to becoming rich at the same time. The search for cheap triumphs, for the honourable title of victor and for the opportunity of indulging a less honourable lust for plunder in Spain and across the Adriatic began to give a sinister twist to the foreign policy of the Republic. During the first century B.C. these questionable practices took a turn for the worse. The hatred the Romans inspired among their subject peoples was revealed in the terrible massacre that took place in 88 B.C. in Asia Minor and in the Greek islands when some 80,000 Latin-speaking southern Italian traders and agents of the greedy and hated Roman business men were slaughtered in one day at the orders, willingly enough obeyed, of Mithridates, King of Pontus.

It was the first step in his grand scheme to organize the northern territories of Asia Minor against Rome, and he launched it when Rome was exhausting her forces in the civil war against Italians. How the command of the army Rome was forced to send against him was entrusted to Sulla, and how Sulla became in consequence the Dictator of Rome, has already been recounted (p. 215). It remains to record that when Sulla returned to Rome his baggage trains were heavy with loot from the Greek temples, from the sale of captives and from wholesale robbery thinly disguised as an indemnity to the amount of 480 million sesterces inflicted upon the unfortunate inhabitants of the Near East, caught between the devil Mithridates and the avenging Romans from the deep sea.

Like an Eastern king rather than a Consul of Rome, Sulla used this vast wealth as he pleased, without giving the customary account of his receipts and expenses. There was therefore no settled, orderly public accounting for any length of time after 90 B.C. and it is impossible to guess what revenues were raised and how much the State Treasury actually received. Until his retirement in 79 B.C. and death in the following year, Sulla was all-powerful and immensely rich. His power and his wealth were something entirely new in the history of the Republic and they had been won for him by his army. No ambitious man could fail to grasp the lesson of this tremendous fact, and the remembrance of it survived to entice others still further along the same road. 'How often', said Cicero, 'have I heard Pompey say "Sulla could do it; shall I not be able to do it?"' There was a new instrument now to help along such ambitions. The army was no longer all the active men of Rome mobilized to defend their farms and their city as in the brave days of old. The new model army created by Marius was largely composed of professional soldiers recruited for long-term service, drilled and disciplined but looking for their rewards to what their army service would bring them, and not to a return, as speedy as possible, to the homes and the farms which few of them now possessed. The army became a new power in the State distinct from the citizen body with which it had from time immemorial been identified.

The campaign which Sulla had begun in the East against king Mithridates was taken up once more by Lucullus. Between 74 B.C. and 66 B.C., after some long and hard campaigning, Lucullus was making a thorough job of his command. He sent hordes of Eastern slaves to Rome and his own gains were large. He distributed 4 million sesterces among his men, paid over 10 million sesterces into the Treasury and became one of the richest men in Rome. But he fought too long. He won battles without winning the war and exhausted his army in the process. Not merely did he not put enough opportunities for enrichment in the way of the business men of Rome but he drastically scaled down some of their more outrageous claims for high interest on outstanding loans, so he lost his command. His name has since remained a by-word for lavish and luxurious living. After a good deal of hesitation the Senate gave his command, with Cicero's strong support, to Pompey (66 B.C.).

Pompey's supporters were numerous among the financial and business classes, who were exasperated by their continued losses through piracy on the seas, by the time it was taking to quieten the East and by the way Lucullus protected their helpless creditors. Pompey was therefore given both tasks of settling scores with the pirates and of finishing the war against Mithridates. In the five years between 67 B.C. and 62 B.C. he succeeded in both commands and returned to Rome with rewards more substantial than glory. So much loot was collected from Asia Minor and especially from Syria, where marauding Roman armies had not before penetrated, that the share-out was impressive.

Pompey had eight legions, each of which had a normal strength of 4,000 men, sixty centurions, and six Tribunes. The share of each man came to 6,000 sesterces, more than twelve years' pay. Centurions received 120,000 sesterces and Tribunes 720,000 sesterces. They fully expected, although in this they were disappointed, an immediate allotment of land in Italy as well. For this they had to wait (p. 239). Over and above the 288 million sesterces paid to the army rank and file, he shared another 100 million with his staff officers, eighteen *legati* and two Quaestors. Supposing Pompey kept 25 million for himself, each of these higher ranking officers would have had over 3 million sesterces.

Five per cent was regarded as a low rate of interest in Cicero's day, but had these officers got no more, their gratuity would have provided them with an income of 160,000 sesterces a year for life, a respectable fortune in itself when compared with the modest incomes of Rome's middle classes (p. 111).

After providing all these huge rewards for the army, Pompey was able to pay for a lavish triumph, a votive offering to Minerva of 8 million sesterces, and later to build a great theatre. He was also said to have paid 480 million sesterces into the Treasury and to have added about 140 million sesterces to the annual revenues of the Republic of 202 million sesterces before 62 B.C. That he added substantially to his own vast fortunes goes without saying. It is also evident that when he succeeded in stopping the losses Roman citizens had been sustaining through piracy, he also made a positive contribution to the national income of Rome.

It was not always necessary to start a war in order to bleed the provincials white. As the provinces increased in number, the governing classes were able to get themselves appointed in charge of them as military and civil governors for a year at a time as proconsuls. The title perpetuated the original military nature of Rome's colonizing activities outside Italy where there were allies, but no provinces except in the Gallic north where the valley of the Po constituted the province of Cisalpine Gaul. Many if not most of these proconsular governors and their staffs looked upon their exile from Rome as having only one compensation, the opportunity to get rich quick at the expense of the provincials and to return to live in Italy in a vastly better style than when they left it.

Not so Cicero. Much against his will and inclination he was forced, as a former Consul, to take his turn in 51 B.C. as proconsul in the large province of Cilicia. With him went two legions and a mere 8 million sesterces for expenses. He devoted himself to the well-being of his province, he both preached and practised justice, did what he could to remedy the wrongs inflicted on the inhabitants by the previous Roman governor, refused to allow his wretched people to be ruined by the tax-collectors, and did his best to restrain his staff and his friends from gouging as much as they could from the natives.

He boasted that 'no expense has been imposed upon them

during my government, and when I say no expense I do not speak hyperbolically, I mean *none*, not a farthing'. The man who had secured the conviction of a scoundrel such as Verres, whose misgovernment of Sicily as Roman Praetor between 73 B.C. and 71 B.C. was an infamous chapter of Roman imperialism, was pledged himself to honourable behaviour.

Some indication of what Roman rule meant to subject races may be gathered from the fact that the inhabitants of the small island of Cyprus used to scrape together 4,800,000 sesterces a year to bribe their Roman ruler not to billet his troops on them. It was a common practice of Roman commanders to keep for themselves the money voted by the Senate for the expenses of their army by quartering their troops on the subject races to be fed and housed at their expense. Cicero, who made his men live under canvas and yet refused the bribe, was regarded by the natives 'with speechless astonishment' and it was all he could do to stop them erecting temples, statues, or marble chariots in his honour. One of the haughty aristocrats battening upon the unfortunate Cypriots was none other than Brutus, 'the noblest Roman of them all', who used to write to Cicero 'in a tone of hauteur, arrogance and offensive superiority', expecting him to help him collect arrears of unpaid interest on loans he had made to the islanders at a rate which Cicero was horrified to discover worked out at 48 per cent a year, 'an impossible sum', said Cicero. 'It could not be paid, nor could I have allowed it.' Cicero offered to get him 12 per cent but his agent refused to take it.

Cicero was vain enough to hope that the modest campaign in which he overcame a few fractious hill tribes might earn him the coveted title of *Imperator* and the claim to a triumph through the streets of Rome, which, however, the Senate did not grant. Those of the enemy he had captured were sold to the slave-dealers for 12 million sesterces.

He thought himself lucky to get away so successfully for he was in mortal terror lest the Parthians should fall upon him and defeat him as they had defeated Crassus two years earlier. His pathetic pleas for reinforcements were not heeded although he sent a dispatch to the magistrates and Senate warning them that the fate of many provinces 'on which the revenues of Rome depend' were in danger. It was, he reported, hopeless to expect anything from Rome's allies because such had been 'the harshness and injustice of our rule' that they were either too weak or so disaffected that they could not be trusted.

His staff were by no means pleased to return from a year in an exposed, lonely and dangerous part of the world with no better reward than their pay, because Cicero had insisted on a strict accounting and the deposit of all credits in the Treasury. 'Of the booty taken by me, no one,' he said, 'except the Quaestors of the City, has touched or will touch a farthing.' He considered himself legally entitled to a modest 2,200,000 sesterces which he was able to bank for himself with business men in Ephesus, but he did not use it himself. A few months later he wrote that 'the whole of it has been appropriated by Pompey' during his fight with Caesar which broke out in the following year, when of course Cicero lost it all because he backed the losing side.

How many honest governors were there, like Cicero? We do not know, but Cicero himself hints that there were several. Had there not been, all the wretched provincials would have been left without a tunic on their backs. Far too many seem indeed to have been reduced to something approaching this condition. Cicero had found 'a province drained by charges for maintenance'; nobody, he said, could be more needy than one of the dependent kings and 'nothing can be stripped cleaner than his kingdom'. Such was the misery under Roman rule of the once relatively prosperous peoples of the Middle East that it has been suggested that in their utter hopelessness they were led to turn for consolation to religions which directed their gaze away from the evils of the world around them, to cultivate instead satisfactions springing from the inward spiritual life, so seeking compensation on the other side of the grave for evils they were unable to remedy during their lifetime.

The pessimism and despair provoked by successive Roman conquerors and, still worse, by the bloodsucking tax-gatherers and leeches in the shape of money-lenders following on their heels, could not be arrested by a solitary Cicero making a brief and very unwilling stay of one short year. Imperialism is a word which has never recovered from the meaning which Cicero's contemporaries gave it. Charged with emotional memories of these bad times it has served as a political 'smear word', often apparently in the absence of any clear notion of its real relevance to the conditions it purports to describe.

Cicero was attempting to revive an obsolete tradition. Sulla, Lucullus, Pompey had shown what profits war could bring, but they were feeble bunglers beside Julius Caesar who, in this sphere of action as in all others, did nothing by halves. It was now obvious that, rightly handled, a Roman army could do anything a resolute man determined it should do to advance him in wealth, power and glory. Caesar's military career, in fact his whole life, has been very generally admired for the glory it brought Rome, less for the power it gave Caesar. Little has usually been said by his enthusiastic admirers about the sources of his great wealth. From his own point of view, riches were probably his most important immediate objective. He went to Spain in 61 B.C., crippled with a debt of 25 million sesterces. War gave him a chance to sack and loot some Spanish towns, so when he returned to Rome a year later, after a vigorous campaign, he had amassed enough to enable him to look his creditors once again in the face. The result of his ten years in the wilderness after 59 B.C., fighting the German tribes and reducing Gaul to dependence on Rome, certainly added enormously to the influence and possessions of Rome. Yet it is not very far wrong to say that in Caesar's eyes there was a more important cause at stake than the safety and glory of the Republic, and that was the personal security and advantage of Julius Caesar himself.

During the ten years in which his army slashed its way along the Rhine about 400,000 of the wretched inhabitants were slaughtered and as many, if not more, men, women and children were torn from their native land, exposed naked on the slave-dealers' block, branded with a red-hot iron and sold into captivity like so many cattle. After destroying human life and all that gave meaning and value to life, it was a relatively small matter that he also looted on a grand scale. Not one of the hundreds of millions of sesterces Caesar collected so diligently in his ten years' piracy seems to have been paid into the Roman Treasury until that became in turn Caesar's own personal property in 46 B.C. Before then all his loot was used to enlarge his army, to bribe his soldiers and to corrupt politicians at home. The ruin such activities brought to the slowly developing civilization in his path was of no concern to him or to any other Roman. Cicero's brother Quintus was with Caesar during some of these exploits, including the expedition to Britain. Cicero himself betrayed the prevalent

Roman attitude when he expressed his anxiety about the outcome of the 'British War'. It had been discovered, he said, that 'the approaches to the island are protected by astonishing masses of cliff. Moreover, it is now known that there isn't a pennyweight of silver in that island, nor any hope of booty except from slaves, among whom I don't suppose you can expect any instructed in literature or music'. No word of extending the benefits of Roman civilization and law to backward areas, nothing about trading opportunities or even of a desirable strengthening of Rome's hinterland, but plain smash-and-grab.

When a cultivated Roman like Cicero spoke like that, it would have been idle to look for nobler sentiments elsewhere. Nothing reveals more clearly the sordid and rotten foundations of Roman imperialism in the Republican era. In his more responsible moods, however, Cicero was as conscious as any man has ever been of the duty of an imperial power towards its subject peoples. The record of his actions as proconsul in Cilicia in 51 B.C. proves that he was no sham and empty preacher of virtue when, in his writings, he earnestly recommended high-minded devotion to the strict path of duty as obligatory upon Roman statesmen.

His service to humanity has been far greater than it was to Rome, for his memory endured as a perpetual guide to the conscience of mankind, not indeed always heard, frequently disobeyed by those who had heard him, but remaining a constant, steady beacon light to direct their wavering steps towards equality, justice, and humanitarian ideals.

The Private Life of a Roman Politician

Large families do not seem to have been the fashion among the wealthier Romans in the declining years of the Republic. In Cicero's family circle there was his wife Terentia, their daughter Tullia, and their only son, called Marcus after his father. The boy was twelve years younger than his sister. Beyond these three, Cicero had only his brother Quintus, married to Pomponia the waspish sister of Cicero's rich friend Atticus, and they had only one child, a boy, two years older than young Marcus Cicero.

Judging by the outcome, both Cicero and his brother had an indifferent success in the difficult art of staying happily married and the still more difficult art of bringing up their children. Cicero and Terentia were united for thirty-one years; then, in his sixtieth year (in 46 B.C.), Cicero divorced her. His brother Quintus, whose temper was more fiery, seems to have had a pretty miserable home life until he at length parted company with Pomponia after a married life of almost twenty-four years.

Not much is known about the children despite the frequent and affectionate references to them in Cicero's letters. He seems to have given some time and a good deal of thought to the education both of his son and of his nephew. But his darling was his daughter Tullia, 'my dear little Tullia, dearer to me than life itself'. For her he had always sunny good humour. But he does not say how the children lived, what games they played, where and how they had their early lessons, whether they went to the public games and festivals as children today go to cinemas, whether Tullia was able to walk alone in the streets of Rome or to go unattended to the houses of friends or relations. The answer to all these and many other questions, which would help, did we but know them, to make the young Ciceros and their fellow Romans seem understandable human creatures, must mostly remain unknown. In comparison with the children of the poor, we may believe that they had an enviable time. In summer they probably spent happy days at Cicero's family home in the hills at Arpinum, wandering along the shady banks of the Liris whose full stream was refreshingly cold in the hottest days of an Italian summer. Or they would be at the seaside where in calm weather Cicero would take them shrimping. Other country recreations are very little mentioned in surviving Roman literature. Sports, and particularly hunting, do not seem to have greatly preoccupied many Roman gentlemen. But the passion for blood-sports, particularly degrading fights with wild beasts and between gladiators in the Circus or theatre, became an increasingly sordid feature of Roman life during the last hundred years of the Republic.

Childhood did not last long, particularly for Roman girls. Tullia was engaged very early and was married in the year her father was Consul, when she was probably not fourteen years old. Her father by no means lost sight of her, for she was frequently mentioned in his letters. Cicero did his best for his two children and tried not to spoil the boy, but it seems that his darling Tullia often got her own way. One April when Tullia was about seventeen, Cicero had to rearrange his time-table. 'On the 1st of May I leave Formiae,' he said, 'intending to reach Antium on the 3rd of May. For there are Games at Antium from the 4th to the 6th of May, and Tullia wants to see them.'

The two boys may have gone to the Games as well but all that remains on the record about them is more serious stuff about their education and training. Cicero gave time and thought to the problem of their upbringing which he could ill spare from the often overwhelming demands made upon his time by his public position.

Yet neither Quintus nor young Marcus Cicero became the model young men Cicero had hoped and planned to develop. His nephew Quintus indeed gave him serious cause for alarm after 10 January 49 B.C., when Julius Caesar had crossed the Rubicon and it was plain that civil war would decide who was to rule Rome. Cicero was prominently identified with the opponents of Caesar. Pompey had in fact put him in command of the Campanian coast.

At that dangerous period young Quintus was nearly eighteen, Marcus was nearly sixteen, and neither of the two lads was so resolutely anti-Caesar as Cicero wished. Referring to his own boy Marcus, Cicero remarked, 'because he is not after all more dutiful than he is, he gives me extraordinary pain'. But young Quintus was worse. 'Oh dear! oh dear!' lamented Cicero, 'it is the keenest sorrow of my life – corrupted no doubt by our system of indulgence, he has gone very far, to a point indeed which I do not venture to describe.' He was indeed thought to have gone to curry favour with Caesar by denouncing his uncle as one of Caesar's enemies. This was bad enough for Cicero; it was tragic for Cicero's brother.

It has recently been said that almost the bitterest and most hopeless tragedies of all are the tragedies of parents with bad children. The tragedy of children with bad parents is no less acute and the childhood of little Quintus was poisoned by the squabbles of his mother and father. His father was now to reap the consequences.

'My brother is prostrate with grief and is not so much afraid for his own life as for mine.' Cicero and his brother must have experienced that anguish of mind which in our own day has been the hard fate of those liberal-minded parents in totalitarian prison-states who were denounced by their own children to the enemies of freedom. Unlike some of the Hitler youth, young Quintus did not apparently succeed in his treachery, if treachery it was, for he came back again to his family. Cicero gave him a good dressing-down. 'I gave it to young Quintus when he returned!' he wrote to the boy's other uncle Atticus. 'I perceive that it was a piece of avarice on his part, and the hope of a large bounty. This is a serious evil enough, but the crime which I feared, I hope he did not commit.'

Cicero said he would school and control him but he began the job rather late in the day, as he seems himself to have realized. He blamed his brother. 'His father has always spoilt him but his indulgence is not responsible for his being untruthful or grasping or wanting in affection for his family, though it perhaps does make him headstrong and self-willed as well as aggressive.' Not a very pleasant picture, but it seems to have been only too common, because Cicero goes on to refer to these disagreeable traits in his character as being 'the results of over-indulgence, but they are pardonable, we must admit, considering what young men are nowadays'.

He flattered himself that he had brought up young Marcus more satisfactorily. 'My own son I keep under control without difficulty. He is the most tractable boy possible.' The evil days into which Cicero had survived made the task of training a son for public life terribly difficult. His responsibility for the boy weakened Cicero's never very firm resolution in times of danger. Cicero could be candid about his own shortcomings. He once wrote: 'If there is anyone who is nervous in matters of moment and danger and who is always more inclined to fear a reverse than to hope for success, I am that man.' Consequently he must have found it difficult to give his son firm guidance. 'My remorseful pity for him makes me less determined in politics,' said Cicero, and 'the more he desires to be staunch the more I fear turning out a cruel father to him.'

As we have seen in the totalitarian countries in our own day, the loss of political liberty poisons the whole of life, leaving no safe refuge, not even in family relationships. So it was with Cicero and his brother. Quintus had been one of Caesar's high-ranking staff officers in Gaul and had done exceedingly well for himself financially in consequence. When, after long and desperate hesitation, Cicero resolved to join Pompey across the sea he persuaded Quintus to accompany him and to bring his son. As soon as Pompey had been hopelessly defeated by Caesar at Pharsalus in 48 B.C., Quintus angrily attacked Cicero for having misled him into deserting his former chief to join the losing side. He quarrelled violently with his brother and took himself with his young son to throw himself on Caesar's mercy. 'They will easily obtain their pardons,' said Cicero, who himself wrote to Caesar accepting full responsibility for having got them to go along with him to Pompey's camp. Cicero was in such danger that he added, 'I only hope that as they will have seen Caesar first, they may choose to aid me with him as much as I should have wished to aid them, if I had the power'.

Unfortunately his brother had not Cicero's generous disposition. Possibly he was still afraid and anxious to show excessive zeal to clear himself of the charge of deserting Caesar. Whatever the motive, the fact remains that he denounced Cicero in wild terms. News about his goings-on soon reached Cicero. Quintus sent letters to several of Cicero's friends which came into Cicero's hands. He sent on all those addressed to people near at hand. 'They immediately came to me boiling with indignation, loudly exclaiming against "the villain". They read me the letters full of every kind of abuse of me. Ligurius raved; said that he knew that Quintus was detested by Caesar, and yet the latter had not only favoured him but had also given him all that money out of compliment to me. Thus outraged I determined to ascertain what he had said in his letters to the rest. For I thought it would be fatal to Quintus himself if such villainy on his part became generally known. I found that they were of the same kind.' Cicero had taken an extraordinary liberty in opening the letters. He sent them on to Atticus saying, 'If you think that it is for his interest that they should be delivered, please deliver them. It won't do me any harm.' But it was a bitter blow and Cicero did not lack other information showing that his brother and nephew were unsparing in their abuse of him. Uncertain as he was of his own position and about the provision he could hope to make for his wife, son, and daughter, this added hazard from his nearest relation with whom he had always been on affectionately intimate terms was crushing. 'These things', he said, 'are a positive torture to me.' In the end Caesar pardoned Cicero with every show of friendship and regard, but it was two years before Marcus and Quintus were again reconciled. His nephew Quintus kept up the animosity still longer. His attacks on his distinguished uncle were notorious. This was not the full story of Cicero's family troubles in these disastrous years.

Terentia, Cicero's wife, is a silent figure in the story. She is often mentioned. Some of Cicero's letters to her are preserved. They are affectionate and emotional enough at the time of Cicero's exile, but they cooled off considerably in the last ten years of his life. After Cicero's flight to join Pompey in the summer of 49 B.C. and his absence from Rome for over two years, the marriage finally came to grief. There is one short letter of Cicero's to his wife, curt to the point of rudeness, which shows that they were hardly on speaking terms at the time when he returned, with Caesar's full pardon, to live once more in Rome. What the cause of the break may have been is unknown. Cicero darkly refers in a letter to a friend to the disordered state of his domestic affairs, to misconduct which left nothing safe within the walls of his house, to intrigues and treachery, but what it was all about we do not know. It can only be guessed that Cicero's wife, who had remained in Italy during those decisive two years, was perhaps not as resolute in opposition to Caesarism as her husband. She, like his brother Quintus, may have reproached him bitterly with his folly in throwing in his lot with Pompey, reproaches which would have cut Cicero all the keener because he more than anyone knew the hollow incompetence of Pompey and the hopelessness of his cause, and he as much as anybody suffered from the disaster which had overtaken the Republic. It is certain at least that no other woman had replaced Terentia in Cicero's affections. Female society had little attraction for him, although, like all prominent figures, he enjoyed a wide circle of acquaintances among the best society of Rome. There is a story of a dinner party, in the year he divorced his wife, at which he found himself in the company of a notorious actress who had been running around with Caesar's lieutenant Mark Antony and who was assumed to be just as ready to take up with any other man. Cicero confessed that he had not known that she would be at the party but it is not necessary to infer that he would have declined the invitation had he known that she was to be among the guests. 'The fact is,' he said, 'that sort of thing never had any attraction for me when I was a young man, much less now that I am an old one.' He was proof against the powerful attractions of the notorious Clodia. She was a Consul's wife but the sister of his arch-enemy P. Clodius, a fact quite sufficient to colour Cicero's views about her. But he seems to have seen her for what she was worth. 'I detest that woman, so unworthy of a Consul' was his verdict, quoting, as he loved to do, an appropriate line of poetry: for "a shrew she is, and with her husband jars".'

When, therefore, at the age of sixty he remarried very shortly after his divorce, it is most unlikely that any grand passion explained his action. His new bride was Publilia, a girl young enough to have been his grand-daughter. Cicero's interest in her arose from the fact that her father had left a large fortune, much of which was bequeathed to Cicero in trust for her. Cicero was in the habit of living in a luxurious style and he was often in need of money. It was a scandalizing match, and Cicero must have felt ashamed of the lengths to which financial pressure had driven him. What did Tullia think of him? We can only guess, but in any case she had short time in which to tell him. For within three months she was suddenly stricken and she died towards the end of February in the following year (45 B.C.). She was little more than thirty years of age. Life had not been very kind to her. She had become a widow before her twentieth year, she was again married, and then divorced. Her third husband, a handsome scoundrel, P. Cornelius Dolabella, who had previously married an elderly lady for her money, was her mother's choice and, it seems, her own also, when Cicero was away in his province of Cilicia. Cicero, who greatly disliked Dolabella, wanted her to marry Tiberius Nero, but a father's wishes evidently counted for little. After four years she was again divorced. Her first child died in infancy. Her second boy did not long survive her. Her own death in such circumstances was the hardest of the many blows which Cicero had to bear. He was consumed by a grief probably not unmixed with remorse and regrets for his broken home life. He looked everywhere for consolation but in vain. He spent whole days wandering aimlessly in woods and thickets, searching in vain for some consolation from philosophy and religion, unable to master the grief which shook him. All that he could think of doing was to try to find some worthy memorial for the one human being for whom he had nothing but tenderness. His young bride is said to have foolishly shown that she had no regrets for Tullia, so Cicero at once sent her back to her mother and made it very plain that he had no desire ever to see her again. Despite his great need of money to repay Terentia's dowry and to buy a garden to be dedicated to the shade of Tullia, he very soon divorced little Publilia. Somehow he had to repay her dowry. Poor Atticus, who was called upon to finance these expensive undertakings, must have winced when he thought of their cost.

Troubles were now crowding thick and fast upon the Republic and upon Cicero. 'The disorganization and confusion are so great, the general dismay and collapse caused by a most shocking war are so complete,' said Cicero, 'that each man thinks the place where he happens to be the most wretched in the world.' When Cicero was at Rome he said, 'I feel no doubt that at the present moment the most miserable place for a good man to be in is Rome.' So he did not stay there.

'Do you wonder at my keeping away from the city,' he asked, 'in which my house has no pleasure to offer me, while the state of affairs, the men, the Forum, and the Senate House are all utterly repulsive to me?'

Having no public occupation, he sought consolation in literature. 'The amount of my reading and writing is such', he wrote, 'that my people find a holiday more laborious than I do working days.' And again, 'The amount I write is beyond belief, for I work in the night hours also as I cannot sleep.'

In the year which followed the death of Tullia, Cicero lived in retirement, devoting his time to writing. Then it was that he composed those moral and philosophical works which helped to popularize Greek thought among his own countrymen and during many succeeding centuries: the *De Finibus*, the *Academica*, and *Tusculan Disputations*, to be followed by others upon which his fame was largely to rest.

The Private Life of a Young Man About Town

Cicero, excusing his nephew by comparing him with 'what young men are nowadays', had many unpleasant examples in his memory and before his eyes; none worse no doubt than his arch-enemy Publius Clodius. Few were as unpleasant and as vicious as he, but it seems clear that, in wild and dissolute behaviour, he led many of his countrymen by a rather narrow margin.

Some aristocratic young gentlemen in Rome's smartest social set took to reckless political adventure rather in the spirit of surf-riders. As ordered constitutional life gave way to anarchy and civil war, many a sedate Roman home became the uneasy scene of hurried intrigues, alarms, plots and counterplots.

The meteoric career of Julius Caesar showed what glittering prizes rewarded audacity, dash and enterprise. From the mad social world of vast expenses, colossal debts, and political intrigue, he had gone to Spain where his one year's command got him a fortune. Then, after epic adventures in Gaul, he returned with the wealth of the world and power to command the world. 'Sulla did it, why should not I do it?' Pompey used to say. Not even the most ambitious may have hoped to repeat Caesar's exploits but they were there to show one sure way to supreme social distinction.

Something of the heights and depths of Roman life and feeling on the more ordinary level of everyday life has been preserved down the ages in the work of one young Italian, Catullus, whose poetic genius lights up for us the gloom and sorrow as well as some of the joys of life in Rome 2,000 years ago. A native of Verona far to the north of Rome, Catullus seems to have been left fairly well provided for when he inherited the family home on the shores of the beautiful Lake Garda. He also had a small farm almost near enough to Rome to be considered fashionable. Like Cicero, he responded to the magnetic pull of Rome, yet he never lost, amid the fascination of the great city, all sense of the joy and well-being that boyhood's memories attached to his northern home.

Before reaching manhood he must have had a thorough grounding in literary studies, particularly in Greek and Latin verse. Literature retained its hold upon him. A case of books went with him to Rome but he said that he had left many more at his country home. Not for him was the public career to which Cicero devoted his days with such whole-hearted devotion. He did indeed, about the year 57 B.C., take a minor appointment on the staff of a Roman Governor sent to manage the province of Bithynia, a move which has been plausibly connected with his reference to his empty purse full of cobwebs and to the heavy mortgage, more damaging than all the winds that blow, by which his property was threatened. A gay life among the city's spendthrifts had soon beggared him. If poverty was his motive in serving abroad, he wasted his time. Bithynia had then been a Roman province for a bare ten years, but war, the influx of Roman tax-gatherers and successive Roman governors and their staffs had left few pickings for their successors. Catullus came back no richer than he went out, an unsatisfactory state of affairs for which he blamed his chief, the Roman governor, Memmius, who was, he said, far too grasping and selfish to take any interest in the welfare or the fortunes of his staff. When people mentioned Bithynia in Rome they thought of the new practice of being carried about in litters in the Asiatic style by the sturdy slaves brought from the new province. In some amusing verses Catullus records his loss of face when a girl, whom he let assume that he too had at least his eight litter-carriers, asked to borrow them. In fact he had not managed to bring back one broken-winded slave. Catullus was by no means alone in his bad luck, for he commiserates with some of his friends whose scanty luggage, easily packed, shows them also to have been unfortunate in seeing service under greedy chiefs.

However, he had his share of the good things of life. Besides his two homes he writes, with an affection unusual for a Roman, in praise of a fast sailing yacht he brought back from the East to his own northern shores. For him, as for gilded youth, and indeed the generality of mankind in all ages, good food and wine enjoyed with congenial companions were prominent among the satisfactions to be had from life. The boundary between normal social life and wilder excesses was however far from being as clearly drawn then as it is in our own day. Catullus, like other Roman poets, protested that his life was more respectable than his verses where he certainly let himself go without restraint. They have an air of realism contrasting sharply with mere products of the imagination, and revulsive enough are the impressions to which some of them give rise.

If, upon a candid review, the seamy side of Roman life bulks so largely, it must be remembered that we judge it in the light of continuous tradition of Christian morality of almost 2,000 years. The grand idea that the greatest crime one human being can commit against another is to treat him or her merely as an instrument or as a means of obtaining some private satisfaction had not, in the days of Catullus and Cicero, been clearly proclaimed for all to hear. The unquestioned acceptance of slavery, indeed the active steps taken to develop it on a scale probably greater than has ever been seen among the white races of mankind, shows how far the Romans were from respecting, in the practical conduct of their lives, a belief in the doctrine of the real, fundamental dignity of the human personality.

While it would be ridiculous to pretend that, in these circumstances, most Romans wallowed in a kind of animal indulgence, it would be equally false to the facts to deny that life was, for many, gross and debasing to a degree that would now seem utterly revolting. The life of the common people was held cheaply, and the vast majority of Romans and Italians were common people. When grossness is widespread throughout a society, everyone runs a risk of infection. Yet all was not black. The gallantry, deep human affection and upright sentiments to be found in the work of Catullus were more than a veneer of nobility of thought and feeling overlaying a turbulent and undisciplined nature.

The two great tragedies of his life were the death of his brother in the East, where he probably went in the service of the Republic, and the unhappy ending of a great love affair. He called the lady Lesbia and it is generally believed, although it is not known for certain, that she was Clodia, sister of Cicero's enemy Clodius, and wife of Quintus Metellus Celer, Consul in 60 B.C., one of the most vigorous of the aristocratic opponents of Caesar and the *populares*. When Catullus first met Lesbia, or Clodia, as we may assume her to have been, she was a brilliant leader in Rome's smartest social set, and her husband was still living. He died suddenly and so unexpectedly in 59 B.C. that he was commonly thought to have been poisoned. Such already was Clodia's reputation that she was suspected of having given him the fatal dose. Catullus, young and ingenuous, fell so hopelessly in love with her that his own life was wrecked and made worthless in his eyes when she threw him over, as she very soon did, for a succession of other lovers, selected apparently with little taste or discernment. Hell has many furies and Catullus showed that a man can rival the fury of a woman scorned. In some searing verses he fastened the most unsavoury reputation upon the enchantress whose charms he used to celebrate with a heartfelt intensity impossible to doubt or to forget.

The experience of another young Roman, who succeeded Catullus in Clodia's affections, seems to prove that Catullus was abundantly justified in his denunciation of an utterly worthless woman. Marcus Caelius Rufus, a former pupil of Cicero's and one of his most sprightly correspondents, had attracted Clodia's attention and had for a short while fallen under her spell. Catullus, who evidently had counted him among his own friends, was bitter at what he thought was the treacherous betrayal by which Rufus robbed him of his beloved. This time Clodia was thrown over, for Rufus soon tired of her. Her fury was unbounded. It was also highly dangerous. Rufus soon found himself before a Roman court (in 56 B.C.) to answer the double charge of robbing Clodia of gold and of attempting to poison her. Cicero had already found that it was no light matter to incur the hatred of the Claudian house, but he very willingly undertook the defence of his wild and reckless young friend. He had some old scores of his own to repay. If Clodia had a reputation to lose, it certainly could not have survived Cicero's attack. Disclaiming any enmity to women, still less to 'a woman who is the friend of all men', he cleverly turned the accusations against Rufus into so many admissions of her own guilt, summoned the shade of old Appius Claudius, the blind Censor of the fourth century B.C., from the underworld to denounce the shameful life of his own descendant, so glaringly contrasted with the strict manners of the good old time; and, without in so many words accusing her of murdering her own husband, referred to his sudden end in language which pointed to only one conclusion. 'Shall that woman,' he asked, 'coming from the house in which her husband died, dare to speak of the rapid action of poison? Is she not afraid of the very house itself, lest it should make some sound? Does she not dread the very walls, which know her guilty secret? Does she not shudder at the recollection of that fatal and melancholy night?'

Rufus was acquitted. There could be but one inference. The Roman court believed Clodia to have been as dissolute, debauched and degraded as Cicero, the enemy of her house, and as Catullus, her passionate lover, had declared her to be. Rufus however was clearly no saint and his future career was stormy. His colossal debts, like those of Caesar, Antony, and Curio and other young aristocrats were the talk of the town and a scandal in the Forum. He kept in with Cicero, was at constant hazards from the enmity of the Claudii, but managed to pursue his career. He was elected as Curule Aedile in 51 B.C., so his year of office in Rome came at a time when Cicero was away in his province of Cilicia. Rufus pursued him there with letters appealing for help to enable him to put on a really magnificent show in the public games, for which, as Aedile, he was responsible. He badly wanted some panthers for the wild beast show and he plagued Cicero unmercifully for them. Cicero however had other notions about the dignity of a Roman governor and does not seem to have bothered himself unduly to put on wild beast hunts for the Roman circus. Later Rufus joined Caesar against Pompey and was Praetor in the year 48 B.C. Mounting financial difficulties at last overtook him and like Catiline, with whom he had had some connexions fifteen years earlier, he tried to introduce some desperate measures to rescue himself from his embarrassments. They failed and, switching his allegiance, he lost his life trying to stir up trouble for Caesar ostensibly on Pompey's behalf in Campania. It was a sordid story. He had emptied gaols and enlisted slaves, gladiators, and any riff-raff he could find. This was not at all the sort of life Cicero had in mind when he sent him the advice with which this book opened (see p. 1). He, like Milo, his accomplice in the grim final scene, met a violent death as did Catiline, Clodius, Dolabella, Cicero's son-in-law, all of whom shared the fate of many of the gilded youth whose revelries at Rome and at the fashionable beach of Baiae had shocked sober citizens. This degeneration, decay, and collapse of a form of culture that had once been fresh, strong, and virile is the momentous climax enacted in the lives of the younger generation of Cicero's Rome.

What happened in the end to Catullus and Clodia is not known. They, like the vast majority of their countrymen and women, soon pass out of sight and record. It is difficult to reconstruct much of their lives upon the basis of the scanty shreds of evidence that have survived. For a brief moment they light up the pages of history and disclose a world in some ways familiar but in others strangely foreign to that of our own experience. Cicero took a poor view of his world. The whole day would not be long enough, he said, to describe the spread of luxury and vice, the scanty regard paid to marriage vows, and the abandonment of what true Romans regarded as moral conduct.

But then, Cicero was as unusual a type in Roman life as a

book-loving philosopher would be in a crowd of football or baseball fans today. His well-earned fame saved him from being dismissed in the way lesser men like him would be dismissed, as a curious oddity completely out of the stream of national life. That stream itself, then as now, flowed silently on and away to eternal forgetfulness. We cannot fully measure today the time in which we live. We each know but little of the vast stream of life in which we are immersed. It is true that in the last few decades serious efforts have been made to select samples of it for measurement and study. Yet we still stand on the threshold of knowledge. In the Roman Republic the very notion that there was anything to be measured, or that study could bring any help in controlling the fate of social groups and classes, seems to have been wanting. Our small knowledge has therefore to be balanced against a vaster ignorance that we shall in all probability be for ever unable to overcome.

Chapter Sixteen

THE CULTURAL LIFE OF ROME

Education

THE influence and importance of outstanding intellectual figures like Cicero in the Roman Republic was all the greater because Romans had been late in developing their schools. The Roman tradition of education, exemplified in the practice of old Cato the Censor, was for every Roman father to bring up his own sons in all the manly arts and to give them as well such political education as he could. With this personal coaching as a foundation, the younger generation then completed the process for themselves in the compulsory comradeship of the army, by frequenting the Forum and by taking part in the public gatherings of the electoral assemblies (the *comitia*). When, in the later degenerate days of the decaying Republic wealthy Romans no longer kept up these ancient customs, but handed their sons over to Greek tutors, both the boys and the State suffered. The wealthy had tutors living in their homes and those who could not afford to employ them sent their sons to schools which seem to have begun to multiply in Cicero's time.

The results were usually poor. For the tutors were mostly slaves or freedmen and could not therefore inspire the respect and affection of a father. They were usually despised more than the father had ever been reverenced. Roman boys therefore not only had little healthy outlet for their imitative instincts but, on the contrary, ceased to associate authority with respect. There were, to be sure, exceptions. Cicero seems to have taken some pains with his own son and nephew. Young Cicero was sent when he was about of university age, as his father before him, to the professional and finishing schools of Athens, which became the spiritual home of Cicero, if not of other educated Romans.

This was a new development. As late as 161 B.C. some Greek philosophers were expelled from Rome, and Cicero's grandfather was probably among the Romans glad to see them go. A vigorous cultural life had nevertheless begun to take shape although it was largely derivative. The Romans had been preceded in every field of cultural and scientific activity by the Greeks, whose creative genius between the years 750 B.C. and 350 B.C. successively developed the arts of music, literature, architecture, sculpture, and painting. Their achievements in these fields as well as in medicine and science were, for that epoch of human history, so complete and so perfect that they made rivalry seem a vain effort. No Mediterranean people except the Romans seemed able even to absorb the lessons Greece had to teach, so there was no question of any other race being able to sustain and carry on her creative activity. The very excellence of the Greek models seemed to stifle effort. The first promise of Roman artistic effort made no headway from its early Etruscan and Italian beginnings, no doubt because of the superior attractiveness and satisfaction to be had from the arts of Greece. To the Romans at least belongs the credit for their good taste in recognizing the excellence of Greek work and in going to great expense to secure examples of it and to copy it as faithfully as they could.

Roman sculpture, painting and architecture seem to have made few noteworthy developments during the entire history of the Republic. Music was never an art to which the Romans contributed anything of significance. The story is the same in science. The attempt to cure sickness and disease had always been one of the earliest stimulants of man's scientific efforts, but here the Romans were also entirely dependent upon the Greeks.

Among the practical arts it has been seen how Greek craftsmen, often enslaved by Roman masters, shaped the jewellery, designed and executed the finer pottery and artistic furnishings of the well-to-do Roman home. Greeks and orientals navigated Roman ships. In building and in such municipal engineering as is involved in providing water and sewerage systems, the Romans were indeed better able to stand alone but, despite the high valuation rightly placed upon the plumber's art (as in modern America), such improvements must be held to stand at the base rather than at the summit of constructive civilization.

Literature

The last two centuries of the Roman Republic did however show a remarkable development and enrichment in literature. The Punic Wars, and particularly the Second Punic War, enormously stimulated Roman self-consciousness and so paved the way for the individual expression of Roman minds. Then began that deepening awareness of the range and glory of Greek civilization, soon to be rapidly developed by the conquest of Greece, and by the import into Rome of large numbers of Greek slaves skilled as craftsmen, scribes, teachers, orators, and secretaries. The limited outlook of traditional Roman ways with its scant provision for cultural activity seemed unbearably cramped and sterile by comparison. The hellenizing process may be said to have begun after the Second Punic War in the first quarter of the second century B.C. and Scipio Africanus, the conqueror of Hannibal, was its leader. It was slow at first in making headway in the traditional custom-bound society of Rome. Yet it was not a movement affecting the wealthy classes alone. In Sicily masses of Roman troops made their first acquaintance with the Greek theatre. They acquired a taste for it which they took back to Rome, so providing a demand for entertainment which was amply supplied. Borrowed largely from the Greek in outright translation or adaptation, the new comic theatre nevertheless began to speak with a thoroughly Roman idiom in the plays of Plautus and Terence. Plautus died shortly after the Second Punic War while old Cato was Censor (184 B.C.). Terence belonged to the next generation but he lived a hundred years before Cicero was at the height of his fame.

Theirs are the only Roman plays of the Republic which have survived. Hundreds of others have perished in common with the great bulk of Roman writing. Nevertheless, it is evident that by Cicero's lifetime a mature and sophisticated literature had suddenly flowered. Cicero himself helped as much as anyone to create it. Mankind has not forgotten the immense service he rendered during the succeeding seventeen centuries in which Latin, which he first wrote to perfection, was everywhere the familiar second language of cultivated men. But it was not merely as a skilful writer of harmonious and eloquent prose that he has been remembered. Among the early fathers of the Church, St Ambrose, St Jerome, St Thomas Aquinas, who looked upon the world from a viewpoint very different from Cicero's, all bore witness to his power. With the revival of humanistic learning Cicero's influence reached new heights with Petrarch and his followers.

For none of his contemporaries can the same claim be made,

although for creative genius and originality there were greater writers than he. He was indeed dismissed by a later writer of antiquity as a man uninspired and with no touch of madness in his soul. The oratorical style he developed soon went out of fashion just as the declamatory style in the theatre, with which actors such as Henry Irving used to thrill Victorian audiences, would now barely get a hearing as an odd turn in a variety performance. Among profounder writers there was Lucretius, little regarded it seems by his contemporaries, who, fiercely scornful of contemporary susperstitions, expounded the philosophy of Epicurus for Roman readers in the majestic lines of his poem *On the Nature of Things*. Pushing the search for personal satisfaction to the farthest point consistent with human happiness and intelligence, Epicurus was led to give the melancholy advice to withdraw from public life and the world. This was no doctrine for a Roman. Catullus, the young country boy from the North, whose story was referred to at the end of the last chapter, wearing his heart on his sleeve, expounded no philosophy. Amid some clever verses of a gay young Roman libertine and some academic experiments in literary versifying, there is his searing story inspired by his passionate love for the worthless Clodia, 'Lesbia of the burning eyes', and a convincing picture of his heart-broken misery when, following her wont, she cast him off to seek new victims elsewhere. The easy facility of his work struck a fresh lyric note not heard in the surviving works of other writers but the testimony which both he and Cicero bear to some of their contemporaries whose works have all perished, is evidence of the vigorous creativity of the Ciceronian age of Roman literature.

The chief actor on the political scene might have rivalled and excelled Cicero in the world of letters had he not forced himself to a life of action with the sword rather than the pen, but in his *Commentaries* on his campaign in Gaul and in his other propaganda effort, an account of the civil war he had precipitated, Julius Caesar left models of terse military narrative in a bare economical prose contrasting markedly with the sonorities, rotundities, and polished periods of Cicero.

Sallust, who wrote after the death of Cicero, had grown rich in Caesar's service. His history of Rome between 78 B.C. and 67 B.C. has not survived. C. Sallustius Crispus, to give him his full name, also wrote a shorter account of the conspiracy of Catiline in which he more or less follows Cicero's own version; and a brief history of the Jugurthine War in which he was concerned to praise Marius, the democratic leader, at the expense of the nobles whose descendants were Caesar's enemies. All such works were addressed to the cultivated classes of Roman society. A publishing trade seems already to have developed, but not upon such a scale as to provide authors with an income from their pen. The motive for writing was not money but fame, renown and influence with the only public opinion which mattered – the social equals and superiors of the writers. The commercial interest in literature, regarded as marketable private property belonging to the authors, was then quite unknown; indeed, it did not develop in England until the eighteenth century.

Books of the time were papyrus paper rolls and much care was evidently taken in their production. Each was of course handwritten and the work was done by slaves. Cicero's banker friend Atticus seems to have employed very many copyists and may be regarded as the Roman equivalent of a publisher. The rolls or volumes so produced he no doubt sold at a profit. Books in this shape were plentiful. Catullus, wishing to damn the boring works of one otherwise unknown writer Volusius, describes them as providing loose wrappings for mackerel in the fish shops when they were not applied to yet baser uses in what Victorian respectability knew as 'the usual domestic offices'.

There were as yet no public libraries, and Romans with literary tastes made their own collections. It was a task to which Cicero gave much thought, energy and affection. His letters abound with references to his beloved volumes, his efforts to add to them, and to see among other collections those he did not himself possess. 'Mind you don't promise your library to anybody, however keen a collector you may find for it,' he wrote to his friend Atticus 'for I am hoarding up all my little savings to get it as a resource in my old age.' 'If I succeed in that I shall be richer than Crassus and look down on any man's manors and meadows.' He must have lost most of his much-prized books when he was driven into exile, but he seems to have recovered a number. A slave, Tyrannio, was employed in rearranging them. Cicero told Atticus that 'Tyrannio has made a wonderfully good arrangement of my books, the remains of which are better than I had expected.' However, he borrowed two library slaves from Atticus to help 'as gluers and in other subordinate work'. They did their work well. 'Your men', he told Atticus later, 'have beautified my library by making up the books and appending title slips.' The result pleased him enormously. 'Since Tyrannio has arranged my books for me,' he writes later, 'my house seems to have had a soul added to it.' This was his villa at Antium in the spring of 56 B.C. Then, as in England before the rise of great public collections in the national libraries, a literary worker depended much upon the generosity of private owners for the sight of rare works. Cicero was fortunate in getting access to the priceless library of Greek works, including the writings of Aristotle, which the dictator Sulla had brought back with him from the East.

The literary life for which Cicero was so well fitted and in which he found so deep and abiding satisfaction was only a part of his busy career. Few Roman aristocrats gave more time to it than he; but there were some exceptions, such as the scholarly antiquary Varro, of whose many and lengthy works only a short treatise on farming and smallholding and a work on the Latin language have survived. Varro was one of Cicero's literary correspondents on whom he depended for books and much miscellaneous information. There seems also to have been a race of professional researchers and historians who made what use they could of the early records and the works of the early annalists of Rome. 'The mere chronological record of the annals has very little charm for us', was Cicero's verdict on these early records. A few men had begun to put together somewhat primitive histories in the century after the two Punic Wars, and in the generation before Cicero more ambitious histories were compiled for a growing semi-educated public. One author, Gellius, filled a work no longer extant, extending to ninety-seven books, with stories of Rome's past, legends of the kings and of the famous Roman families. One successful but partisan and inaccurate romantic historian before Cicero was Valerius Antias, whose writings have also perished. A more critical spirit slowly developed so that Cicero and his friends took more than the proverbial pinch of salt before swallowing everything written by these earlier authors. So much is clear from Cicero's letters themselves, one of the best remaining indices of the degree of vigour in the intellectual interests of the time. Yet for Cicero, until the final defeat of the Republic by Caesar, literary interests and pursuits were forced to take second place, sandwiched between the more urgent and practical matters demanding the time of a prominent Roman statesman. Cicero in one quite shameless letter shows how, for him, a political reputation was more important than historical truth. One of his acquaintance, L. Lucceius, was writing a history of the times, and Cicero confessed to him that 'I am inflamed with an inconceivably ardent desire, and one, as I think, of which I have no reason to be ashamed, that in a history written by you my name should be conspicuous and frequently mentioned with praise.' This was bad enough, but he goes on to say, 'I again and again ask you outright both to praise those actions of mine in warmer terms than you perhaps feel, and in that respect to neglect the laws of history' and even 'to yield to your affection for me a little more than truth shall justify'.

No words have done more damage to Cicero's reputation in the eyes of posterity than these of his own deliberate writing, perhaps because we mistakenly suppose that there was no need for the public men of the past to employ publicity agents or to devise tactics which are commonplace enough in our own world of business, entertainment and politics.

Letters were usually scratched on waxed tablets. They were also written upon paper made from papyrus, an old Egyptian export, or on parchment, and were sent sealed by wax or a kind of gypsum or clay on which was stamped the device on the writer's signet ring.

It is all the more remarkable that so much of Cicero's correspondence should have survived. So surprising indeed that in our own time the ingenious theory has been proposed, by M. Jérôme Carcopino, that the collection was published about ten years after Cicero's murder at the instigation, or to gain the favour, of Octavian, during his conflict with Antony. The object of publication was to discredit Cicero completely by revealing in the clearest light Cicero's vanity, weakness and timidity, love of luxury, carelessness over money-matters, self-seeking, shameless flattery of friend and foe, political manoeuvring and trickery. After trying to blast the reputation of Cicero and his circle, Carcopino then argues that Atticus had this aim in publishing the letters for he was seeking to curry favour with Octavian, who had connived at Cicero's murder. An epicurean such as Atticus would not merely regard loyalty to a dead friend as of no account but would, for his own profit, be very ready himself to be the tool by which his friend's reputation was destroyed. Certainly this bad effect was produced upon some of Cicero's admirers during the Renaissance when the letters were rediscovered, as the anguished remarks of Petrarch survive to prove, but subsequently readers have discovered in them the whole man and have balanced Cicero's many amiable qualities and his great abilities against his private but candid revelation of human weaknesses.

Plausibly as Carcopino presents his theory, it has not won general acceptance. If the letters were published around 34 B.C. as he contends, Cicero to most Romans would have been a dim figure from almost another world whose influence would be unlikely to cause Octavian any uneasiness. Indeed it has been argued that Augustus, far from wishing to discredit Cicero, regretted his crime in proscribing him. In 39 B.C. he had pardoned young Cicero, later promoting him to be a priest and Consul. Whatever may have been the motive or occasion of their publication, the important thing is that from Cicero's correspondence, written as he said himself 'in the language of everyday life', we are able to gain some insight into the nature of the hundreds of thousands of letters by which Romans managed their private affairs, pursued their fortunes, maintained their friendships, discussed politics, business and pleasure, while the framework of their Republican system of government was cracking and decaying around them. Despite the sophistication of society there was no independent class of critics and intellectuals such as that which developed in Europe during and after the eighteenth century, free to comment upon public affairs and to try to agitate, influence and guide public opinion, often on the strength of little or no practical experience and usually free from any personal responsibility or liability for their actions. Such classes, shrewdly described in our own day as embracing 'the rhetorical professions', had no outlet for their activities before the days of the free press. Newspapers did not exist in Cicero's world although, as Consul in 59 B.C., Caesar had created the rudiments of a news service and a report of the proceedings in the Senate. The only avenue to political influence was an active part in the life of the Forum leading up to election to political offices with their sobering responsibilities.

When, in spite of Cicero and his friends, Caesar abolished the

Republic and ruled as uncrowned king of Rome, Cicero no longer had full scope for his talents. His only refuge was in literature. 'If no one will employ us,' he wrote to a friend, 'let us compose and read "Republics". And if we cannot do so in the Senate House and Forum, yet at least (after the example of the most learned of the ancients) on paper and in books let us govern the State, and investigate its customs and laws.' It was on that basis that Cicero set himself up in his old age to guide and instruct his countrymen in three outstanding works, *The Republic*, *On The Laws*, both of which have been largely lost, and the work on Duty, *De Officiis*. Powerless to deflect the tremendous struggle surging around him, they remained, after the battles had died away, to stimulate and illuminate succeeding generations of men.

Medicine and Surgery

In creative thought, philosophy and science, no Roman work remains giving the smallest indication that Rome would have been able at any time to match the creative genius of the Greeks. The Romans, it has been said, invented nothing. So sweeping a judgement is perhaps too harsh. In art, and especially in literature, the record is by no means so one-sided, although here also the unmistakable pre-eminence of the Greeks and the largely derivative nature of Roman work are pronounced features of the cultural life of Rome throughout the Republican era.

So marked was the brilliance of the Greeks and so poor by contrast the known achievements of all other peoples of antiquity, that inevitably the sudden flowering of the human spirit in ancient Athens has been thought to point to the existence of some special quality of their minds, to be explained, if it can be explained at all, on the basis of racial characteristics. If this is true, then the Romans, who did not possess this quality, were by nature incapable of the unique effort put forth by the Greeks, and in consequence there is not much point in seeking other explanations of their admitted inferiority. Their failure to progress in the one line above all others in which for us progress now seems to consist, would then be part of the nature of things and no more need be said. 'Order, not progress was, as it still is, the mission of Rome.' It is not without interest, however, to note some factors arising from the Roman character, which delayed the emergence of a scientific outlook upon the world. Of these the Roman religion was undoubtedly one. A view of the world which invented spirits to account for any and every normal or unusual occurrence was not one to advance a deeper knowledge of nature or of men. Sickness and disease have everywhere been the first and most urgent stimulants to a better understanding of the physical world; but when every disease was supposed to be the work of a supernatural agency, inquiry was obviously stifled at birth. 'Even the itch was not without its goddess.' To placate and pacify the gods or demons who, they thought, were directly responsible for their pains, their fevers and their sickness, was therefore the first reaction of the Romans in illness and distress. Unlike certain worthy folk in our own day who otherwise resemble them in adopting a purely religious attitude towards disease, they did not neglect drugs. But their drugs were often more horrible than their diseases. The more strange and far-fetched, the more revolting in taste or stench, the more eagerly were the remedies sought and swallowed. The superstitions which created so formidable a pharmacopoeia were also manifested in other directions. Faith was put in votive offerings, in the interpretation of dreams, in holy wells and ceremonial washings. There were ritual incantations, laying-on of hands, accompanied often by the repetition of antique formulae from long-forgotten languages devoid of any known signification, which were in fact no better than gibberish. Names had a peculiarly satisfying effect, just as today patients often cannot be quieted until some label is found for their symptoms. Great reliance was placed in magic numbers, mystic correspondence of marks and in the pronouncements of astrologers.

Against this lumbering impediment, this sub-human heritage from the cave and the pit, man the thinker has waged and must continue to wage perpetual war. For, even today, strong forces are still at work to prolong this martyrdom of man, to drag whole peoples down once more to the morass from which twenty-five centuries of stubborn struggle have barely freed them. Because medicine was closely linked with religion, every *paterfamilias* was the medical officer of health as well as the high priest of his household. He was in charge of the medicine chest which had an honoured place in the store cupboards over which presided the *penates*, reverenced by the Romans as the spirits of the home. The religious powers of the father of the household left no room for a large class of priests; neither did they permit the rise of a medical profession. It seems probable that the army made provision for medical and surgical treatment of its sick and wounded but nothing is known about whatever arrangements were made. The troops do not seem to have been served by specialists who might have become doctors in civil life. Great as have been the misfortunes which mankind can justly attribute to the ignorance, the conservatism and the vested interests of the professions of priest and doctor, it is evident that neither religious thought nor medicine could have progressed without them. Support for such a view seems at least to be available from the experience of the Romans. The fathers of the Republic in its heroic age would have nothing to do with Greek physicians, many of whom would have been willing to practise in Rome. Not until about 220 B.C., a little before the war with Hannibal, was there a Greek physician in Rome. He had few immediate followers. The traditional suspicion and dislike of the Greeks was sufficient to keep them away. Old Cato reasoned that the Greeks who thought nothing of causing the death of a barbarian and who made no secret of the fact that in their eyes the Romans were among the barbarians, would speedily spread disease and death if they were allowed a foothold in the sacred city.

The Romans were the losers, for although the medical science of the Greeks was not very profound, they did not make the mistake of thinking superstition a substitute for it. They tried to look facts in the face and they studied their patients with calm but inquisitive detachment. They seem also to have arrived at the wisdom of relying as far as possible upon the unaided power of nature to effect cures. They sought to aid this *vis medicatrix naturae*, often the principal element in the prescription of many eminent practitioners of our own day, less by drugs than by gentler remedies of rest, simple diet, baths, and exercises. This in itself was no mean achievement. Slowly their superior insight gained them a surer welcome in Rome, despite Cato and his reliance upon the household remedies he had inherited from his grandparents and their forebears. Many of his recipes are useless, some can only be called indecent. The great reliance which he and his kind placed upon the cabbage seems one of their few notions with some scientific justification. The Italian winter is not as long as ours but it may still have been long enough to make it very necessary to have a remedy against scurvy – caused, as we now know, by the lack of vitamin C. The cabbage, in an age which was ignorant of the potato, no doubt provided enough of that vitamin to correct deficiences in the plain hard fare of the puritanical ancient Romans.

By Cicero's day the Greek physician, whether as a slave or freedman, occupied an important place in Roman private life and was frequently either very expensive to buy or highly rewarded when he was able to work for fees. Cicero was not another Cato who considered himself fully competent to dose and cure his family. He thought highly of his friend and doctor, Asclapo. Recommending him to a friend, he said, 'I found his society very agreeable as well as his medical skill, which I had experience of in the illnesses of my household. He gave me every satisfaction both by his knowledge of his profession and by his kindness.' Cicero's own notions on how to keep well were mostly matter-of-fact common sense. 'Individual health', he told his son, in his last work, *On Duty*, 'is preserved by studying one's own constitution, by observing what is good or bad for one, by constant self-control in supplying physical wants and comforts but only to the extent necessary to self-preservation), by forgoing sensual pleasures, and finally, by the professional skill of those to whose science these matters belong.' Sometimes Cicero took a less practical view of illness. Finding himself suddenly freed by violent sickness from a persistent feeling of depression, he wrote to his wife, 'I was at once so much relieved, that I really think some god worked the cure. Pray make full and pious acknowledgement to the god, Apollo or Aesculapius, according to our wont.' Perhaps he was doing no more than finding some outlet for the greater religious feelings of his wife at a crisis in their fortunes, for he had just left her on his way to join Pompey in the civil war against Caesar.

Medical practitioners multiplied and thrived in Rome. Yet there was no professional training, no standard of qualification and consequently nothing to prevent plausible quacks setting themselves up as doctors. The fate of many a wretched Roman must have been grim indeed when he became the helpless prey of some ignorant fellow possessed of no better qualifications for treating illness than conceit and impudence. A far more efficacious treatment is now available for our farm and domestic animals

than the wealthiest Roman invalid could command in the mos
flourishing age of the Republic.

We are heirs to more ills than the Romans seem to hav
known, but there was misery and suffering enough calling alou
for any aid that Greek skill could render. Consumption, typhus
dysentery, and amoebic infection seem to have been prevalen
and for them no cure was known. Digestive diseases and gou
were also widespread, particularly after the simple fare of th
early Republicans had given way to the luxurious life of the wel
to-do in the days of Cicero. Some diseases which modern hygien
and medicine have succeeded in controlling and reducing almos
to vanishing point were then rampant and destructive. Anthrax
rabies, tetanus and the bubonic plague wrought havoc amongst
people ignorant alike of their cause and cure. Unable to arres
their progress, the Romans must have seen them sweep throug
whole communities like a forest fire. The Romans also saw th
advance of malaria. This insidious malady was probably a wors
disaster to Italy than all her civil wars put together. The ruin
had wrought in Greece probably goes far to explain the sicknes
which had already overcome the spirit of Hellas, for as early a
the time of Plato and Aristotle the land had become widely an
seriously malarious. From the South of Italy, through Campan
and the Latin plain the malady spread insistently throughou
Italy. During the war against Hannibal, in the year 208 B.C., it
recorded that 'a serious epidemic attacked both the city an
country districts, but it resulted more frequently in protracte
than in fatal illness'. It was very likely malaria. The enfeeblin
character of the disease among adults is marked, but amor
children its ravages can be far more deadly. The numbers as we
as the strength and vigour of the people of Italy were probab
seriously reduced by a high death-rate of children from malari

The disease was worse in the country than in the better-draine
towns. When the fresh healthy country-bred families were smitte
that which should have been a source of strength to the Republ
was turned into a source of weakness. The Romans did not kno
as indeed with all the resources of modern science we ourselv
discovered only yesterday, that malaria is caused by the bite of
insect and that the insect is the anopheles mosquito. They ha
however discovered that the mysterious disease was more like
to be caught near swampy ground. Cicero's friend Varro ca

tioned would-be farmers to choose a healthy site for their farm-house and never to build near swampy ground because, he said, 'certain minute animals, invisible to the eye, breed there and, borne by the air, reach the inside of the body by the way of the mouth and nose and cause diseases which are difficult to be rid of'. This was the nearest any Roman came to guessing the germ theory of disease. Varro's opinion may have seemed as far-fetched to the Romans around Cicero as it did eighteen hundred years later to a learned German who, with the rash dogmatism of ignorance, asked, 'Am I to believe that Varro attributed lingering diseases to these small gnats? Never did any doctor ancient or modern make such an assertion.'

Land policy and public health, had the Romans but realized it, marched hand in hand. As smallholdings and a large peasant population gave way to large cattle ranches there was no longer the numerous labour force which used to look after the drainage and conservation of the soil. Marshes began to increase and with them came the mosquito. It would have been impossible to re-populate the deserted plains even had the landowning classes been prepared to sacrifice their holdings. Julius Caesar seems to have realized what was involved when he made plans for the proper drainage of the Campagna, a policy which was still wait-ing for Mussolini to undertake in modern times.

The Romans, deficient in theoretical speculation, were sound technicians and their surgery was, for an age so primitive in the scientific sense, by no means so contemptible as their medicine. Their military campaigns had no doubt provided an all too rich field for practice from the earliest years of the Republic. They operated for gall-stones and undertook trepanning. Anaesthetics were of course unknown, and in the course of their treatment Roman patients had ample opportunity to show the ancient Roman virtue of courage. But many diseases and disorders, such as appendicitis, which modern surgery can cure, then proved fatal to the Romans. (Plate 26b.)

General Science

The example set by the Greeks in such subjects as mathematics and geometry was barely understood, much less followed or developed by the Romans. During his service as Quaestor in

Sicily Cicero discovered in a neglected and overgrown cemetery the tomb of the great Greek mathematician and scientist Archimedes who had been murdered nearly 140 years earlier by a Roman legionary during the Roman campaign in Sicily in 212 B.C.

It is questionable whether Cicero was aware that the cylinder and sphere which marked the grave commemorated what Archimedes regarded as his most important discovery: the ratio of the circumference to the diameter of the circle. However that may be, there is small doubt that Cicero's countrymen cared as little for the discoveries of Archimedes as they did about his last resting-place. An 'Archimedean problem' was Cicero's name for an unsolvable perplexity. Yet by his time a succession of Greek thinkers had not merely laid the foundations, but had developed mathematics and astronomy to a degree that was not to be surpassed until the seventeenth century.

Judged by our own standards, in geography or geology, the Greek scientific achievement was undoubtedly slight. In medicine biology, physics, and still more in chemistry, it was so insignificant that any comparison is ludicrous. Relatively small as was the achievement of the Greeks in these fields it was joined to a far deeper contribution to the study of politics, society and philosophy which first set the minds of men moving upon the road to knowledge. The Greeks, moreover, with their balanced, humanistic ideal of the development of the whole man, sought to advance upon all fronts at once without cramping and limiting their outlook on life by narrow specialization. Thus it was that they remained, throughout the Roman era and far beyond, the master of those who know. Lucretius gives some measure of the comparative ignorance of the Romans. 'It is a hard task', he wrote 'to set clearly in the light the dark discoveries of the Greeks above all when many things must be treated in new words, because of the poverty of our tongue and the newness of the themes.'

Cicero generously acknowledged the debt of Rome. When his brother Quintus went as Roman governor (or propraetor) to Asia in 61 B.C., Cicero wrote him a long lecture on his duties to the Greeks – 'a race of men', he said, 'in which civilization not only exists but from whom it is believed to have spread to others'. He added this personal confession: 'Whatever I have accomplished I have accomplished by means of those studies and principles which have been transmitted to us in Greek literature and schools of thought, wherefore over and above the general good faith which is due to all men, I think we are in a special sense under an obligation to that nation to put into practice what it has taught us among the very men by whose maxims we have been brought out of barbarism.' Narrow national feeling clearly had not blinded Cicero's vision and regard for the truth as it had limited the outlook of the earlier generations of Romans whose spokesman was Cato the Censor. Cicero spoke in the name of true humanism, and his words remain to shame all who seek to fetter the minds of their fellow-creatures by the cramping restrictions of a control and censorship designed either to promote pseudo-values narrowly conceived on national or racial lines or to impose some crude economic or political ideology serving their private or sectional interests.

There could be no more convincing evidence of the reality and depth of Cicero's feeling of gratitude to the Greeks than the very intensity of effort he put forth to introduce Greek thought to his countrymen. The long hours spent in reading in his library and the odd moments snatched as he was carried on his travels in a litter were matched by work at his desk before dawn, in the daytime and late at night as he strove to pass on in his own matchless Latin something of the inspiration he had found in the imperishable writings of those Greeks he was proud to acknowledge as his masters. Not merely was Greek thought more widely popularized in Rome as a result of Cicero's devotion, but the accidents of time were to make his writings one of the main sources from which a few men in the dark ages of medieval Europe were first able to learn something of the wisdom of the ancient world and to gain some knowledge of the thought of Greece by which that wisdom had chiefly been inspired.

Chapter Seventeen

THE COMMON PEOPLE

The Wretched Starveling Mob

THE developed and modern way of life of cultivated Roman society did not extend at all deeply. The voice of the common man and woman finds little or no echo in the pages of Cicero or of his contemporaries. Such references as are made to them are rarely respectful, often contemptuous. Millions of Romans and Italians around Cicero, peopling the soil of Italy, working in the fields, vineyards and olive plantations, crowding the market-places, marching to wars, laughing, cheering and yelling in the public circuses and theatres, jostling in the streets as they watched the triumphant processions of their victorious generals, have vanished, leaving no account of their daily lives, their loves, hates, hopes and fears.

Although they made up the Roman Republic, their fate seems to have been of scant concern to the men who depended upon their votes for the privilege of ruling over them. Despite the fine stoic sentiments he was fond of uttering about the dignity and brotherhood of mankind, Cicero, the most urbane of men (to employ a word he was fond of using), in his more intimate and candid moments called the masses the scum of the earth.

Their condition was indeed unenviable. What little we are able to piece together about the life of the common people of Rome shows a depressing picture of poverty and neglect. Life, while it lasted, was supported at a minimum cost. Their food was of the plainest – wheat porridge or simple wheat cakes flavoured, if at all, by a few herbs or vegetables and an occasional cheese, dried salt fish and olive oil. Sugar was unknown and honey was probably beyond their means. They did not drink milk, but cheap wine, mixed perhaps with water. Coffee and tea were of course not known until eighteen hundred years later. Meat they saw so rarely that masses of the Romans never seem to have acquired much taste for it. On one of Caesar's campaigns it was apparently accounted a hardship when Roman soldiers were forced to eat meat because their corn supplies had been exhausted. A little higher in the social scale, however, there was more meat-eating; mainly of pork. Poultry was also available for the better-off classes.

The needy Roman citizen was, however, assured of free water and cheap corn. From 58 B.C. to 46 B.C. corn was supplied free to all Roman citizens who cared to go to get it. A public water supply has never been thought to make men less inclined to work for their own support. But free bread raises different emotions, and any suggestion of it has always met violent opposition. Roman experience is very often quoted in evidence of the evils to which it may be expected to lead. 'Bread and circus-races' has become a by-word in referring to the degeneracy and corruption of the Roman proletariat. But bread and water alone make depressing fare and it has been suggested above that cheap or free bread was not so much the cause of the rot in Roman life as merely one of its symptoms. Cicero did not object to a well-managed corn supply. If it was not likely to exhaust the Treasury, he thought it 'both practicable for the State and necessary for the common man . . . a blessing therefore both to the citizens and the State'.

The violence and unrest which made life in Rome so unpleasant for Cicero were certainly not caused by free corn doles. All alike were symptoms of a great evil calling aloud for firm treatment. The corn dole naturally did not improve matters and it alone became a serious financial problem. No doubt it was for this reason that Cicero referred to the masses of Rome as 'the wretched starveling mob, the bloodsucker of the Treasury'. Leeches they were indeed, but it must not be forgotten that the hand that applied them to the body politic of Rome was that of Caesar's agent, Clodius. Was it a deliberate move to drain the Treasury so that Caesar's senatorial opponents should find themselves without the wherewithal to equip armies against Caesar? Whether so intended or not, the free corn policy undoubtedly added heavily to the embarrassments of the Senate.

The shattered condition of public affairs was such that when Caesar eventually fought his way through chaos to supreme control of the Republic he reaped the whirlwind he had himself stirred up, and among many other worries he inherited the unpleasant responsibility of finding grain for about two-thirds of the free population of the city of Rome. This probably required about 300 tons out of the 500 tons of wheat needed to feed the population every day. Suddenly to reduce this tremendous outlay was an unpleasant task, and the man who undertook it obviously had to be sure of his own position. Caesar in 46 B.C. was the first man to have achieved such security since the retirement of Sulla in 79 B.C. He dared not do what Sulla had done and abolish the dole, but he cut down the names on the free list for corn to 150,000 – eloquent testimony to the shallowness of the devices by which, as leader of the *populares*, he rose to power. In this way he was able to halve the annual cost to the Treasury of the corn dole of 72 million sesterces. The free corn policy had been Caesar's in opposition. He did not intend it to be more than a means of gaining power. No doubt he then realized that unless the supply of free wheat in Rome was drastically reduced, his policy of large-scale emigration for Rome's unemployed would be all the more difficult to achieve.

The great mass of the poor had nothing resembling the home over which Cicero waxed so eloquent when on his return from exile he claimed compensation for the destruction of his fine house. There, he said, had been his household gods and the family divinities of his hearth, and what could be more holy or more fitting a subject for religious respect than the house of a Roman citizen? However florid and artificial his language seems to our ear, and however convincing it no doubt was to thousands of Roman householders, it must have sounded somewhat hollow to the thousands of destitute Romans whose home was at the best some mean room in one of the many-storied lodging-houses crowded together in the depressions between the hills which were reserved for the better homes. To build within the protecting walls of Rome the Romans were forced to run the tenements as high as they dared. There the masses were huddled together, many without heat, water, or adequate light, often lucky if they were able to retain a roof over their heads, for there were frequent collapses of some of the crazy structures, and others often caught fire. Free corn may well have meant the difference between life and death from starvation to many of the poverty-stricken inhabitants of Rome's teeming tenements. No wonder therefore that the management of the public wheat was high up on the list of burning political questions.

Of course not all the citizens and electors of Rome were on the margin of starvation. There were grades among the totally unemployed. Some would be clients of the well-to-do, paying an obsequious call every morning which, for the price of servility to the rich man's door-keepers and personal servants, might yield a coin or two to satisfy their landlord, as well as a few scraps of food. Among this crowd would be many former slaves who had been given their freedom. Within one generation, in Cicero's lifetime between 81 B.C. and 49 B.C., it has been estimated that half a million slaves were freed and let loose in Rome. There was therefore a vast recruiting-ground for private bands of thugs and bullies. Most poor Romans were probably not unemployed but made up the hard-working artisans and shopkeepers who kept alive the free commerce and industry of the city: bakers who were also the millers, leather workers, shoemakers, fullers who were the only laundrymen and dyers, as well as makers of cheap clothes – for the old days were long past when every Roman girl and woman from the highest to the lowest spent hours spinning and weaving. There must also have been thousands of porters and carriers. The Roman masses, like the masses in all ages, worked largely for each other, no doubt on very slender margins of profit. The rich provided so much for themselves by the work of their slaves that the small artisan, unless he was an exceptionally skilled worker or engaged in some luxury trade like jewellery, did not have wealthy clients. The average Roman could truly have been called 'the man in the street'. For the masses escaped from their cramped, dirty and inconvenient homes as often as they could by living on the street and in the Forum. There was no Sunday or 'week-end' but there were about one hundred public holidays every year. Hence the demand for public games, the 'circus-races'. Because these events provided the one staple means of temporary escape from the sordid realities of daily life, they were immensely popular and filled much more of the waking thoughts of the average Roman than we can now easily imagine. The crowded, cheap public baths that were to form a second relief from the boredom and tedium of poverty had not attained their full development during the Republic, but already in Cicero's lifetime they were becoming popular. Open from sunrise to sunset at a very low fee, they provided a public resort and meeting-place of a type unknown to dwellers in our modern cities. Daily life on this level was not likely to breed conservative opinions in politics.

Over all these struggling folk hung the constant fear of great discomfort from bad seasons, a cold winter, drenching rain or torrid summer heat, as well as the more serious menace of sudden catastrophe: illness, loss of a patron, robbery and violence against which there was no police protection, sudden collapse of the market, failure of the free wheat, as well as less frequent but by no means unknown risks of the collapse of their crazy tenements or their destruction by fire, against which also there was no public fire brigade to fight for them. Among Cicero's property were some shops, two of which had entirely collapsed, and the rest seemed likely soon to follow them. He regarded the matter with what he considered philosophic detachment, refused to be annoyed and jokingly remarked that not the tenants alone but the very mice had migrated.

Shops below, crowded tenements above, narrow busy streets, were the setting for the feverish life of the city. Parts of it devoted to public affairs had a dignity and spaciousness contrasting all the more vividly with the squalor and uneasiness of the poorer quarters. There was one source of satisfaction denied to the dwellers in most of our industrial towns. The sight of some of the temples, public buildings, statuary and memorial buildings was free of cost to all whose eye delighted in beauty. But the Roman people were to benefit more in this respect from rulers who came after Cicero and Caesar than they had ever done under the Republic. The 'puritan tradition' of the Roman Republic is seen in Cicero's opinion that the expenditure of public money was justified 'when it is made for walls, docks, aqueducts, harbours, and all those works which are of service to the community'. But, despite his friend Pompey's initiative in providing new public buildings, Cicero confessed at the end of his life to doubts about the propriety of building 'theatres, colonnades and new temples'.

The cost of living for the poorer classes was very low. Vegetables, a little cheese, some dried salt fish, dried beans and olive oil were a cheap addition to the free or low-priced public wheat. The cheaper grades of wine mixed with water furnished a very popular and inexpensive drink.

In this way the masses struggled to keep body and soul together, although in a style of life that seems miserable enough to us today, if we could forget the years in Europe after 1940 when hundreds of thousands were forced by the miseries of war and invasion to reduce their level of consumption even below that of the dregs of society in ancient Rome.

Low State of Public Health

Little enough is known about the more serious epidemic diseases of Rome; still less has survived from which it would be possible to get a reliable picture of the general level of public health. It is difficult to believe that it was good. The low state of medical knowledge and above all ignorance of the elements of hygiene combine to forbid optimism on the subject. The mere lack of soap alone must have been an immense disadvantage. Handicapped in the effort to clean dirt from their bodies and their clothes, they were equally hard put to it to clear the dirt, refuse and sewage from their dwellings, their towns and cities. Everyone in Rome was vulnerable to dirt and disease; some classes were more affected than the rest. Ignorance of the way to avoid maladies arising from the various trades and industrial processes undoubtedly carried off thousands of Romans at an early age. Some occupations were so notoriously unhealthy that they were reserved for criminals and slaves. Such were the metal mines. Before any mechanical aids in ventilating and draining were invented, work in quarries and in underground mines was necessarily particularly dangerous. Explosives were unknown, so that the only method of shifting huge rocks and stones was to crack them by lighting great fires. The heat and fumes of the fires, apart from any poisonous gases they might create by acting on metal ores, were alone a sufficient hazard. Lead workers and sulphur workers were also dangerously exposed and their expectation of life was small. So also was that of workers in stone and marble. Silicosis, against which it has not yet been found possible to protect workers completely, found them defenceless.

Trades which would not now be regarded as dangerous then held many risks. The peculiar processes of the fullers have been mentioned. Their work in confined small rooms must have been extremely unpleasant from the smells and from the possibly infected nature both of their materials and of the clothes they had to clean. To be exposed to burning sulphur, as they were in their bleaching processes, was an additional danger.

There were more offensive trades than the fullers', particularly that of the tanners and leather-makers, and efforts were made to segregate them beyond the Tiber. Candle-makers and oilmen, whose oil came from olives, no doubt also deserved to be included in this class.

The millers and bakers had a less pleasant occupation than they mostly have today. Nearly 200,000 tons of wheat consumed in Rome every year had to be carried at some stage in sacks on the workers' backs. To this exhausting toil must be added the hard work of grinding corn by hand in the days before water-mills and windmills were common. No true Roman would endure to see his wife at a grinding-mill. The threat of being sent to work at grinding corn was sufficient to make most slaves tremble. Covered in perspiration and flour, the millers and bakehouse workers needed frequent baths which it is very questionable whether many were able to get. The unpleasant association of lice with the milling and baking trade endured long enough in Italy to make it probable that it also existed in Cicero's Rome. Before the public-bath habit became regular, the resources of such citizens as believed in cleanliness was a daily wash of the arms and legs and a weekly bath in the scullery. It was a possibility open to few of the poorer tradesmen and to fewer still of the more numerous slaves.

It has taken a new form of warfare to bring home to the city-dwellers of today what they owe to modern sanitation and to supplies of water, soap, gas and electricity. Not until such services, formerly taken for granted, are suddenly interrupted or destroyed, does their vital link with civilization become evident. In ancient Rome there was of course neither gas nor electricity. Sanitary services left much to be desired; none of the appliances to which we are accustomed had then been invented.

It is important, therefore, not to assume that life in Republican Rome had anything like a modern physical background. Our standards of public health and cleanliness are on a vastly better scale.

Just as we are apt to forget the low standards of public health and cleanliness in Rome, so in this age of machines it is difficult to realize what life was like when all work had to be done by human muscles aided to some extent by the help of animals. Not merely the loading, unloading and distribution of the tremendous tonnage of food and supplies but all forms of manufacturing and

construction depended upon the physical strength of the men of
Rome. What that means in carpentry and woodwork alone is
sufficiently obvious when it is realized how much hard work is
involved in the various processes between felling a tree and the
production by hand of the planed and polished woodwork
required in furniture and building.

The sheer physical burden of all this toil, apparent in the
strained muscles, arteries and hearts of the labouring classes,
their premature ageing and death, would have been a melancholy
commentary upon the pleasing delusion of some contemporary
moralists that nobody has ever been killed by overwork. Death,
when it came, increased the hazards of the survivors. Burial was
indeed forbidden within the precincts of the city, but immediately
beyond were the vast common graves into which the dead bodies
of the poor were thrown indiscriminately at night. In their
funeral customs the Romans further sharpened the contrast
between rich and poor. The magnificent torchlight processions
accompanying the funeral train of the rich and powerful, the
musicians, the mourning women, and above all the men imper-
sonating the deceased's ancestors, on their way to the magnificent
tombs lining the wayside on the main approaches to the city, all
threw into sharp relief the social gulf between the best people
and the dregs of the city.

This would not be the only shock for us if we could visit
Cicero's Rome. We should find it crowded, noisy, dirty, with
unusual and forbidding stenches, swarming with vast crowds of
people, many of whom would seem almost sub-human types
marked by disease, mental deficiency, malformation and mutila-
tion, and all under the threat of sudden death. The general impression of Rome might well have been sickening, even frightening. Very little of the glib cynicism which amuses itself by throwing
doubt upon the reality of modern material progress would be
likely to survive such an experience.

When the masses lived or rather existed in such conditions, it is
not surprising to learn that no provision was made for educating
them. By Cicero's time also, compulsory army service had begun
to be of less importance to the State than the professional army;
so the average Romans missed this opportunity of being taken
out of their sordid surroundings and being given some form of
organized training. The growing race of slaves and descendants of

slaves in any case would never have had this experience of corporate life and discipline in the service of a great cause. They were therefore entirely and, for an imperial race with responsibilities towards a vast subject world, shamefully ignorant, neglected and uncontrolled. Not benefiting, as did the Romans of the heroic age, from a firm family and social discipline, not the bearers of that high tradition of self-control, self-discipline and devotion to public duty, they were but poor stuff. Yet into their unskilled and incompetent hands was committed the great heritage of the golden age of the Republic.

If, as Samuel Johnson believed, one test of a civilization is the way in which it treats its poor, it is indeed difficult to take a rosy view of the quality of life in the Roman Republic. There are other measures of the relative standard of material civilization in different countries. In modern times it has been well said that the average expectation of life is one good measure. It is a figure which varies today from just over thirty years of life in India to nearly seventy years in New Zealand. The lack of adequate actuarial statistics in the ancient world, where life assurance was an unknown science, makes it impossible to apply this modern test to Ancient Rome.

The Organization of Labour

In the heroic age of the Republic the citizen army of Rome acted as a strong unifying force welding together Roman manhood in common experiences and common exertions in the face of common dangers. Many a time during an arduous campaign the whole army became a vast labour battalion building stockades, digging huge ditches and erecting great earthworks which would dominate the walls of a besieged town and serve as a mount for the battering rams and other military gear.

The army was the Republic in action. The habit of corporate effort which it fostered was reflected in the guilds or co-operative bodies found at an early date in nearly all the separate crafts in which Roman workers engaged. These guilds or corporations of workmen bear no resemblance to modern trade unions, because they do not seem to have been organized with any special economic aims in view such as to raise wages, to improve working conditions or to shorten the hours of labour. They were not bargaining weapons in an economic class war. It would be misleading to apply this modern notion to a society inheriting strong traditions about class privileges and run very largely on slave labour. It would be truer to regard them as benefit or friendly societies, but their aims were limited, for they provided their members with little more than burial expenses and an occasional commemorative dinner.

Their real purpose was, or had been, religious: to bring their members together before some common shrine. All paid special veneration to the temple of Ceres on the Aventine hill of Rome but later they probably helped to spread the new Eastern religions brought to Rome by slaves.

To a people condemned, as most free Romans of the poorer class were, to a life of hard toil for very small wages and with very little hope of earning more, their guilds must have provided some warmth of fellow feeling and some substitute for the lack of a satisfying personal religion. The members of these guilds, assembled together at a modest feast provided by one of their number in a generous mood or by the interest on an endowment bequeathed to the guild by a deceased member, would for a brief moment experience something of the strengthening influence of human solidarity and feel that they were not entirely alone and friendless in a hard and hostile world. They must have needed all the consolation they could get in this way because it was no part of the Roman idea of duty, still less of Roman religion, to believe that the State ought to come to the aid of the poor and needy. Hospitals, lunatic asylums and almshouses were unknown. The free corn dole of the later Republic was given only to citizens, and great numbers of the inhabitants of Rome were not proud possessors of this right. Apart from this very modest form of assistance there was no public relief for homeless, destitute Roman citizens and certainly none therefore for anyone else.

Cicero could however write that it should 'be the duty of those who direct the affairs of the State to take steps to see that there shall be an abundance of the necessities of life'. Such a general counsel of perfection could not be carried very far into practice because of the sheer lack of adequate administrative machinery to manage the business it would have involved. It would of course be exhibiting a complete lack of historical understanding to criticize the Romans for not having discovered that principle of planned, State-managed social services provided largely by nationally administered insurance schemes which is a feature, still by no means unanimously welcomed, of twentieth-century England.

What Plato in a well-known passage says about the fate of a workman in Athens overtaken by illness was no doubt just as true for great numbers of the Roman poor also:

When a carpenter is ill he asks his doctor to give him an emetic or a purge to expel the trouble or to rid him of it by cautery or the knife. But if he is advised to take a long course of treatment, to keep his head wrapped up and all that sort of thing, he soon replies that he has not time to be ill ... and goes back to his ordinary way of life. Then he either regains his health and lives to go about his proper business, or if his body is not equal to the strain, gets rid of his troubles by dying. ... That is the right attitude towards medicine for a man of his class.

The application of this doctrine was not confined to the poor. 'Each one', said Cicero, 'must bear his own burden of distress rather than rob a neighbour of his rights.' There could hardly have been any other doctrine in a predominantly agricultural community recognizing the possession of private property as a primary, sacred right. Cicero himself repeated, in his last work, *De Officiis*, the opinion of a philosopher of Rhodes, that 'the private fortunes of individuals are the wealth of the State'. Everyone had his duty, therefore, to maintain and increase his own wealth, although not by unjust and unfair practices. The State had the duty of safeguarding and protecting private rights and therefore private property. Men ought however to use their wealth with care. Cicero singles out for special approval the duty of ransoming prisoners and relieving the poor. These, he said, are forms of charity that are of service to the State.

So poor Romans in distress had to rely upon relations and neighbours, as the poor have mostly had to do throughout the history of mankind. It must not be imagined that they looked in vain for aid. The Stoic doctrine of the brotherhood of man was becoming known, and Cicero did much to gain adherents for it. In its name Cicero denounced those 'who say they will not rob a parent or brother for their own gain but that their relation to the rest of their fellow citizens is quite another thing'. ... To deny that one is bound to one's fellow citizens by mutual obligations, social ties or common interests, would, said Cicero, 'demolish the whole structure of civil society'. Noble sentiments such as these shared the fate of similar noble sentiments in all ages in being imperfectly translated into practice. There seems on the whole to have been remarkably little corporate activity or organization for mutual aid against the normal accidents of life in the Roman Republic apart from the guilds, and it seems evident that they never went far.

Later in their development, probably in the year before Cicero became Consul (i.e. 64 B.C.), some of the workers' guilds or brotherhoods seem to have begun to develop political interests. They were then banned by the Senate, which would not allow the party of the *populares* to gain such a potential organized support.

Cicero's enemy, Clodius, as might have been expected, did his best to revive them and to harness them to the cause of Julius Caesar a few years later. That they continued to be a vexation is shown by a decree of the Senate in 56 B.C. which Cicero mentions: 'That political clubs and associations should be broken up and that a law in regard to them should be brought in, enacting that those who did not break off from them should be liable to the same penalty as those convicted of riot.' With the lack of responsibility of a true demagogue, Clodius, drunk with a sense of power, was evidently indulging in political excitement much too wildly for his backers. Apart from the exploits of Clodius, however, there is insufficient evidence to show whether the civil commotions in Rome were the work of organized societies of workmen, or whether these societies took any considerable part in them. Indirect testimony to their nuisance value in political life may be seen in the action of Julius Caesar, who, as soon as he achieved undisputed mastery, abolished all except the oldest and most respectable clubs. Other successful politicians in all ages have shown, with a cynicism like Caesar's, that ladders up which they climbed to power can be kicked away as soon as a dominating position has been reached.

Low Social Status of Workers in Industry and Trade

Farming and fighting were the two occupations of ordinary men upon which immemorial Roman tradition had set the seal of respectability. Other ways of earning a living might become increasingly important but they did not attain the same prestige.

Cicero made plain the traditional attitude in a well-known passage in one of his best-known books, *On Duty* (*De Officiis*). In it he condemned all incomes which could only be earned at the cost of public revulsion and dislike, mentioning tax-gathering and money-lending as examples. It is not very surprising that he shared with Plato and Aristotle the opinion that labourers working for money are disreputable. Their work he thought degrading and their wages a badge of servitude. 'All mechanical labourers are by their profession mean, for no workshop is a place for a gentleman.' 'We are likewise to despise', he goes on 'all who retail goods from merchants for prompt sale, for they would make no profits unless they lie abominably.' The least respectable of all, according to him, were 'those trades which cater for sensual pleasures', among which he listed fishmongers, poulterers, butchers and cooks. Such traditional snobbishness was, to say the least, ungrateful, for never before in the whole history of the Republic had Romans given themselves up with less restraint to the enjoyment of the pleasures of eating and drinking. It was as though they sought to compensate their own diminished self-respect by affecting to despise the means of their selfish indulgence. A somewhat similar attitude was noticeable in some sections of Victorian England to 'mere traders' and mechanics. It was necessary for any member of such classes to receive the label 'respectable' or 'very respectable' before 'the gentry' could publicy avow much social contact with him.

Our Victorian ancestors were without the excuse which Cicero had, that in his time the rich employed slaves for such work in their own households. Again therefore the pernicious system of slavery degraded the personal worth of a free labourer to much the same level as that of a slave. Did not both do the same kind of job? As Aristotle had pointed out, the free labourer was worse off than the slave who 'shared in his master's life'. In Rome there was little distinction between a slave cook and a free cook, particularly as the latter probably worked for a very small margin of profit. Great numbers of free workers were moreover ex-slaves or freedmen or their descendants. Cicero, who, no doubt for such reasons, could write so slightingly of the workers who contributed to the comfort of his own and other Roman households, yet realized well enough his debt to them and to their predecessors. He did not, in so many words, call attention to that division of labour in society which Adam Smith was first to emphasize as the foundation of the economic prosperity of nations, but he came very near it when he called attention, with many examples, to the evident facts that 'without the association of men, cities could not have been built or peopled' and that 'by giving and receiving, by mutual exchange of commodities and conveniences, we succeed in meeting all our wants'.

Poor Reputation of Business Men and Financiers

Trade on a large scale enjoyed much better esteem in Cicero's eyes. It could be undertaken only by men owning a considerable capital, and such men Cicero had always treated with consideration. From them much of his own wealth was derived in the shape of gifts and legacies. Yet Cicero's words lack warmth. 'Merchandising on a small scale', he said, 'is mean, but if it is extensive and rich, bringing in a variety of goods from all corners of the earth and providing large numbers with a livelihood, it is not so despicable.' The most he would say in its praise was that it 'even seems to deserve the highest respect if those who are engaged in it, satiated or satisfied with the fortunes they have made, make their way from the port to a country estate'.

There was a great social gulf between the small craftsman in his tiny booth or shop and the wealthy business men. The one would be little more than a slave in the eyes of Cicero and his aristocratic friends, except on election days when Roman citizens, however poor, might give their votes to new laws or for new magistrates. The other, enrolled among the class of *equites*, had a special social standing of his own. He did not normally try to become a Senator since he would not forsake a financially profitable career to seek election to high political office which was the way to secure automatic admission to the Senate. He might be enrolled as a Senator by the Censor, but before Sulla (p. 215) such a distinction would have been exceptional. In the last century of the Republic Gaius Gracchus gave the *equites* the right to become jurymen, who were really judges or assessors in the Court of Claims. This was a privilege they had long sought, to enable them to influence trials of a commercial or business nature. Their social position was also improving. They were accepted as friends and guests at the dinner parties of liberal-minded public men. Cicero, whose father was one of them, could not have been so stand-offish as to find anything unusual in that. Senatorial and aristocratic families in financial difficulties had for long found it useful to arrange marriage contracts for their own children with the sons or daughters of wealthy *equites*. For all his somewhat distant words about them, it is plain that Cicero frequently exerted himself on behalf of his business friends and clients. His own most intimate and trusted friend Atticus was a member of this class. They had been educated together. Cicero relied upon him for help and advice more than he did upon his own brother Quintus Cicero who married Pomponia, the bad-tempered sister of Atticus (p. 296). Despite their wealth and, no doubt, their self-importance, the business men never became an important force in Roman politics. Success in industry, business or commerce was never an avenue to political influence and well-organized political pressure groups or lobbies of business interests were quite unknown.

In marked contrast to the business men and aristocrats, the common people of Rome had little or no possibility of enlarging their experience, developing their personalities or expanding their minds. They may, together with humanity throughout the ages, be credited with this urge to realize something of the promise of the spirit of man. Not capable perhaps of great progress, they may instinctively have sought to achieve that better self, of which, like all men, they were capable. If this is so, anyone who seemed able to make good a promise of the smallest enlargement of their narrow circumstances and stunted lives would then inevitably have had their support. If, in addition, he was a man of tact, charm, high achievement and great eminence, he might indeed count upon their devotion.

Julius Caesar alone won this outstanding position. After consolidating his personal fortunes and securing an impregnable position for himself, which he achieved with little regard for others, there remained the crying need to restore order and stability to his sorely tried country. But he had spent himself in his long fight for power. His time was too short. To halt the decline into anarchy for a year or two, which is all he was able to do, was not progress.

Personal Religion of the Romans

What religion can mean to mankind often remains a personal secret, and we shall probably never succeed in understanding the religious experience of the Roman people. At no time had the Roman religion much to say about the human soul. Theirs was neither a very profound nor an intellectually satisfying religion, but it provided practical observances for all the normal occasions of life and so seemed to bring some outlet and some aid and comfort in all perplexities. It therefore suited the matter-of-fact, hard-working Roman farmer. To such country folk the earth was filled with forces (*numina*) whose wishes had to be respected and whose wills had to be propitiated by proper observances and sacrifices. Every place had its own spirit. Those supposed to guard the family hearth (*Vesta*) and the family stores of food and necessaries (*di Penates*) were specially reverenced. The Vestal Virgins who ministered to the spirit of Vesta, protectress of the city, in her circular temple in the heart of the Forum always kept an honoured position in Roman life. There were also spirits of the woods, groves, mountains, springs and floods. At the worst such supernatural influences merely filled them with superstitious, irrational fears. At best they may have inspired a Wordsworthian sense of deep-seated awe, but of this there is little evidence, for the Roman attitude does not in the main seem to have been spiritual reverence for what is 'holy' in the sense, for example, described by a religious thinker of modern times with the Roman word 'numinous'. The average Roman's religious observances, if he indulged in any, centred around the details of the cult as such. Little curiosity was shown in the reasons for, or the object of, the cult, which had the practical aim of getting some material benefit or to avoid some threatening danger or calamity.

Every rustic labourer in field and vineyard unquestioningly joined in the many ritual observances accompanying all the activities of the farming year. Some special festivals stood out, chief of which were the *Saturnalia* or sowing, the *Robigalia* to ward off blight and mildew, and the *Consualia* on storing the harvest.

Such observances were duties spontaneously undertaken in every farming household. Their performance did not depend upon the ministrations of any organized priestly body. Public religion in the sense of temple worship and an active professional priesthood never had much importance in Roman eyes, and by Cicero's time they were scarcely heeded at all. At home, however, things had always been different. Every old Roman home was also a chapel. Daily ministrations at the household shrine had been a duty to the gods and a privilege of true Roman citizens. No plebeian or slave was capable of conducting these rites. Hence the rigid class distinction and the early attempt to bar marriage between the two orders, patrician and plebeian.

Every house had its own shrine dedicated to the *di Penates*, spirits of the store cupboards, and to the *Lar*, spirit of the fields, and the house whose worship the Romans shared with their slaves. The *Lar* was represented by a little figure in a niche in the wall, carefully tended and often decorated with flowers. Every house had its altar or hearth upon which burned the sacred fire. Old rites demanded prayers and devotions before it at least twice a day. The fire was not extinguished save on the New Year's Day of the old Romans, the first of March, and it was forthwith relit by the father of the house in the presence of his whole family. Because the sacred fire had to be kept alight, the Roman home could not be left unattended for a single day. Desecration of his altar and hearth was the supreme calamity for a Roman. To fight 'for hearth and altar' meant that everything was at stake. Little of this intimate communion with the spirits of the past survived in the crowded urban conglomeration of Rome. (Plate 25a.)

The care of the family grave and the cult of the family dead, the *di Parentes*, like that of the whole great community of Roman dead, the *di Manes*, was not a form of worship so much as the expression of reverence and fear. Allied with such domestic devotions was the respect, amounting to worship, of the spirit or *genius* of the head of the family, the *paterfamilias*. The idea of the *genius* neither implied divine origin nor gave any promise of immortality, but it symbolized the continuity of family life and, in earlier times, the perpetuation of the family ties with the wider clan or *gens* with which it had been connected. (Plates 23, 24b.)

The traditional personal religion of the Romans did not at any time offer the inspiration and guide to conduct in daily life such as the East was already receiving from Buddhism, or such as later ages in the West were to derive from Christianity. The high moral code of the best age of the Roman Republic embodied what later generations venerated as the habits of their ancestors (*mos maiorum*). It was against this standard that they were able in some degree to measure their own conduct and that of their contemporaries. A well-developed community spirit, combined with a genuine respect for justice and animated by courage and self-sacrifice, formed the core of a Roman's practical creed. It was sufficient in the earlier conditions of life, but as the city and its dependent Empire grew vast, the sense of community of interest was unable any longer to sustain the tremendous new burdens or to preserve the old Roman way of life against the continual invasion of floods of newcomers.

The rich, with homes of their own and their closed society, could no doubt provide themselves with elegant *Lares* and *Penates*, and for ceremonial rather than truly religious reasons they kept alive the observances attending marriage, birth, coming-of-age and death. But myriads of the poor had neither hearth nor altar. The great Dictator, Sulla, at the outset of his career, is said to have lived without either in a cheap apartment. Lacking the occasion and the means for taking part in any religious ceremony, the common people had nothing to take them out of themselves and their sordid surroundings or to lead them to think about the grand questions of life, death, time and the destiny of mankind.

When their world began to go to pieces in civil strife, the Romans lost faith in their own firm strength of purpose, the old Roman *virtus*, and thought of themselves as the sport of blind Fate, whom they sought to evade or propitiate by paying increasing reverence to *Fortuna*, Goddess of Chance.

Public Religion

Although the Romans had already taken the decisive step of linking religion with the State, there was nothing in the Republic like the churches of our present-day organized religion, nor our one day in the week set aside for divine service. It is true that the many public holidays (a hundred a year in Cicero's day) often had some religious origin, but the fact was not always remembered or observed. In primitive times the worship of gods in human shape did not form part of the old Roman religion, which was preoccupied with the mystic forces of nature. Such, for example, were Janus, God of the beginning of activities (hence

January), and Consus, God of the ending of activities (hence the festivals of the stored harvest on 21 August and of the end of the old year on 15 December, both known as the *Consualia*). Influenced, however, first by the Etruscans, the Romans began to give their ancient tribal gods human form in terracotta. The worship of these figures at Rome was soon swamped by the invasion of many others derived from the Greeks. The Romans learned the names of their deities from the lumbering verses of old Ennius:

> *Juno, Vesta, Minerva, Ceres, Diana, Venus, Mars,*
> *Mercurius, Jovis, Neptunus, Vulcanus, Apollo.*

These were Jupiter, the Supreme God, Juno, goddess of married life, Minerva, patroness of Science, Art and Learning and hence of the trade guilds (of which her temple on the Aventine was the centre), Vesta (Protectress of the Domestic Hearth and of the Hearth of the City), Apollo (the God of Healing), Diana (the Moon Goddess), Venus (Goddess of Love and Beauty), Ceres the Earth Mother (Goddess of Corn and Agriculture), Mars (God of War), Neptune (Lord of the Sea), Vulcan (God of Fire) and Mercury (God of Trade and Commerce). To these principal deities a whole host of others was added from time to time and from place to place. Observances were also paid to what may be called the personification of actions and of moral qualities.

It was as though the Romans paid homage to the mysterious forces of nature apparent to them in the earth, in fire, in mildew and blight; forces which seemed the embodiment of a will-power (*numen*) not at first supposed to spring from any person or divine being but existing in its own supernatural right. Similar awe attached to such places as the entry to a city or a house (of which Janus became the guarding spirit). Not surprisingly in an overcrowded land of smallholders, frontier markings and boundary stones also had their spirits. This tendency to reverence moral qualities and forces persisted, and it is seen in the temples and sacrifices offered to Courage (*Virtus*), Honour (*Honos*), Good Faith (*Fides*), Hope (*Spes*), Modesty (*Pudicitia*), Fortune (*Fortuna*), Victory (*Victoria*), Peace (*Pax*) and others.

The two aspects of the religious veneration of the Romans, these impersonal forces and the later personal gods and goddesses, characterized the older cults which before Cicero's day had been changed by a great influx of new practices and new deities, for one result of Rome's many conquests up to the time of the Punic Wars was the bringing to Rome of strange gods, many of them from surrounding cities. Possibly to avert the wrath of those gods whose cities and temples they had despoiled, the Romans offered them hospitality within their own walls. The more there were, the safer the Romans seem to have felt. Great importance was attached towards the end of the Second Punic War in 204 B.C. to the transference from Phrygia, the fabled home of the Roman people, of a goddess known as Cybele, or the Great Mother (*Magna Mater*), and her installation in Rome was attended by scenes of wild enthusiasm. The goddess was accompanied by priests whose inhuman frenzies and weird rites soon created so great a scandal that the puritanical city fathers forbade Romans to join them. Public enthusiasm was diverted instead into annual Games, the *Megalensia*, in honour of the new deity of whom but little is subsequently heard.

Wars in the Eastern Mediterranean subsequently introduced other cults into the city. The wealth brought by foreign conquests also had the effect of greatly increasing the lavishness, the splendour, and the display connected with religious observances. The old primitive simplicity was giving way to spectacular cere- monies, to games and to banquets. At the same time decidedly less healthy influences made headway and there was a great increase in dubious mysticisms, soothsayers, sign-readers and professors of the occult. The new materialistic culture, fed so lushly on the spoils of foreign conquest, had less and less place for the old simple pieties of the early Romans. Religion, which had always been associated with public and private law, increasingly became one of the departments of State with appointment to the priestly offices as a matter of public election, just as the Quaestors, Aediles, Praetors and Consuls were elected by the people. Candi- dates came forward moved by their personal ambition for place and power, not by any genuine religious feeling, so the elec- tions went on with an increasing accompaniment of canvassing, bribery and corruption. The fact that Julius Caesar, at the age of thirty-seven, a notorious political schemer and man-about-town, could become the Chief Priest or *Pontifex Maximus* by popular election shows how deep-seated was the rot. Public worship could not survive in such an atmosphere, neither could it possibly have coped with the multiplication of cults and ceremonies. Roman piety was correspondingly weakened although it was never entirely driven out of Roman homes, particularly in the homes farthest from the contamination of the great city.

Yet the conventional language of respect towards the supernatural was preserved. Cicero larded his public orations with deferential references to the religious ceremonies and observances of the Republic and he complimented his country indirectly by expressions of gratitude for the divine favours upon which the greatness of Rome was supposed to rest. His letters also had little religious tags: 'may the Gods avert', 'through the favour of the Gods', 'may the Gods approve'; but perhaps they meant less to him than the initials D.V. often did to our Victorian ancestors. In any event, the decay of public religion seems to have gone far by Cicero's time. The very temples were falling into decay and no public money was devoted to their restoration. Many of the gods and goddesses of earlier times had been so far forgotten that industrious antiquarians like Cicero's friend, the scholar Varro, could discover nothing about them. Lucretius denounced contemporary idolatries with bitter scorn. Cicero was therefore by no means alone in having a difficult task when he tried to find his own way through the mass of nondescript deities available for Roman adulation. He endeavoured to clear his own mind and to help his countrymen to a better view of the question in his book *Of the Nature of the Gods*. In it he poured scorn on many 'puerile tales' to be found about such beings and he condemned authors who had 'mustered up a numerous band of unknown gods; so unknown that we are not able to form any idea about them'. Apart from such obvious absurdities he held that 'the superior and excellent nature of the Gods', in whom he believed because everybody else had done, 'required a pious adoration from men because it is possessed of immortality and the most exalted felicity'. In writing in this fashion Cicero seems to have been prescribing for others, rather than for himself.

As far as can be judged from his letters, the nature of the gods was not a problem which had ever caused him much concern in the practical business of everyday life. There was no Victorian Sunday in the Roman calendar, and politicians were much more likely to acquire a bad reputation by being absent from the Games than from the Temple of Jupiter. The notion that religion should be allowed to interfere with private life, let alone mould and guide every action, would have appeared just as quaint to many a sophisticated Roman as it now seems to be to his modern counterpart. Nevertheless, some notions were too deeply ingrained to be easily lost. Jupiter, Father of Heaven, Light-giver and Father of the Latin peoples, retained his pre-eminent position. An oath taken before Jupiter remained of binding force and helped to preserve Roman fidelity and reverence for truth.

How the patrician ruling class of Rome sought to retain its monopoly of power in earlier times by using religious observances and superstition to defeat the ambitions of the plebeians, has been recounted in an earlier chapter (pp. 179–186). Very much weakened in Cicero's time, it was a device by no means entirely given up. Bad as that record was, at least the Romans never fell under the sway of a tyrannous priesthood. Their priests were apt to be politicians in another form. Among a democratic body of electors, many of whom were daily performing religious duties in their own homes, the members of the priestly orders, like the magistrates, gained great dignity from their high station, but no longer from the monopoly of any vitally important religious powers or secrets of State. Cicero himself had been elected into the venerable College of Augurs at the age of fifty-three and it seems evident that he derived a good deal of satisfaction from the honour. In his book on *The Laws* he plainly stated his 'sincere belief' in the art of divination 'and that the flight of birds and other signs which the Augurs profess to observe, form a part of this divination'. He did not know, he said, why anyone should deny the existence of such an art 'when we grant the existence of the Supreme Gods, their intellectual government of the universe, their benevolent concern for the interests of the human race and their power of granting us intimations of future events'.

But he had a very difficult case to defend. The system of sacrifices, omens and revelations from on high would not stand examination. Old Cato the Censor, a conservative and die-hard if ever there was one, had said that he could not understand how two *haruspices* or diviners could pass in the street without grinning at each other. Cicero could not forget this fatal thrust and often repeated it. More recently than Cato, one of the best-known Roman Augurs had written a book in which he plainly declared that the auspices were merely got up for the interests of the

State. Nor could Cicero deny their usefulness as a method of government. He knew well enough that they had often 'furnished a plausible method of adjourning useless or mischievous assemblies. For in this way it has often happened that the Gods have suppressed by means of auspices the unjust impetuosity of the mob'. If the Augurs had indeed the power Cicero boasted they possessed 'of dismissing the assemblies of the people ... of annulling their enactments ... of commanding Consuls to lay down their office ... of granting or refusing permission to form treaties ... of abrogating laws, of ratifying edicts of the magistrates' they might have been the rulers of the Republic. How little all this supposed power amounted to was quickly shown by Marius and Sulla a generation before Julius Caesar declared the Republican constitution to be no more than a sham. In 59 B.C. Caesar, as Consul, was pushing ahead with his land reforms to the dismay of the best citizens, when his colleague Bibulus tried to hold him back by frantic protestations that all business must stop because he was going 'to look for lightning'. Caesar soon showed him how little religious obstacles meant to a determined man. And Caesar had been elected *Pontifex Maximus* a bare four years earlier, purely of course for the political wires the office enabled him to pull.

Cicero himself was inconsistent in his remarks, for in his treatise on *Divination* he states all the rational objections to belief in the practice, illustrated by many examples drawn from Roman history, and concludes; 'Let us reject, therefore, this divination of dreams as well as all other kinds. For to speak truly, that superstition has extended itself through all nations and has oppressed the intellectual energies of almost all men and has betrayed them into endless imbecilities.' But although Cicero and the men of his age had no real faith in the traditional religious beliefs of the Roman people, they had by no means proceeded to complete atheism or a clear affirmation that there were no gods.

Cicero on the Good Life

For the sake of a quiet mind Cicero advised his countrymen to forsake superstition in favour of 'a religion united with the knowledge of nature'; otherwise they would find no rest 'whether you consult a diviner, or have heard an omen, or have sacrificed a victim, or beheld a flight of birds; whether you have seen a Chaldean or a soothsayer; if there is lightning or thunder; if anything is struck by lightning; if any kind of prodigy occurs; some of which events must be frequently coming to pass so that you can never rest with a tranquil mind'. While believing that if he could entirely eradicate all such superstitious errors he would be doing great service to his countrymen, he was careful to point out that there was no fear 'that true religion can be endangered by the demolition of this superstition; for it is the part of a wise man to uphold the religious institutions of our ancestors by the maintenance of their rites and ceremonies'. He seems to have tried to combine what most appealed to him in the Epicurean and Stoic teachings.

Like all Romans, the real bent of his mind was towards the practical problems of everyday life, and when he came at the end of his days to sum up for the benefit of his son, in his book *De Officiis*, his ideas on the rules a man should follow if he is to lead a good life, he had not much to say about religion. He based his plan upon men as they are, concentrating however upon their unique possession of reason. Not for him, however, was the pursuit of wisdom or the contemplative life the supreme ideal. He found other human characteristics – the urge to self-preservation and the perpetuation of the race, and the strong tendency towards human co-operation in society – more congenial as a foundation for a Roman way of life. Consequently thoughts about justice, by which alone society can be preserved and maintained, loom large in his work. Following, in the fashion of Socrates, where the argument led him, he did not hesitate to condemn, as contrary to justice, many features of the life of his time. He declared against the use of naked force instead of argument and negotiation, whether in domestic concerns or in foreign relations. War as a means of getting rich, of winning power or glory, he accordingly condemned. What was not permissible among neighbouring nations should also be forbidden at home, and Cicero's was one of the few resolute voices of antiquity demanding humane treatment for slaves. This was at a time when most Romans were probably content with the attitude displayed by Varro, one of his contemporaries, who in his book on agriculture repeated the division of 'the instruments of agriculture', current at the time, into 'the class gifted with speech' (slaves), 'that which has inarticulate voice' (oxen), and 'that which is voiceless' (waggons).

With his pronounced emphasis upon humanity and the social virtues, Cicero was not prepared to consider courage as a supremely glorious quality. It must, he thought, be exhibited on behalf of other virtues, notably justice, before it can unreservedly be praised.

The last of Cicero's cardinal virtues, temperance, is also clearly related to the pre-eminent position he gives to justice in the life of society. It must qualify the otherwise natural love of distinction which drives everyone forward. It must also, like justice, teach men to moderate their thirst for wealth and power. Here he had in mind not only the rich, like Crassus, and the great, like Caesar ('wild beasts in human form' he called them), but all the army of tax-gatherers, money-lenders and business men whose avid competition for the means of their own self-satisfaction gave no thought to the good of the Republic as a whole. He did not deny that the pursuit of things useful to life (*bonum utile* or economic aims) had its place but, as we have seen, he rated them below the supreme values of justice, truth, and goodness (*bonum honestum*). On the value of beauty and the arts of life (*bonum jucundum*) he had, like most of his countrymen, no special teaching to offer.

In his subsequent book on *The Laws*, Cicero prescribes the sort of religious observance, he would like to see in a reformed Republic. It was essential, he thought, 'to persuade our citizens that the Gods are the lords and rulers of all things and that what is done, is done by their will and authority; that they are likewise great benefactors of man, observing the character of every individual, what he does, of what wrong he is guilty and with what intentions and with what piety he fulfils his religious duties'

On such a foundation a State would, he thought, be securely based, 'for surely minds which are imbued with such ideas will not fail to form true and useful opinions'. He proceeds to draw up a religious system and a series of injunctions in the best tradition of the early Republic. For he agreed when his brother pointed out that his plan 'does not differ a great deal from the laws of Numa and our own customs'. Numa was the legendary king who, at the end of the eighth century B.C., was supposed to have succeeded Romulus, the founder of Rome, and to have drawn up the earliest laws and the earliest religious code of the City. Cicero infuses something of real religious earnestness into his moral law, which begins by commanding that the people 'shall approach the gods in purity, bringing piety and leaving riches behind'. In the main Cicero is harking back to the best practices of the olden time, and he does not advance matters much beyond the practical matter-of-fact round of customary rites and practices hallowed by long observance. Upon this unimaginative, yet on the whole decent, code of clean living and respect for higher things, Christianity was later to exert its revolutionary influence.

By Cicero's day the earlier joyous confidence that Greek thought would succeed in solving the riddle of the universe had departed. The successors of Plato and Aristotle, as commonly happens when a critical age succeeds an age of inspiration, were running up one blind alley after another and a sense of disillusion was turning men's thoughts from the great problems of meta-physical philosophy into narrow questions of ethics and con-duct. The Stoics and Epicureans to whom Cicero had listened had brought him to a sceptical conclusion. 'Our school', he said, 'maintains that nothing can be known for certain. ... We say', he went on in a curiously modern tone, 'that some things are probable, others improbable.' Here he follows, as often, the views of the Academics, as the successors of Plato are called.

Nevertheless his letters abound with expressions of the im-mense resource which his studies were to him. 'My one refuge is philosophy and literature,' he said in the dark days. It was a devotion that increased as time went on. 'Could I have kept alive had I not lived with my books?' But there were not many like Cicero, for the philosophers in all ages have been a small minority.

It is true that many well-to-do aristocratic Romans were in the habit of employing a Greek philosopher in their house-hold, somewhat in the same way that wealthy Englishmen of the Renaissance and later had their own clergyman as a private chaplain and tutor. Of vastly greater moment were the foreign beliefs brought to Rome by the hordes of slaves, particularly those from the East. Religious persecution was unknown in Rome during the Republic. The worst the Senate would undertake against unsavoury religious practices was to forbid them within the city walls but not to interfere with them beyond the city limits. In this way some new currents in the world of thought and reli-gious emotion began to permeate Roman society. There were, to be sure, some strange, un-Roman doctrines among them. Alexandria, the meeting place of Greek, Egyptian, and Oriental influences, was one of the main centres from which, in the first century B.C., came the more striking of the new notions about the nature, mission and destiny of man. Compounded of older Greek theological, other-worldly and mystical doctrines associated with thinkers such as Pythagoras, and blended with ascetic teachings of the Jews of Palestine and Syria – derived perhaps by them in turn from Buddhist missionaries of a previous century – they invited the old-style Roman to take a view of the world very different from that which he had learned from his elders and ancestors. For he was now told to reject the world and all the manifold temptations he was so eager to embrace. Personal possessions, according to the new doctrines, must be renounced in favour of a communal life in which property would be held in common. Meat-eating and wine-drinking were to be given up along with animal sacrifices. Instead of loyalty to ancestral habits and traditional morality sufficing as a guide to life, a new model, to be found in the life and the deeds of one ideal man, was proposed for veneration. To Romans of the old school this was a new way of thought, for they never seem to have believed that a man could become godlike, still less a god.

To achieve perfection on this new plan, men were invited to live apart from the rest of the world in religious communities or as hermits, thereby introducing the new notion of spiritual leadership quite foreign to Roman notions, to whom a priest was but a very respectable kind of public servant or magistrate. With this call to a new way of life went a distrust of the power of purely intellectual reasoning on Socratic lines and a marked preference for trusting instead to spiritual intuition and mystical illumination. The first faint beginnings of such influences in Rome are traceable in men such as Cicero's friend P. Nigidius Figulus, scholar astrologer and mystic, but apart from a very few such oddities without real influence, the Romans had no inkling of the fact that men preaching a new doctrine, destined truly to turn the world upside down, would one day come among them also.

Cicero himself, despite his matter-of-fact Roman way of life and Greek ways of thought, stood in considerable and somewhat strange contrast to his own large circle of aristocratic, cultured friends. Indeed, he found it necessary to explain and to apologize for habits that kept him in his library when he was expected in the Forum, at the Games or at some social gathering. And he stood in still more marked contrast to the uneducated mob of Rome. They would never read Cicero, still less Plato or Aristotle. Denied the guidance of religion and without the consolations of philosophy, they weltered in conditions sufficiently sordid to provoke despair, the sudden outbursts of violence to which despair is naturally prone, and a curiosity, passive at first but easily stimulated into an active desire for some new thing, perhaps even for a new way of life.

Aristocrat and pauper shared a common spiritual destitution. No spark had as yet kindled the blaze that was to light a beacon to guide their footsteps into the way of peace. Long years of torment and suffering were to pass before in that new dawn fresh meaning and value were to be added to the impoverished lives of the sons and adopted sons and daughters of Romulus.

Cicero on Roman Law

Religion in the first century B.C. had no stirring message of hope for the masses in Rome. Ethical and philosophical thought were above their heads. They were also hardly touched by the development of Roman law which already was showing signs of becoming the stabilizing force in society that it was later to be. Roman law began to make steady progress after the early days of the Twelve Tables. It had become progressively freed from the shackles of the priesthood. For this improvement the Praetor had been largely responsible. The annual edict or declaration of broad legal rules made by successive Praetors had gradually formed a compact body of law. Every Praetor had previously served an apprenticeship in the art of ruling since none but Quaestors and Aediles could be elected as Praetors. They would all be Senators, accustomed therefore to debate and deliberation upon public questions. Many would, like Cicero, have begun their career defending and prosecuting before Roman Praetors in the Forum. In relation to the modest development of law in Republican times they were as well-equipped to serve as judges themselves as are the barristers and counsel from whom our own legal bench is recruited today. Cicero said that most of his contemporaries thought that the place to look for the real core of Roman legal

doctrine was in the Praetorian edicts. It was an eminently concrete, matter-of-fact body of doctrine dealing with persons and
things and having little to do with abstractions, with jurisprudence
or with legal philosophy. Very few Romans, apart from Cicero,
took any interest in such general ideas. Law was a practical means
of getting practical advantages. There were no Law Reports but a
small body of men became experts as *juris consulti* and acted as
professional advisors, in theory without reward. They did not
appear in Court where decisions in many disputes were swayed
by the spell-binding rhetoric of advocates such as Cicero in a
style which would not be allowed today.

The *Praetor peregrinus* (p. 174) had done still more to encourage the notion that law and justice were not mere racial
privileges of the Roman people but the birthright of mankind.
It was new for this idea to become operative in human society, yet
already two centuries before Cicero's day and long before they
first encountered Greek thought or any other philosophy the
Romans, thanks to the influence of this court, were acting,
whether they realized it or not, on the principle that equity
should be the basis for the decisions of their courts. The doctrine
was not lost upon Cicero. He had not been a student of Plato in
vain, whom he called 'that divine man who had inspired me with
such admiration'. Cicero followed Plato in believing that the law
depended upon the principles of right which it was the business
of philosophy to teach mankind. He was able therefore to see
further into the problem than many of his contemporaries, so
that for him the law was a sacred subject, not 'a thing contrived
by the genius of man nor established by any decree of the
people but a certain eternal principle, which governs the entire
universe'.

In a magnificent passage in his book on the *Commonwealth* or
Republic which has survived as a quotation in a book of a later
writer, he gave imperishable expression to this great idea. 'True
law is indeed right reason, conformable to nature, pervading all
things, constant, eternal. . . . It is not lawful to alter this law, to
derogate from it or to repeal it. Nor can we possibly be absolved
from this law, either by the Senate or the people; nor may we
seek any other standard by which it may be explained or inter-
preted. It cannot be one law for Rome and another for Athens,
one thing today and another tomorrow; but it is a law eternal

and unchangeable for all people and in every age; it becomes as it were general master and governor, the one God of all, itself its own author, promulgator, and enforcer. He who does not share this sentiment flies from himself and nature as a man despised.'

Again in his work on *The Laws* Cicero returns to this theme: 'Law is neither a thing contrived by the genius of man nor established by any decree of the people, but a certain eternal principle which governs the entire universe, wisely commanding what is right and prohibiting what is wrong.'

The voice is Cicero's, the thought is ·Greek; for, of all the human race, the Greeks first discovered that general terms or concepts or categories of thought, such as Justice or Right, had an independent validity of their own. They first identified the qualities that give supreme meaning and value to life as being the values of Truth, of Beauty, and of Moral Worth (or Goodness, Right, or Justice). Cicero, without putting the matter in this summary form and without having much to say on the subjects of scientific truth or of beauty or aesthetic satisfaction (but not ignoring them) nevertheless revelled in the immense enlargement of human powers of reflection that the Greeks had made possible and, what is much more important, he succeeded in communicating some of his enthusiasm to others down the ages.

Romans did not, as the people of Israel, achieve the unifying belief in a single God, but thanks to their sound democratic instinct aided to some extent by Greek inspiration they were capable, as these passages from Cicero show, of rising to the grand philosophical idea of a universal principle of justice. Their ultimate failure firmly to build on this early foundation is no part of the history of the Republic. Nevertheless, long after Greek had become an almost forgotten language, men read and pondered Cicero's words so that they entered into the stream of European civilization, guiding men's thoughts about the nature of law to an extent that no other non-religious writing was so well able to do.

Cicero cannot be blamed if his vision of justice was not shared by the narrow-sighted men of his time. Had it been, the worst disasters by which the Roman Republic was overtaken might have been averted. Instead, those able to seize power in the Republic selfishly sought to use it for their own personal advantage.

Chapter Eighteen

THE SICKNESS OF ROMAN SOCIAL LIFE

HAVE the facts, so far narrated in this work, provided a sufficiently sound basis for general conclusions about the social condition of the latter age of the Roman Republic which may serve as clues to the reason for its disintegration and collapse? Probably we shall never know enough to warrant any confident pronouncement on the subject. Yet we must make the best of what facts we have and use them to devise some general picture, however tentatively drawn.

The Changed Social Outlook

Rome in Cicero's day was clearly a busy, complicated, and very troubled place. It was also modern in the sense that its inhabitants looked out upon their world very much as most people do today. That is to say they concentrated upon their personal interests, upon the everyday things and practical problems of this workaday world. It is so much our own attitude that the question naturally arises, 'What else might they be expected to have done?'

It seems clear that all classes of the ancient Romans of the early Republic, like many of the English and French in the early Middle Ages, would have found an answer to this question with an ease denied to ourselves today or to the Romans around Cicero. Doubtless, in those earlier days, they took care to get enough to eat and drink, to provide themselves with clothing and shelter. But this was not that part of their lives which seemed most important to them. They found the real satisfaction of living in taking part with their families and their fellows in traditional common social and religious observances. Beyond the means of sustaining and enjoying their daily life, their minds and therefore their interests were occupied in following the routine devised for them by their ancestors and paying observance to the remote and unknown forces which their forefathers had imagined or invented to account for all the mysterious happenings around them which they were otherwise at a loss to explain – earthquakes storms, drought, disease. Life had a kind of pre-established social harmony to which each individual contributed and beyond which he or she never thought to stray.

Such a society had its own meaning and purpose. As long as the men and women composing it were content to go on in the old ways the harmony was preserved and with it the strength which came from internal union. It knew evil and distress, but they came mainly from external causes – famines or wars. A uniform, automatic social pressure was sufficient to curb any rebellious characters who sought to create disturbances. For power in social matters is no twentieth-century novelty. Rigid and uncompromising as the power of custom was, it was also able to make the necessary compromises when altered circumstances made change essential. So year after year, without pause or question, Consuls succeeded Consuls, citizens came forward for their military service, paid their taxes, grew their crops, maintained their modest homesteads, sacrificed to the gods, met in their political assemblies to elect officials from their own ranks and to decide their public business with a minimum of fuss and bother, employing very few civil servants and no policemen. Then came the marvellous expansion of Roman power. Within one or two generations the leading Romans acquired what, for them, was a great fortune. It provoked a crisis and sudden change. The individual atoms making up Roman society no longer kept their accustomed place. So many began to break out of their old orbits that social harmony was shattered. A tremendous release of energy thereupon occurred, as it does when a chemical atom is split. But the energy lacked direction. The rule became 'everyone for himself'. At first this social revolution was probably confined to the relatively few leading political and financial families of the city of Rome and the fashionable resorts near by. But it must soon have had wider repercussions. For the emphasis was increasingly put upon private wants, private ambitions, private possessions, personal enjoyment and ease of life; on all the things which divide instead of unite man with man. They also greatly inflame social discontents. They set the poor against the rich, for in an age when all the emphasis is upon wealth, great is the frustration of those forced to remain poor. It is no very profound discovery of our own time that frustration, sufficiently intense and prolonged, usually tends to develop strongly aggressive attitudes in the victims. No wonder therefore that violence and street battles on a scale unheard-of began to disfigure life in Rome. That nearness of some men to the beast of which the most frightening modern symptom has been the rise of the prison-state, became revoltingly apparent. The Roman mob clamoured increasingly for blood-sports, delighted in watching gladiators kill each other and revelled in wild beast fights in the arena. The poison infected everybody.

> Now Roman is to Roman
> More hateful than a foe
> And the Tribunes beard the high
> And the Fathers grind the low.

All such symptoms pointed to a fundamental malady, as Cicero was sufficiently aware. 'Today', he declared, 'our moral sense is depraved and demoralized by our worship of wealth.' Was not his plaintive motto '*concordia ordinum*' or 'co-operation between the Senators and the *Equites*' a plea for the restoration of a vanished social harmony? No remedy indeed, but a description of the state of society which a remedy ought to produce, could it have been found.

Hence, it was wishful thinking, academic and antiquarian, because harmony could not be restored by the spellbinding oratory of which he knew himself capable. That was merely waving a magic wand. Although Cicero's tactics were poor it would be unfair to leave the impression that his message was valueless. It was 'academic' in the best sense, in that it taught a good doctrine, although at the time it was beyond Cicero's power to make the product of his own insight effective as a motive to action in the minds of his fellow men. For 'philosophy has never touched the mass of mankind except through religion,' and Cicero was no religious prophet. Nevertheless, his political and ethical teaching influenced the later reconstruction of Roman government, and it endured to guide thinkers of the Middle Ages long after oxen grazed over the buried site of that Forum in which he had so long and so earnestly sought to persuade his fellow-countrymen to take the path of harmony and of peace.

This contrast between a society living a life of traditional routine and one dominated by self-seeking speculative rationalism and the urge to acquisitive adventure seems to provide a dividing line which helps to explain a great deal of what has happened in the past.

When the old settled way of life of the early Romans, given over as it was to simple agriculture and handwork and governed by immemorial rites and practices handed down from father to son, began to change, and when the old religious and social routines gave way under the influence of vastly greater material comfort and luxury won by foreign conquests, then came the time of stress and strain for Romans also. The old ordered framework of life began to break up and nothing took its place save a sudden breathless haste to conquer, possess, and enjoy the untold riches of an almost defenceless world. The opportunity was undoubtedly enormously stimulating and the Romans, in grasping it, put forth an immense effort which radically changed their country and themselves. What were they to do with their new Empire and their fabulous wealth? That was in itself a difficult problem, but they might have found a solution if they had been able to answer the still more difficult question, what were they to do with themselves?

They did not know, and therein lay their tragedy. It was this Roman tragedy which was later to provoke the tremendous words 'What shall it profit a man if he gain the whole world and lose his own soul?' They had indeed gained the whole world and most of them seemed in the process to have forgotten they ever had a soul to lose. They were rarely reminded of the fact, because the Roman religion cannot be said to have ranked as a powerful force to promote either individual peace of mind won through other-worldliness and spiritual development or that social cohesion or harmony which Cicero saw was lacking among all classes of his countrymen. Groping for some clues to the disaster, the Romans themselves, followed by later writers, have blamed the decay of religion. But can it be believed that the religion of the primitive Romans was an excellent system which, had it been preserved, might have saved the State? It was on the contrary merely one quality of the vanished old ways, superseded by new conditions of life that could by no means be reversed. The breakdown of the Roman machinery of government was not due to irreverence shown to the ancient gods of Rome by Gnaeus Pompeius and Julius Caesar. The real point is that without a new system of beliefs and values to replace the old religion, the sophisticated Romans had no aim or purpose in their lives save the gratification of their senses and the enjoyment of their material prosperity. Now whatever values the old Roman religion may have had, they did not include the germ from which higher spirituality and more refined ethical and moral standards might develop.

There have been other completely unhistorical attempts to explain the fate of the Republic, less plausible than the decline of religion. Such for example is the notion that the death of the Republic was a stage in the class war and was due to an attempted uprising of the proletariat against their capitalist exploiters. Such catch-phrases, usually a substitute for thought today, certainly have no relevance to the world of ancient Rome. The poverty-stricken masses of Rome, completely subordinated economically by the competition of slaves, were and remained politically insignificant, cowed by the sight of a few armed troops. Despite the instinctive support they probably gave to legitimate government, they were ready to cheer any substitute for it clearly able to command them. If Caesar's assassins had made good their defeat of one-man rule, as at one time they seemed likely to succeed in doing, the Republic might have been pulled together on traditional lines by Brutus, Cassius, Casca, Cicero and their friends. The masses would then have accepted their lead, probably very much more readily than they bowed down before Antony and Octavian. In the long run they stood to prosper more under a healthy Republic than they were ever to benefit from their Emperors, because a Republic could have provided many of them with that political freedom, education in self-government and responsibility they were for evermore to be denied. But the words 'a healthy Republic' beg a large question and it is an unrewarding occupation to pursue the 'ifs' of history.

Caesarism was no great manifestation of popular will. It was not a popular political movement at all in the sense that there was a large 'Caesarist party'. What above all dismayed Cicero was the indifference of the great mass not merely of the middle classes, but of the leaders of Roman society to the consequences of the duel between Pompey and Caesar. His scorn of the 'fish-breeders' has already been quoted (p. 149). When the struggle was beginning, his friend Atticus had tried to encourage him by speaking of 'the loyalists'. 'I don't understand whom you mean by "the loyalists"', was Cicero's embittered reply. There were, he admitted, individuals who were loyalist, 'but when it is a case of political divisions, what we have to look for is classes and sets of loyalists. Do you regard the Senate as loyalist when it is owing to it that the provinces have no governors with *imperium*? ... or the *publicani* [the tax-gatherers and contractors] who, having never been staunch, are now warmly in favour of Caesar? Or the financiers or the farmers whose chief interest is peace?' Such men, Cicero saw plainly, cared little for the form of government as long as they were left in peace. Perhaps there were many Romans who saw nothing in the dispute except the clash of two ambitious military leaders. The fight may not have seemed their fight since no political principle was clearly involved. Both Pompey and Caesar paid satisfactory lip-service to the Constitution. Neither fought under a revolutionary banner. But Cicero was more alert. He considered that too many of his fellows were 'lacking in spirit, as indeed most of us were who have lived the life of free men in a State that was itself wealthy and free'. He wrote this to one of his aristocratic friends, but everywhere it was the same. 'People living in the country towns and the country folk also talk a great deal to me,' he said. 'They don't care a farthing for anything but their lands, their poor villas, their paltry pence.' Habit and conservatism may have made them disbelieve in the possibility of any radical change, but in any case Cicero could not get them to admit that supreme values of personal independence or of political liberty were at stake for which they should make a determined stand.

'As to your question about the state of public affairs,' Cicero wrote to a friend in his old province of Cilicia, 'there is a most profound difference of opinion, but the energy is all on one side. For those who are strong in resources, arms, and material power, appear to me to have scored so great a success from the stupidity and lack of resolution of their opponents that they are now stronger in moral influence as well.' Caesar's terrific drive and energy swept everything before him. His opponents, conscious of their inadequacy, had no stomach for the fight. Many of |them were appeasers at heart. Cicero, who saw more plainly than the rest what was at stake, was in a most unenviable position. After struggling for months in acute mental distress he resolved, against his better judgement, to join Pompey whose many grievous short-comings were thrown into sharp relief when he matched himself against Caesar. Cicero was urged along partly perhaps because of his youthful admiration for Pompey, partly by his exaggerated sense of gratitude for the little Pompey had done to get him recalled from banishment, but above all by mere class- or herd-instinct. Most Senators reluctantly chose Pompey as the lesser of two evils. Confronted with the stark necessity of joining one side or the other and knowing that neither Pompey nor Caesar would restore the old Republic, Cicero at least confessed that he would do 'just what animals do who, when scattered, follow the flocks of their own kind. As an ox follows a herd, so shall I follow the loyalists or whoever are said to be loyalists, even if they take a disastrous course.' Cicero was no coward but clearly he was not of the stuff of which great leaders are made. Yet a generous view of this confession would see in it a blind faith in what he thought was the party of liberty against tyranny. In rallying to such a cause, doomed although it was, he may have felt himself in harmony with the verse from the *Iliad* he was fond of quoting:

> Nay, not the coward's death nor shorn of fame,
> But after some high deed to live for aye.

The Roman Revolution, then, was no class war, no uprising of down-trodden masses, no crusade for great political principles. Neither was it, despite the hero-worshippers of Julius Caesar, a necessary though painful incident in the career of a superman bringing a new economic, political, social and moral gospel to guide benighted humanity along new paths to higher things. Pompey had no title to consideration in this respect. No new idea on any subject is recorded as having originated with him. In the bitterness of disillusion at seeing the Republic of his philosophical meditations lost beyond recovery, Cicero said that Pompey was a bungling fool and that his aim was not different from Caesar's: 'The object of neither is our happiness,' he wrote. 'Both want to be supreme'; *regnare* – as though both wanted to reign as kings.

To accuse a Roman of royal ambitions was of course about as far as political hatred could go. Disregarding the word 'king' as a 'smear-word', what Cicero meant was that neither Pompey nor Caesar really cared a rap for the constitution of the Republic. Clearly they had only a totalitarian solution for the state of confusion which they found around them and which they, above all Caesar, had done much to create. Not that Caesar was a Hitler or Mussolini of the ancient world. So to describe him would be to import into the past a whole mass of ideas which had no meaning in those very different days. So to describe them might also suggest that these sordid figures of our own time, who conspired in an attempt to wreck Western civilization, possessed something of Caesar's genius and humanity, which they very plainly did not. Nevertheless, the seamy side of Caesarism needs exposing, particularly because Caesar has for centuries figured as one of the heroic types of the successful general and statesman and has been glowingly written up in consequence. Few hero-worshippers have gone so far in their praise of Caesar as Theodore Mommsen, who showed how unreserved can be the servility and adulation which a great scholar will lavish upon the wholesale butchers of men.

Uncertain as we are of Caesar's real nature, his schemes and intentions, it seems plausible to believe that, without at first planning to become the supreme ruler of Rome, he was gradually forced to secure that position because his activities and ambitions stirred up so many enemies that he was driven to the point at which he could have no personal security unless he was in full control of the State. His own character and ability undoubtedly made his success possible, just as they explain his moderation and humanity in the exercise of supreme power.

Cicero, who often spoke and wrote of him, paid him this tribute five months after his assassination: 'In that man were combined genius, a power of reasoning, memory, literary skill, accuracy, depth of thought and energy. He had performed exploits in war, which, though calamitous for the Republic, were nevertheless mighty deeds. Having for many years aimed at being a king, he had with great labour and much personal danger accomplished what he intended. He had conciliated the ignorant multitude by presents, by monumental buildings, by largesses and by banquets; he had bound his own party to him by rewards, his adversaries by a show of clemency. He had already brought a free city, partly by fear, partly by indulgence, to a habit of slavery.'

These last words sum up Cicero's charges against Caesar, and they are formidable. As he reminded the Senate, there was nothing more shameful than for a Roman to become a slave.

'There is literally no life at all for one who is a slave. All foreign nations can endure slavery, our State cannot.' 'We have been born to dignity and to liberty; let us either preserve them or die with dignity.' In the sense that their freedom to pursue an open career in politics and to influence public affairs had vanished, the Senators were indeed the slaves of Caesar. Was so ignominious an end really merited by the 'chief men of the most honourable council on the whole face of the earth', as Cicero called them? Caesar has usually been excused on this ground. It is said that the Senators of Rome were no longer fit to rule and that consequently it was necessary in the interests of peace and security to put one man in charge. We should know by now how dangerous it is to approve such a 'totalitarian' solution merely because it results in neater and more efficient public administration. Tyranny in fact is destructive. It cannot create, for creation must come from the free development of individual lives, which is precisely what totalitarianism and one-man rule cannot possibly allow. We should be false to the message of a thousand years of British history, and false to the very clear lesson of our own experiences from the Bolshevik revolution in Russia, the Fascist Revolution in Italy until the defeat of the Axis in 1945, if we took any other view of the matter than this. Between Caesarism, however attractive as a short cut to efficiency, on the one hand, and the Rule of Law on the other hand, even if it means muddling through, there can be only one choice. Cicero saw this very clearly. 'Do you call slavery peace?' he thundered at the Senators. 'Our ancestors', he reminded them, 'used to take up arms not merely to secure their freedom but also to acquire an Empire. Do you think we ought to throw away our arms in order to become slaves? What juster cause is there for waging war than the wish to repel slavery in which even if one's master be not tyrannical, yet it is a most miserable thing that he should be able to be so if he chooses?'

While Romans spoke like this it is plain that they were by no means all of the feeble decadent type which the apologists of Caesarism like to pretend. Neither would so many of them have become irresolute had they not been weakened by the unlawful shock tactics of Caesar himself. For the habit of stirring up social unrest so as to be able to exploit the alarm, distress, and misery it creates, in the guise of the strong man who alone can restore peace

and security, was not a piece of political jugglery left to Hitler to
invent. Caesar, who, said Cicero, had 'wasted all the power of
genius which he had in a most brilliant degree, in a capricious
pursuit of popular favour', also 'had this peculiar characteristic:
whomever he knew to be utterly ruined by debt, and needy, even
if he knew him also to be an audacious and worthless man, he
willingly admitted him to his intimacy'. This is the principle upon
which gangsters always proceed. How else can they get a following? Desperate characters are needed for desperate deeds. While
Caesar had these dogs upon a leash, there was some hope of
keeping them in check. But what a dangerous situation for
Rome! The blind forces which Caesar had controlled broke loose
at his death. Looking back on that troubled time from our own
experience of government and social life, longer by 2,000 years
than that of the Ciceronian age, it is not easy, after describing
and explaining Rome's troubles, to suggest a remedy for them
ourselves. Yet unless some answer is attempted it is surely rather
arrogant to adopt the high moral tone to be encountered in some
books on the Roman Republic where the many shortcomings of
the Romans are described and denounced without any effort
being made to set up the attainable standards the Romans might
have been expected to reach.

A Policy of Reform for the Roman Republic

To begin with, there are two traps into which it is very easy to
fall when thinking about the problems of the Roman Republic
and ways in which they might have been solved. In the first place
it is almost impossibly difficult to shed our own experience and
to look at the problems themselves as Cicero and his contemporaries would have done. But assuming that the problems
themselves are seen in their true proportions from a Roman
point of view, there is in the second place a serious risk that our
answers to them will be suggested by our own experience which
naturally no Roman could properly understand.

Either mistake would be as ludicrous as a picture of Cicero in
Mr Gladstone's top hat and frock coat. Added to these two
difficulties is the further fact that, despite great progress in the
twentieth century, we do not yet sufficiently understand the interaction of the complicated network of forces in play in any society,

our own included, in order to be able to foresee with complete confidence all the direct and indirect results of undertaking any one line of social action.

If therefore the knowledge and mental energy of the average person today does not provide a satisfactory understanding of our own society, as it clearly does not, how can we expect to succeed in interpreting the society of Rome, in stating its problems or in recommending ways of solving them? No doubt we may rely upon certain broad principles that must guide every society. We may believe that history is fundamentally the story of human liberty. We should then hold that the aim of Cicero's enlightened ruler should have been, without suddenly and dangerously limiting the liberties and freedom of the aristocracy, to begin a programme of social betterment, increasing political activity and increased prosperity for the common people. But such generalities do not advance matters very far. A reformer's programme for Rome needs to be much more concrete, with a series of detailed recommendations on all the major problems of the time. At the risk – and it is serious – of being unhistorical in addition to being inadequate and possibly wrong, an attempt may be made to outline what should have been, from our twentieth-century vantage point, the main projects in a five years' or ten years' reconstruction scheme for Republican Rome. Look first at the economic problems. There was, in the face of mass poverty, unemployment, and a generally low standard of living, a great need to raise the level of production in agriculture, manufacturing and distribution.

The Economic Problem

The agricultural problem in Roman eyes was above all a problem of land-tenure, because they were looking at the unemployed city mobs and ex-soldiers with one eye while the other eye saw the huge cattle ranches north and south of Rome, bare of human habitation. Yet because of the underlying geological factors (Chapter 3) and the easy import of cheap grain, the ranches were undoubtedly the most economical and efficient use to which that land could then be put. The mild coastal plain assured winter feed in the open, while the mountain pastures were green in summer when the coastal plain was scorched brown. Aided by the skill of the Carthaginians, whose agricultural

wisdom had been summed up in a book in the Punic tongue by
Mago that had been translated by order of the Senate around
140 B.C., it is unlikely that the Romans did not know their
business. The ranchers worried no more about the fate of the
displaced smallholder than the sheep-owners in sixteenth-century
England worried about the social results of the enclosure movement they found personally profitable. In much the same way,
'sheep, the devourers of men', as Sir Thomas More was to call
them, together with oxen and horses left no room for the small
cultivator in Rome of the second and first centuries B.C. Then,
as in the sixteenth century, the social effect of the untrammelled
operation of economic forces raised strong complaint on moral
grounds. Such laments can evoke little sympathy from an econo-
mist, whose concern is and must be to apply all the factors of
production in such a way as to maximize output and to minimize
waste and inefficiency. Instead of deploring the cattle ranches as
the ruin of Italy, as the moralists did, they might have sought
compensation elsewhere for the dispossessed, by a vigorously
maintained emigration scheme for example to the rich plain of the
Po in the Gallic north. Instead, the Roman Republic exhibited
very little interest in colonies inside or outside Italy after the need
for them as military outposts had disappeared. Caesar however
seems to have intended to embark upon just such a policy.

One modern remedy of trying to create centres of new industries
was not open to the Romans, who witnessed little industrial
expansion and who made no striking inventions. Rome never was
and has never become a place of manufacture for export. Consequently the Romans were unable to seek economic progress as
the modern world has done by combining the accumulation of
capital resources with mechanical inventions. The land was always
the main source of wealth in Italy in Ancient Times.

In agriculture and in industry, the Romans were heavily handicapped by one of the resources they did most to develop. That
slavery impoverishes and cannot enrich a nation may seem a
paradox, particularly in an economically primitive age when, as
in Rome, all the activities in the farming calendar, except perhaps ploughing and harrowing, depended upon the muscular
exertions of men. The cheaper the labour, the better, it might be
thought. There can be no doubt that the slave-owner's profits
were larger than they would have been had he employed free

labourers at a wage, but this very fact demonstrates that he got his profits at the expense of the Roman nation which is another name for the total population of free men and women. Farmers may have been able, as Cato's figures show (Chapter 4), to maintain two slaves for the cost of one free labourer, but for every two human animals they bought from the slave-traders they necessarily decreed the elimination of one free Roman and his family. And farmers were by no means the only people profiting from this sordid traffic in human flesh and blood. Slaves may have yielded profits to their employers in agriculture and industry, but if one fact is abundantly clear from the doctrines of political economy it is that the motive of human co-operation in agriculture, industry and commerce is not merely that employers may make profits but that mankind may more effectively provide for its wants by dividing up the world's work and by getting everybody to specialize in certain parts of it. When large numbers of men and women are slaves working for one master's needs, the effective division of labour in society is lamed and impeded both by the inability of the slaves to work for others and by their equal inability to consume, in exchange for their products, those goods and services that would have been placed upon the market by their fellow inhabitants had there been any call for them. Gresham's law that bad money drives out good has its parallel in the field of labour where honest toil cannot compete against artificially depreciated labour. Caesar must also have seen this for as Dictator, in 45 B.C., he made a rule that one-third of the shepherds on the huge cattle-ranches had to be men of free birth.

If every Roman had owned one or two slaves to work mainly for him alone slavery might have been an economic advantage to the nation, but even then it would have been an advantage to be had only at the cost of a great reduction in the total number of free Romans. And, of course, the fatal political and social evils that follow in the wake of slavery would still have to be taken into account. The economic disadvantages of slavery moreover are not exhausted by its adverse effects upon the current production and exchange of goods and services. They extend into the future by removing the stimulus to invention. Without slavery to provide a cheap motive power and a source of energy, the Greeks and perhaps the Romans might have been driven to seek those methods of increasing productivity by mechanical means that for us so decisively divide the new world from the old. In that event they might, in time, have succeeded in improving their knowledge of fuels and metals and so have enormously stimulated their industrial production and their means of communication.

Irrespective of such highly speculative possibilities, it seems evident that despite the delusive appearance of rapid progress occasioned by successful war which brought loot, slaves and tribute to Rome, the economy of the ancient world as a whole was, in relation to that of the modern world, stationary, instead of being dynamic and progressive. This economic clue to the fundamental nature of the social life of the ancient world is not usually given the emphasis it merits. It puts a sharp limit to the notion that the material conditions of life could have been much improved for the masses by economic action. The great principle of securing progressively increasing returns to human labour in industry still lay undiscovered. In agriculture, far from there being hope of securing increasing returns, the Roman farmer was ousted by the contrary principle as he saw the returns to his labour on the fields diminish owing to the exhaustion of the soil and the lack of manures with which to restore it.

The conclusion must be that it could not have been merely through an economic plan that an enlightened ruler of Rome would have been able to rescue his fellow countrymen. Every available device had already been tried a hundred years previously by Tiberius and Gaius Gracchus (pp. 67–74). Caesar himself had nothing strikingly new to offer.

The Political Problem

This verdict that there was but little real hope of a cure for Rome's troubles by economic remedies has rarely been declared, no doubt because economic grievances were not, after all, as serious a cause of public unrest as they would be today. They certainly should not have been able to wreck the constitution of the Republic for they were after all very largely local difficulties at Rome. By far the greater part of Italy remained self-sufficient, hard-working, with a reasonably adequate livelihood.

Such a state of affairs stimulates the far greater attention that has always been devoted to the political difficulties of the Republic. For it is in the world of politics rather than of economics that the inadequacies of the Roman State, when they have been sought in any systematic way, have usually been located. They were indeed serious, yet, as the argument of this book has been concerned to show, it does not follow that a more efficient political and administrative machinery would by itself have guaranteed health and prosperity to the Republic.

It is true that the foundation of the State upon the people's will, admirable in theory though it might appear, was in fact most imperfectly secured. The adequacy of the franchise is not alone in question. More serious was the limited influence of the electors, who always voted simply for or against some specific proposal and never with any expectation or promise that an intelligent programme of continuous State activity would be undertaken in any one direction apart from war. A series of plebiscites provides altogether too feeble, too disjointed and too spasmodic a means of constituting a government. The Romans had not hit upon our practice which is to leave policy-making to political parties and to vote for or against those parties, not for or against specific proposals except on the rare occasions when, as in the United States, there is a referendum to the people on one important issue such as Prohibition. The party given the greatest number of votes then becomes the government and proceeds to direct the executive and administrative machinery of State to carry out its policy. In Anglo-Saxon countries it can normally count upon several years of office. Because party politics were unknown, there could be no professional specialization in politics for broadly national purposes. Without a system of representative government the crude and clumsy device of the plebiscite was the nearest the Romans were able to get to the reality of democratic action in politics. The policy-making function of the State was therefore never as properly effective as it should have been, neither was it well co-ordinated with the executive arm of government. On the contrary it lent itself in a marked manner to clever manipulation. A demagogue had only to devise a cunningly framed question to get public support. A wider franchise with elections held not in Rome only but throughout Italy, combined with a more vigorous local campaign by candidates for political office, would alone have provided a remedy. But the time had not come for such a development which is none other than the invention of a Parliament.

The internal weaknesses of the governmental machine as such have been analysed already (Chapter 9) and it is unnecessary to say more in general upon them than that they contributed to aggravate inefficiency and ultimately to paralyse the State as soon as harmony and concord in society were replaced by competition and strife. The very remedies then sought for a political situation getting dangerously out of hand, including as they did bargaining, bribery, intimidation and violence, served but to aggravate the prevalent uneasiness and to contribute notably to the final collapse.

So the Romans lacked a system of popular voting, political parties and administrative machinery. In a very real sense, therefore, they hardly had a government at all as we know it. The lack of anything so massive as a 'government' may not have been a very great embarrassment in the affairs of a small town, which is all Rome was in primitive times, but an Empire cannot be run without one. There are too many things to decide, too much to learn and to remember, too great a need to understand and to observe fixed principles of action, too vast a responsibility and too much to do and to plan, for it to be possible to leave things to run themselves.

Government, in short, means directed activity towards certain approved ends and it implies the possession of the means of action. In the Roman Republic the sole effective means of executive action by the State in a time of crisis was provided by the army. In a very real sense therefore military dictatorship was able to supply the first essential of government. It had no rival. We may say that the army should have been subordinated to the civil power. But there was no civil power. There were Senators squabbling among themselves and business men making life difficult for Senators. There were individuals playing their own hand who grew reckless as the stakes mounted and the gamble became more hazardous and more exciting. 'The Republic is merely a sham.' These actual words may not have been Caesar's but he saw clearly that the time had come to write this epitaph. He was correct and the people seem to have realized the fact. They gave their support to any man who would get something done. The Senators did not qualify for their support, because they were more interested in trying to find ways of tripping up and removing the demagogues and agitators – as they would call them –

than in looking for remedies for the discontents and evils upon which the power of the agitators was nourished. The troubles continued. The agitators grew louder and the prestige and influence of the Senate steadily declined.

Failures in Loyalty and Leadership

Economic and political troubles cannot of course be isolated from each other and separately treated. Economic grievances, for which there was no short-term remedy, were exploited as political weapons and both stimulated division and rivalry. Consequently they merged into the whole complex pattern of life itself as it was formed by more obscure but deeper forces at work in the country as a whole. Old habits making for fixity and stability had been undermined. Manners, morals and religion therefore were unable to exert their customary restraints making for docility, conformity and unquestioning obedience to the ways of ancestors whose example no longer evoked admiring reverence. Under these and other pressures, such as those arising from the growing consciousness of the Italians of their stake in the Roman Republic, the rapid admixture of alien peoples with the Roman people and the growth and expansion of Rome itself, the social fabric of Rome was greatly changed.

Reflective Romans perceiving this state of affairs were at a loss to know what to do. Energies were wasted upon flaying the degeneracy of the age, on extolling the virtues of the past and on inviting loyalty to an obsolete and possibly misinterpreted model of society.

Confusion about the proper ends of political action paralysed the will to act. For any plan to succeed, one preliminary condition had to be fulfilled. The Romans needed the will to reform and a courageous faith that joint action and persistent patient effort would see them through. Their political and social system collapsed because they lacked this inspiration. Every problem and every possible solution therefore are involved in an initial difficulty: how could such a common front and co-operative endeavour have been mounted? Had a genius arisen able to propose a true new model, the possibility of gaining assent for it was slight. There were no schools, no newspapers, no means of appealing to the masses who were avid for cheap bread, gladiator

shows, wild beast fights, circus-races and any temporary excitement. In such circumstances the temptation to direct action
by one man could not become strong until he was backed, or
thought he was backed, by a powerful body of friends and
retainers and above all with a loyal army behind him. Strong
leadership might emerge from such a situation which indeed
clamoured loudly for just such guidance, but it would not necessarily have been leadership under the rule of law, without which
we have in our own time seen leadership to be the biggest curse
great nations have ever been forced to endure.

It seems that to many Romans there was no alternative but to
trust in a leadership that might easily spell ruin. There was no
help for it. All alike seemed driven by some desperate necessity
to their fate. Cicero at least, one of the wisest and most intelligent of Senators, would not have known what to do had some
miracle suddenly put him in the place of that enlightened ruler
for whom he longed. Despite his inadequacy, he was on the side
of the angels, for in comparison with his contemporaries, Julius
Caesar included, he stood out as a great advocate of the eternal
values of the human spirit.

A Statesman's Manual

Yet those Romans who, like Cicero, had read the works of
Plato and Aristotle must have known that Rome's troubles were
not new in the ancient world. Aristotle, who died over 200 years
before Cicero was born, describes in his writings called *The
Politics* the causes of political troubles very like those of Rome.
There was, he said, a form of democracy 'in which not the law
but the multitude have the supreme power and supersede the
law by their decrees. This is a state of affairs brought about by the
demagogues.' It needed but a short step for a demagogue to set
himself up as a tyrant or dictator. History had already proved to
Aristotle that 'almost all tyrants have been demagogues who
gained the favour of the people by their accusation of the
notables'.

He preferred to see social justice established otherwise than
through a revolution caused by economic discontents. Everything
possible should of course be done to relieve the troubles of the
poor. They should, he thought, be helped by being given an

opportunity to help themselves. Let them be set up in trade or agriculture by being enabled to buy a small farm. He was against free
doles because then 'the poor are always receiving and always
wanting more and more. Such help is like water poured into a
leaky cask'. Cicero must have thought of Caesar's creature Clodius
and his free corn dole to almost every family in Rome when
he read those words. Aristotle knew that political and social
problems cannot be solved merely by economic action. Much
more than the struggle for wealth and possessions is involved.
Economic activities are driven forward by acquisitive desires and
'it is of the nature of desire not to be satisfied' although 'most
men live only for the gratification of it'. It is true that the aim
should be to produce a State 'composed as far as possible of
equals and similars and these are generally the middle classes', for
'great is the good fortune of a State in which the citizens have a
moderate and sufficient property'. Beyond that he was not interested to go because he believed that the mere pursuit of
wealth is no worthy purpose for any man wishing to lead a good
life.

The contrary notion that a State in which no man possesses
more than his neighbours might provide a short way to salvation
for society did not deceive him. He admitted that a law to equalize
everyone's income had 'a specious appearance of benevolence …
men readily listen to it and are easily induced to believe that
in some wonderful manner everybody will become everybody's
friend.' But he was under no illusion that men will begin to love
their neighbours as soon as those neighbours prevent them from
becoming rich. Not money or possessions, but 'a very different
cause, the wickedness of human nature' was for Aristotle the root
of all evil.

With deeper insight, he saw that 'it is not the possessions but
the desires of mankind that require to be equalized'. Consequently he held that the moral reformation of man through education alone offered much hope of realizing that political and social
progress he believed to be possible. Despite their hard-headed
good sense, the Romans do not seem to have grasped this essential
truth. The diverse elements composing a State should, said
Aristotle, 'be united into a community by education'. For him
'the adaptation of education to the form of government' was the
influence above all others to which he looked to 'contribute to

the permanence of constitutions'. Such education, he thought, should be the same for all because 'women and children must be trained by education with an eye to the State ... for the children grow up to be citizens and half the persons in the State are women'. Slaves should have nothing to do with it. The aim should be to establish good moral values without losing sight of the fact that 'the first principle of all action is leisure': leisure in which the good life is to be lived.

In his analysis of the causes of revolutions and the manner in which dictatorships are established and maintained, Aristotle used language which any free Roman might have regarded as a sentence of doom upon his liberties and as a compelling incitement to kill any man by whom they were threatened. He sought further to show how constitutional governments should be preserved and how they should be administered. Here he laid great stress upon 'the administration of justice ... the principle of order in political society'. 'There is nothing', he said, 'which should be more jealously maintained than the spirit of obedience to law, more especially in small matters; for transgression creeps in unperceived and at last ruins the State, just as the constant recurrence of small expenses in time eats up a fortune.' On this great theme Cicero certainly followed Aristotle, whose words upon the supreme importance of the Rule of Law may well have inspired Cicero's own emphasis upon it (p. 354). 'He who bids the law rule', said Aristotle, 'may be deemed to bid God and Reason alone rule, but he who bids man rule adds an element of the beast, for desire is a wild beast, and passion perverts the minds of rulers, even where they are the best of men. The law is reason unaffected by desire.'

The Romans, who suffered a Clodius to make war upon them for five years, shamefully ignored this first principle of government. Aristotle's teaching contained plain warnings on other matters the Romans had begun to neglect, such as the rule against allowing the same persons always to rule or the same men to hold many offices, the danger of allowing men to buy their way into public office, as wealthy Romans did by providing free gladiatorial contests and other ruinously expensive displays. 'Those who have been at the expense of purchasing their places will be in the habit of repaying themselves,' he said. The Romans and still more their dependent peoples had good cause to agree with his caution that 'special precautions' should be taken to ensure that 'above all every State should be so administered and so regulated by law that its magistrates cannot make money'.

There was therefore no lack of sound wisdom and good advice on how to manage a State in Cicero's day. But the traditional wisdom of the Greeks helped the Romans no more than the far longer experience of mankind has aided our own contemporaries. For in our own day we too have seen the bankruptcy of government on a scale far more vast and more disastrous than that of the catastrophe by which the Roman Republic was engulfed. We have seen self-appointed leaders, a Duce and a Führer, allowed to create and to develop a private force to such an extent that by luck, by bluff, and by an extravagant combination of propaganda and intimidation, they succeeded in overawing and replacing the government of their countries amid the rejoicings of a large number, if not indeed a vast majority, of their fellow citizens who apparently despaired of relief or salvation from other quarters. What we witnessed was the surrender of liberty by millions of Italians and Germans. They gave up one right after another, accepted new laws and consented to new restrictions until they were reduced to political slavery in which any attempt to resist was so brutally repressed that none save men of the greatest resolution dared to disobey. We have seen how these same Nazi gangsters proceeded to apply the same tactics to their neighbours and by how narrow a margin and at what frightful cost they were withstood in order that civilization and humanity might be rescued from the rule of the jack-boot and the revolver. We too have been forced to realize that 'when periods of barbarism and violence are approaching it is only for the vile and the foolish that the ideal becomes unfreedom and slavery'. Cicero would have been able to say, 'That is what I also believed.'

The Verdict of History

Today more than ever before it is important to get the story right. How many people, misled by thoughtless praise of Caesar's genius, have in succeeding centuries right down to our own time been blinded to the danger of one-man rule? Not merely in Italy but in other parts of the world Mussolini's propaganda successfully suggested the notion of a revived Caesarism as a cure for the blunders of democracy. Cicero's example and his teaching were unfortunately then forgotten. He may not have been alert to discover and repair the imperfections in the Republican constitution, but he did not make the mistake of thinking that abject surrender to an autocrat was their cure.

The quarrel between Cicero and Caesar has been perpetuated down the ages. Each has had his loyal partisans and equally bitter critics. But attitudes of praise and of blame, if they are to be assumed, must rest upon deep reflection and upon a scale of values which cannot be extracted from the bare narrative of events alone. History is a Muse, not a hanging judge, and what we should seek from her inspiration is understanding before verdicts. The temptation to continue the battle between these two great men is naturally strong because their fight seems to have been renewed in our own time on a grand scale in the struggle between the rule of law on the one hand and dictatorship by totalitarian prison-states on the other.

Cicero has the enduring honour of having been one of the most eloquent champions of social harmony and of the rule of law. To many of his countrymen he may have appeared as one preaching a new doctrine. The tragedy of Rome lay in that fact. Yet he was not doing more than to distil for them, possibly in too literary and too philosophical language, the essence of the political experience of their countrymen as they had worked it out in hard trials through the centuries. The Romans of Cicero's day, having turned their backs upon the traditional morality, manners and customs of their grandfathers, were unable to advance rapidly enough to give their loyalty, as Cicero urged them to do, to an abstract ideal of a body politic governed by the rule of law and to revise their public and private lives so as to make it a living reality. More compelling urges and narrow personal ambitions blinded them to the grand principles of social unity and drove them, as such primitive urges always will, to seek short cuts to ease and happiness. How, in consequence, their government broke down, has been the theme of much of this work. The separate forces in it, particularly the elected magistrates, the sole and annually renewed legal source of executive authority in the Republic, were – in Cicero's day – no longer sustained in their sense of duty and kept in their proper place by the almost instinctive obedience their predecessors of the heroic age had unquestionably rendered to that tradition of Republican government handed down to them by their forefathers.

Forgetful of their historic past, without having had a schooling in the philosophy of civil polity such as that which Cicero himself so enthusiastically absorbed from Plato, Aristotle and their successors, and not being interested in the forthright Roman form in which he tried so hard to pass it on to them, his fellow citizens had for the most part no other guide in the desperate confusion of their times than the promptings of their own desires and their own short-sighted self-seeking. They were unable to sink their selfish interests in self-effacing service to a greater cause than their own private hopes and ambitions as their ancestors of the heroic age were unreservedly willing to do. Here lay the real change and here is the explanation of the decline and fall of the Roman Republic.*

Whatever may have been Caesar's defects, he was not as short-sighted as the selfish politicians of Rome. Did he not choose to sacrifice ten of the best years of his life to endure the boredom and hardships of camp life and campaigning in Gaul? He saw more clearly than Cicero that the old traditions of the Republic no longer had the power to activate the political and administrative machinery by which Rome rose to greatness. Yet the first necessity of the State was that the government should be strong. With the sure instinct of the born administrator and statesman, Caesar set about restoring, or rather creating for the first time as a permanent feature in the government of Rome, that unified line of command which had hitherto existed spasmodically when a Dictator had been created to deal with a special crisis in the country's fortunes. There can be no question but that Caesar was right in his strenuous and momentarily successful effort to vitalize the executive power of the Republic. All that we have since learned about the principles of public administration confirms that without a line of responsibility, authority, or unified command, executive and administrative action is lame or paralysed.

But government is more than administration and executive action. These activities supply the means of government. The ends of action, the purposes which government and administra-

* A fuller treatment of the underlying causes of historical change on these lines is attempted in Cowell, F. R., *History, Civilization and Culture.* (Thames and Hudson, 1958) and *Culture in Private and Public Life* (1959).

tion are to achieve, have their source elsewhere. In the heroic age of the Republic, men were content to have traditional morality as their guide and as the source of their executive and administrative purposes and authority. When the men around Cicero no longer looked to tradition they ought, as he urged them to do, to have enthroned social harmony, social justice and the rule of law in its place. But his doctrine was too abstract, the law insufficiently developed, and the penalties of ignoring it not sufficiently appreciated, for many to be likely to listen to him.

Should loyalty to an undoubted leader of men have been a sufficient substitute for law or tradition as the guide and source of authority in the State? Caesar had nothing else to offer. At a high cost in Roman bloodshed and ruin he was prepared to prove that the State could be made to work on his basis of one-man personal leadership, and for a time he succeeded. It was not enough. Caesar's genius could not discover, declare and pursue the purposes and the welfare of the millions of human beings inescapably united and bound together in the great society known as the Roman Republic. A state runs a desperate hazard when its fate hangs upon the slender thread of one man's insight, life and health. If Caesar had lived would he not have saddled Rome with the burden of an absolute monarchy on Oriental despotic lines? These were the fears which turned Cicero's early admiration for Caesar into mistrust and aversion. For all his energy and far-sighted practical measures of reform, Caesar had no recipe for reviving the poor and deflated morale of his subjects. He had no great cause to put before them to which all could dedicate themselves. As great a genius as Napoleon, he had no foreign enemies against whom, in the heat of battle, he could forge some spirit of unity and common resolution in his people.

Beyond this, and beyond any mere economic and political adjustments, lay the supreme task of getting masses of human beings in time of peace to accept new meanings and values by which to direct their lives. In this truly superhuman task they had no guide or leader. Caesar perished and instead of a statesman and military genius the Romans had Caesar's sword to rule them. Mere military dictatorship had still smaller chances of survival than rule by genius.

Caesar, in contrast to Cicero, has often been praised for his creative vision and ability to see in advance the shape of things to come, as though, of the men of Roman antiquity, he alone was clear-headed with his eyes upon the future, while Cicero has been dismissed as a muddler chained to the past and unable to see a future different in any essential way from that past. The matter is not so easily settled. Cicero was not muddled upon the question whether the rule of law is preferable to rule by gangsters. He may not have been a tremendously strong character but he tried to exert his strength, not for himself alone, but on behalf of his fellow men, and this in an age where by no means all public men strove to the limit of their powers, and when strength was too often displayed in mere brutality or grasping, limitless self-indulgence.

Pompey, Brutus, even Cato, may stand as examples of men who might have done more for mankind. Marius, Lucullus, Crassus and others, including the great Sulla, may typify those whose undoubted strength and energy brought little but misery to their fellow men.

If Caesar stands above such of his contemporaries so also, although on another plane of achievement, does Cicero. Neither spared themselves; both, but again in different degree, sought to realize their own vision of what the Roman Republic should be.

The world-shattering events of our own time have enabled us to see more clearly the desperate calamity with which Cicero and Caesar were forced to grapple. We may admire Cicero's resolute stand for the grand principles of political freedom which alone make life tolerable for men of spirit. Many generations of Romans were to suffer cruelly because these principles were no longer honoured. We may equally admire Caesar's stronger and more resolute determination to have done with drift and flabby lack of purpose; to hack his way through the appalling confusion in Rome and at all costs to make the machinery of government work so that administrative energies might begin to achieve worthy purposes in society. By adopting his policy, those who succeeded him were to renew the might of Rome and to spread ordered government and the rule of law throughout Western Europe and the Mediterranean lands. We may admire both points of view, and without pretending that the question between the two men is completely exhausted by the distinction implied, take our stand upon it at this particular epoch in world history. We may then say that the predominantly reflective genius of Cicero and the predominantly practical genius of Caesar were of different orders of excellence; that both were needed then as they are needed in government everywhere; that their tragic story should be given a broader setting than that merely of their own characters, ability, performance, and fate because it deserves to be regarded as part of the great loom of human destiny upon which all men work out their lives.

To see Caesar and Cicero, their friends and enemies and the millions of Romans whom they never knew, against this broad historical background will be to get as near as it is yet given to mankind to that vision of humanity *sub specie aeternitatis*; that godlike, unattainable comprehension which finds a place for all the relevant facts, which at the same time makes clear their explanation, their meaning and their message, and so guides and directs our footsteps as we, like Cicero and Caesar before us, wrestle with our own difficulties and encounter our own fate.

Fifteen years after Caesar perished, when peace came again at last to the troubled city of Rome, it was achieved partly because many of the actors in the great drama of Cicero's age had died, committed suicide, been killed, or had exhausted themselves and their countrymen in the miseries of a civil war too long drawn out. The young men in the rising generation at Rome hardly knew the meaning of political liberty, neither had they had any experience of stable, orderly government. The new peace was also partly due to the skill of that most unlikely young man, Octavianus, born in the year of Cicero's consulship, whom Cicero flattered but in whom he detected little sign of greatness. He was Caesar's great-nephew and adopted son. His was the great advantage of fighting under Caesar's colours and becoming the heir therefore to a mighty name and to the following it inspired amongst thousands of Romans. He was a young man. He had learned much from the failures of the elder generation of Roman statesmen, of Crassus, Pompey, Cicero, Cato, Antony, and of the great Julius Caesar. If he also is regarded as a political gangster on the grand scale, he was a successful one, for he eliminated all his rivals. Thereafter he had a lifetime in which to make his experiments in ruling, backed by overwhelming power as a virtual dictator. He was helped too by the desperate desire of millions for peace and security at almost any price. He had a free field. Patiently, persistently and firmly he devised and dressed up a more plausible source of State authority so that the executive and administrative power of government could be more intelligently directed to serve public purposes and so ultimately to win acceptance by the majority of the peoples dependent on Rome. On such a foundation was to be based that mighty Empire whose civilizing mission was to make Roman ways and Roman thought part of the very fabric of Western European civilization and of the national being of hundreds of generations knowing little or nothing of Cicero, Caesar, or the Roman Republic.

So the edifice which Octavianus, as Augustus Caesar, the first Roman Emperor, erected upon the ruins which the bankrupt Republicans had pulled down upon themselves as they slaughtered Julius Caesar, was a more subtle and more complicated construction than Caesar could have devised or would have had the patience to build. Pompey might perhaps have recognized it as a solution he had fumbled to find. It would have made little appeal to Cicero despite his wish for an enlightened ruler, but then no true Republican could have welcomed it wholeheartedly because it was designed for a new age and for a different race of men.

BIBLIOGRAPHY

THE vast literature devoted to the history of the Roman Republic is listed in the full bibliographies given in *The Cambridge Ancient History*, vols. 7–10 (Cambridge University Press, 1928–34). The following are some of the books likely to prove most interesting and rewarding.

I. Roman and Greek Classical Works

Texts and translations include:

The Loeb Library, published by Messrs Heinemann, especially Latin works by Caesar, Cato, Cicero, Livy, Ovid (the *Fasti*), Plautus, Terence, Sallust and Varro, the Greek works by Appian, Dio, Polybius and Plutarch. The Loeb Library gives the original text and an English translation page by page. A similar series for French readers is the *Collection Guillaume Budé* (Société d'Edition 'Les Belles Lettres').

Cicero *Letters to Atticus* are newly edited and translated by Shackleton Bailey, D.R. Cambridge University Press 1965–

Translations alone are available in such well-known series as:

Bohn's Classical Library (Messrs Geo. Bell & Sons), containing an excellent translation of Cicero's Letters by E. S. Shuckburgh (4 vols., 1904) and older translations of Cicero's other works; Varro on Farming, translated by Lloyd Storr-Best; Appian (2 vols.); Livy (4 vols.); Plautus (2 vols.); Pliny (6 vols.); Plutarch's *Lives* (4 vols.) and *Morals* (2 vols.); Quintilian; Sallust; Terence.

The Oxford Translation Series, including Aristotle's *Politics*, translated by Jowett (1885) and later (1946) by Sir Ernest Barker.

Macmillan's Series of Translations, including Polybius, translated by E. S. Shuckburgh.

Everyman's Library, published by J. M. Dent & Sons Ltd.

Lewis, N., and Reinhold, M. *Roman Civilization Selected Readings*, Vol. I. Columbia University Press, 1951.

II. General Reference Works

There is no exhaustive modern encyclopedia in English, but there is a wealth of nineteenth-century scholarship in the following works by Sir W. Smith, published in various editions by John Murray:

Dictionary of Greek and Roman Antiquities, 3rd edition. 2 vols.

Dictionary of Greek and Roman Biography and Mythology. 3 vols.

Dictionary of Greek and Roman Geography. 2 vols.

The French encyclopedia is Daremberg, Ch. et Saglio, E.: *Dictionnaire es antiquités Grecques et Romaines*. 10 vols. 1877–1919.

The great German encyclopedia is Pauly-Wissowa's *Real-Enzyklopädie der klassischen Altertumswissenschaft.* 1894 – (still in course of completion. Four summary volumes are in the press.)

Enciclopedia dell 'Arte Antica. Rome, 1958 – (in course of publication.

Single-volume works include:

   The Oxford Classical Dictionary. Oxford University Press, 1950.

   A Companion to Latin Studies. Cambridge University Press, 1929.

   Map of the Classical Lands of the Mediterranean. National Geographic Society, Washington, D.C., 1940.

   Van Der Heyden, A.A.M., and Scullard, H.H.: *Atlas of the Classical World.* Nelson, 1959.

III. General Histories

Cambridge Ancient History, vols. 7–10. Cambridge Univ. Press, 1928–34.

Ferrero, Guglielmo: *The Greatness and Decline of Rome* (transl. A. E. Zimmern). Heinemann, 1907.

Frank, Tenney: *A History of Rome.* Holt & Co., New York, 1924. *Roman Imperialism.* Macmillan, 1914.

Greenidge, A. M. J., and Clay, A. M.: *Sources for Roman History 133–70 B.C.,* ed. Gray, E. W. Oxford University Press, 1960.

Heitland, W. E.: *The Roman Republic,* 3 vols. Cambridge University Press, 1923.

Holmes, T. R. E.: *The Roman Republic and the Founder of the Empire* 3 vols. Oxford University Press, 1923. *Caesar's Conquest of Gaul* Macmillan, 1903.

Marsh, F. B.: *A History of the Roman World from 146 to 30 B.C.* Methuen, 1963.

Meyer, E.: *Caesars Monarchie und das Principat des Pompejus.* Stuttgart, 1918.

Mommsen, Theodor: *History of Rome* (transl. W. P. Dickson). 5 vols. Macmillan, 1894; also in the Everyman's Library (Dent) in 4 vols. *Römisches Staatsrecht,* and, with Marquardt, J.: *Römische Staatsverwaltung.* 7 vols. 1871–82.

Rostovtzeff, M. I.: *A History of the Ancient World,* vol. 2: *Rome* (transl. J. D. Duff). Oxford University Press, 1930.

Scullard, H. H.: *A History of the Roman World from 753 B.C. to 146 B.C.* Methuen, 1961.

Syme, R.: *The Roman Revolution.* Oxford Univ. Press, 1939 and 1960.

IV. Books on Special Subjects

Adcock, F. E.: *Roman Political Ideas and Practice.* University of Michigan Press, 1959. Adcock, F. E.: *Caesar as a Man of Letters.* Cambridge University Press, 1956.

Allbutt, Sir T. C.: *Greek Medicine in Rome.* Macmillan, 1921.

Altheim, Franz: *A History of Roman Religion* (trans. Harold Mattingly). Methuen, 1938.

Anderson, W. J.: Spiers, R. P., Ashby, T.: *The Architecture of Ancient Rome.* Batsford, 1927.

Aymard, J.: *Essai sur les Chasses Romaines.* Boccard, Paris, 1951.

Badian, E.: *Foreign Clientelae, 264–70 B.C.* Oxford Univ. Press, 1958.

Balsdon, J. P. V. D.: *Roman Women,* Bodely Head, 1962.

Beare, W.: *The Roman Stage.* Methuen, 1955.

Berriman, A. E.: *Historical Metrology.* J. M. Dent & Sons, 1953.

Bieber, M.: *History of the Greek and Roman Theatre.* Oxford Univ. Press, 1961.

Botsford, G. W.: *The Roman Assemblies, from their Origin to the End of the Republic.* Macmillan, 1919.

Broughton, T. R. S.: *The Magistrates of the Roman Republic,* 2 vols. American Philological Association, 1951–2. *Supplement* 1960.

Carcopino, Jérôme: *Cicero: The Secrets of his Correspondence,* transl. by E. O. Lorimer. Routledge & Kegan Paul, 1951.

Cary, M., Warmington, E. H.: *The Ancient Explorers.* Methuen, 1919.

Charleston, R. J.: *Roman Pottery.* Faber, 1955.

Clarke, M. L.: *Rhetoric at Rome.* Cohen and West, 1953.

Cochrane, C. N.: *Christianity and Classical Culture.* Oxford University Press, 1940 and 1960.

Cowell, F. R.: *Everyday Life in Ancient Rome,* Batsford, 4th ed. 1966.

Cramer, F. H.: *Astrology in Roman Law and Politics.* American Philosophical Society, 1954.

Cumont, F.: *Les Religions Orientales dans le Paganisme Romain.* Geuthner, Paris, 1929. *Mysteries of Mithra,* Dover, 1956.

Dorey, T. H., Dudley D. R. *eds: Cicero,* 1965; *Lucretius,* 1965; *Roman Drama,* 1965. Routledge & Kegan Paul.

Earl, D. C.: *Tiberius Gracchus: A Study in Politics.* Latomus, Brussels 1963.

Ferguson, J. and others: *Studies in Cicero.* Centro di Studi Ciceroniani Editore, Rome, 1962.

Fowler, W. W.: *The Roman Festivals of the period of the Republic.* Macmillan, 1899. *The Religious Experience of the Roman People.* Macmillan, 1911. *Roman Ideas of Deity.* Macmillan, 1914. *Social Life at Rome in the age of Cicero.* Macmillan, 1908. *Roman Essays and Interpretations.* Oxford University Press, 1920. *Julius Caesar and the Foundation of the Roman Imperial System.* Putnam, 1892.

Frank, Tenney: *An Economic History of Rome,* 2nd edition. Cape, 1927. (ed.) *An Economic Survey of Ancient Rome,* vol. I. Johns Hopkins Press, 1933. *Aspects of Social Behaviour in Ancient Rome.*

Harvard University Press, 1932. *Life and Literature in the Roman Republic*. Cambridge University Press, 1930.

Frisch, H.: *Cicero's Fight for the Republic*. Copenhagen, 1946.

Gardiner, E. Norman: *Athletics in the Ancient World*. Oxford University Press, 1930.

Gjerstad, E.: *Early Rome I–III*. Swedish Institute, 1953–60. Gjerstad, E.: *Legends and Facts of Early Roman History*. Lund, 1962.

Grant, M.: *From Imperium to Auctoritas*. A Historical Study of the Aes Coinage, 49 B.C.–A.D. 14. Cambridge University Press, 1946. *Roman Literature*. Cambridge University Press, 1954. *Myths of Greece and Rome*. Weidenfeld & Nicolson, 1962. Editor: *The Birth of Western Civilization*, Thames and Hudson, 1964.

Greenidge, A. H. J.: *Roman Public Life*. Macmillan, 1901. *Legal Procedure in Cicero's Time*. Oxford University Press, 1901.

Grimal. P.: *Les Jardins Romains*. Boccard, Paris, 1943.

Haarhoff, T. J.: *The Stranger at the Gate*. Longmans, 1938.

Halliday, W. R.: *History of Roman Religion*, 1922, *The Pagan Background of Early Christianity*. Liverpool University Press, 1925.

Hammond, Mason: *City State and World State*. Harvard, 1951.

Hardy, E. G.: *Some Problems in Roman History*. Oxford University Press, 1924. *The Catilinarian Conspiracy*. Blackwell, 1924. *Six Roman Laws*. Oxford University Press, 1911.

Haskell, H. J.: *This was Cicero*. Secker & Warburg, 1942.

Heitland, W. E.: *Agricola*. Cambridge University Press, 1921.

Higgins, R. A.: *Greek and Roman Jewellery*. Methuen, 1961.

Hill, H.: *The Roman Middle Class, Republican Period*. Blackwell, 1952.

Jolowicz, H. F.: *Historical Introduction to Roman Law*. Cambridge University Press, 1952. *Roman Foundations of Modern Law*. Oxford University Press, 1957.

Kenyon, Sir F. G.: *Books and Readers in Ancient Greece and Rome*. Oxford University Press, 1932.

Louis, Paul: *Ancient Rome at Work*. Kegan Paul, 1927.

Maiuri, A.: *Roman Painting*. Skira, 1953, *Pompeii*. Novara, 1957.

Mattingly, H.: *Roman Coins*, 2nd edition. Methuen, 1960.

Mau, August: *Pompeii* (transl. F. W. Kelsey). Macmillan, 1902.

Mortiz, L. A.: *Grain Mills and Flour in Classical Antiquity*. Oxford University Press. 1958.

Nash, E.: *Pictorial Dictionary of Ancient Rome*, 2 vols. Zwemmer, 1961–2.

Pais, Ettore: *Ancient Legends of Roman History*. Sonnenschein, 1906.

Palmer, L. R.: *The Latin Language*. Faber. 1961.

Petersson, J.: *Cicero, a biography*. Univ. of California Press, 1920.

Samburksy, S.: *Physics of the Stoics*. Routledge Kegan Paul, 1959.

Scullard, H. H.: *Roman Politics, 220–150 B.C.* Oxford University Press, 1951. *From the Gracchi to Nero*. Methuen, 1959.

Sherwin-White, A. N.: *The Roman Citizenship*. Oxford University Press, 1939.

Smith, R. E.: *The Failure of the Roman Republic*, 1956; *Cicero the Statesman*, 1966. Cambridge University Press.

Stahl, W. H.: *Roman Science*. University of Wisconsin Press, 1962.

Stenico. A.: *Roman and Etruscan Painting*. Weidenfeld & Nicolson, 1963.

Strachan-Davidson, A. L.: *Cicero and the Fall of the Roman Republic*. Putnam, 1894. *Problems of the Roman Criminal Law*. Oxford University Press, 1912.

Strong, E.: *Art in Ancient Rome*, vol. 1. Heinemann, 1929.

Syme, R.: *Caesar, the Senate and Italy*. British School, Rome, 1938.

Taylor, Lily R.: *Party Politics in the Age of Caesar*. Cambridge University Press, 1949. *Voting Districts of the Roman Republic*. American Academy, 1960.

Teuffel, W. S., and Schwabe, L.: *History of Roman Literature*. G. Bell & Sons, 1891.

Thiel, J. H.: *Studies on the History of Roman Sea-Power in Republican Times*. North-Holland Publishing Co., 1946.

Toynbee, A.: *Hannibal's Legacy*, 2 vols. Oxford University Press, 1965.

Toynbee, J. M. C.: *The Art of the Romans*. Thames & Hudson, 1965.

Wilkins A. S.: *Roman Education*. Cambridge University Press, 1905.

Wilkinson, L. P.: *Letters of Cicero, a new selection in translation*. Bles, 1949. *Golden Latin Artistry*. Cambridge University Press, 1963.

Wirszubski, Ch,: *Libertas as a Political Idea at Rome*. Cambridge University Press, 1950.

The historical study of Rome is fostered in Great Britain by the Society for Promotion of Roman Studies (31 Gordon Square, London, W.C.1), whose valuable annual Journal and specialized collection of books, periodicals, and pamphlets offer the strongest inducement to all interested to become members.

ACKNOWLEDGEMENT

In addition to general indebtedness to the sources mentioned above. special acknowledgement must be made to Messrs G. Bell & Sons Ltd, publishers of E. S. Shuckburgh's translation of Cicero's Letters, L, Storr-Best's translation of Varro on Farming and of Bohn's Classical Library, and to the Johns Hopkins Press of Baltimore, U.S.A. publishers of Professor Tenney Frank's *Economic Survey of Ancient, Rome* for permission to quote material from those works.

INDEX